JOURNAL FOR THE STUDY OF THE PSEUDEPIGRAPHA SUPPLEMENT SERIES
29

Editors
Lester L. Grabbe
James H. Charlesworth

Sheffield Academic Press

Turbulent Times?

Josephus and Scholarship on Judaea in the First Century CE

James S. McLaren

Journal for the Study of the Pseudepigrapha
Supplement Series 29

For
Margaret E. McLaren

Copyright © 1998 Sheffield Academic Press

Published by
Sheffield Academic Press Ltd
Mansion House
19 Kingfield Road
Sheffield S11 9AS
England

Typeset by Sheffield Academic Press
and
Printed on acid-free paper in Great Britain
by Bookcraft Ltd
Midsomer Norton, Bath

British Library Cataloguing in Publication Data

A catalogue record for this book is available
from the British Library

ISBN 1-85075-891-3

CONTENTS

As with most books, a long journey has been undertaken in the completion of this text. In one sense it began in my undergraduate years when I first encountered Josephus in 1981 in a course on Roman history. Although it was purely by chance that my initial interest in Josephus coincided with what has since become an increasing level of scholarly activity regarding his writings, this book is not simply a desire to join the 'bandwagon'. Rather, it reflects my continuing interest as a historian in a particular period—Judaea, between 200 BCE and 150 CE—and in the use of ancient sources in historical inquiry.

The main impetus for this particular book came from what began as a history of first-century BCE–CE Judaea. One of the main concerns was to consider the validity of a widely held view that turmoil and unrest were the hallmarks of the situation in Judaea. The final product, however, is somewhat different. The history, as such, has not been written. In effect, what was meant to be the introduction has become the focus of the entire book.

The book is not intended to be a lament nor an attempt to 'stir the pot' simply for fun. I am conscious that comments are made regarding the existing scholarly use of Josephus without allowing others to view how I use him in any detail. Here the reader is requested to be patient and await my reconstruction in a later manuscript. The final chapter of this book, however, does provide an example of the direction the reconstruction will take and it indicates the importance of examining the events through Josephus but outside his terms of reference. The reader is encouraged to encounter the book as it is intended: an expression of a desire to contribute to the realm of historical inquiry into first-century Judaea, one which is fraught with the complications of our subjectivity and that of the sources upon which we are dependent.

There are many to whom I owe thanks in the completion of the book. I am grateful for the support of my institution, Australian Catholic University, especially in terms of six months' study leave in

1995 and financial assistance towards travel to Israel and England while on leave. The time away was a window of opportunity to break from the hectic schedule of teaching across diverse fields of study that is now part of university life in Australia. My colleagues within the School of Theology (Victoria) have provided valuable support, in particular Barbara Stead and Terry Curtin. While on leave I had the pleasure of returning to Pembroke College, Oxford, as a Senior Associate for Michaelmas Term. The college, and Oxford in general, provided a wonderful environment in which to work through many of the issues associated with the book. For those who graciously offered comments to papers given at the University of Oxford and the University of Sheffield I also offer my thanks. In particular, I would like to express my appreciation for the comments and observations of Martin Goodman and Philip Davies. I benefited greatly from the perspectives they offered regarding the line of argument I have presented. My thanks also to Lester Grabbe for his comments and acceptance of the text in the series. Any faults the reader may detect in the views put forward lie entirely with me, not with any of those who have kindly offered their assistance along the way. I am also grateful for all the help provided by the staff at Sheffield Academic Press.

Several friends have asked how I managed to complete the book. I have assumed that their curiosity pertained to matters of time, not ability! The simple answer is that it has demanded much of those most precious to me: my family. To my wife, Mary-Rose: thank you for ensuring that we have all remained sane. I am blessed by your love. My daughters, Georgina and Alexandra, have been so patient and tolerant of the long nights and 'lost' weekends—thank you, girls. On telling them that I had finished the book their response was mixed. They were happy that their daddy might be able to spend more time with them but also sad in that it would probably mean I will write another one. Their wisdom belies their age! Although not around at the time of writing, a special welcome to our third child, Fergus. Finally, the experience of seeing what my family has done over the past two years has helped me arrive at a clearer understanding of the sacrifices my mother made for me over many years as I found my home in the study of history. In an effort to publicly mark my appreciation, therefore, I dedicate this book to Margaret McLaren.

ABBREVIATIONS

ABRL	The Anchor Bible Reference Library
ALGHJ	Arbeiten zur Literatur und Geschichte des hellenistischen Judentums
ANRW	*Aufstieg und Niedergang der römischen Welt*
BSJS	Brill's Series in Jewish Studies
CBQ	*Catholic Biblical Quarterly*
CRINT	Compendia rerum iudaicarum ad Novum Testamentum
CSCT	Columbia Studies in the Classical Tradition
ClQ	*Classical Quarterly*
HDR	Harvard Dissertations in Religion
Hist.	Tacitus, *Histories*
HTR	*Harvard Theological Review*
IEJ	*Israel Exploration Journal*
JJS	*Journal of Jewish Studies*
JQR	*Jewish Quarterly Review*
JRS	*Journal of Roman Studies*
JSJ	*Journal for the Study of Judaism in the Persian, Hellenistic and Roman Period*
JSNTSup	*Journal for the Study of the New Testament*, Supplement Series
JSOT	*Journal for the Study of the Old Testament*
JSPSup	*Journal for the Study of the Pseudepigrapha*, Supplement Series
LCL	Loeb Classical Library
NTS	*New Testament Studies*
NovT	*Novum Testamentum*
NovTSup	*Novum Testamentum*, Supplements
RB	*Revue biblique*
SCI	*Scripta Classical Israelica*
SJLA	Studies in Judaism in Late Antiquity
SJT	*Scottish Journal of Theology*
SPB	Studia postbiblica
TSAJ	Texte und Studien zum antiken Judentum
WUNT	Wissenschaftliche Untersuchungen zum Neuen Testament

INTRODUCTION

History is a story of relationships. It involves mystery, and requires commitment and a willingness to encounter change, toil and pleasure. Furthermore, this range of human expressions is at play in several directions because there are numerous liaisons at work at any given moment. At the base is the relationship between the events or issues and the people who decided to write about them. For the modern reader, however, most energy is focused on a second relationship, that is, the one that exists between themselves and the period of history which they are concerned to explore. Here, the historian desires to establish a dialogue with a society and culture of another era, giving life to still voices. Cultures and events associated with them are locked away in the scattered physical remains and trapped within the text of literary accounts. These echoes of a past existence are honoured with the status of being 'matchmaker'—the go-between that fosters and feeds the relationship between past and present. My aim is to explore the expression of one such relationship: the use of Flavius Josephus in connection with the scholarly reconstruction of the state of affairs in first-century CE Judaea.

There are a number of different sources at the disposal of historians as they seek to enter the relationship with the past. As further archaeological work is undertaken, the material remains of the first century BCE–CE are providing a glimpse of various aspects of urban and rural life in the region. Aspects of economic life, such as land settlement and possible ethnic location, are being drawn to the attention of the historian. It is apparent that no comprehensive discussion of the period can be undertaken without reference to this expanding mountain of material remains.[1] To rely only on literary accounts of the period is to turn away from an important partner in the

1. The excavations at such cities as Sepphoris and Caesarea Maritima are examples of how archaeological work is indispensable for a 'full' study of the culture and society.

relationship that the historian is seeking to establish. Despite this, most
energy is unequivocally focused on giving life to the period through
detailed exposition of the available literary sources. Various bodies of
literature can be explored, such as: the writings from Qumran; the
early Christian texts—canonical and apocryphal; Philo's writings; the
tannaitic literature; the Pseudepigrapha and related texts; Tacitus; and
the writings of Josephus. These various texts fall into two broad categories: narrative accounts and thematic writings. The narrative texts
tend to be episodic in format and because of the nature of their content can be related to specific occasions in time and space. The
thematic texts, however, do not always allow the reader to readily
identify the content with specific periods of Judaean history, nor with
particular groups within the community. They are conceptual in
nature and often appear deliberately to avoid reference to particular
moments in time and space. Furthermore, questions regarding the
dating, prominence and purpose of some of the writings have resulted
in a narrowing of which material is deemed relevant for a historical
reconstruction of first-century CE Judaea.[2]

Discussion of the available sources tends to result in the promotion
of Josephus as the leading 'go-between' for the historian. Writing in
the last 30 years of the first century CE about some events in which he
could claim first-hand knowledge, combined with the fact that he
deliberately set out to describe events that took place in Judaea, help to
ensure that Josephus has pride of place as scholars seek to engage in a
relationship with the first century CE. On an even more fundamental
level, Josephus is the only major extant narrative account of affairs in
Judaea for this period of history. Irrespective of what view scholars
have of Josephus as a person or as a writer and historian, therefore,
his narrative must hold centre stage. Only Josephus provides an
episodic account of events up to the capture of Jerusalem in 70 CE.
Philo describes a few specific incidents, as does the early Christian literature. Tacitus provides a brief summary of what happened in Judaea
in connection with the 66–70 CE revolt, while it is possible that allusions to actual events are made in elements of the Pseudepigrapha and
Qumran literature. The tannaitic literature, especially the earliest
corpus, the Mishnah, probably contains a number of traditions that

2.   For example, the dating of the traditions within the tannaitic literature as indicated by J. Neusner, *The Rabbinic Traditions about the Pharisees before 70*, III
(Leiden: E.J. Brill, 1971).

originate in the pre-70 CE period which pertain to historical situations. These traditions, however, are isolated and it is difficult to establish the extent to which they have been preserved free of later editing. In short, an investigation into the flow of events in Judaea is almost entirely dependent on Josephus's account. Other sources can be called upon to provide testimony to specific incidents but for any attempt to construct a narrative of what happened in the period we must rely primarily on Josephus.

The existence of Josephus's narrative is cause for celebration while the dependence on him is of crucial significance. We cannot overestimate the importance and relevance of Josephus for the status of the relationship between the historian and the period of history being examined. Without Josephus's account we would be struggling to say very much at all about what happened in the region during the first century BCE–CE. Furthermore, Josephus has provided the modern reader with two accounts of many of the events he describes. We may be dependent on one author but between the parallelling within *War–Ant.* and *War–Life*, much of what Josephus narrates can be compared against his own word.

The survival of Josephus's work is nevertheless a double-edged sword. The positives are matched by what is a major cause for concern in how the relationship between historian and source operates. Any discussion of the state of affairs in Judaea is dependent, almost entirely, on the witness of one writer. Recognition of the implications of this material dependency on the scholarly reconstruction of Judaea in the first century CE has influenced the way this particular study has unfolded. It has resulted in a shift of the agenda away from the writing of a history of the period to the examination of an underlying methodological issue.[3] There are two related questions which drive this investigation into the interaction between Josephus and scholarship. First, what is the nature of the relationship between the historian, Josephus, and his narrative? Second, what is the impact of that relationship on the way scholarship reconstructs the first century CE?

Concern over material dependence on a single source is not unique to the reconstruction of the first century CE. In fact, comparison with

---

3. In effect, this study has become a necessary preliminary work with the intended history of Judaea being 'delayed'. Writing a 'history' is the next step, with this study laying the foundation for the direction to be taken.

other areas of historical interest tends to offer reason for hope rather than despair. I have in mind here examples closely related to the time frame of this study. One is the examination of the early Christian movement. Scholarship has long struggled with the dependence on the Acts of the Apostles for information about the initial spread and development of the movement. Apart from occasional references in the Pauline corpus that pertain to historical events (such as Galatians 2), Acts is the only extant near-contemporary account of the early years. This situation has drawn various responses, ranging from total acceptance to the complete rejection of the Acts narrative as a reliable source of historical information.[4] A similar example is the desire of some scholars to examine the historical figure of Jesus. The various 'quests' have faced the vexed question of deriving historical information regarding Jesus of Nazareth's career through the surviving narrative. Here the primary concern is not that historians are dependent on a single source, but that each of the sources is derived from the same basic perspective of faith. As such, what is recorded in the Gospel narratives pertains to theological claims rather than a desire to preserve an account of what Jesus actually did and said.[5]

The dependency on Josephus appears to be quite promising in comparison to the dependency on Acts for the early Christian movement, and to the Gospel narratives for Jesus of Nazareth. Concern over possible theological motivation is not an issue in Josephus's narrative. He actually sought to write a history; his stated aim was to preserve an account of actual events. He may have held particular views regarding the parameters within which certain events should be explained, but

4. For a review of the various opinions expressed, see G. Luedemann, 'Acts of the Apostles as a Historical Source', in J. Neusner, P. Borgen, E.S. Frerichs and R.A. Horsley (eds.), *The Social World of Formative Christianity and Judaism* (Philadelphia: Fortress Press, 1988), pp. 109-25. It is interesting to note that Luedemann's positive conclusion regarding the reliability of the parts of Acts that can be compared with Pauline material is matched by his recognition that the many parts where there is no other source must be assessed simply on the grounds of comparison with examples of the Lukan redaction.

5. Other examples include the reliance on the tannaitic literature regarding post-70 CE Judaism and Thucydides for the so-called Peloponnesian war. On the latter, see E. Badian, 'Thucydides and the Outbreak of the Peloponnesian War: A Historian's Brief', in J.W. Allison (ed.), *Conflict, Antithesis and the Ancient Historian* (Columbus: Ohio State University Press, 1990), pp. 46-91; V. Hunter, *Thucydides: The Artful Reporter* (Toronto: Hakkert, 1973).

his agenda was to be a 'historian'—to provide for his reader an account and explanation of what took place. To understand the role of Josephus in the construction of a modern account of the first century CE, however, we must still explore the relationship between Josephus and his narrative and the impact of that relationship on scholarly reconstructions of the period. Without resolving these questions it will not be possible to establish appropriately the distinction between when, if ever, Josephus's narrative is to be viewed as his interpretation of a given situation and when it is an accurate description of what actually happened.[6]

The test case through which these questions are examined is the state of affairs in first-century CE Judaea. The choice is deliberate. It is an area of historical interest for which Josephus provides a substantial narrative and to which scholarship has also devoted a significant amount of energy. The combination of these two points has also meant that the use of Josephus as a source in historical inquiry has featured prominently in scholarly discussion of the first century CE.

By far the overwhelming outcome to this line of scholarly discussion has been to malign Josephus as a historian, with scholarship readily proclaiming the need for independence from Josephus's interpretation of the situation. It is a central tenant of this study that all the existing discussion within scholarship that purports to establish independence from Josephus's interpretation is fundamentally flawed. Despite the various claims of scholarship, the existing relationship is one of conceptual dependency on the interpretation of Josephus. This line of argument will be developed along two related paths. The first, which incorporates the major portion of the study, establishes the lack of recognition given to the all encompassing nature of Josephus's interpretation of how he presents the first century CE. Scholarship gives an unwarranted and unsubstantiated prominence to an interpretation, with its picture of Judaea being constructed entirely within the parameters established by Josephus. The second path is more positive in outlook. The focus will be to outline a means by which we are able to establish conceptual independence from Josephus—to draw on his

---

6. I am presuming here that there is a desire to go beyond identifying the interpretation of a particular source to an exploration of the actual incidents that are being narrated. I am not, however, implying that the former is any less relevant or legitimate than the latter. On this aspect of historical inquiry see the discussion in Chapter 6.

interpretation but not be bound to his framework for how to understand the dynamic of what was happening in the first century CE. In
effect, a mechanism for employing Josephus in historical inquiry will
be presented, with a view towards fostering the relationship between
Josephus and scholarship.

The two paths dictate the direction of the study. Chapters 1–5 are
devoted to the first path: the lack of recognition given to the all
encompassing nature of Josephus's interpretation and its impact on
scholarly discussion. In Chapter 1 the concern is to outline Josephus's
picture of the state of affairs in first-century CE Judaea up to 66 CE.
The narrative of *War*, *Ant.* and *Life* will be examined. Through this
description it will become evident that Josephus's narrative is
'crafted', being constructed around two basic pillars. These pillars are
that Judaea was a place of increasing turmoil and that the revolt was
bound to take place. Chapter 2 then explores the manner in which
Josephus has developed this crafted narrative of the first century CE.
The account of events is part of what is described as the 'interpretative
framework' of Josephus. This interpretative framework is absolute.
The way the subject matter is narrated, and the actual choice of subject matter, are shaped entirely by the two pillars of how Josephus
understands the first century CE. There is, therefore, no separation
between commentary and narrative, and what we read in Josephus is
an interpretation of what took place in Judaea. The third chapter is
devoted to a detailed description of the various elements of the interpretative framework as they function in *Life*, *War* and *Ant.*
Recognition of the interpretative framework raises the question of its
accuracy and how it is used in the historical inquiry into the first century CE undertaken by scholarship.

With such a gauntlet laid down, Chapters 4 and 5 shift attention
forward to how scholarship interacts with Josephus's narrative.
Chapter 4 commences with a survey of the picture of the state of
affairs in Judaea that is presented by contemporary scholarship. The
most notable feature of this survey is the overwhelming consensus that
the period is framed by Josephus's two pillars: an escalating level of
turmoil; and the inevitability of armed conflict between the Jews and
the Romans. The clear parallel between the picture presented by Josephus and that constructed by scholarship is explored in Chapter 5, in
an effort to explain its presence. Here it is argued that contemporary
scholarship has generally proclaimed conceptual independence from

Josephus but has failed to achieve this goal. Fundamental to this failure is the inability to comprehend fully the exact nature of Josephus's interpretative framework. As a result, in the guise of historical inquiry, scholarship has—more often than not—unconsciously assumed that an interpretation of the first century CE actually stands as the framework from which to understand the period.

The last two chapters look forward to the direction in which the relationship should move. In Chapter 6 an approach that enables the reader to be in dialogue with Josephus but not to be conceptually dependent on him for the means of understanding what happened in first-century CE Judaea is outlined. Where the agenda is to undertake a historical inquiry it is argued that standing outside the interpretative framework is crucial. This view is upheld, not necessarily because Josephus has inaccurately portrayed how to understand the dynamic of the first century CE but because his accuracy, or otherwise, must be substantiated rather than assumed. Discussion of this part of the relationship—the ground rules under which the dialogue can take place—incorporates two separate elements. One pertains primarily to the reader, the other to the text being read. For the reader, rather than trying to claim definitive lines of interpretation regarding the role of such factors as hindsight or the mechanisms of measuring the state of affairs, it is argued that these factors need to be borne in mind as the narrative of Josephus is explored. The other element is what is labelled as the 'case study approach'. This is the means by which the narrative of Josephus is to be employed in a historical inquiry while maintaining conceptual independence. Fundamental to this approach (a development of a method I have employed elsewhere) is that incidents be examined separately. Attempts to draw conclusions are reserved until the synthesis, after all incidents have been discussed individually.

The final chapter provides a sample of how the case study approach operates. Taking one specific year, 66 CE, the various incidents that are contained in Josephus's narratives are identified and three are selected for investigation. Given the brief nature of the example undertaken no attempt is made to suggest definitive conclusions regarding 66 CE. What is evident from the three incidents considered, however, is the effectiveness of the case study approach to provide conceptual independence from Josephus's interpretation of what took place in 66 CE.

This book is essentially a methodological study, exploring the dynamic of the relationship between Josephus, the events he narrates and contemporary scholarship. It is apparent that the existing relationship is far from healthy and that the integrity of scholarship's claims is continually undermined by the approach it adopts. The current use of Josephus is flawed in a fundamental manner. Scholarship generally desires, and asserts, conceptual independence in its use of Josephus within historical inquiry of such topics as the situation in first-century CE Judaea. Unfortunately it fails to achieve this goal. If the intention is to employ Josephus in historical inquiry, then a major shift in approach is required. Conceptual independence is a legitimate goal and it is attainable through the application of the case study approach. The fruits of this approach in the reconstruction of the first century CE are exciting and challenging. The relationship can prosper, but first—as the readers—we must leave the comfort of Josephus's interpretative framework.

Chapter 1

JOSEPHUS'S JUDAEA

'I will now open my narrative with the events named at the beginning of the forgoing summary' (*War* 1.30).[1] With this statement Josephus commences his account of events in *War*. The significance of this account and that located in *Ant.* and *Life* cannot be overstated. Any attempt to describe and explain what happened in Judaea in the period leading up to the revolt must draw heavily on Josephus. My contention is that the appropriate starting point for such an investigation is to let Josephus's accounts be read 'in situ' and at face value. Hence, what follows is a summary of Josephus's narrative, not an attempt to establish 'historical reality' by clarifying, deleting or adding 'corrections'. Instead, it is the ambience of Josephus's description and its possible implications regarding how he should be perceived as a writer that are of concern. We need to begin by taking Josephus as we find him.[2]

A few preliminary comments regarding the approach adopted in the following summary are necessary. The three narrative texts, *War*, *Ant.* and *Life* provide an account of the first century CE period prior to the revolt in varying detail. Although it is important that the integrity and independence of the three texts be preserved, only one overall account will be given. Josephus did not repeat his description of the war in *Ant.*, but he obviously saw no problem with going over

---

1.   The translations of Josephus provided in this work are based on the Loeb version and those of the author. The Greek is cited in brackets after the translation on those occasions where the interpretation of the word or phrase is significant for the discussion. See, in particular, Chapter 7.

2.   P. Bilde also argues for the importance of beginning with what Josephus has to say for himself (*Flavius Josephus between Jerusalem and Rome: His Life, his Works and their Importance* [JSPSup, 2; Sheffield: JSOT Press, 1988], p. 24). It will become apparent in the course of this study, however, that I diverge from the remainder of the approach adopted by Bilde.

the same period in *Ant.* as presented in *War* prior to the revolt. As such, to present one summary, is, in part, an artificial task. However, to provide separate summaries would result in unnecessary repetition. Furthermore, despite the fact that we are dealing with texts written some 20 years apart, it is the work of the one author.[3] Where differences exist in the information contained in the individual accounts they will be cited. In a similar vein, where only one text describes a particular incident it will be acknowledged. Where Josephus repeats himself, however, we will refrain from doing likewise. There are two further comments that relate to the selection of the subject matter. First, I will not describe events which are not directly relevant to the situation in Judaea, such as the machinations in Rome or Alexandria. The second is that the narrative sequence of the texts will not be broken to include material that Josephus locates elsewhere in his accounts. At present, my purpose is simply to encounter the subject matter where it is placed by Josephus.

Our introduction to the first century CE is an event that takes place in 6 CE. In that year Archelaus, appointed ethnarch by Augustus in partial agreement with the request of Herod's final will (*War* 1.664; *Ant.* 17.188-90), was sent into exile. According to *War* 2.111 this occurred in the ninth year of his rule, while in *Ant.* 17.342 it is in the tenth year. The decision to depose Archelaus is presented as being the initiative of Jews and Samaritans (described as 'the first men' in *Ant.* 17.342), rather than a change of Roman policy. The exact nature of the 'brutality' (*War* 2.111) or 'brutality and tyranny' (*Ant.* 17.342) of which Archelaus was accused is not stated. The only detail Josephus provides regarding the end of Archelaus is reference to the latter's dream, foretelling his downfall (*War* 2.112-13; *Ant.* 17.345-48).[4]

---

3. The debate regarding whether Josephus underwent a significant change in attitude between the writing of *War* and the later works *Ant.*, *Life* and *Apion* will be considered in the following chapter. Irrespective of what conclusion is drawn on the issue it is important to acknowledge that we are dealing with the same author and that more is held in common than is disputed in the description of events in first-century CE Judaea. For a discussion of the main approaches to this issue see Bilde, *Flavius Josephus*, pp. 123-71. For the divergent opinions compare T. Rajak, *Josephus: The Historian and his Society* (London: Gerald Duckworth, 1983); S.J.D. Cohen, *Josephus in Galilee and Rome: His Vita and Development as a Historian* (CSCT, 8; Leiden: E.J. Brill, 1979).

4. There is also reference to the dream of Archelaus's wife, which predicted her imminent death (*War* 2.114-16; *Ant.* 17.349-53).

The deposition of Archelaus marked a major change in the nature of the relationship between the Jews and Romans in Judaea.[5] The territory became a province placed under the direct control of a governor (prefect). The first governor, Coponius, was an equestrian (*War* 2.117; *Ant.* 18.2). He was given 'full authority' (*War* 2.118; *Ant.* 18.2), which Josephus claims only in *War* 2.118 as including the right to inflict capital punishment. At this juncture we strike a significant difference in the *War* and *Ant.* accounts. In *War* 2.118 Josephus states that Judas, a Galilaean, 'incited' fellow Jews to rebel against the Romans. The motivation for rebellion is expressed in terms of allegiance, with Judas proclaiming that the Jews should not pay taxes to the Romans because they already had a master—namely, God. Exactly when Judas 'incited' the Jews is not stated; Josephus merely locates Judas within the governorship of Coponius. There is also no information provided regarding the fate of Judas. Josephus simply states that Judas founded a unique 'sect' and then proceeds to outline the three existing Jewish philosophies (*War* 2.119-66).

From the very plotted *War* account we move to *Ant.* In *Ant.* 17.355, 18.1 we learn that Quirinius was appointed by Augustus to be the legate of Syria with a commission to carry out a census of Syria and Judaea. Furthermore, Judaea came under the control of the Syrian legate (*Ant.* 17.335, 18.2). Among the detail included by Josephus is the involvement of Joazar, the serving high priest, who was instrumental in convincing Jews to comply with the census and declare their property for assessment (*Ant.* 18.3). Judas, however, was not willing to cooperate. In league with Saddok, a Pharisee, Judas declared that God alone was their master and that the census was a form of 'slavery' (*Ant.* 18.4-5, 23). For Josephus, this 'invention' was the subsequent cause of disaster for the Jews (*Ant.* 18.5-10, 24). Despite the long editorial comment, however, we are left without any information as to the fate of Judas, Saddok and the followers they obtained. We do not even know whether there was a rebellion. As in *War*, Josephus introduces a digression on the Jewish philosophies (*Ant.* 18.11-25). Here the philosophy founded by Judas is identical to the Pharisees except for their 'passion for liberty' (*Ant.* 18.23).[6] Josephus then returns to

5.   Philip and Herod Antipas remained in control of the territory that was allocated to them by Augustus in accordance with Herod's will (*War* 2.167; *Ant.* 18.27).

6.   Much of the detail contained in the description of the philosophies varies between *War* and *Ant.*, especially in relation to the Essenes. For an interesting

the narrative of events in 6 CE. Quirinius completes the census and replaces Joazar, appointing Ananus b. Sethi as high priest (*Ant.* 18.26). The change is explained as a result of Joazar being 'overpowered by a popular faction', whoever it may have been.

At some point during Coponius's term as governor an incident took place in the temple that is narrated only in *Ant.* 18.29-31. Despite uncertainty as to the exact wording of the text it appears that some Samaritans used a Passover festival as an opportunity to enter the temple and place human bones throughout the temple precinct.[7] As a result, the priests made certain changes to restrict access to the temple. The next events relate to the governorship of Gratus, and again these appear only in *Ant.* Gratus made several changes to the high priesthood. Not one of the changes is explained; each is simply stated in the course of the narrative. Ananus was replaced by Ishmael b. Phabi, who was then replaced by Eleazar b. Ananus (*Ant.* 18.33). After a year Eleazar was deposed in favour of Simon b. Camith (*Ant.* 18.34). In turn, Simon, lasting less than a year, was followed by Joseph Caiaphas (*Ant.* 18.35). Apart from these changes no events are mentioned for the ten-year governorship of Gratus, nor of those who held the office between Coponius and Gratus: namely, Marcus Ambivulus and Amnius Rufus. The only other events narrated by Josephus prior to his description of the governorship of Pilate relate to the building activities of Philip and Herod Antipas. The former constructed Caesarea Philippi and developed Bethsaida Julias (*War* 2.168; *Ant.* 18.28), while the latter, having already restored Sepphoris, went on to construct Tiberias (*War* 2.169; *Ant.* 18.27). According to *Ant.* 18.36-38, many of the residents of Tiberias were forced to settle there by Herod Antipas.

Tiberius replaced Gratus with Pilate in 26 CE. Although both governors held office for a similar period of time it is the latter who is involved in events that Josephus narrates in some detail in *War* and *Ant.* Two incidents are presented as being initiated by the governor,

attempt to explain this distinction see T. Rajak, 'Ciò che Flavio Giuseppe vide: Josephus and the Essenes', in F. Parente and J. Sievers (eds.), *Josephus and the History of the Greco-Roman Period* (SPB, 41; Leiden: E.J. Brill, 1994), pp. 141-60.

7. There appears to be a lacuna in the text. See L.H. Feldman *et al.*, *Josephus. IX. Jewish Antiquities* (LCL; London: Heinemann; Cambridge, MA: Harvard University Press, 1965), p. 27.

both attracting a significant response from the Jews. In the first, troops sent to Jerusalem by Pilate entered the city at night bearing effigies of Caesar on their military standards (*War* 2.169; *Ant.* 18.55). According to *Ant.* 18.55, the purpose of this visit was to house the troops for winter. Furthermore, Pilate was the first governor to allow troops to enter the city bearing effigies (*Ant.* 18.56). At daybreak the Jews expressed their outrage at the 'attack' on their laws (*War* 2.170; *Ant.* 18.55). Jews from Jerusalem and the countryside gathered together to protest. They travelled to Caesarea and remained there for five days, refusing to end their protest (*War* 2.171; *Ant.* 18.57). On the sixth day Pilate brought the situation to a climax, calling a public meeting where he intended to attack the Jews by using disguised troops (*War* 2.172; *Ant.* 18.58). Although threatened by the troops the Jews held fast in their resolve and it was Pilate who relented, ordering the effigies to be removed (*War* 2.174) and returned to Caesarea (*Ant.* 18.59).

In the second incident, Pilate used funds from the sacred treasury for the construction of an aqueduct for Jerusalem (*War* 2.175; *Ant.* 18.60). According to *War* 2.175, the treasury was actually known as the Corbonas. The length of the aqueduct is either 400 furlongs (*War* 2.175) or 200 furlongs (*Ant.* 18.60), and its function, whether for general or a specific usage, is not indicated. A protest takes place, involving many Jews (*Ant.* 18.60). The timing of the protest is unclear. According to *War* 2.175, rather than travel to Caesarea to voice their outrage, the Jewish protest takes place in Jerusalem during a visit by Pilate. The governor dispersed troops among the crowd of protesters (*War* 2.176; *Ant.* 18.61). Failing to curb the protest, Pilate ordered his troops to use force. Although in the ensuing panic a large number of Jews died no further protest is mentioned (*War* 2.177; *Ant.* 18.62).[8]

Ant. contains two further incidents associated with the governorship of Pilate which are absent from *War*. The first is the Testimonium Flavianum (*Ant.* 18.63-64). The possibility of Christian editing makes establishing the exact nature of Josephus's account regarding Jesus of Nazareth difficult to ascertain.[9] The other incident helps to explain

8. At the conclusion of his narrative of the incident in *Ant.* 18.62 Josephus states that there was no further outbreak of 'sedition'.

9. See E. Schürer, *The History of the Jewish People in the Age of Jesus Christ*, I (rev. trans. G. Vermes, F. Millar and M. Black; Edinburgh: T. & T. Clark, 1973), pp. 428-41.

the decision to recall Pilate from Judaea. At the instigation of a Samaritan, many of his compatriots were gathering at Tirathana in preparation to climb Mt Gerizim (*Ant.* 18.85-86). Many Samaritans arrived, bearing arms, in the expectation of being shown the location of the sacred vessels (*Ant.* 18.86). Pilate intervened, sending troops with orders to attack those who had gathered. Representatives of the Samaritan community from 'the boule' (*Ant.* 18.88) sent a delegation to Vitellius, protesting at Pilate's harsh suppression of the gathering. The legate then ordered Pilate to report to Rome to explain his actions. Marcellus was sent to Judaea as Pilate's replacement by Vitellius (*Ant.* 18.89).

In *Ant.*, Vitellius toured Judaea after removing Pilate. While in Jerusalem at Passover he removed taxes on the sale of agricultural goods in the city, and placed control of the high priest's vestments in the hands of the Jews (*Ant.* 18.90). After the deposition of Archelaus, the Romans had taken over responsibility for housing the high priest's robes in Antonia (*Ant.* 18.93). Although the priests and custodians of the treasury were involved in the process of storing the vestments it was the 'warden', presumably a Roman official associated with Antonia, who controlled the robes (*Ant.* 18.93). Vitellius handed over the control of the vestments to the priests, agreeing to allow them to be stored in the temple (*Ant.* 18.95).[10] A final action associated with Vitellius's tour was the removal of Caiaphas from the high priesthood and the appointment of Jonathan b. Ananus by the legate (*Ant.* 18.95).

The next three brief references to events are also located only in *Ant.* The first is the death of Philip the tetrarch (*Ant.* 18.106), whose territory was annexed to the province of Syria by Tiberius (*Ant.* 18.108). In the course of narrating the war between Herod Antipas and Aretas, Josephus describes the second incident. Josephus cites one explanation for Herod's defeat that circulated around the territory— the vengeance of God for Herod's order that John the Baptist be executed (*Ant.* 18.116). Herod, fearing that John and his increasing band of followers would cause 'sedition' to erupt, had John taken to Machaerus where he was put to death (*Ant.* 18.117-19). The other minor incident is associated with Vitellius's preparations for the campaign against Aretas. 'The first men', concerned that Vitellius would

10. In *Ant.* 15.405 Josephus claims that Vitellius was responding to a request made by the Jews in a letter they sent to Tiberius.

march through Judaea with military standards bearing images, urged the legate to take an alternative route (*Ant.* 18.121). Vitellius willingly complied with the request, sending the troops via the Great Plain (*Ant.* 18.122). After agreeing to the request, Vitellius and his associates travelled to Jerusalem, arriving for the celebration of one of the pilgrim festivals. Again, Vitellius took responsibility for removing the incumbent from the high priesthood, Jonathan b. Ananus, presumably in the context of the festival (*Ant.* 18.123). The change was internal as the new high priest was Theophilus b. Ananus, the brother of Jonathan.

The narrative of *War* and *Ant.* then turns to the rise of Agrippa I. The accession of Gaius was to be for the benefit of Agrippa. A friend of Gaius's in his youth, Agrippa was rewarded by the emperor who made him king of what had been the tetrarchy of Philip (*War* 2.181; *Ant.* 18.237). According to *Ant.* 18.237, Judaea remained under Roman control with Marullus being sent as 'commander of the cavalry'. Apparently angered at Agrippa's good fortune, Herod Antipas and his wife Herodias sought an increase in their standing. Agrippa countered the claims of Antipas, with the end result being that Gaius transferred the tetrarchy of Antipas to Agrippa (*War* 2.181-83; *Ant.* 18.240-56).

The general silence regarding what was happening in Judaea is abruptly broken in 40 CE. Gaius's order that statues of him should be erected in the temple is recorded in *War* 2.184-203 and *Ant.* 18.261-309. The order was, according to *War* 2.184, an expression of Gaius's impiety. *Ant.* 18.260-61 gives another, more immediate context: the conflict between Jews and Greeks in Alexandria. Whatever the reason, Petronius, the new legate of Syria, began marshalling his troops and set out to Judaea with either three (*War* 2.186) or two (*Ant.* 18.262) legions and accompanying auxiliaries with orders to place the statue in the temple by agreement, or, if necessary, by force. Petronius's first major stop was Ptolemais, where, according to *Ant.* 18.262, he intended to stay for winter. At Ptolemais he encountered the first wave of Jewish protest (*War* 2.192; *Ant.* 18.263). Large numbers of Jews travelled to Ptolemais to declare their unwillingness to defy their law and comply with Gaius's order. At this juncture Josephus begins to cast Petronius as a man of reason. Rather than ignoring the pleas of the Jews he attempts another approach in an effort to persuade the Jews that the emperor's order must be fulfilled. Petronius, leaving the

bulk of his army and the statues at Ptolemais, travelled to Tiberias
(*War* 2.192), apparently accompanied by his associates, according to
Ant. 18.269. At Tiberias the dialogue continued; Petronius tried to
convince the Jews that they must comply with the order, while the
Jews remained determined not to defy their law. Exactly which Jews
Petronius spoke to is not clear. In *War* 2.193 he is described as
demanding the presence of 'the multitude' and 'all the notable' of the
community, holding public meetings with 'the people' and private
conferences with 'the powerful' (*War* 2.199). In *Ant.* 18.273, Aristobulus (Agrippa's brother), Helcias the elder and 'the noblest' of
Agrippa's house together with 'the first men' appeal to Petronius. The
seriousness of the issue is evident by the length of the protest. Over a
period of 50 (*War* 2.200) or 40 (*Ant.* 18.272) days the fields had been
unattended. Eventually Petronius chose to make a 'brave' decision in
terms of his personal safety. He wrote to Gaius, recommending that
the emperor rescind his order as its fulfilment would require a major
war (*War* 2.201; *Ant.* 18.277). According to *Ant.* 18.279-83, Petronius, informing the Jews of his decision, also implored 'the leading'
Jews to ensure that the unsown fields be attended to immediately (*Ant.*
18.284). In this instance Josephus claims that God's providence was at
work with the sudden downpour of rain (*Ant.* 18.285).

War and *Ant.* differ as to how the incident was resolved. In *War*
2.202-203 Gaius was angered by Petronius's letter but his response
arrived after news reached Petronius that the emperor had been murdered, despite the fact that the emperor's letter had been sent much
earlier. In *Ant.* 18.289-301 Josephus incorporates a story that Agrippa
I, then residing in Rome, had successfully requested that Gaius rescind
his order during a banquet held in the emperor's honour. Gaius wrote
to inform Petronius that if his order had been fulfilled then he was to
let matters rest as they were, but if he had not yet placed the statue in
the temple he was to return it to Antioch (*Ant.* 18.301). It was after
writing this letter that Gaius received Petronius's communiqué, but
news of Gaius's death reached the legate before the second letter of
Gaius arrived (*Ant.* 18.305-309).

Whatever the role of Agrippa I in the case of the statue, he was
soon to benefit from the political machinations in Rome. Most of the
detail is located only in *Ant.* Agrippa sided with Claudius in the
aftermath of Gaius's assassination, and was rewarded for this support
by being made king of the territory controlled by his grandfather,

Herod. The Jews were again placed under the kingship of a Herodian (*War* 2.215; *Ant.* 19.274-75). Only in *Ant.* are a few incidents cited from Agrippa I's reign. On his arrival in Judaea he travelled to Jerusalem to make an offering in the temple (*Ant.* 19.293) and provided financial assistance for a number of Nazarites (*Ant.* 19.294). He also sought to gain support in Jerusalem by reducing the tax placed on every house (*Ant.* 19.299). Two further changes instituted at the beginning of his reign were the replacement of Theophilus as high priest with Simon Cantheras b. Boethus (*Ant.* 19.297) and the appointment of Silas as commander of his army (*Ant.* 19.299). These two appointments were to be changed at a later date. Agrippa proposed to restore Jonathan b. Ananus to the high priesthood by removing Simon (*Ant.* 19.313). Although Jonathan declined the offer, his family retained the office. On Jonathan's recommendation Agrippa appointed Matthias b. Ananus, Jonathan's brother (*Ant.* 19.314-16). Silas, a long-time friend of Agrippa, was removed from office and imprisoned, having over-extended his position by vocalizing his sense of superiority (*Ant.* 19.318-19). Although Agrippa apparently offered to release Silas, the latter refused to accept Agrippa's change of heart and was, therefore, confined to prison until the end of Agrippa's reign (*Ant.* 19.320-25). The one incident which is narrated in *War* and *Ant.* is Agrippa's decision to fortify the new portion of Jerusalem. In *War* 2.218-19 the project was not completed because of Agrippa's death. In *Ant.* 19.326-28, however, it is the order of Claudius to cease work conveyed by Marsus, the legate of Syria, that brought an abrupt end to the project.

According to *Ant.*, at some point during his reign Agrippa defended his actions in relation to the temple. In a brief aside used by Josephus to display Agrippa's kindness the king is challenged and criticized by a resident of Jerusalem, Simon, who was 'accurate in the law' (*Ant.* 19.332). Although warranting a visit to Caesarea by Simon and the holding of a public assembly to proclaim his displeasure, Simon was not punished (*Ant.* 19.333-34). Shortly before his death Agrippa again changed the high priest, returning the office to the family of Cantheras in the hands of Elionaeus (*Ant.* 19.342). The death of Agrippa brought two notable, immediate responses. One was the swift action of Herod of Chalcis and Helcias, the 'prefect'. Before Agrippa's death became public knowledge, these men ordered that Silas be executed (*Ant.* 19.353). The other response was the way the people of Caesarea and Sebaste greeted the news of Agrippa's death (*Ant.* 19.356-57). Their rejoicing was viewed with displeasure by Claudius, who ordered that they be reprimanded (*Ant.* 19.364). Furthermore, he ordered that the auxiliary troops drawn from the two cities be transferred to Pontus (*Ant.* 19.365).[11]

After the short period of direct Jewish rule (41–44 CE) Judaea reverted back to being a Roman province. Adhering to the advice that Agrippa I's son was too young to be entrusted with his father's kingdom, Claudius sent Fadus to act as governor of the province that included Galilee for the first time. Here Josephus's narrative of *War* and *Ant.* presents a different picture of the situation. Fadus's governorship and that of his successor, Tiberius Alexander, are dismissed in *War* 2.220 as times when the governor did not interfere with 'the customs of the country'. In *Ant.* 20, however, especially with Fadus's term of office, Josephus offers quite a different picture. Fadus arrived to find himself required to resolve armed conflict between the Peraean Jews and the residents of Philadelphia. The issue was a territorial dispute over the village of Zia and the behaviour of its inhabitants. Fadus is described as being angered that the Peraean Jews had taken matters into their own hands (*Ant.* 20.3). As a result he had three of their 'first men' imprisoned, executing one named Annibas and exiling the two others, Amaramus and Eleazar (*Ant.* 20.4). Fadus later captured and executed Tholomaeus, 'the brigand chief', who had been active in Idumaea and Arabia. This action, Josephus claimed, marked a point in the history of Judaea that brought an end to the activity of 'brigands' in the province (*Ant.* 20.5).

The other incident associated with Fadus's governorship appears to be in sharp contrast to the claim in *War* that Fadus refrained from interfering in the 'customs of the country'. In *Ant.* 20.6 Fadus ordered the 'chief priests' and 'the first men of Jerusalem' to return the high priest's robes to Antonia to be held under Roman control. Longinus, sent by Claudius to replace Marsus as legate of Syria, decided to travel to Jerusalem with troops, apparently concerned that Fadus's order would result in a 'rebellion' (*Ant.* 20.7). The response of the Jews was to refuse to relinquish control of the robes. Furthermore, they requested that a delegation be sent to Rome to allow them to present their case before Caesar (*Ant.* 20.7). Fadus and Longinus

---

11. According to *Ant.* 19.366 this order was not actually carried out.

agreed to the request on the condition that some children were handed over as hostages, to which the Jews complied (*Ant.* 20.8). Claudius received the envoys, apparently through the agency of Agrippa II (*Ant.* 20.9-10). Josephus quotes the letter in which Claudius cites the precedent established by Vitellius and friendship with Herod of Chalcis, his son Aristobulus and Agrippa II as reasons for granting the request of the envoys, who are named as Cornelius b. Ceras, Tryphon b. Theudas, Dorotheus b. Nathanael and John b. John (*Ant.* 20.10-14).

A final incident during Fadus's governorship described only in *Ant.* 20.97-99 was the capture of Theudas. After a substantial break in the narrative (*Ant.* 20.17-96) Josephus returned to Judaean affairs, briefly describing the activity of Theudas and the response of the Roman officials. Theudas, an 'impostor' (*Ant.* 20.97), had managed to convince a number of the people to travel to the Jordan, carrying their possessions. He claimed to be a prophet who would cause the river to part to allow his followers to cross over. Fadus's response was to send a detachment of cavalry who quickly overwhelmed Theudas and his followers, bringing the head of Theudas to Jerusalem to be put on public display (*Ant.* 20.98).

At some point in time Herod of Chalcis successfully requested that Claudius give him control of the temple and the responsibility to appoint the high priest (*Ant.* 20.15). Before his death Herod made two changes to the office bearer, at first removing Elionaeus b. Cantheras and appointing Joseph b. Camei (*Ant.* 20.16). Herod then had Joseph replaced by Ananias b. Nedebaeus (*Ant.* 20.103). On Herod's death, authority over the temple and the territory of Chalcis were given to Agrippa II by Claudius (*War* 2.223; *Ant.* 20.104).

Two incidents during the procuratorship of Tiberius Alexander are noted in *Ant.* One was a 'great famine' that affected all of Judaea. Some relief from the famine was provided by Queen Helena and her son, Izates, who paid for the purchase of corn from Egypt (*Ant.* 20.101).[12] The other incident was the capture and crucifixion of James and Simon (*Ant.* 20.102). They were sons of Judas the Galilaean who, Josephus reminds the reader, had encouraged the people to rebel against the Romans at the time of the census conducted by Quirinius. The nature of their activities and their offence are not mentioned.

Of the next procurator, Cumanus, Josephus narrates incidents in

12. The assistance given by Helena and Izates is also mentioned in *Ant.* 20.51-53, when Josephus narrates the decision of Helena to convert to Judaism.

both texts. His description of them gives the clear impression that the situation in Judaea was becoming increasingly insecure. The first outbreak of trouble took place during a Passover festival (*War* 2.223-27; *Ant.* 20.106-12). It began when one of the soldiers standing guard on the porticoes exposed his genitals. The Jews present in the temple called for Cumanus to punish the soldier. According to *War* 2.225 some of the Jews, 'hot-headed young men and seditious people in the crowd', began throwing stones at the assembled troops. In *Ant.* 20.108, it is 'the bolder' Jews who undertake the protest. Cumanus responded by calling for reinforcements. The arrival of extra troops struck fear among the crowds and in the ensuing panic many Jews were trampled to death by their compatriots as they tried to flee. As a result, the festival became a time of mourning (*War* 2.227; *Ant.* 20.112).

Following the trouble at Passover, a further incident brought conflict to Judaea (*War* 2.228-31; *Ant.* 20.113-17). Here the instigators were 'brigands' (*War* 2.228) or 'seditious revolutionaries' (*Ant.* 20.113), who robbed a slave of Caesar named Stephen as he travelled the open road near Beth-horon, according to *War* 2.228, or 100 furlongs from Jerusalem according to *Ant.* 20.113. Cumanus dispatched troops to punish the villages located near the scene of the robbery. They were to bring 'the most eminent' (*Ant.* 20.114) or 'the inhabitants in chains' (*War* 2.229) to account for not pursuing the 'brigands' (*War* 2.229). In the process of fulfilling the orders one of the soldiers discovered a copy of the law in a village. He either tore up the book and threw it in a fire (*War* 2.229) or yelled obscenities as he ripped it apart (*Ant.* 20.115).[13] News of the action stirred many Jews to demand Cumanus to punish the soldier, taking their protest to the governor at Caesarea rather than waiting for him to act. The energy of the Jewish protest appears to have had a positive impact on Cumanus. In *Ant.* 20.117 Josephus adds details stating that Cumanus feared 'another revolution of the multitude' and consulted with his associates. The governor chose to acquiesce to the demands of the protesters, ordering the execution of the soldier, apparently after he had been paraded before his accusers (*War* 2.231). According to *Ant.* 20.117, by beheading the soldier, Cumanus had thus prevented the

---

13. Playing on the metaphor of fire, Josephus colourfully describes that all the Jews were enraged as though the entire country 'had been consumed in the flames' by the soldier's action in *War* 2.230.

'sedition' when it threatened to begin for a second time.

The final incident associated with Cumanus's governorship was also to be the cause for his removal from office. It began as a dispute between Galilaeans and Samaritans, only to be resolved finally in a hearing before the emperor in Rome. While travelling through Samaria on the way to Jerusalem for one of the pilgrim festivals, either a single Galilaean (*War* 2.232) or many Galilaeans (*Ant.* 20.118) was/were murdered by Samaritans, from the village of Gema (*War* 2.232) or Ginae (*Ant.* 20.118). In the response that follows *War* and *Ant.* provide a different sequence of events. According to *War* 2.333 many Galilaeans gathered together in preparation for an attack on the Samaritans while 'the notable' Galilaeans travelled to see Cumanus to voice their protest and seek his aid to punish the murderers in an effort to restore order. Cumanus, however, dismissed the Galilaeans without offering to resolve the trouble. In *Ant.* these actions are reversed. 'The first' Galilaeans go to Cumanus (*Ant.* 20.119). He refuses to help, having been bribed by the Samaritans and then the Galilaeans call on the 'Jewish multitude' to take up arms 'and to assert their liberty' (*Ant.* 20.120).

Here the narratives converge in the sequence of events, if not in all the detail. In *War*, when the news of the murder reached Jerusalem 'the people' who had gathered there for the festival immediately set out for Samaria, without any 'generals' and ignoring the pleas of the 'magistrates' (*War* 2.234). The 'brigands and insurgents' were led by Eleazar b. Deinaeus and Alexander (*War* 2.235). They attacked the border territory of Acrabatene, killing many of the inhabitants of the villages. According to *Ant.* 20.121, although the 'leading men' offered to take the case to Cumanus again, 'the masses' took up arms, calling Eleazar b. Deinaeus, a long-time 'brigand', to their aid and they began to attack Samaritan villages.

Cumanus decided to intervene, marching from Caesarea with the Sebastenian cavalry, infantry and, according to *Ant.* 20.122, armed Samaritans. He attacked and defeated the Jews. The 'magistrates of Jerusalem' (*War* 2.237) succeeded in convincing 'the people' to disperse (*War* 2.238). In *Ant.* it is those of 'rank and birth in Jerusalem' who plead with 'the rebels' to cease their activity for the sake of their families and country (*Ant.* 20.123). Convinced, the masses dispersed and the 'brigands' fled to their hideaways (*Ant.* 20.124). Any sense of order, however, was superficial according to Josephus. Bands of 'brigands' (*War* 2.238; *Ant.* 20.124) roamed the countryside from this point in time onwards.

'The powerful' (*War* 2.239), or 'the first' (*Ant.* 20.125) Samaritans did not let matters rest. They went to see Quadratus, the legate, in Tyre to accuse the Jews of destroying their villages (*War* 2.239; *Ant.* 20.125). According to *Ant.* 20.126, the nature of the Samaritan charge was that the Jews had taken matters into their own hands rather than awaiting Roman adjudication. The Jews also travelled to Tyre to register their own protest (*War* 2.240; *Ant.* 20.127). *War* 2.240 names among the Jewish 'notables' the high priest Jonathan. They laid responsibility for the trouble at the feet of the Samaritans and Cumanus because he refused to punish the culprits. According to *Ant.* 20.127, Cumanus had been bribed. Quadratus decided to delay any judgment until he reached the scene of the crime. Once in Caesarea (*War* 2.241) or Samaria (*Ant.* 20.129) he ordered the execution of the prisoners held by Cumanus. *Ant.* 20.129 adds that Quadratus investigated the case while at Samaria, levelling blame at the Samaritans and also ordering the execution of Samaritans and Jews that had participated in the 'revolution'. Travelling on to Lydda he allowed the Samaritans a further hearing. Quadratus then ordered the execution of other people deemed involved in the trouble—all of whom were Jews. In *War* 2.242 there are 18 who are beheaded while in *Ant.* 20.130 it is five of the instigators that are executed, one of whom is named as Doetus. Next Quadratus decided to pass the final resolution of the matter over to Caesar. The 'most distinguished' Samaritans (*War* 2.243) or 'the first men' (*Ant.* 20.132) along with Cumanus and the military tribune Celer were ordered to travel to Rome (*War* 2.244; *Ant.* 20.131). The Jewish delegates named in *War* and *Ant.* are different. In *War*, the high priests Jonathan and Ananias, two others of 'the most powerful men', Ananus b. Ananias and some other 'notable' Jews are sent (*War* 2.243). In *Ant.* 20.131 Josephus names Ananias, the high priest, Ananus the captain and their followers as being sent to Rome, apparently in chains. Finally, Quadratus decided to visit Jerusalem, according to *Ant.* 20.133, because he feared a 'revolution' by the Jews. His arrival coincided with a festival, which is identified as Passover in *War* 2.244. Satisfied that all was in order in Jerusalem he departed for Antioch (*War* 2.244; *Ant.* 20.133).

In Rome, Cumanus and the Samaritans were supported by prominent Romans while Agrippa came to the aid of the Jews (*War* 2.245;

Ant. 20.135). According to *Ant.* 20.135, Agrippa managed to influence Claudius through the agency of Agrippina. On hearing the case Claudius found in favour of the Jews, ordering the execution of the Samaritan deputies (*Ant.* 20.136) or three of their 'most prominent men' (*War* 2.245), Cumanus to be exiled and Celer to be returned to Jerusalem where he would be publicly executed after being dragged through the city (*War* 2.246; *Ant.* 20.136).

The narrative of events during Felix's incumbency is even more detailed and suggestive of increased trouble than that of his predecessor, Cumanus. Territorial realignments took place when first Claudius and then Nero adjusted the kingdom of Agrippa II. Claudius transferred Agrippa from Chalcis to what had been the tetrarchy of Philip and the kingdom of Lysansias (*War* 2.247; *Ant.* 20.138). On his accession Nero confirmed Felix as governor of Judaea but also gave Agrippa II control of several cities and their toparchies previously under the control of the governor—Abila (not in *Ant.*), Julias, Tarichaeae and Tiberius (*War* 2.252; *Ant.* 20.159). In Judaea 'brigands and impostors' were active throughout the country (*Ant.* 20.160). In his efforts to restore order Felix managed to capture and send to Rome for trial Eleazar b. Deinaeus, a 'brigand chief' (*War* 2.253; *Ant.* 20.161). According to *War* 2.253 Eleazar had been active for some 20 years, and in *Ant.* 20.161 his capture was achieved by the use of a rouse. In *War* 2.253 Josephus adds that other 'brigands' were executed and many of the 'populace' were punished.

War 2.254 then introduces a new type of brigand group that began in Jerusalem, the sicarii. Mingling among the crowd of worshippers in Jerusalem, especially at festivals, they murdered people, the first being Jonathan, the high priest (*War* 2.255-56). Their activities caused great fear and anxiety among the Jewish people (*War* 2.256-57). *Ant.* describes the death of Jonathan in a different manner. There Felix is the instigator, wanting to remove Jonathan because of his vocal criticism of the governor, someone that the high priest had originally supported (*Ant.* 20.162). Felix bribed Doras, Jonathan's trusted friend, to use 'brigands' (*Ant.* 20.163). They mingle with the crowd at the festivals, disguise their daggers under their cloaks and then carry out further murders in the safety of their anonymity (*Ant.* 20.164-66).

Matters worsened because 'deceivers and impostors' became active (*War* 2.259; *Ant.* 20.167). They fostered 'revolution' and persuaded many of the people to flock to the desert to witness signs of deliverance being performed (*War* 2.259; *Ant.* 20.168). Felix was quick to respond, dispatching troops to punish the crowds that gathered (*War* 2.260; *Ant.* 20.168). One particular example of such an impostor is the Egyptian 'false prophet' (*War* 2.261; *Ant.* 20.169). *War* 2.261-63 and *Ant.* 20.169-72 differ in a number of the details regarding the account of the Egyptian. According to *War* 2.262 the Egyptian travels through the country, taking a circular route before arriving at the Mount of Olives. The prophet intended to force entry into Jerusalem, overpower the Roman garrison and set himself up as 'tyrant'. According to *Ant.* 20.169-70, however, declaring himself to be a prophet on his arrival in Jerusalem, he persuaded many of the masses to go out to the Mount of Olives where he would demonstrate his power, commanding the walls of Jerusalem to fall, and allowing entrance to the city. For the remainder of the story the sequence of the two texts agree. Before the Egyptian could do anything, Felix sent out a detachment of troops which attacked the Egyptian. According to *War* 2.263, 'the people' joined in the attack. Although many of his followers were killed or imprisoned, the Egyptian managed to escape capture. The end of the Egyptian episode, however, only marked the beginning of even more 'impostors and brigands' being active and working together (*War* 2.264). In *Ant.* 20.172 it is only 'brigands' that are active. Attempting to turn the people towards war with Rome, they attacked those that refused to comply and looted the property of the wealthy (*War* 2.264-65; *Ant.* 20.172).

Felix also found himself having to deal with conflict between the Jewish and Syrian portion of the population at Caesarea (*War* 2.266-70; *Ant.* 20.173-78). This dispute was to reappear on several later occasions during the governorships of Festus and Florus. At issue were the respective rights of 'citizenship' for each group in the city. The Jews claimed they had the 'right' because the city was founded by Herod, while the Syrians claimed that the place had been inhabited by Syrians prior to the founding of Caesarea (*War* 2.266; *Ant.* 20.173). The dispute, initially verbal, soon involved open violence, despite the efforts of the older Jews trying to constrain their 'own insurgents' (*War* 2.267). The 'prefects' tried to control the situation in which the wealth of the Jews was matched by the military support of the Roman troops for the Syrians (*War* 2.269; *Ant.* 20.176). The conflict reached the point where Felix intervened after one skirmish. When the Jews refused to retire, Felix ordered his troops to attack. They killed many Jews and then ransacked their properties (*War* 2.270; *Ant.* 20.177). According to *Ant.* 20.178, the troops were stopped when 'the eminent' Jews appealed to Felix. The *War* account mentions that the 'sedition' continued until eventually Felix selected 'notable' Jews and Syrians to take their case to Nero (*War* 2.270).[14]

The narrative of *War* and *Ant.* takes quite a different shape from the end of Felix's governorship until 66 CE. *War* is extremely brief in its discussion of affairs under Festus and Albinus while with Florus there is a very lengthy account of events in 65/66 CE. In *Ant.*, on the other hand, the bulk of Josephus's attention lies in affairs associated with Festus and Albinus; Florus draws only a very brief mention. According to *Ant.* 20.179-81 either just before or after Festus's arrival, Josephus narrates trouble that was developing in Jerusalem. Agrippa II's appointment of Ishmael b. Phabi as high priest marked the occasion of conflict between the chief priests on one side and the priests and 'the first men of the population of Jerusalem' on the other. Working as 'factions' they gathered together bands of 'the most reckless revolutionaries' (*Ant.* 20.180). Their conflicts were verbal and physical, with the chief priests even going so far as to deprive many priests of the tithes by sending their 'slaves' to the threshing floor to take the offerings (*Ant.* 20.181).

Of Festus, the *War* narrative only briefly states that he attacked the 'brigands' (2.271). In *Ant.* 20.185-88 Festus is faced with 'brigands' ravaging the country. Especially prominent at the time were the sicarii (*Ant.* 20.186). Festus is also described as taking action against an 'impostor' active in the countryside (*Ant.* 20.188). The troops sent by the governor killed the impostor and many of his followers. In *Ant.* 20.189-96 Festus soon became embroiled in a dispute that arose between Agrippa and some of the prominent Jews in Jerusalem. Agrippa extended the height of his palace in Jerusalem by adding an extra chamber (*Ant.* 20.189). As a result he was able to view the activities in the temple. 'The eminent men' of Jerusalem were angered, believing Agrippa to have broken the established tradition, and they responded by building a wall to block the view (*Ant.* 20.191). This action not only blocked Agrippa's view but also that from the western portico, thus inhibiting the Romans' ability to see in the

14. In *Ant.* 20.182 Josephus states that 'the first men' among the Caesarean Jews travelled to Rome in order to protest about Felix when he was deposed.

temple precinct (*Ant.* 20.192). Both Agrippa and Festus were angered and the governor ordered that the wall be pulled down (*Ant.* 20.193). The Jews declined, requesting that the matter be decided by Nero. The request was granted by Festus, with Ishmael b. Phabi, Helicas, the treasurer and ten of 'the first men' acting as the delegates (*Ant.* 20.193-94). Although Nero found in favour of the Jewish envoys Poppaea had Ishmael and Helicas detained in Rome (*Ant.* 20.195). With the high priesthood now vacant Agrippa chose Joseph Cabi b. Simon as the replacement (*Ant.* 20.196).

Festus appears to have died in office and before his replacement, Albinus, arrived a further incident took place that is described only in *Ant.* 20.197-203. Joseph Cabi's stay as high priest was short-lived. He was replaced by Ananus b. Ananus (*Ant.* 20.197). Soon after his appointment Ananus had a number of Jews tried and executed on an unspecified charge, including James, the brother of Jesus (*Ant.* 20.200). Residents of Jerusalem—'the most fair minded and accurate in observance of the law'—complained to Agrippa II and the new governor, Albinus (*Ant.* 20.201). The latter threatened the high priest with punishment while Agrippa deposed Ananus and replaced him with Jesus b. Damnaeus (*Ant.* 20.203).

During Albinus's term of office the situation in Judaea is presented as deteriorating even further. In *War* 2.272-76 Josephus continues to provide only a brief description of events, casting Albinus in a very negative light. He plundered and stole property, used extraordinary taxes to exact more money and accepted ransoms for the release of people from prison, with only those who could not afford to pay anything remaining in captivity (*War* 2.273). In Jerusalem, 'the powerful among the revolutionary party' bribed Albinus to give them a free hand (*War* 2.274). Leaders of these bands acted like 'brigand chiefs', plundering and tormenting the people, who constantly lived in a state of fear (*War* 2.275-76).

This bleak picture is not entirely mirrored in *Ant.* 20.204-15. Albinus began his term by attacking the sicarii (*Ant.* 20.204). In Jerusalem, Ananias managed to extend his prominence with gifts of money for the governor, the serving high priest and the people of the city (*Ant.* 20.205). Ananias's servants, however, in league with 'the most reckless men', confiscated most of the tithes from the threshing floor, resulting in many poorer priests starving to death (*Ant.* 20.206-207). The sicarii undertook a new tactic. At a festival they kidnapped 'the secretary' of Eleazar b. Ananias, demanding a ransom for his release (*Ant.* 20.208). Ananias intervened and managed to convince Albinus to agree to the terms—the release of ten sicarii from prison (*Ant.* 20.209). The success of this first venture only encouraged the 'brigands' to repeat the action, targeting the staff of Ananias (*Ant.* 20.210). Further trouble among the Jews was sparked by Agrippa's replacement of Jesus b. Damnaeus as high priest with Jesus b. Gamaliel (*Ant.* 20.213). As rivals these men and others, such as Costobar and Saul, gathered together bands of 'the most reckless men'. Ananias remained the most prominent thanks to his ability to offer bribes (*Ant.* 20.214). Finally, with the news that he was to be replaced, Albinus cleared the prisons. Those deserving death were executed while others imprisoned on only minor charges were released. To Josephus the effect of this action was that Judaea was 'infested with brigands' (*Ant.* 20.215).

Ant. closes its narration of events with four incidents associated with Agrippa II, without giving an exact chronological location. Two requests were made of Agrippa II as custodian of the temple. The Levites successfully requested that they be allowed to wear linen robes just as the priests, rather than their previous robes (*Ant.* 20.215-17). A further request for a change in practice was that those who sang the hymns be allowed to learn them by heart (*Ant.* 20.218). To Josephus these changes marked an unwarranted departure from the established custom. The third incident was associated with the completion of all the work on the temple. To provide employment and use surplus funds Agrippa was requested to grant permission for the raising of the east portico (*Ant.* 20.221). Although Agrippa refused this request he did allow the city to be paved in white stone (*Ant.* 20.222). Finally, Agrippa removed Jesus b. Gamaliel from the high priesthood, replacing him with Matthias b. Theophilus (*Ant.* 20.223). Exactly when the change took place is not stated.

Around the time that Florus became governor an incident only recorded in *Life* has Josephus travelling to Rome to defend several priests (*Life* 13). These priests, known to Josephus, had been sent to Rome by Felix on a 'slight and trifling charge'. They appear to have been released, thanks to the aid of Poppaea, but we are not informed as to their exact fate (*Life* 16).

The structure of the narrative in *War* and *Ant.* is reversed in the description of Florus's governorship. In *Ant.* 20.254-55 Josephus provides no account of any specific events. The two years before the war were a time of escalating trouble, largely resulting from the actions of Florus. He joined together with the 'brigands' seeking to acquire whatever spoils he could (*Ant.* 20.255). Many Jews left the country under the increasing burden, while those who remained were eventually forced into a situation where they had to rebel (*Ant.* 20.256-57). *War* cites the criminal depravity of Florus but also includes a description of some events. Justice became obsolete, brigandage was acceptable on the payment of money and cities were pillaged, with Florus seeking to extend his wealth (*War* 2.277-79). Josephus states that although the Jews did not send a deputation to Cestius in Antioch, when the legate visited Jerusalem at Passover he was greeted with protests regarding the behaviour of Florus (*War* 2.280). Guaranteeing that Florus would be more lenient, Cestius returned to Antioch (*War* 2.281). The result of the protest was the exact opposite to that intended: instead of relief, the departure of Cestius marked an increased effort by Florus to protect himself from censure by pushing the Jews to the point of rebellion (*War* 2.282-83).

The situation in Caesarea apparently provided Florus with the opportunity to further his cause. Nero had found in favour of the Syrians, giving them authority over the Jews (*War* 2.284). According to *Ant.* 20.183, Nero's assistants were bribed. Tension was high in the city. The Jews wanted to purchase a plot of land that adjoined their synagogue (*War* 2.285).[15] The Greek owner of the land refused all offers and decided to build workshops, obstructing access to the synagogue. Some Jews, the 'hot-headed youths', tried to stop the construction work (2.286). Florus intervened to restore order. At this juncture John, the tax-collector and other 'notable' Caesarean Jews bribed Florus in an effort to call a halt to the building (2.287). After taking the money, however, Florus left Caesarea and travelled to Sebaste without ordering the work to stop. The following day, the sabbath, was marked by further violence. The Jews gathered at the synagogue to find that a Caesarean 'insurgent' had placed a pot outside the entrance on which he was sacrificing birds (2.289). The Jews were outraged and soon 'the insurgent, passionate youths' were in conflict with the Caesareans (2.290). The cavalry commander, Jucundus, tried to quell the trouble without great success. As a result the Jews took

15. All subsequent references to the text of Josephus in this chapter will be to *War* unless otherwise stated.

their copy of the law and fled for Narbata (2.291). Twelve of 'the leading men', including John, went to see Florus at Sebaste to protest at his lack of support, only to be arrested for having taken the copy of the law away from Caesarea (2.292).

Attention soon turned to Jerusalem. News of the situation at Caesarea caused much anger. Florus made matters worse by issuing an order that 17 talents be paid to him out of the temple treasury (2.293). Jews gathered at the temple to voice their indignation while some 'insurgents' made a mock collection of money (2.295). Florus reacted by gathering his troops to march on Jerusalem to acquire the funds, ignoring the situation in Caesarea. Josephus states that the people decided to greet Florus as he approached the city, but were turned away by Capito (2.297-300). Florus entered the city and resided in the palace. On the following day he demanded that the 'chief priests, powerful men and most eminent citizens of Jerusalem' hand over for punishment the men responsible for making the mock collection (2.301). They pleaded with Florus that the 'foolish youths' should be excused if he wished to preserve peace in Judaea (2.303). Florus responded by sending troops to attack the agora. Many people were killed, others had their property looted and some, including those of equestrian order, were scourged and crucified (2.305-308). A witness to what happened, Bernice, sent some of her officers to plead with Florus to bring an end to the rampaging (2.310).

On the next day Jews gathered in the upper agora to express their anger. Concerned that Florus would respond with further violence, the 'chief priests' tried to placate the crowd, while Florus, apparently wanting to rekindle the conflict, devised a plan to cause further trouble (2.318-20). He called for reinforcements from Caesarea, telling the troops not to accept any greeting offered by the Jews as they approached Jerusalem. However, to the 'chief priests' and 'the notable men' the governor said that the Jews could prove their loyalty by greeting the troops coming from Caesarea. At a meeting in the temple the chief priests tried to convince the people that they should display their loyalty (2.320). At first the 'insurgent party' and the people refused to comply. All 'the priests' and all 'the ministers of God' pleaded with the people, appealing 'by name to each of the notables individually' (2.321-24). In time they prevailed, curtailing 'the insurgents' and leading the people to welcome the troops (2.325). Following Florus's order the troops ignored the Jews and drew the expected

response, with 'the insurgents' verbalizing their anger against Florus
(2.326). The troops then attacked the crowd. As the people fled into
the city they were followed by the troops who were trying to seize
control of the temple. At the same time Florus sent troops from the
palace in an effort to reach Antonia (2.328). Both attempts failed,
with the Jews forcing the Romans to retreat (2.329). After 'the insurgents' destroyed the porticoes linking Antonia with the temple, Florus
decided to leave the city (2.330). He gave responsibility for affairs in
Jerusalem to the 'chief priests' and the 'boule', who requested that he
leave one of the cohorts that had recently arrived from Caesarea to
maintain order (2.332).

Florus dispatched a report to Cestius, claiming the Jews were
rebelling, while 'the magistrates' of Jerusalem and Bernice also sent a
report laying blame with Florus (2.333-34). Cestius decided to send
Neapolitanus to investigate the situation. He was accompanied on his
tour by Agrippa, who had returned from Alexandria. At Jamina,
Agrippa was met by the 'chief priests, powerful and boule' to express
their concern (2.336-38). Neapolitanus's visit was without event; he
toured the agora, went to the temple and returned to Cestius to report
that all was in order (2.339-41).

In response to requests by the populace that an embassy be sent to
Nero, Josephus records a lengthy speech made by Agrippa in an effort
to quell their animosity (2.345-401). Initially the Jews followed the
advice of Agrippa, began repairing the porticoes and collected the
taxes that were required (2.405-406). However, when he encouraged
them to accept Florus as their governor until a replacement was sent,
he was banished from the city (2.406). As a final action Agrippa sent
'the magistrates' and 'the powerful' to Florus so that the governor
could appoint some among their number to collect the tribute (2.407).

What followed was the open fragmentation of the Jewish
community in Judaea. Eleazar b. Ananias convinced 'the ministers' to
cease accepting the offerings on behalf of foreigners (2.409). At the
same time Masada was captured by 'the most ardent promoters
of war' (2.408). The 'chief priests' and 'the notables' (2.410) and then
the 'chief priests', 'the powerful men' and 'most notable Pharisees'
(2.411) tried to persuade Eleazar and his associates, which included
'the most vigorous of the revolutionaries', to repeal their action
(2.410). Having failed in their efforts, those in favour of peace
sent requests to Florus and to Agrippa for aid, but only the latter

responded positively (2.418-21). The city was now divided in two. The pro-peace group, which included Agrippa's troops, the chief priests and some of the people occupied the upper city, while the lower city and the temple were occupied by 'the insurgents' (2.422). After seven days of skirmishing between the two groups, the Jews in the temple were joined by some of the sicarii, who gained entrance to the temple (2.425). The pro-peace group were forced to flee the upper city (2.426). The rebels destroyed the house of Ananias, the palaces of Agrippa and Bernice and then the public records archives, which housed debt records (2.426-27). Ananias, Ezechias, Saul, Costobar and others fled to the palace of Herod (2.429).

On the next day 'the insurgents' captured the Antonia and killed the garrison (2.430). It was about now that Josephus apparently sought refuge within the temple (*Life* 20). Then the attack on Herod's palace commenced. In this task 'the insurgents' were accompanied by Menahem, who had entered Jerusalem to act as leader of the revolt with his brigands as his bodyguard (2.433-36). Eventually those inside the palace of Herod sued for terms. Menahem and 'the leaders of the insurrection' allowed the royal troops and other Jews to leave, but barred the Romans from departing (2.437), who then fled to the towers that adjoined the palace. Menahem's forces captured and then killed Ananias and his brother as they tried to hide (2.441). Angered at this action, Eleazar, his followers and the people turned on Menahem, who was killed along with many of his supporters (2.443-45). Those who survived fled to Masada (2.447). With the death of Menahem and 'the first men of the brigands', Josephus left the temple and met with the 'chief priests' and 'the first Pharisees' (*Life* 22). In Jerusalem, Eleazar turned his attention to the Roman troops still in the towers—the only group still in the city actively and openly opposed to the rebels. The Romans sought and received terms for their safe passage out of Jerusalem (2.451). However, when the troops laid down their arms they were murdered by Eleazar's supporters (2.453). According to Josephus this deplorable action took place on the sabbath (2.456).

As Cestius prepared to march on Judaea trouble broke out in Caesarea and other cities between the Jews and Greeks (2.457-60). Cestius marched from Ptolemais with the twelfth legion, aided by troops from Agrippa (2.499-502). He dispatched Gallus to deal with Galilee (2.510-13). Cestius then marched on Jerusalem, destroying Antipatris and Lydda on the way (2.513-16). The Jews attacked the Romans with a frontal and rear assault. After this initial conflict Cestius managed to push back the Jews (2.517-22). Camping at Mt Scopus, the legate made preparations for an attack on the city. 'The insurgents' abandoned the new city (Bezetha) for the safety of the temple and the inner city (2.530). Cestius quickly occupied the territory left vacant with the view towards attacking the royal palace but was persuaded against this by Tyrannius, who had apparently been bribed by Florus (2.531). Among the Jews, Ananus b. Jonathan, encouraging 'the notable citizens', planned to open the city to the Romans (2.533). 'The insurgents', on hearing of Ananus's intentions, had him and his associates removed from guarding the wall (2.534). Cestius then launched an attack on the north side of the temple. The Roman troops began to undermine the wall. However, for some unstated reason Cestius decided to raise the siege (2.540). His retreat turned into a disaster. After a fighting retreat to the pass of Beth-horon Cestius fled overnight, leaving most of the baggage to be captured by the Jews (2.546-50). The pursuit of the Romans continued as far as Antipatris (2.554). The revolt had begun.

Three observations that direct our attention beyond the text to focus on the author stand out from the forgoing summary of Josephus's description. The first relates to the relationship of the narratives in terms of the subject matter they provide. For the period between 6–66 CE there are more occasions where the same incident is narrated in *War* and *Ant.* than there are incidents recorded in only one text. Furthermore, where the texts overlap there is a substantial amount of agreement in the content of each version. However, *Ant.* is not simply a copy or amplification of the *War* account. For example, the Galilaean–Samaritan dispute and the statue of Gaius are littered with differences in minor detail. These differences can be explained by several plausible arguments, ranging from the use of different sources to authorial laziness. It is also evident that some of the differences do not greatly alter the structure of the incident. For example, whether the strike over the statue of Gaius lasted 40 or 50 days does not change the outcome, nor the motivation of Petronius to take action. Their presence in the narrative, however, indicates that *War* and *Ant.* are an interpretation of the event. One or both texts may accurately preserve the historical details of particular incidents, such as who was involved, when things happened and in what order. The presence of the differences alerts the reader to the issue of authorial historical perception and the notion of interpretation in the construction of the narrative. Josephus may be writing 'history', but in what sense and for what purpose? Furthermore, given the differences in content between *War* and *Ant.*, what type of influences controlled the narrative that Josephus constructed?

The second observation echoes the concerns raised in the first. The *War*, *Ant.* and *Life* appear to be 'crafted texts'. That Josephus does not simply narrate all known events in a chronological sequence is apparent in a number of ways. For example, the narrative of the events is laced with numerous overt editorial comments. Often Josephus's comments are directed towards explaining why people acted as they did or the implication of certain events as in the case of the protest at Passover while Cumanus was governor. Even the nature of the subject indicates that the texts are crafted by Josephus. For example, mention of high priests in *Ant.* is relevant as part of the 'history' but not relevant for the pre-war summary of *War*.

Two further important indications that the texts are crafted also relate to the presentation of the content. One is that not all information regarding events is presented in its appropriate chronological sequence, let alone in all the texts. Prime examples include the 'census' of 65/66 CE (*War* 6.422-23) and the activity of Jesus b. Ananias (*War* 6.300-309). These details regarding historical events are located in sections of *War* where they fit a particular thematic scheme. Their inclusion, therefore, is deliberate. The other indication is the selective nature of the subject matter included. What Josephus provides is a very potted account. There are many periods of silence. After the governorship of Coponius, apart from Gratus's appointment of high priests, it is not until Pilate's term of office that any event is mentioned. These gaps can be explained in terms of either a lack of sources, a lack of anything to record or maybe a lack of interest. These 'holes' aside, many of the incidents recorded contain large grey areas. For example, names are not used to identify those who make the mock collection or those who capture Masada. These gaps pertain to significant elements of the basic narration of incidents that Josephus deemed relevant for his texts, but for some reason or another did not clarify. One reason that must feature prominently among those given for the greyness is choice on the part of the author as he crafted his narrative to comply with certain agendas.[16]

The third observation relates to the picture of first-century CE Judaea that emerges from the texts. Although each account conveys a distinctive edge to the picture of the situation, underlying their individual touches is a common thread that portrays two central pillars. One is that there were many disputes in Judaea and that trouble on a communal level was escalating into open conflict. The 'mood' of the description is that Judaea is engulfed in a pressure cooker atmosphere where the momentum of affairs is towards war, especially in the period after the return of direct Roman rule in 44 CE. In this context, the second pillar is that the revolt in 66 CE comes as an inevitable pinnacle: the explosion is the culmination of intensifying political and social disintegration in a territory that was tossed from one crisis to another. Within this framework Josephus describes the revolt as the responsibility of an unrepresentative minority in the Jewish community. Judaea was a place where the situation was out of hand, in which a rogue subsection of the community, acting as a disease, was able to foster trouble until it drove Judaea into conflict with Rome. Exasperating the situation was the inability of some governors to contain, and the deliberate provocation of others to nurture, the 'disease' within Jewish society. In this world-view a central position is given to the revolt, especially the disastrous climax in 70 CE. The description of the first century CE acts as a channel, a means by which Josephus directs the attention of the reader to the catastrophe that unfolded.

The preceding summary of Josephus's Judaea raises important questions that must be addressed regarding the use of his narrative. In what sense is it a history of Judaea? What was his attitude to writing? What was his understanding of 'history', especially in terms of determining the appropriate subject matter and means of constructing his narrative? These questions are all the more important because of the monopoly Josephus holds as a window into what was happening in Judaea during the period prior to the revolt. They point to a fundamental issue associated with how Josephus's narratives of the first century CE should be treated. Are they primarily 'inanimate' descriptions of events which have been subject to some minor tinkering by

---

16. There are two further examples of the text being crafted. One is the prominence of individuals, especially rulers, and incidents relating to Jerusalem, in the narrative. The other example is the disproportionate weight of the narrative in *War* 2 where the events of 66 CE constitute the vast majority of Josephus's attention.

the author? Alternatively, are they 'animate' entities, crafted by the author? To further address these questions our attention turns directly to Josephus, to explore his self-consciousness as reflected in his texts.

Chapter 2

JOSEPHUS THE WRITER:
EXPLORING THE NATURE OF HIS INTERPRETATIVE FRAMEWORK

The events that took place during Josephus's lifetime make him a
person of interest. He witnessed and survived events that had a dramatic and permanent impact on the functioning of Jewish society. In
fact, his direct involvement in the revolt, particularly his survival in
the Roman camp, have made him a major target for criticism. That
Josephus was also an active participant in many of the events and subsequently decided to record some of them, especially the revolt of 66–
70 CE, makes him an important source for a scholarly inquiry into the
dynamics of second-temple-period Jewish society in Judaea. The
veracity of his narrative, however, has long been questioned—an
activity that Josephus openly exposes himself to through such obvious
discrepancies as the *War* and *Life* accounts of his actions as a general
in Galilee.

The primary focus of this chapter is to explore the personal perspective of Josephus, particularly how he worked as an author. The
key issue is to establish how Josephus interacts with his narrative and
in turn, therefore, how the reader should approach the texts. The
central contention is that his narratives are animate works. They are
not neutral and lifeless but narratives steeped in hindsight and formed
by what I term the 'interpretative framework' of Josephus. The choice
of this term is deliberate. By interpretative framework I mean not
only the explicit summary comments, where it is clear we are receiv-
ing Josephus's interpretation, but also the choice of subject matter
itself, as well as the way that the material is recorded. This interpretative framework is all encompassing, controlling all aspects of *War*,
Ant. and *Life*.[1] The following discussion focuses on the theoretical

---

1. Although *Apion* also should be understood as the product of Josephus's
interpretative framework, it will not be discussed in any detail in this study as the

and conceptual nature of the interpretative framework. Here, the way Josephus uses sources, the relationship between his life experience and the texts he constructs, how he understands the task of writing history and an outline of the four main elements of the framework will be considered.

We commence with the issue of sources. The relevant sections of Josephus's three texts are all narrative based, with a broad chronological structure.[2] They are attempts at providing a description of historical events, not novels or abstract philosophical treatises. In this task Josephus is dependent on sources, whether they be his personal recollections or the written or oral records of others. As a result, in assessing the construction of the interpretative framework, some attention must be paid to the role played by these sources, especially in terms of the extent to which the narrative of each text is controlled by the sources of information Josephus employs. If the account of events in Judaea is essentially a compilation of those sources then it may appear unnecessary to think in terms of Josephus's interpretative framework.

The issue of sources in Josephus is a vexed one. There is no question that he actively used sources, not only for the period of history prior to his lifetime but also in relation to his own career (*Life* 358; *Apion* 1.55-56). A major part of the problem is that most of the possible known sources of Josephus for the first century CE are no longer extant—such as Nicolaus of Damascus and the Memoirs of Vespasian and Agrippa II. The only points of direct comparison that can be made relate to the earlier periods of Josephus's narrative.[3] Even here,

focus is on the narrative based texts.

2.   Cohen, *Josephus*, pp. 62, 69, 91, provides a contrasting view, arguing that *War* is a thematic text, which he believes helps explain some of the differences in the structure of *War* and *Life*. Although it is likely that themes operate within each of the texts their core structure is chronological: *War* moves from Antiochus Epiphanes IV to the capture of Masada; *Ant.* moves from creation to the outbreak of war in 66 CE; and *Life* moves from Josephus's family heritage to his later years spent in Rome.

3.   Some scholars, such as D.R. Schwartz, seek to identify where Josephus may draw upon a different source in a single narrative or within two accounts of the one issue. For example, see D.R. Schwartz, *Agrippa I: The Last King of Judaea* (TSAJ, 23; Tübingen: J.C.B. Mohr [Paul Siebeck], 1990), pp. 30-32, regarding a possible reconstruction of how Josephus used different sources for his accounts of Agrippa I. In a similar vein, D.R. Schwartz, 'On Drama and Authenticity in Philo and Josephus', *SCI* 10 (1989/90), pp. 113-29, presents a line of argument which seeks to

we cannot exactly be certain as to what version of the Bible Josephus used.[4] Where we can compare versions of the same events in which Josephus has probably used written sources, such as with the Hasmonean period, they indicate that he was not bound to the source. Changes to the narrative have been made in the form of additions, alterations in detail and the omission of material.[5] Even if some of the changes could be explained by the use of a different source, our attention is directed toward Josephus. It is his choice to make the changes. This discussion, however, all pertains to the period prior to the first century CE.

The apparent imbalance in the narrative of the first century CE has

identify changes in the text of Josephus in terms of how strictly he adheres to his sources. Note the qualifications to this interpretation suggested by D.S. Williams, 'On Josephus' use of Nicolaus of Damascus: A Stylometric Analysis of *BJ* 1.225-273 and *AJ* 14.280-369', *SCI* 12 (1993), pp. 176-87, who argues that even when Josephus appears to be following Nicolaus closely in *Ant.* he is still rewriting the source. See also D.R. Schwartz, 'KATA TOYTON TON KAPION: Josephus' Source on Agrippa II', *JQR* 72 (1982), pp. 241-68, where he notes Josephus's apparent lack of 'discernment' to ensure that differences between sources are adjusted.

4.   The continuing debate regarding whether Josephus used a Greek and/or Hebrew version of the Bible in part reflects the difficulty of not having a version that we know he would have been able to consult. One example of this problem is the conclusion reached by E. Ulrich, that Josephus was dependent on a Greek text for 1–2 Samuel ('Josephus' Biblical Text for the Books of Samuel', in L.H. Feldman and G. Hata [eds.], *Josephus, the Bible and History* [Detroit: Wayne State University Press, 1989], pp. 81-96). See also L.H. Feldman, 'Introduction', in L.H. Feldman and G. Hata (eds.), *Josephus, the Bible and History* (Detroit: Wayne State University Press, 1989), pp. 21-22.

5.   There is a general consensus on this point, whether it is in terms of the Bible or such sources as Nicolaus of Damascus and 1 Maccabees. For example, see B.Z. Wacholder, 'Josephus and Nicolaus of Damascus', in L.H. Feldman and G. Hata (eds.), *Josephus, the Bible and History* (Detroit: Wayne State University Press, 1989), pp. 147-72; I.M. Gafni, 'Josephus and 1 Maccabees', in L.H. Feldman and G. Hata (eds.), *Josephus, the Bible and History* (Detroit: Wayne State University Press, 1989), pp. 116-31; and L.H. Feldman, 'Josephus' Portrayal of the Hasmoneans Compared with 1 Maccabees', in F. Parente and J. Sievers (eds.), *Josephus and the History of the Greco-Roman Period* (SPB, 41; Leiden: E.J. Brill, 1994), pp. 41-68. Even D.R. Schwartz, 'Josephus on Hyrcanus II', in F. Parente and J. Sievers (eds.), *Josephus and the History of the Greco-Roman Period* (SPB, 41; Leiden: E.J. Brill, 1994), pp. 210-32 (229-32), accepts that some of the changes can be accredited to Josephus's own interests.

often been noted, with the paucity of information for the period prior to 44 CE being the cause of much speculation. Prominent among the discussion is that the 'silence' of Josephus for the years between 6–26 and 36–40 CE is due to the absence of a source for him to employ. The availability of sources, however, should not be viewed as the only criterion Josephus used for the inclusion of material, let alone the most important one. Certainly, Josephus drew upon sources where they were available. However, he was not merely the preserver of existing traditions. Josephus was also an author in his own right and he should be approached from this perspective first and foremost. The fact that Josephus did not always ensure a consistency in different accounts of the same event may be considered as 'sloppiness'. Such possible sloppiness, however, is significant. It clearly indicates that the versions of events are interpretations, not just neutral descriptions of historical events. Changes are not to be related simply to a dependence on, or independence from, a particular source, but to decisions taken by Josephus that are best explained by his personal circumstances. The focus of our attention should lie on Josephus the author rather than Josephus as a compiler, describing anything and everything on which he could lay his hands.[6]

With our attention directed towards Josephus it is appropriate to consider his career. Our concern is to establish the possible links between what Josephus did and what he wrote. Discussion of Josephus's career indicates the extent to which he is in control of the reader of his texts. Our understanding of Josephus's personal career is entirely dependent upon what he allows the reader of his texts to know. We can compile a list of his activities but we remain bound by the limits defined by the author as there is no extant external witness. The synchronicity between *War* and *Ant.* and especially between *War* and *Life* do allow us to construct a picture that is two dimensional but it would be a mistake to assume that the comparison allows a full picture to be formed. What this process does is help highlight

6. For a contrasting conclusion see D.R. Schwartz, *Agrippa I*, p. 32, where he states that 'Josephus' own contribution was mainly that of extractor, compiler, and seamster' in relation to the account of Agrippa I. It is important to recognize that Josephus was consistent in his desire to use sources where he could for the period before his lifetime and he conformed to the contemporary expectations of historiography. See Cohen, *Josephus*, pp. 28-33, and P. Villalba i Varneda, *The Historical Method of Flavius Josephus* (ALGHJ, 19; Leiden: E.J. Brill, 1986), pp. 266-74.

the importance of recognizing and defining the extent of Josephus's interpretative framework. Many of Josephus's comments regarding his background are framed in an apologetic defence of his character.[7] Allowing for exaggeration it appears that he was born into the mainstream of Jewish society. From his mother he could claim a link with the Hasmonaean family (*Life* 2). He was a priest, familiar with the temple cult and appears to have been a resident of Jerusalem (*Life* 1-2). Although educated, it is not clear to what extent he was versed in Greek prior to his move to Rome after the revolt.[8] Most of his life before the war was lived under direct Roman rule. He appears to have been involved in public affairs on the basis of the reference to his trip to Rome to defend two fellow priests (*Life* 13-16). The debate regarding his possible allegiance to the Pharisees in daily life is not directly relevant to this study (*Life* 12). Josephus definitely knows of and expresses opinions regarding the Pharisees, Sadducees and Essenes (*War* 2.119-66; *Ant.* 13.171-73, 297-98; 18.11-22). Discussion of his possible allegiance, however, should not be allowed to overshadow the constant recognition of the priesthood within the functioning of Jewish society.[9]

---

7.   For an unusual reconstruction of Josephus's pre-war career that does not give sufficient recognition to this context see G. Hata, 'Imagining Some Dark Periods in Josephus' Life', in F. Parente and J. Sievers (eds.), *Josephus and the History of the Greco-Roman Period* (SPB, 41; Leiden: E.J. Brill, 1994), pp. 309-28.

8.   Regarding the assistance provided for Josephus in the writing of *War* see Rajak, *Josephus*, pp. 233-36.

9.   See M. Smith, 'Palestinian Judaism in the First Century', in M. Davis (ed.), *Israel: Its Role in Civilization* (New York: Harper & Row, 1956), pp. 67-81, and D. Goodblatt, 'The Place of the Pharisees in First Century Judaism: The State of the Debate', *JSJ* 20 (1989), pp. 12-30; cf. S.N. Mason, 'Was Josephus a Pharisee? A Re-examination of *Life* 10-12', *JJS* 40 (1989), pp. 31-45, and D.S. Williams, 'Morton Smith on the Pharisees in Josephus', *JQR* 84 (1993), pp. 29-42. In terms of the recognition of the presence of priests among the events narrated, a few examples include the chief priests in *War* 2, especially among the generals named in *War* 2.562-68. Although presented in a more negative light priests are prominent in *Ant.* 20. Even in *Apion* 2.184-89, where Josephus presents a very positive picture of Jewish government, it is priests that are given a crucial role. In relation to the extent of influence the various groups hold within the society see E.P. Sanders, *Judaism: Practice and Belief, 63 BCE–66 CE* (London: SCM Press, 1992) and J.S. McLaren, *Power and Politics in Palestine: The Jews and the Governing of their Land 100 BC–70 AD* (JSNTSup, 63; Sheffield: JSOT Press, 1991); cf. S.N. Mason, 'Chief Priests, Sadducees, Pharisees and Sanhedrin in Acts', in R. Bauckham (ed.), *The*

Despite the length of Josephus's narrative regarding the 66–70 CE revolt, the description of his activities during this crucial period of Jewish history is piecemeal. Josephus became involved in the revolt at its outset. His motivation for involvement is a matter of some debate, but it is clear he had sufficient profile to be one of the generals in the army of the initial wartime administration. His posting to Galilee is interesting. Presuming that Syria was the point of embarkation he was likely to be the first to confront the Roman response to the defeat of the twelfth legion. The appointment appears to have originated in Jerusalem and was part of an administration in which priests were prominent (*War* 2.562-68). Although Josephus provides a colourful description of his prowess in outwitting the Romans at Jotapata and in gaining the respect of the Galilaean population, he was captured at the downfall of Jotapata (*War* 2.569-71; 3.141-289, 316-44). The capture of the city and the general did not mark the end of the Galilaean campaign but it did mark the beginning of a new stage in Josephus's career. As a prisoner of the Romans he became an interpreter for his captives in the 69–70 CE campaign. His tasks incorporated parleying with the Jewish rebels in an effort to seek terms for their surrender during the siege of Jerusalem. Exactly how Josephus acquired this task is open to debate, depending primarily on the veracity allotted to his story of surrender at Jotapata and the prophecy regarding the rise of Vespasian (*War* 3.345-408).[10] Josephus does not indicate whether he also provided the Romans with logistical information regarding Jerusalem, its layout and defences.

It is apparent that Josephus was rewarded for his actions in the latter part of the war by the Flavians. The protection of Vespasian saw Josephus move to Rome after the revolt, where the new emperor provided him with a house and pension. To this were added estates in

Book of Acts in its First Century Setting. IV. *The Book of Acts in its Palestinian Setting* (Grand Rapids: Eerdmans, 1995), pp. 115-77.

10. For an example of the different approaches to this issue compare A. Schalit, 'Die Erhebung Vespasians nach Flavius Josephus, Talmud und Midrasch: Zur Geschichte einer messianischen Prophetie', *ANRW* 2.2 (1975), pp. 208-327 and H.R. Moehring, 'Joseph ben Matthia and Flavius Josephus: The Jewish Prophet and Roman Historian', *ANRW* 2.21.2 (1984), pp. 864-944 (918-44). Despite Moehring's strong criticism of Schalit there are signs of agreement between the conclusion both scholars draw regarding Josephus's attitude towards the war—one of opposition.

Judaea and Roman citizenship (*Life* 422-23). It is while Josephus was in Rome that his literary activity began. Although living in relative peace and prosperity, Josephus appears to have been subject to criticism and slander, via Jonathan and Justus (*Life* 338, 424-25). Exactly when Josephus died is not known and it appears that he saw his literary activity extending beyond the four extant texts (*Ant.* 20.267).[11]

It is apparent that Josephus displayed a remarkable ability to be a survivor during his life. He was confronted by a number of flash points which could have threatened his personal safety. They include: the trip to Rome; the beginning of the revolt; his time as general in Galilee, especially the siege at Jotapata and his capture; and the accusations against him after the war. To each of these challenges Josephus was able to adapt himself. Irrespective of what commentators may wish to say regarding his integrity, he was, in modern political terms, a 'survivor'.[12] Of particular interest here are two observations. One is that Josephus was not only directly involved in and effected by the 66–70 CE war, but also that these events continued to have personal ramifications for him well into the 90s CE. The second observation is that Josephus continued to perceive himself as a Jew. The rationale provided for his support of the Roman war effort and acceptance of Flavian sponsorship are cast in Jewish terms. In this context the literary activities reflect a continuing allegiance to his heritage. Irrespective of how other Jews interpreted Josephus's career changes, he continued to label himself as a Jew.

The first observation—the continued influence of the 66–70 CE revolt on Josephus's life—is probably most obvious in *Life*. Whereas the expression of personal concerns needs to be extracted from *War* and *Ant.*, their presence in *Life* is explicit. A major concern of this apologetic tract is to defend Josephus against accusations made by Justus of Tiberias in his account of the revolt. Clearly, chronological distance did not mean that Josephus could lay to rest the events of the revolt, whether he wanted to or not. Although Josephus did not see direct reference to the events of the revolt as a necessary element in *Ant.*, he was obliged to revisit the revolt because of what others said

11. Note that Josephus also provides a very brief, offhand reference to his wives and children (*Life* 414-15, 426-27).

12. It is possible that Josephus's willingness to let the reader understand this point is deliberate, with the reader 'free' to acknowledge that he was one who upheld the principle expressed in *Ant.* 1.14.

and wrote.[13] Some 20 years had passed since the revolt but the nature of Justus's claims regarding Josephus's involvement in the Galilaean campaign resulted in Josephus deciding it was appropriate that he defend himself. Josephus's integrity, in the period prior to the revolt and in the years that followed 70 CE, is outlined along with a detailed account of his actions in Galilee before his first major engagement with Roman troops.

Further evidence of the ongoing impact of 66–70 CE for Josephus is contained in the way he expresses his concern to explain the revolt in *War* and *Ant*. In *War*, Roman responsibility is primarily linked to the actions of Albinus and Florus, while 'rogue' Jews actively foster a climate of conflict (*War* 1.4, 10; 2.265, 277-79, 283). In *Ant.*, however, the Roman factor and 'rogue' Jews are not the only ones held responsible for the revolt. Internal strife within the Jewish community takes on a new dimension in *Ant.*, with Ananias b. Nedebaeus and other leading Jews portrayed as active agents in causing instability (*Ant.* 20.180-81, 205-207, 213-14). Josephus has stopped short of repeating his narrative of the war in *Ant.* He has not, however, shied away from taking the opportunity to elaborate upon the nature of the factors that contributed to the outbreak of the revolt. By implication, this continued interest in the revolt is an expression of how the ramifications of 66–70 CE were still being lived out by Josephus in the 90s CE.[14]

The second observation, a continued adherence to his Jewish heritage, is asserted overtly and implicitly. It is evident in *War* through his explanation of the destruction of Jerusalem; in *Ant.* it is through the attempt to present the antiquity and privileged status of the Jews; and in *Life* it is through the claims regarding his status before the war.[15] In the 90s CE, as Josephus constructed his defence in *Life*, the

13. In *Ant.* 20.267, Josephus claims he will write another account of the war. For the possible dating of *Life* and its relationship with *Ant.* see Bilde, *Flavius Josephus*, pp. 104-106.

14. Most scholars accept that Josephus was concerned with post-70 CE issues. For example, see Moehring, 'Joseph', pp. 864-913, Cohen, *Josephus*, pp. 232-42, Bilde, *Flavius Josephus*, pp. 173-91 and S. Schwartz, *Josephus and Judaean Politics* (CSCT, 18; Leiden: E.J. Brill, 1990), pp. 210-16. It is important to acknowledge that the ongoing interest in Jewish affairs is primarily dictated by the events that took place before 70 CE, as indicated by Bilde, *Flavius Josephus*, pp. 73, 110.

15. *Apion* reinforces Josephus's continued allegiance.

bulk of the details regarding his heritage clearly locate him within Jewish society in Jerusalem. Here Josephus reaffirmed what he proudly proclaimed in the introduction to *War* (1.3). Josephus appears to have lost none of his desire to promote his prominent heritage within Judaism. The two large narrative texts, *War* and *Ant.*, clearly express Josephus's allegiance to his heritage in the themes and subject matter presented. *War*, written in the aftermath of 70 CE, seeks to provide a narrative account of the revolt, briefly describing the events that lead up to the outbreak of hostilities in 66 CE. Of central importance for Josephus in the description of the war is his concern to explain the defeat of the Jews. The explanations offered by Josephus are Jewish. For Josephus, the unthinkable—the destruction of the temple and the burning of the city—was to be understood in terms of the will of God. Roman prowess, military might and the integrity of their generals, especially Vespasian and Titus, were important. However, Josephus declares that the Roman victory was possible only because God had deserted the Jews. The destruction of Jerusalem was punishment from God because of crimes committed by the Jews. In effect, the Jews defeated themselves. Their crimes against one another, especially their faction fighting during the war, polluted Jerusalem (*War* 6.250-51). Whether Josephus believed this to be the case at the time, as he stood watching the city burn in 70 CE, is open to debate. By the time he wrote *War*, however, it is a stated and implied understanding of the underlying reason why the Jews were defeated.[16]

A crucial element of the explanation was that Josephus be able to isolate the Jewish 'guilt'. Such a task was fraught with difficulty. He and many of his friends were obviously directly involved in the war effort, yet to accept responsibility for the war would adversely compromise his post-war status and the image of insight he wished to convey that he had regarding what was happening in Judaea. Josephus's solution is the 'brigands', who later, during the war, are under the leadership of three 'tyrants'—John of Gischala, Eleazar b. Simon and Simon b. Gioras (*War* 5.2-12, 21; 7.254-74). It was a small, isolated proportion of the population that wanted war; through their actions they drew the wrath of God upon the city and temple, and caused God to employ the Romans as the means of retribution. In

---

16. See Bilde, *Flavius Josephus*, pp. 176-79, 180-89, for a positive interpretation of Josephus's use of his 'cultural language' to explain what had happened in Judaea.

effect, it was possible to remain a loyal Jew throughout the war—the test lay in recognizing the will of God, that victory lay with the Romans.[17] Josephus's involvement at the beginning of the revolt, and that of his associates was one of restraint. In the context of the narrative as it is constructed, they were the counter to the brigands; they were people concerned for the welfare of the Jewish community, seeking a peaceful resolution to the conflict. The defeat of Josephus and his decision to surrender is portrayed as part of the cosmic drama. Josephus's duty was to God, to be the messenger that announced divine blessing on Vespasian (*War* 3.354). The protection Josephus found from the Flavians was an extension of his attempt to convey the true nature of what was happening in the revolt. Jerusalem was cast under God's wrath; the path of mercy lay with acceptance of Roman rule. It was a rule that Josephus implies rested in the hands of people who held no lasting animosity towards the Jewish people, hence Titus's efforts to save the temple (*War* 6.260-66).

These explanations of issues directly relevant to Josephus's personal career have been voiced in scholarship often as expressions of his bias. They have even resulted in *War* being labelled a piece of Flavian propaganda. Serving Flavian interests is clearly part of *War*. It is important, however, to recognize this process as originating from within the personal career of Josephus, not as something that was imposed upon him. Even if he was concerned to return favours or promote the supposed integrity of certain sections of the Jewish community, the way Josephus seeks to do this is through language and concepts that are from his own cultural background. This point will become more apparent as we turn to the second of Josephus's texts, *Ant.*

Published in the 90s CE, *Ant.* reiterates the importance of the observation that Josephus continued to present himself as a Jew. The text seeks to provide an account of the Jewish people from the beginning of time until the outbreak of the revolt in 66 CE. Woven within the narrative, Josephus clearly gives voice to three ongoing concerns that are derived from his personal circumstances. They include explaining

---

17. For the possible influence of such prophetic figures as Jeremiah and Daniel on Josephus see D. Daube, 'Typology in Josephus', *JJS* 31 (1980), pp. 18-36, and S.N. Mason, 'Josephus, Daniel, and the Flavian House', in F. Parente and J. Sievers (eds.), *Josephus and the History of the Greco-Roman Period* (SPB, 41; Leiden: E.J. Brill, 1994), pp. 161-91.

the present status of the Jews, the revolt of 66–70 CE and Josephus's continued allegiance to Judaism. Aware of polemic against the Jews, Josephus seeks to explain that, despite their recent defeat at the hands of the Romans, they remained a respected and legitimate ethnic group within the empire. Apart from asserting the antiquity of the Jews, Josephus devotes space in his narrative to citing the privileged status of Jews in various cities of the Graeco-Roman world (*Ant.* 16.160-78). The depiction of Jews as rebels is outweighed by recognition of the Jews as friends. Hence Josephus does not shirk from expressing his Jewish heritage. Furthermore, the providence of God is used to explain events, and in terms of the subject matter there is a marked focus on issues pertinent to the expression of lifestyle among the covenant people.[18]

The direct nature of the relationship between career and texts is significant for the examination of the interpretative framework Josephus constructs. The importance of Josephus's career in determining what he wrote about and how he wrote is not surprising. The very fact that we are dependent on Josephus's texts for information regarding his career indicates that their author is not personally distanced from the events narrated. Josephus, the survivor, was probably primarily interested in self-justification. This does not mean he avoided trying to explain what had happened in his lifetime in a critical manner as best he could. However, what it indicates is that the whole process of Josephus's writing needs to be examined when we seek to understand his interpretative framework. It is not the comments alone that are relevant but it is the entire process of constructing the narrative that needs to be considered. Whether or not it is historically appropriate to argue that the events prior to 66 CE actually pertained to what happened during the revolt, such an association is legitimate from Josephus's perspective. He was one of many who were presumably trying to make sense of four years that had dramatically altered the nature of their entire existence. We have in Josephus, therefore, a person trying to explain 66–70 CE and come to terms with the implications of the revolt.

The significance of the two observations lies primarily in the impact they have for understanding the relationship between Josephus and his

18. Some examples include the Samaritan affair (*Ant.* 18.29-30), the housing of the high priest's robes (*Ant.* 18.90-95; 20.6-14) and the tenure of the various high priests (*Ant.* 18.33-35; 20.179, 213, 224-51).

literary products. The *War*, *Ant.* and *Life* are not the work of someone who became a disinterested witness with the passing of time.[19]
Although geographically separated from the battlefields, and with the
activities of the temple now only a memory, Josephus's life remained
intimately involved with what had happened in Judaea between 66–70
CE, in trying to explain the revolt and in coming to terms with life
after the revolt. Although Josephus's career went on beyond the
revolt, he remained intimately concerned with the events that culminated in the disaster of 70 CE. After the revolt it was the past that
dominated Josephus, both in life and literature.

Given Josephus's personal interest in what he narrated, we are com-
pelled to direct our attention to the next factor associated with
establishing the nature of his interpretative framework: namely, his
attitude to the process of writing history. The concern here is not to
address the motivation associated with the construction of any one
particular text. Instead, by drawing upon general explicit statements
and insights implied through the narration of events, the task is to
establish the mindset of Josephus when he approached the task of
writing. Possibly in part because of the nature of the subject matter of
his texts, Josephus provides the reader with numerous clues regarding
the task of writing. We are able to comment on three areas: the credentials necessary to be a writer of history; the reasons why a person
decides to write; and Josephus's guiding principle in writing his narrative, a concern for 'truth' (ἀλήθεια). It is notable that there is
consistency in Josephus's attitude regarding these three areas in each
of the narrative based texts.[20]

19. In contrast, see Rajak, 'Ciò', p. 160, who claims that Josephus had lost his
'communicative passion' as his 'Palestinian roots had been dislodged'. In the context
of dismissing the notion of Flavian propaganda being a dominant factor in Josephus's work, M. Goodman has pointed out that Josephus chose to write, he was not
forced to do so ('Josephus as a Roman Citizen', in F. Parente and J. Sievers [eds.],
Josephus and the History of the Greco-Roman Period [SPB, 41; Leiden: E.J. Brill,
1994], pp. 329-38).

20. It is possible that Josephus is just following the established literary conven-
tion in his various introductory comments. Whether Josephus actually adhered to
what he claimed to be required, and whether it was possible to do so, can only be
determined in the light of studying his narrative. It is clear that Josephus perceived
himself as working within the contemporary principles of historiography. See
Cohen, *Josephus*, pp. 27-32, Villalba i Varenda, *Historical Method*, pp. 242-66,
272-77, Bilde, *Flavius Josephus*, pp. 201-205, H.W. Attridge, *The Interpretation*

Josephus's discussion of the credentials he considers necessary for writing history is an issue of direct significance for *War* and *Life*. In these texts, particularly the latter, Josephus's legitimacy and integrity were at stake. To defend and sell his work Josephus declares what he believes are the essential credentials—all of which he happens to possess! Josephus states that being an eyewitness to the events narrated is crucial. In his aggressive attack on Justus of Tiberias's account of the revolt, Josephus is quick to point out that Justus was not involved in the events that took place in the city (*Life* 357). In *War* 1.3, Josephus boldly declares that he was a participant at the beginning of the revolt and then an eyewitness of what happened in Jerusalem.[21] In contrast, the accounts of others who had chosen to narrate the revolt are criticized because they had not taken part in the war (*War* 1.1).[22] After the qualification of being an eyewitness comes the requirement to analyse the appropriate available sources. Again Josephus is loud in his criticism of Justus, for failing to consult contemporary accounts of what happened in Jerusalem (*Life* 357-58), and of those who narrated the revolt without being eyewitnesses because they used hearsay (*War* 1.1; *Apion* 1.45). Indeed, Josephus claims that producing appropriate evidence is an important aspect in the process of writing (*Life* 41, 342, 344).[23]

---

of Biblical History in the Antiquitates Judaicae of Flavius Josephus (HDR, 7; Missoula, MT: Scholars Press, 1976), pp. 43-60, and S.N. Mason, *Flavius Josephus on the Pharisees: A Composition-Critical Study* (SPB, 39; Leiden: E.J. Brill, 1991), pp. 376-83. The exact nature of the relationship between Josephus and his literary context within the Graeco-Roman world is a topic beyond the scope of this study. See G.A. Press, *The Development of the Idea of History in Antiquity* (Montreal: McGill-Queen's University Press, 1982), pp. 37-67, for an outline of the context in which Josephus could regard the writing of history as an established genre with defined boundaries and expectations. The statements Josephus makes regarding the work of Justus in *Life* 357-60, those who have written accounts of the revolt in *War* 1.7-9, 13-16 and of Greek 'historians' in *Apion* 1.44-46, 53-56, clearly indicate an awareness of a standard by which he should seek to structure his own 'history' (*Apion* 1.57).

21. See also *Ant.* 1.4, *Apion* 1.45-49 regarding the importance of being an eyewitness.

22. The example of the capture of Masada indicates that being an eyewitness of *every* event was not deemed as a pre-requisite.

23. Josephus boldly claims that *War* was published while other eyewitnesses were still alive (*Life* 357-67; *Apion* 1.50-52) so that the 'truth' of his account could be confirmed by others. According to Josephus, writers such as Justus failed to

Josephus states that there are a number of reasons why a person may decide to write a history. As with the necessary credentials, personal agenda is close to the surface in the discussion of this principle. In the introduction to *Ant.*, Josephus outlines four motivations for writing. One is a desire to display literary skill, the second is a desire to promote the well-being of the subject matter of the narrative, the third is a desire to narrate significant events in which the author was personally involved, and the fourth is a desire to pass on knowledge of important matters of which the public are ignorant (*Ant.* 1.1-3). Josephus claims that it is the latter two motives which apply to his work (*Ant.* 1.3). Josephus believes those who are motivated by an interest in style and a desire to gratify their subject are worthy of criticism. Previous accounts of the war, even when constructed by eyewitnesses, were nothing more than attempts to gratify the Romans (*War* 1.2, 7). As a means of defence, Josephus also attacks those who see contemporary events as unworthy of recording. As evidence Josephus points out that 'ancient historians' deemed their contemporary events appropriate for preservation (*War* 1.14).

Josephus's concern to state some of the appropriate credentials and approved reasons for writing history indicate a sensitivity to validate his activity. The crowning point in this concern is Josephus's discussion of what he declares to be the guiding principle in the process of constructing a historical narrative. This guiding principle—the presentation of 'truth'—is also extremely important for an understanding of Josephus's interpretative framework. More than any other point, it helps explain what Josephus claims he was doing. The following analysis of Josephus's comments regarding this third area of the process of writing is based on explicit claims made by Josephus and on the structure of the narrative, particularly in terms of the subject matter chosen.

In all his texts Josephus reiterates the claim that 'truth' is the guiding principle for how he narrates events. This claim is based on his declared belief regarding the central task of a historian: namely, 'truth is incumbent upon a historian' (*Life* 339).[24] Indeed, the harshness of

---

subject their work to such scrutiny.

24. For further expressions of this view see *Ant.* 14.1-3; 16.187; *War* 1.26, 30; 5.257; 7.455. Villalba i Varenda emphasizes Josephus's concern to provide an apodictic account, going beyond the recording of important events to the realm of explaining them, exposing the 'truth' of the situation (*Historical Method*, pp. 258-

Josephus's criticism of others lies primarily in their distortion of the 'truth' (*Life* 41, 336-37; *Ant.* 1.4; *War* 1.2, 15-16). Although partly excused because his narrative was written to promote the well-being of Herod, Nicolaus is taken to task by Josephus for not upholding the 'truth' when he failed to describe Herod's pillaging of money from David's tomb (*Ant.* 16.163-87).

At the end of *War*, Josephus states 'as concerning truth, I would not hesitate boldly to assert that, throughout the entire narrative, this has been my single aim' (*War* 7.455). Consistent with Josephus's declared intentions such a claim could have closed any of his narrative texts. The claim, however, is meaningless without a context. Clarification of what Josephus means when he states that 'truth' is his guiding principle is required. Here, we are given ample clues by the author to define 'truth' and at the same time to unravel his attitude regarding what was legitimate to include in a narrative of history. We also gain an insight into some of the methodological limitations of Josephus as a writer of history.

It is apparent that Josephus believed 'truth' should be understood as the subject matter—the events that are being narrated. For this definition we are dependent primarily on *War* and *Life*. At the end of *War* 7 Josephus states that he has fulfilled his objective, 'to relate with perfect accuracy for the information of those who wish to learn how this war was waged...' (*War* 7.454). This narration of 'information' was 'the truth' (*War* 7.455). In Josephus's criticism of Justus, the link between 'truth' and subject matter is clear. Justus has presented a narrative of events in an attempt to distort the 'truth' of what happened at Tiberias (*Life* 40). Implicit here is the notion that an individual can corrupt the description of incidents to distort the 'truth' of a situation. Such a view is also evident in the criticism of other accounts of the revolt (*War* 1.2, 7), where flattery dictates over and above a desire for historical accuracy. Josephus, on the other hand, states that he will 'faithfully recount the actions of both combatants' (*War* 1.9). It appears Josephus believes that any given author has at their disposal incidents which they can choose to narrate in a corrupt, false manner or accurately. Such a view is confirmed by an important distinction that Josephus upholds: namely, it is possible to separate the narration of events, where veracity is the guiding principle, from personal

66). See also Mason, *Flavius Josephus*, pp. 78-79, regarding Josephus's concern for accuracy in *War*.

reflection and comment. After declaring his intention to narrate the actions of Jews and Romans involved in the revolt, Josephus declares that he will also include 'reflections on the events'. Furthermore, he states that it is not possible to 'conceal my private sentiments, nor refuse to give my personal sympathies scope to bewail my country's misfortune' (*War* 1.9). Josephus did not go so far as to claim that 'truth' was connected with his reflections and comments. If anything, Josephus was careful to distinguish 'truth' from the reflections. 'Truth' lies in the realm of the events narrated properly within a context. Hence the claim is made that writing history was the place for a narrative of events, not for personal lamentation (*War* 5.20). Josephus recognized that his comments might not be well received by his readers (*War* 1.11-12). He also acknowledged that controlling the amount of personal comment was prudent and he restrained himself from engaging in too much lamentation or personal attack (*Life* 339). Reiterating his sensitivity to possible criticism of the personal comments he makes in his history, Josephus reaffirmed the division between narrative and commentary by appealing to the reader to 'credit the history with the facts, the historian with the lamentation' (*War* 1.12). 'Truth' in a historical narrative is not achieved by including personal reflection, let alone pre-determined apologetical agendas that control the account. Given sufficient care, the 'facts'—the correct narrative of events—will stand on their own right.

Whatever Josephus may claim about the presence of such a divide between reflection and 'truth', there is ample evidence to question its presence in his accounts. The narrative of events and personal comments go hand in hand. As Josephus states that the 'laws of history' means he must restrain from 'personal lamentation' and simply narrate the events in *War* 5.20, his attempt to re-establish the thread of the narrative is governed by his interpretation: 'I therefore proceed to relate the after history of the sedition' (*War* 5.20). The use of 'sedition' (στάσις) is, in itself, an interpretation determined by Josephus of how the events in Jerusalem should be perceived by the reader. Even more damning is when Josephus praises his own efforts to describe contemporary events in his text. Prominent among the virtues of historians is that they must construct their own framework (*War* 1.15). Josephus may assert that this framework is presenting the 'truth' regarding the revolt and that he is merely recording the full detail of what was happening by describing the events. As Josephus claims, his narrative allows the reader 'to follow their own opinion as to where the facts may lead them' (*War* 5.257). What is narrated, however, is controlled by the author as an interpreter.

It is apparent that Josephus tries to proclaim a distinction between author and subject matter. In so doing, though, he unconsciously contradicts himself. In this instance the interpreter is a person who was directly involved in the subject matter of the texts and remained directly affected by those events when he constructed his accounts. The narrative of the events allegedly shows the 'truth' and the author must control the personal commentary to allow the proper description of events to hold centre stage. That such a distinction exists is clearly artificial. A brief glance at some of the contents and the way they are presented in *War*, *Ant.* and *Life* effectively illustrates this point.

A process of selection is used by Josephus in all the texts. The explicit guiding principle may be a desire to present the 'truth'—a narrative of the facts free from distortion. However, what determines the choice is the interpretation of Josephus. Sources available to him are not the sole factor at work. For example, *Life* cannot be considered as more than a potted narrative of Josephus's life. Furthermore, of the information included much is of a very summary nature. The trip to Rome is a prime case. It is tantalizing, not so much for what is narrated, but for what is presumably left out, such as the charge against the priests, their identity, the timing of the trip, the choice of Josephus, the identity of any companions and the fate of the priests. In this instance the silence cannot be because of a lack of sources. Presuming that the event did take place, the lack of detail is the decision of the author to control the nature of what is divulged to the reader. Josephus is determining what is important enough to be narrated.

Authorial choice is evident in other aspects of the subject matter. Within the confines of the chronological boundaries of this study there is a clear bias in the narrative to describe affairs associated with Jerusalem and issues associated with the leadership of the Jews, particularly changes in the leadership. Apart from the occasional interludes on affairs outside Judaea, normally regarding Jews in foreign territory, the narrative rarely diverges from its description of the various leaders. Clearly Josephus knew other subject matter could be included but decided that it was not appropriate. Hence in *Ant.* he indicates that detailed discussion of the laws, customs and traditions of the Jews should be discussed elsewhere (*Ant.* 20.268). The existence of an authorial process of selection is also evident in comments of Josephus that explain the inclusion of information relating to members of the Herodian family as being pertinent to his history (*Ant.* 17.354; 18.127). 'Truth' may be the declared principle, but on what basis can it be deemed that Josephus is not just 'cooking the books', only giving material he thinks relevant? More importantly, even if the events narrated are only those relevant to the state of affairs in Judaea, is his interpretation of them balanced and accurate?

That a process of selection was employed by Josephus is further reinforced by the way the material is presented. Within each text Josephus made choices regarding not only what to narrate but also what details to include. Here Josephus is his own worst enemy. By comparing the elements of *War–Life* and *War–Ant.* that are parallel it is apparent that questions regarding Josephus's reliability need to be addressed. More often than not this has resulted in a negative assessment of Josephus. In the context of establishing the interpretative framework of Josephus, however, this comparison is extremely beneficial. There are numerous differences in the *War–Life* narrative of events, in the details included and the order of events.[25] Prominent examples include the commission of Josephus as a general in Galilee and the description of the petition to remove Josephus from his command. Clearly Josephus controls the contents of the text. It is claimed that both texts are guided by the principle of 'truth', yet the end product of the narrative of some of the events in Galilee is very different in *War* and *Life*.[26] In a similar vein, *War* and *Ant.* provide a comparative narrative of events prior to the revolt. Many of the events are recorded in both texts but there are numerous minor differences in the detail provided. Sources may explain some of the variations but the differences are also apparent in events narrated from Josephus's lifetime.[27] 'Truth' in Josephus, therefore, is the product of

25. It is important to keep a sense of 'balance' as there are also many aspects on which the two accounts agree.

26. Although answered in very negative terms it is an issue that Cohen, *Josephus,* pp. 1-2, 8-12, 181-82, and U. Rappaport, 'Where was Josephus Lying—In His *Life* or in the *War*?', in F. Parente and J. Sievers (eds.), *Josephus and the History of the Greco-Roman Period* (SPB, 41; Leiden: E.J. Brill, 1994), pp. 279-89, explore.

27. Although still a teenager, one example is the dispute during the governorship of Cumanus when Samaritans attacked Galilaean pilgrims (*War* 2.232-46; *Ant.* 20.118-36).

his interpretation; it is how he believes the events and issues described should be understood.

Discussion of Josephus's use of sources, his career and his attitude to the task of writing history all point to the need to acknowledge the direct involvement of Josephus in constructing his narrative. In turn, it is necessary to outline the principles associated with the consequence of this involvement, namely Josephus's interpretative framework.

Josephus's interpretative framework functions on two levels which are intrinsically linked. One level is the nature of the subject matter that is chosen for inclusion. It is Josephus who decides what incidents he will describe and they are an expression of his interpretation of what was appropriate to include in his texts.[28] The second level pertains to the manner in which Josephus presents his narrative. There are four distinct elements in this second level of the interpretative framework. All of them are different types of commentary incorporated in the description of the subject matter. One is the reflection on the general situation in Judaea. These comments stand alone in the text. The second type of commentary is found in the reflections on events that are alluded to but which are not narrated by Josephus. The third is the reflections provided on incidents that Josephus narrates in his texts. More often than not these two types of comment seek to identify the significance of the incidents that have been referred to or described. The fourth type of commentary differs in its location. It is the comments that are included within the narration of an event. This type of commentary is particularly evident in the description of participants and the discussion of their possible motivation.

We are left with a problem of timing, trying to establish how the various reflective comments and commentary interact with the subject matter. Discussion of Josephus's attitude towards writing history would suggest that he narrated the events impartially with occasional insertions of personal reflections. Clearly Josephus does not adhere to this theory. There appear to be two plausible models for explaining how the two levels of the interpretative framework are put together. One accepts that Josephus's reflections act as the guiding principle. Steeped in hindsight, Josephus decides the appropriate subject matter

---

28. Obviously how extensive Josephus's account was for the period before his lifetime would be, in part, dictated by how many sources of information he could draw upon.

to include and the manner in which it should be recorded. The other model allows for more interaction. As Josephus collates various subject matter he reflects on the significance of those events and, in turn, focuses more sharply on particular types of material. Here, in a sense, Josephus is thinking as he writes. Only in the light of examining his texts will it be possible to speculate as to which of these models is more plausible for explaining the dynamic of how this interpretative framework was put together by Josephus.

It is evident that the narrative of events contained in Josephus's texts should not be taken at face value. The interpretative framework as outlined indicates that to distinguish between the comments and the narration of events is not possible. It is not simply a matter of dismissing Josephus's interpretation, nor a matter of working out which version of an event is accurate. The interpretative process is more fundamental: it controls the entire choice of subject matter and, therefore, the overall picture that is being conveyed. We must now contend with the possibility that although we can make conclusions and observations regarding what Josephus narrates, what we can conclude is, in itself, the product of an interpretation. In other words, the picture being used to understand the first century CE in Judaea may not necessarily provide the reader with a 'full' or 'balanced' representation of what was happening in the territory. In effect, our major resource for examining the period is itself a constructed picture.

Chapter 3

WRITING FROM HINDSIGHT:
JOSEPHUS'S INTERPRETATIVE FRAMEWORK IN OPERATION

Our attention turns to examining how Josephus functioned as an author
in practical terms. The purpose is to explore how the interpretative
framework that Josephus constructs for each text actually operates,
primarily in *War* and *Ant.*[1] I will discuss the purpose of each text,
both that stated in, and implied through, the narrative in an effort to
display the framework that is built by Josephus and on which the
reader is dependent. Our particular concern is to consider how the
framework is expressed in terms of the depiction of the situation in
Judaea during the first century CE. Here it will be apparent that there
are two central pillars in the framework: namely, Judaea is portrayed
as a place where conflict and turmoil were dominant and that the
trouble escalated to the point of the inevitable explosion—the 66–70
CE revolt. In effect, what characterizes Judaea was turmoil and
conflict which was fated towards disaster. Furthermore, it is evident
that the framework is a personal construction, dependent on Josephus's own circumstances. Although this last point is most obvious in
Life, it equally applies regarding *War* and *Ant.* The texts are not
simply laced with comments of Josephus, they are a commentary from
beginning to end. Whether this picture is historically accurate to the
period in question is not an issue that will be considered at this stage.
The focus is entirely on the picture Josephus constructs and how he
achieves this task.

1.   The outline of this interpretative framework, the two pillars, was established
in Chapter 1. Here the intention is to dissect Josephus's narrative to understand how
those 'pillars' were constructed.

1. *Life*

Although it is *War* and *Ant.* that provide the bulk of pertinent information regarding the state of affairs in Judaea I will begin with *Life*. It is chosen as a starting point primarily because it most clearly illustrates the degree of authorial involvement in the construction of the narrative and helps to clarify the nature of the relationship between the two levels of the interpretative framework: that is, the choice of material and the commentary on that material. *Life* has long been acknowledged as an apologetic text with personal concerns being paramount.[2] As a result, the first level—the selection of subject matter—is clearly dependent on authorial choice. The issue is not, therefore, simply the degree to which Josephus is providing a historically accurate account, but that in *Life* the content is determined by what equates with the authorial agenda. The second level, the various forms of commentary, is also an obvious part of the text.

Life is notable for the absence of an introduction. In part this may be explained by the possible origin of the text as an addition to *Ant.* The summary statement in *Ant.* 20.266 appears to indicate the nature of the subject matter for *Life*. Josephus notes his intention to 'recount briefly' his lineage and the events of his life (*Ant.* 20.266). The epilogue to *Life* (430) suggests that the narrative is a description of all the events related to Josephus's life (παντὸς τοῦ βίου). A hint at the purpose of this narrative of Josephus's life is provided in the statement that follows: 'let others judge as they will of my character' (*Life* 430). What Josephus is concerned to do is present information pertinent to an assessment of his 'character'. These few comments aside, the reader is given very little explicit direction as to what *Life* is designed to achieve. At best, we can suggest that personal apology regarding the character of Josephus may be involved. Far more illuminating are the

---

2. Discussion regarding the purpose of *Life* has attracted a significant amount of scholarly interest, which reveals varying degrees of scepticism about Josephus's intentions. For an extreme view that is highly critical of Josephus see R. Laqueur, *Der jüdische Historiker Flavius Josephus: Ein biografischer Versuch auf neuer quellenkritischer Grundlage* (Giessen: Munchow, 1920), pp. 6-55; and A. Schalit, 'Josephus und Justus: Studien zur Vita des Josephus', *Klio* 26 (1933), pp. 67-95. Varying contemporary opinions are expressed by Bilde, *Flavius Josephus*, pp. 104-13, Rajak, *Josephus*, pp. 146-48, Cohen, *Josephus*, pp. 101-80, and Mason, *Flavius Josephus*, pp. 311-24.

insights that can be derived on an implicit level from the subject matter included and the accompanying comments. Combined, they indicate that *Life* was far from a complete description of the career of Josephus. It is first and foremost a personal apology regarding specific issues.[3]

Although Josephus claims to have given an account of his 'whole life' the text is more notable for what is missing than for what it includes. Brief mention is made of Josephus's ancestry, education and of his personal circumstances after the revolt. In terms of the Jewish revolt, the beginning of the war is narrated only briefly. All the other information regarding the revolt and, indeed, the vast bulk of the entire text, pertains to Josephus's generalship between his leaving Jerusalem and the first encounter with Roman troops in the spring of 67 CE. This narrative of affairs focuses on matters in Tiberias, with particular reference to the relations between John of Gischala and Josephus. Events at Jotapata and his involvement in other parts of the revolt are deliberately ignored by Josephus (*Life* 407-13). The list of subject matter makes it hard to accept the idea that the text is an account of his 'whole life'. The escape from Jotapata—such an important issue in the narrative of *War*—is not discussed, nor is the process of his selection as a general. These absences cannot be explained simply by their presence in *War*, despite the fact that Josephus refers the reader to that text for such information (*Life* 412-13). The wartime events narrated in *Life* are described in *War*, not necessarily in the same detail, but they are present.[4] The process of selecting material for *Life* lies elsewhere. It is here that the various comments associated

---

3.   Cohen, *Josephus*, p. 109, states that Josephus was also trying to provide an apology in the form of an autobiography. Bilde, *Flavius Josephus*, pp. 110-13, is even more forthright in affirming Josephus's statements in *Ant.* 20.266 and *Life* 430 by claiming that the text should be regarded as 'a genuine autobiography'. Much of the recent disagreement may be due to issues of definition and emphasis. Although *Life* clearly deals with material that pertains to the activities of Josephus (the autobiographical element) the choice of subject matter is very selective (the apologetical element). Even Bilde, *Flavius Josephus*, pp. 109-10, acknowledges that *Life* is 'an autobiography of a very special kind, one which is concentrated on the decisive events in the life of the author'. One 'decisive event' that is not included is the capture of Josephus and his meeting with Vespasian. The crucial point is to acknowledge that it is the apologetical element that determines the shape of the autobiography and explains Josephus's decision to write *Life*.

4.   For example, see the list provided by Cohen, *Josephus*, pp. 3-7.

with the subject matter become relevant, indicating the importance of authorial choice in the construction of the narrative.

Life is a puzzling text. Of the material relating to his wartime activities that is contained in *War*, only a very small proportion is re-narrated in *Life* and it is done in much greater detail, especially the embassy from Jerusalem (*War* 2.626-31; *Life* 189-332). Some other details regarding Josephus are cited for the first time: for example, his trip to Rome and his post-war career. There are two related agendas that control the subject matter and comments: a desire to provide a defence of himself; and a concern to launch savage attacks on certain opponents. The defensive element of *Life* contains four categories of information: Josephus's family; his education; his pre-war and post-war activities; and his activities during the war. The information provided regarding the war can be further divided into three time spans: the events in Jerusalem at the outbreak of the revolt; the commission of Josephus in Galilee; and some of his activities as a general in Galilee. In relation to his family heritage, Josephus responds to the 'detractors' (*Life* 6) by showing that his family is not 'ignoble' but is of 'noble birth'. This view is reinforced by referring to the priestly and royal ancestry of his family (*Life* 1-2). Regarding his education, the second part of the defence, Josephus highlights his prowess. He presents a picture of an accelerated learner (*Life* 14, 16, 19) to whom even 'the chief priests and leading men of the city' deferred for exact guidance in the laws (*Life* 9). Josephus exposed himself to all the main 'sects' and controlled his encounter with lifestyles, eventually reaching a decision at the age of 19 as to how he would live his life (*Life* 12).

The third part of the defence is the inclusion of information relating to Josephus's career before and after the revolt. What material is provided is very brief in nature and there is a somewhat puzzling lack of material relating to the pre-war period, especially in the light of his alleged educational standing. The events narrated share a focus on highlighting aspects of Josephus's character and status. The integrity of Josephus is apparent in his concern to defend the priests sent to Rome (*Life* 14, 16), his desire to free friends after their capture in 70 CE (*Life* 419-21) and his choice of declining the offer to plunder the country and accepting only 'a gift of sacred books' (*Life* 417-18). Josephus's prowess is evident in the reference to the shipwreck on the journey to Rome (*Life* 15). The intervention of God in the shipwreck story also highlights the special standing of Josephus (*Life* 15), while his prominence is implied by the reference to the gifts he received from Poppaea (*Life* 16).[5] The treatment of Josephus by Vespasian, Domitian and especially Titus as described in *Life* also indicate his privileged status (*Life* 428-29). Friends are released at the request of Josephus, even those being crucified (*Life* 421); he is granted land (*Life* 422), a pension, Roman citizenship and lodgings in Rome (*Life* 423); and his property is exempt from taxation (*Life* 429). Such was Josephus's prominence that it even became the cause of envy among other Jews (*Life* 424-25). In the light of the information provided regarding the post-war career of Josephus, any criticism of him is also, by implication, a criticism of the Flavian emperors. Josephus leaves no doubt: he intends the reader to recognize that the Flavians had directly provided him with his status in Rome and that the character they were assessing (*Life* 455) had been judged favourably.[6]

The fourth part of the defence is the narrative of war events. All the information provided displays the integral link between the subject matter and the comments, helping to provide a defence of Josephus. In relation to events in Jerusalem in 66 CE Josephus offers little detail. The *Life* account (17-27) exonerates Josephus from any responsibility for encouraging the outbreak of hostility. We are informed that he arrived in Jerusalem after the move to rebel had already commenced (*Life* 17), that he actively advised against rebellion (*Life* 17-19), of his need to seek protection from the rebels (*Life* 20-21) and of his decision to participate in the revolt only in an effort to contain the level of conflict (*Life* 22-23). Although the unsuccessful attack of Cestius is mentioned (*Life* 24), the tension and conflict in Jerusalem is only alluded to in vague terms (*Life* 21).[7]

It is notable that a description of the process of selecting the generals and the issue of authority at the outbreak of the revolt is ignored.

5. In *Life* 425 Josephus explicitly refers to being the recipient of God's providence in the years that followed the revolt.

6. What is interesting regarding this feature of *Life* is that the text was published in the years that follow the revolt of Antonius, when the emperor is portrayed as becoming less popular (see Suetonius, *Domitian* 10–11).

7. This focus on a peaceful, conciliatory role echoes a theme of Josephus's attack on Justus and John of Gischala—they incited trouble, not Josephus. It also corresponds with the narration of Josephus's policy as general in Galilee and of his commissioning (*Life* 28-29). The lack of detail regarding this part of the war suggests Cohen's theory about *Life* being used to explain why Josephus became involved in the war is not entirely correct (*Josephus*, p. 100).

Instead, the commissioning simply indicates the nature of Josephus's command as one of controlling the level of conflict—one of limiting the carrying of arms to the military (*Life* 29). Later, in the context of describing his activities as general in Galilee, it is interesting that an emphasis is placed on highlighting the source of Josephus's authority—the 'common council' of Jerusalem (*Life* 62, 77-83, 185-88). The events regarding Josephus's command of Galilee which he chooses to narrate either display something about the nature of his character or the policy by which he performed his task as general. The events highlight his prowess, prominence, integrity and intelligence. Not one of the events is without some relevance in describing a feature of Josephus. More often than not, this link is implied in the nature of the contents, such as the military preparations undertaken by Josephus (*Life* 77-79) and his first encounter with Roman troops (*Life* 114-21).[8]

Josephus's policy as a general is also evident in the narrative of the events in Galilee. In all encounters Josephus actively tried to avoid bloodshed with other Jews and to prevent the escalation of conflict (*Life* 84-103, 121). This policy is in direct contrast to the activities of those subjected to Josephus's written attack, Justus and John of Gischala (*Life* 73-74, 85, 87, 122). The description of the situation in Galilee when Josephus arrived offers a parallel to the expression of the policy of the general. Josephus was not responsible for the situation in Tiberias, Sepphoris, Gamala or Gischala, the only cities mentioned at this stage of the narrative (*Life* 30-61).[9] If Josephus was subject to accusations of being a promoter of trouble in Galilee, then the narrative of his activities as a general as described in *Life* could not do much more to clear his name, in terms of what is narrated and the way it is presented.[10] The defence of Josephus is a triumph of the comments and subject matter in *Life*. Even if the reader did not wish to pay too much attention to the overt presentation of Josephus's actions, the choice of subject matter alone speaks volumes for his

8. For example, see also *Life* 62-69, 84-103, 104-11, 112-13, 114-21, 126-31, 132-48, 149-54, 155-78, 204-15, 398-406.
9. The one city constantly assisting Josephus in the narrative, Tarichaeae, is not mentioned in the survey of the situation when the general arrived. The silence here is curious, to say the least.
10. Further examples include *Life* 70-76, 103, 155-78, 368-72, 373-80, 381-90.

integrity and earnest desire to prevent the war from escalating.[11]

The other element of *Life*—the open attack on opponents—also displays the overlap between comments and content. The subjects of Josephus's attack are two individuals, John of Gischala and Justus of Tiberias. The attack on Justus appears to provide an explanation for the inclusion of much of the defensive element of the text, and probably to the published form of *Life*. Josephus's explicit comments are concentrated in four sections of the narrative, 40-41, 336-44, 354-67 and 390-93. Although Justus is harshly condemned, along with the inhabitants of his native city, it is John of Gischala who receives the greater amount of attention in the narrative. Josephus criticizes Tiberias as a city eager for conflict and lacking in loyalty to one cause (*Life* 155-78, 345-53), and within this context he introduces the reader to Justus by combining comment and narrative. Josephus acknowledges Justus's learning (*Life* 40) but summarizes his character as one of 'general depravity' (*Life* 40). This view is easily substantiated by the context of events that Josephus establishes. Justus is the ringleader of the pro-war group at Tiberias (*Life* 36), whose motives were a desire for power (*Life* 36). He used 'charlatan's tricks' (*Life* 40) to persuade the people to join him, with the end result being that he 'forced many to do so against their will' (*Life* 42). Josephus reveals the reason for his intense attack: Justus's account of the revolt was an attempt to 'disguise the truth' (*Life* 40). Such is Josephus's condemnation that he claims 'our ruin was almost entirely due' to Justus and his brother (*Life* 41). Josephus promises to present the proof of this view in the course of the narrative (*Life* 41). Certainly, on the occasions that Tiberias features in the narrative, Justus (*Life* 88, 177) and his brother Jesus (*Life* 185, 132) are prominent as the instigators of trouble, but he fails to substantiate the claims in *Life* 41 with any evidence.

The importance of Justus's version of events as the main explanation for the published form of *Life* is evident in the three other sections where Josephus focuses his narrative on Justus (*Life* 336-44, 354-67, 390-93). Josephus indicates his intention to defend himself against

---

11. This approach is a feature of numerous scholars who assert that Josephus's commission in Galilee was one of curtailing the level of conflict, where the description of events are deemed to stand as an 'external' witness to Josephus's comments. See Rajak, *Josephus*, pp. 154-64, Bilde, *Flavius Josephus*, pp. 43-46, and Rappaport, 'Where was Josephus Lying', pp. 284-86.

false accusations. This activity does not take place in those sections where Josephus directly addresses Justus. Instead, it is the material cited earlier within the defence of Josephus, the references to the family, education and pre-war and post-war career, with their focus on the nature of Josephus's character, which formed the basis of the desire to respond to 'false allegations'. Josephus clumsily tries to defend himself against the charge of causing Tiberias to rebel (*Life* 336-44), but the bulk of Josephus's energy is devoted to attacking Justus's character and failure to hold the necessary qualifications to write an account of the revolt. Josephus refers to Justus's failure in public life (*Life* 354-56), particularly his troubled relationship with Agrippa II and his fear of Josephus. Whereas Josephus was the legitimate commander appointed by the Jerusalem authorities, Justus promoted himself out of a desire for power, having persuaded the people of Tiberias to rebel (*Life* 390-93). As a writer, Justus is criticized for his lack of personal knowledge of the events, having fled to Agrippa II at Berytus (*Life* 357). He failed to consult the commentaries and he deliberately withheld publication until the relevant witnesses were all dead (*Life* 357-67). In comparison, Josephus presented his text to his Roman superiors and Agrippa II and could cite letters of recommendation. Clearly the need to respond to the criticism levelled at Josephus by Justus was a crucial factor in the way *Life* was presented. It helps explain the focus on Tiberias, its negative comparison with Tarichaeae and Sepphoris and the defensive elements of the text—the autobiographical details.[12]

Although Justus and the inhabitants of Tiberias are harshly condemned, Josephus pays much greater attention in the narrative of *Life* to John of Gischala. There is no obvious link between what Josephus wants to say regarding Justus and John, unless Justus's account happens to promote John as a legitimate Galilaean leader. This concept, however, is not evident in the comments.[13] Whatever the origin of the

12. For discussion of Justus see T. Rajak, 'Justus of Tiberias', *CQ* 23 (1973), pp. 345-68, and T. Rajak, 'Josephus and Justus of Tiberias', in L.H. Feldman and G. Hata (eds.), *Josephus, Judaism and Christianity* (Detroit: Wayne State University Press, 1987), pp. 81-94. It would be interesting to speculate what type of reconstructions scholarship would provide if Justus's narrative survived and Josephus's had been lost.

13. The extensive reference to John of Gischala is not given due weight by the existing arguments which view *Life* as an apology and/or autobiography. Cohen,

attack on John, it constitutes a substantial proportion of the text (*Life* 43-45, 70-76, 84-103, 122-25, 189-335, 368-72). Much of the detail of *Life* not included in *War* is associated with the attack on John, especially in relation to the embassy from Jerusalem that John instigated. In the initial reference (*Life* 43-45), Josephus displays a neutral attitude toward John. If anything, his actions in arming the people of Gischala and attacking the neighbouring Syrian cities are explained as a legitimate retribution. On all other occasions, however, John is the object of much criticism. He is eager for revolution, motivated by a desire for power and envious of Josephus's prominence and respect (*Life* 70, 84, 122, 189). These observations regarding John are mirrored by the events in which John is involved. John continually tries to overthrow Josephus, even to the point of trying to kill him (*Life* 70-76, 84-103, 122-25, 189-335). The most significant of all plots— the request sent to Jerusalem for the removal of Josephus—is cast in the context of being motivated by John's envy (*Life* 189). This embassy is portrayed as lacking popular support in Jerusalem and in Galilee—it is the work of intrigue, averted only by the providence of God, the ingenuity of Josephus and the loyalty of the populace (*Life* 230-31, 262, 289, 309, 324). The victory of Josephus over John and, therefore, the triumph of his character, is complete when it is stated that John is forced to remain in Gischala because of his lack of a following (*Life* 368-72).[14]

It is not possible to read *Life* assuming that a distinction can be drawn between Josephus's commentary and the subject matter narrated. Although some comments can be identified above and beyond the narrative, to assume that what remains is an account devoid of interpretation would be to ignore the fundamental nature of the interpretative framework. What is narrated in *Life* and how it is presented is dictated by Josephus. The specific agendas used to control *Life* are

Josephus, p. 79, suggests that *Life* may have been constructed in two stages. Such a schema of construction may help explain the dual but apparently unrelated focuses of *Life* on Justus and John.

14. See U. Rappaport, 'John of Gischala in Galilee', in L.I. Levine (ed.), *The Jerusalem Cathedra: Studies in the History, Archaeology, Geography and Ethnography of the Land of Israel* (Jerusalem: Yad Izhak Ben Zvi Institute, 1983), III, pp. 46-57, and U. Rappaport, 'John of Gischala: From Galilee to Jerusalem', *JJS* 33 (1982), pp. 479-93, for a positive biography of John and his involvement in the various stages of the revolt.

an apology that tries to defend the credentials of Josephus and an attack on his rivals—namely, Justus and John. What aspects of Josephus's character and, therefore, information relating to his career, that need to be explained are dependent on the accusations made by Justus in his work. The reason for the sustained attack on John in *Life* is not readily explained. Although possible that Justus's narrative included reference to John, Josephus does not make this link. The attack does explain the nature of much of the content in *Life*. The emphasis on events in Galilee between Josephus's appointment and the first Roman sallies, especially the embassy sent from Jerusalem, are all the result of Josephus's decision to attack John of Gischala.[15]

The discussion of *Life* illustrates the need to explain the choice of content of the text as well as the way it is narrated. In *Life* we see Josephus's interpretative framework almost without disguise. The two levels of the framework—the selection of material and the commentary on that material—are working hand in hand to substantiate one another in the justification of their author. Josephus crafts his words to apparently apply the motto 'actions speak louder than words'. *Life* is clearly the result of Josephus's reflection controlling subject matter. By implication, although it may purport to be a full or accurate account of the events narrated, it cannot be more than a single interpretation, one face of the prism.

The same principle of the link between content and commentaries applies to *War* and *Ant*. The difference is the topic. No longer is it a matter of what Josephus himself did. With *War* and *Ant*. the issue is primarily the overall state of affairs in first-century CE Judaea. Simply because the topic has shifted from the individual to the communal situation does not alter the need to be aware of how the interpretative framework functions. If anything, it is all the more important because authorial choice does not appear as such an obvious factor in *War* and *Ant*. as it does in *Life*. The following analysis will consider *War* and *Ant*. separately, with the discussion of each text divided into two sections. The first will focus on exploring the declared aims of the texts. The second section will be devoted to establishing how the two levels of the interpretative framework actually

---

15. As a result, the disposition of *Life* suggested by Bilde, *Flavius Josephus*, p. 107, does not provide sufficient recognition of the two agendas; cf. Cohen, *Josephus*, pp. 114-70, and Mason, *Flavius Josephus*, p. 322, who also do not highlight John in their discussion of the aims.

function in relation to Josephus's description of the state of affairs in first-century CE Judaea. Attention will be paid primarily to the content of the texts, the purpose as implied rather than proclaimed. With both texts I will then turn to elements of the second level of the interpretative framework, outlining the reflective comments on the general situation and the reflective comments on events alluded to but not narrated, before turning to the reflective comments on the events that Josephus actually describes. From there, I will turn back to the first level of the interpretative framework, the nature of the subject matter included. Finally, I will consider the comments Josephus makes as he narrates events. The analysis will conclude by noting several observations pertinent to how Josephus combines the comments and the subject matter. Through this analysis we will be able to develop a picture of how Josephus constructs an account of Judaea in the first century CE, where conflict and turmoil escalating to open war in 66 CE are the key features which dictate what is said and how it is said.

2. War

2.1 Declared Aim(s) of the Text

Josephus provides a rather detailed introduction to *War* in which the focus of the text and the intended subject matter are identified.[16] In general terms the subject matter is the war between the Jews and the Romans (*War* 1.1), a focus confirmed in the epilogue (*War* 7.454).[17] Josephus provides further detail, listing the contents of the narrative (*War* 1.17-29). Of events prior to the war Josephus starts his account with Antiochus Epiphanes IV. The material included in the list of pre-war contents is curious. Although Josephus states that he will be brief in how he deals with the incidents prior to his own lifetime, his choice of events to be signposted is far from complete. The Hasmonaeans, Pompey, Herod, the revolt at Herod's death and then the outbreak of the war of 66–70 CE, particularly the fate of Cestius, are noted. No reference is made to the events between 6–66 CE, which actually

16. The following discussion is focused almost entirely on *War* 1-6. For the dating of *War* 7 see S. Schwartz, 'The Composition and Publication of Josephus's "Bellum Judaicum" Book 7', *HTR* 79 (1986), pp. 373-86; cf. Bilde, *Flavius Josephus*, p. 79.

17. On the title of *War* see Bilde, *Flavius Josephus*, pp. 71-73; cf. Rajak, *Josephus*, pp. 210-12.

occupy approximately half of *War* 2. The paucity of the first part of this list is in sharp contrast to the fullness of the list of events mentioned in relation to the war. Josephus says he will narrate the preparations of the Jews, the appointment of Vespasian by Nero, the campaign in Galilee (with digressions on the Roman army and the geographical features of the region), the sufferings of prisoners captured in the campaign, the Roman civil war, the second invasion, a description of Jerusalem (its walls and the temple), the brutal treatment of the Jews by the tyrants, the civil war in Jerusalem, the clemency of the Romans, Titus's effort to save Jerusalem, the suffering of the Jews caused by the war, famine and tyranny, and the capture of the tyrants (*War* 1.21-29). Although no explicit reference is made to Josephus's career, especially his prophecy, the only substantial part of the narrative not cited in this list is the subject matter of *War* 7.

Several aspects of this list indicate that a process of selection was involved in the construction of *War*. First, Josephus openly states that he is deliberately refraining from narrating events prior to Antiochus Epiphanes IV (*War* 1.17-19). The explanation given is that these events have already been recorded by other Jews and that they have been subsequently translated into Greek. Although this may explain some omissions and act as the starting point of the text, it does not clarify why Josephus chooses to narrate the events that he does. We have no indication of the basis on which the subject matter has been chosen. The absentees from the list of pre-war events in the introduction forms a second indicator that Josephus selected material. The list is lengthy but it does not include all the events that Josephus in fact describes. The third aspect of the list which highlights the active control of Josephus over the text is the way in which the subject matter is cited and the descriptive terms used. Titus's actions are openly labelled as an attempt to save Jerusalem (*War* 1.27). What is unique here is that it is the only part of the list in which Josephus expresses the motivation of the participant. A further example of Josephus's control is the description of the events in Jerusalem during the war as 'sedition', and the labelling of the leaders of the later stage of the revolt as 'tyrants' who stand apart from the people (*War* 1.27).

It has already been established that the narration of the subject matter is allegedly controlled by an overriding concern to present the 'truth' about the war. Josephus laments the failings of other accounts,

whether from lack of first-hand knowledge (*War* 1.1) or an attempt to
flatter the Romans (*War* 1.7-8). In contrast, he states that his own
account will faithfully recount the actions of both combatants (*War*
1.9). The war was a major event (*War* 1.6) that warranted due
recognition and Josephus's text was directed only to 'lovers of the
truth' (*War* 1.30). Furthermore, Josephus believed he achieves this
truthfulness throughout the narrative (*War* 7.455). He will add nothing to the narration of 'the facts' (*War* 1.26). As such, the claims
made by Josephus regarding why the war took place and why the Jews
were defeated in 70 CE are not personal comment, but sentiments of
fact. Therefore, that 'sedition' was the cause of the 'ruin' of the Jews
and that the 'tyrants' caused the Romans to attack the temple is true.
Furthermore, it was the 'Jewish revolutionary party' that seized the
opportunity for war and continued to strive for conflict (*War* 1.4).
Proof that this was true can be derived from the witness of Titus, who
actively called upon the 'insurgents' to allow the temple and populace
to be spared (*War* 1.10-11). In other words, the list of contents
reflects the 'truth' of Josephus's stated view of how to understand the
war. As presented in the introduction, the subject matter and comments work together.[18]

2.2 *The Two Levels of the Interpretative Framework*
2.2.1 *Reflections on the general situation*. With this declared aim in
mind, what follows is an examination of the two levels of the interpretative framework in operation in the contents of *War* regarding the
first century CE. The first aspect of Josephus's commentary to be considered is the scattered reflective comments that Josephus makes on
the general situation. These comments stand alone, they are not related
to any specific event cited in the text. In *War*, there are six such

18. Much of the debate regarding the purpose of *War* has been dictated by the
issue of whether or not the text was apologetical propaganda for the Flavians or a
genuine attempt to construct a history of the war. For recent expressions of the main
approaches see Bilde, *Flavius Josephus*, pp. 65-78, Rajak, *Josephus*, pp. 78-
103, Cohen, *Josephus*, pp. 84-100, H.W. Attridge, 'Josephus and His Works', in
M.E. Stone (ed.), *Jewish Writings of the Second Temple Period: Apocrypha,
Pseudepigrapha, Qumran Sectarian Writing, Philo, Josephus* (CRINT, 2.2; Assen:
Van Gorcum, 1984), pp. 185-232 (196-203), C. Sauliner, 'Flavius Josèphe et la
propagande Flavienne', *RB* 96 (1989), pp. 545-62 and Mason, *Josephus on the
Pharisees*, pp. 57-81.

statements and they all convey a sense of doom. The first two are located in the introduction. In *War* 1.4 Josephus claims that the 'Jewish revolutionary party' was responsible for beginning the war, trying to prosper while Rome was faced with internal conflict. Then in *War* 1.10 Josephus expands upon the situation, stating that the defeat of the Jews and the destruction of the temple were laid at the feet of the tyrants. The four other reflections on the general situation are located in the narrative of events during the war. In *War* 2.650 Josephus summarizes the situation in Jerusalem towards the end of 66 CE in bleak terms: 'In short, the city before the coming of the Romans wore the appearance of a place doomed to destruction'.

The location of the other reflections are in the context of discussion of various rebel factions, implying a link between the two. In the wake of having described the factional groups that dominated Jerusalem, Josephus laments the predicament of the Jewish people who were 'labouring under the three greatest calamities: war, tyranny, sedition—to the populace the war was comparatively the mildest' (*War* 4.397). Even more critical of the situation in which the Jews found themselves, Josephus makes plain his hatred of the tyrants in *War* 5.442-45. Because of the tyrants 'no other city ever endured such miseries, nor since the world began has there been a generation more prolific in crime' (*War* 5.442). For Josephus, the tyrants were 'the dregs of society and the bastard scum of the nation' (*War* 5.443).[19] Any possible inhibition is shed in the final reflection on the general situation. Having outlined the areas in Jerusalem occupied by the rebel factions, Josephus declares 'that it was the sedition that subdued the city, and the Romans the sedition, a foe far more stubborn than her walls, and that all the tragedy of it may properly be ascribed to her own people, all the justice to the Romans' (*War* 5.257). For Josephus, the reflections on the general situation are an avenue for proclaiming the 'doomed' state of affairs in Jerusalem.

2.2.2 *Comments on events alluded to in the narrative.* The reflective comments on events alluded to but not narrated in *War* relate to the activity of some Roman administrators and of certain Jewish groups and individuals. While the comments about Roman administrators involved in incidents can be either positive or negative, they are all

---

19. Josephus confirms his view that these people were the cause of the disaster in his review of the various criminal groups in *War* 7.253-74.

critical regarding the Jews. We commence with the events that pertain to the Roman governors, all of which are linked to the period after 44 CE. In a brief aside, Josephus refers to the governorship of Fadus and Tiberius Alexander: these officials, 'who by abstaining from all interference with the customs of the country kept the nation at peace' (*War* 2.220). Nothing further is added by Josephus regarding the term of office of either Fadus or Tiberius Alexander. Later, Festus's governorship is also briefly mentioned. All that Josephus informs the reader of is that Festus attacked the 'principal plague of the country' by capturing and executing many brigands (*War* 2.271). Although a positive comment regarding the activities of Festus, it is apparent that trouble within Judaea required the governor to act as he did. In contrast, Albinus and Florus are strongly criticized with Josephus reflecting negatively on the effect of their activities. Albinus is introduced with the claim that 'there was no form of villainy which he omitted to practice' (*War* 2.272). He used his office to impose extraordinary taxes, and to steal, plunder and accept ransoms for the release of prisoners (*War* 2.273). He is even bribed by 'the powerful men of the revolutionaries' who, in turn, act like 'brigand chiefs' with gangs that terrorize the citizens (*War* 2.274-75). The net result of Albinus's governorship was that 'none could now speak his mind, with tyrants on every side; and from this date were sown in the city the seeds of its impending fall' (*War* 2.276). Albinus is not directly accused of responsibility for the revolt, but his method of governing is portrayed as providing the fertile ground in which that seed of conflict could grow.

According to Josephus, the situation deteriorates dramatically because of the activities of the next governor, Florus. Where Albinus was bad, Florus was deplorable.

> Such was the character of Albinus, but his successor, Gessius Florus, made him appear by comparison a paragon of virtue. The crimes of Albinus were, for the most part, perpetrated in secret and with dissimulation; Gessius, on the contrary, ostentatiously paraded his outrages upon the nation, and, as though he had been sent as hangman of condemned criminals, abstained from no form of robbery or violence (*War* 2.277).

With this introduction the reader is then informed that Florus was responsible for stripping cities of their wealth and allowing brigandage to flourish (*War* 2.278). Florus's actions resulted in widespread desolation and many Jews deciding to flee their homeland in an attempt to seek refuge outside Judaea (*War* 2.279).

The location of these negative reflections is most illuminating. Josephus provides no description of events under Festus or Albinus—their governorships are merely summarized by reflective comments. While Josephus deemed it important to say something, he did not choose to narrate any events as examples of evidence of his understanding of the situation. Furthermore, equal time is not given to Festus and Albinus in his summary. Josephus lays greater emphasis on Albinus, the subject of the negative reflection. The reflection on events which are only alluded to regarding Roman officials continues into the governorship of Florus. Josephus goes on to narrate and comment on events associated with Florus, but it is notable that he begins his description by reflecting on the purpose and effect of Florus's governorship. Josephus sets the tone in which the events that follow are to be viewed. This structuring of the text is pertinent when we seek to explain Josephus's attitude to the situation in Judaea and the origin of the revolt. The authorial hand appears to be accentuating the sense of unrest irrespective of whether the events warranted such a view.

Reflective comments are also provided on the activities of various 'rogue' Jews which are not described. All the people mentioned are deemed to be causing trouble in Judaea. In a very brief reference Josephus states that Judas 'incited his countrymen to revolt' (*War* 2.118). Judas is introduced as being a Galilaean and his message is summarized as a criticism of the Jews as 'cowards for consenting to pay tribute to the Romans and tolerating mortal masters, after having God for their lord' (*War* 2.118). He 'was a sophist who founded a sect of his own, having nothing in common with the others' (*War* 2.118). Josephus's narrative then digresses into a description of the three philosophies (*War* 2.119-66). However, there is no indication of how successful Judas was in inciting the Jews, the response of the authorities to his message, or exactly when during Coponius's governorship Judas began his activities. If anything, it is the silence and blandness of Josephus that distinguishes the description of Judas.

For the other Jews mentioned Josephus explicitly focuses on the negative impact of their activity. Notably, these people are all linked with the period from the governorship of Felix onwards. The brigand chief, Eleazar, who was eventually captured by Felix, has his career summarized as one of having 'ravaged the country' (*War* 2.252). The 'deceivers and impostors' active during Felix's governorship are portrayed even more poorly. As their title suggests, Josephus is extremely critical. Although they may not have been guilty of murder, they were a 'body of villains with purer hands but more impious intentions' than the sicarii (*War* 2.258). They were 'fostering revolutionary changes', persuading the populace to follow them to the desert with claims that God would show them 'tokens of deliverance' (*War* 2.259). These 'deceivers and impostors' reappear, grouped with the 'brigands' (*War* 2.264-65) to be an even greater cause of trouble. In graphic terms Josephus presents these 'rogue' Jews as a disease afflicting 'a sick man's body', inciting people to rebel, threatening to kill those who associated with the Romans (*War* 2.264) and pillaging the property of the wealthy (*War* 2.265). By implication, to remain loyal to Rome was to place one's life in peril. Josephus summarizes the significance of their activities in terms of 66–70 CE: 'The effects of their frenzy were thus felt throughout all Judaea, and every day saw this war being fanned into fiercer flame' (*War* 2.265). Finally, early in the revolt, the activities of Simon b. Gioras created trouble in the region of Acrabatene. He stole from the wealthy, having 'devoted himself to rapine' (*War* 2.652). When forced to flee the region Simon continued to engage in brigandage after relocating himself at Masada.

Josephus's reflective comments on events alluded to are very important. Most relate to the period after 50 CE and are associated with the negative impact of the activities of certain Roman officials and 'rogue' Jews. They present Judaea as a place under attack. Unrest was increasing and war was imminent. Without actually narrating events, Josephus is able to establish a picture of Judaea simply by referring to the impact of various incidents.

2.2.3 *Comments on events narrated.* The third aspect of Josephus's commentary—his reflective comments associated with specific events which he narrates—are located throughout the text. With the exception of Pilate's introduction of standards bearing images of Caesar, all the pre-war events narrated by Josephus include reflective comments that pertain to their significance. Several factors are common to the pre-war narrative. First, the incidents are described as occasions of trouble. Second, these comments are placed at the beginning of the account of the event. Josephus declares to the reader the impact of what is about to be narrated. The third factor is that most of these incidents are placed in a context where they are linked with other events.

Pilate's decision to use money from the Corbonas to construct an aqueduct is introduced as 'further trouble' (*War* 2.175). For Josephus there was a link between this incident and the decision of Pilate to introduce standards bearing images into Jerusalem. The other pre-44 CE incident that Josephus comments on is Gaius's order to erect statues of himself in Jerusalem. Although the incident stands alone, reflective comments are placed at the outset of the account. Gaius's order is presented as an expression of the emperor's 'impiety' (*War* 2.184). The tone, therefore, in which the incident is to be viewed is set at the beginning.

It is mainly in the period after 44 CE that a sense of incidents being linked together is evident. Cumanus is introduced by claiming that 'under his administration disturbances broke out, resulting in another large loss of Jewish lives' (*War* 2.223).[20] The first of these disturbances, the soldier exposing himself at Passover, is then narrated (*War* 2.224-27). Here, Josephus concludes by reflecting on the consequences of what had occurred. Instead of the festival being an occasion for celebration it became a time of mourning because of the many people who had died (*War* 2.227). Josephus then proceeds to draw a link between the trouble at Passover with the next incident he describes—the attack on Stephen, the emperor's slave (*War* 2.228). This process is repeated in *War* 2.232, where Josephus links the Galilaean–Samaritan dispute with the attack on Stephen. According to Josephus, these three incidents from Cumanus's governorship are a sequence; there is a movement from one expression of trouble to another. It is notable that this sequence of events is on a sliding scale of intensity. The minor incident is described first, then comes a more serious disturbance, and finally the climax comes in the large scale conflict over the Galilaean–Samaritan affair.

Later, in Josephus's description of Felix's term of office, this process of weaving together incidents is repeated and the sliding scale is employed on a second occasion. The rise of the sicarii is introduced in *War* 2.254 as a 'crisis' that replaced the one which Felix had just dealt with, the activity of Eleazar, the 'brigand chief' (*War* 2.253). As one 'pest' is removed a new one appears—the sicarii. The success of the sicarii, in part attributed to their secrecy, is explained in terms of the

20. It is probable that Josephus is referring to the previous occasion that he mentioned the death of Jews in his narrative, the protest over the aqueduct during the governorship of Pilate (*War* 2.177).

consequences for the community: namely, widespread fear (*War* 2.256-57). The next incident Josephus narrates—the activities of the Egyptian—is also introduced in an attempt to locate him in this picture of increasing turmoil. The Egyptian is deemed to be 'a still worse blow' for the Jews (*War* 2.261). The other incident before 66 CE that is narrated by Josephus—the dispute at Caesarea—is also introduced and linked to other material in general terms. Again, Josephus labels the incident as an expression of disorder (*War* 2.266). It is apparent that the reflective comments establish a continuity in the narration of events in the period prior to 66 CE. At the beginning of almost every incident which Josephus describes it is signposted that Judaea was burdened by conflict. One crisis was followed by another.

At no stage in his reflection on the events for the period prior to 66 CE does Josephus overtly claim the war was inevitable. However, any reluctance he may have had with such a view disappears when it comes to reflecting on the events from 66 CE onwards. If anything, the reverse applies—Josephus appears to be eager to explain the significance of incidents in terms of the war and, in particular, the defeat of the Jews in 70 CE. Trouble in Caesarea during 66 CE is described as the 'ostensible pretext for the war' (*War* 2.285). Then, in *War* 2.409 it is the decision of Eleazar b. Ananias and his associates to cease accepting sacrifices on behalf of foreigners that is deemed to have 'laid the foundation of the war with the Romans'. Such a view is reiterated as Josephus concludes his description of the negotiations among the Jews as to whether or not to reinstate the offerings. The support given to Eleazar b. Ananias by the 'ministers' is viewed as being 'instrumental in bringing about the war' (*War* 2.417). Much later, in *War* 6, when Josephus outlines the numerous oracles that were popular near the beginning of the revolt, he reflects on their significance in terms of helping bring about the conflict. The oracles of 'charlatans' had deluded the populace (*War* 6.288). Although God had displayed care by giving the 'premonitory signs', the people failed to understand the warnings (*War* 6.310).[21]

---

21. Josephus displays his practice of combining comment and narrative in the sense of assertion and evidence within this section of *War* 6. The assertion is made in *War* 6.310 and the evidence is the narrative that follows, *War* 6.311-15, the oracles of 70 CE regarding the temple and the response of the people who gathered in the hope of deliverance. On the misinterpretation of other oracles see *War* 2.648-50.

Josephus's numerous reflective comments on events which he narrates during the revolt even more explicitly indicate that the destruction of Jerusalem was inevitable. More often than not Josephus proclaims that it was God who had determined that Jerusalem would suffer punishment. Cestius's decision not to continue with the siege in 66 CE is cast in terms of God having determined that the war would go on (*War* 2.539).[22] The death of Ananus is also portrayed in terms of God's decision that Jerusalem would be destroyed (*War* 4.323). Although Ananus would have been able to help save the city (*War* 4.151, 318-20), God had already decreed that Jerusalem must be punished. In this context Josephus calls on the activities of 'rogue' Jews, citing numerous incidents as occasions in which the true significance of what happened related to God's decision to punish the Jews. The zealots' attack on the populace (*War* 5.3-4), their murder of worshippers in the temple (*War* 5.19), their burning of the supplies (*War* 5.26), their recapture of the second city wall (*War* 5.343) and John's pillaging of the temple (*War* 5.566) are all portrayed in this light. In no sense could the events that culminated in 70 CE be deemed as accidents. The significance and consequence of what is narrated by Josephus makes it apparent that the fate of Jerusalem was sealed. This admission is actively made throughout the narrative of the war.

One further type of reflective comment that Josephus makes in relation to certain events warrants brief mention. Occasionally Josephus comments on the attitude of the Jewish people to what happens. For example, mourning and panic are a consequence of the riot associated with the action of the soldier at the festival (*War* 2.227), while the murder of the Roman garrison also became the cause of mourning (*War* 2.455). During the revolt the faction fighting led to panic (*War* 4.142) and the old men and women turned to the Romans as their rescuers (*War* 5.28). Furthermore, the people, far from helping the 'tyrants', wanted peace (*War* 5.52), a fact that Titus recognized (*War* 5.335).[23]

---

22. In *War* 2.532, however, Josephus claims that Cestius had been bribed by an agent of Florus.

23. Other examples of panic include *War* 2.649-50; 3.435-38; 4.125. One further type of reflective comment pertains to the extent of tragedy that is associated with a particular incident. Two separate events are claimed as the greatest single disaster during the war—the massacre at the Jordan (*War* 4.437) and the murder of deserters by the Roman allies (*War* 5.522).

The reflective comments associated with the events narrated point towards Josephus presenting a view of Judaea as a place of turmoil. Josephus is concerned to highlight the significance of events. Although Josephus does not explicitly deem the war as inevitable prior to the events of 66 CE, he does weave these events together. Almost every incident is signposted as a cause of trouble. As one conflict is resolved another unfolds. There is a process, a movement from conflict to conflict, in which an escalation in the level of turmoil is made evident. These reflections provide a setting for the narrative of the revolt where Josephus sheds any inhibition he may have held. What happened in 70 CE was inevitable. The events narrated are explained as part of the process which culminated with God punishing the 'godless' generation.[24]

2.2.4 *Choice of subject matter*. The next section to discuss is the first level of the interpretative framework: the nature of the subject matter of *War*. For convenience, it is appropriate to view the subject matter in five separate categories: information regarding the leadership of the Jews and Romans; territorial arrangements in the region; changes to certain practices and the response to those initiatives; relations between communities residing in Judaea; and activities of individuals and groups, whether Jews or Roman officials.[25] The following discussion of these categories will be divided along chronological lines, commencing with the material included for the period prior to the disturbance at Caesarea in 66 CE. The second part will incorporate the subject matter devoted to the revolt. It will become apparent that the nature of the subject matter itself leads to the view that Judaea was a place of turmoil and conflict.

The first two categories—material pertinent to the rulers and the territorial arrangements—are dealt with in a very brief, cursory manner in the pre-war section of *War*. Josephus refers to the Roman emperors and comments on the general tenor of the reign of Gaius and Nero (*War* 2.184, 250-51). Noticeably, the material pertaining to Gaius immediately precedes the narration of his order that statues of him be erected in Jerusalem (*War* 2.184). Of the governors, the

24. The instrumental role of God is also indicated in such passages as *War* 4.104, 323; 5.559; 6.250-51, 268, 315, 399, 408, 433.

25. The geographical digressions are different; they will not be discussed in any detail here.

account for the period prior to 41 CE is very potted. After naming
Coponius, the next and only other one mentioned is Pilate. All the
governors between 44–66 CE, however, are named, even if Josephus
does not actually provide any description of what happened while several incumbents were in office, as in the case of Fadus, Tiberius
Alexander and Festus (*War* 2.220, 271). The Jewish rulers of the
Herodian family are named, along with when they acquire their position and when they are replaced (*War* 2.167, 181-83, 214-17, 223,
247, 252). Reference to the second category—the territorial arrangements in relation to Judaea—is directly related to the naming of the
various rulers, whether they be Roman governors or Jewish rulers.
Although only given a minor standing in the narrative, the references
to leadership and territorial arrangements have a common feature—
they describe changes that took place.

The third category—the changes to practice and the accompanying
response—is also only a minor feature of the pre-war subject matter.
There are only two examples of this type of subject matter, and both
attempts to alter the existing customs or practice are the initiative of a
Roman official. One is the work of Pilate, who introduced into
Jerusalem standards with images of Caesar (*War* 2.169-74). The other
is the order of Gaius that statues of him be erected in Jerusalem (*War*
2.184-203). In response to both initiatives the Jews protested. In turn,
the Roman officials, Pilate and the legate Petronius, backed down.
Whether Gaius would have made other arrangements to ensure his
order was fulfilled is not stated as the 'timely' death of the emperor
allowed the incident to be resolved without conflict. These two incidents are examples of attempts by certain Roman officials to impose
upon the Jews practices they were not willing to accept. They are
changes that portray conflict.

The subject matter that describes the relations between communities
residing in Judaea, the fourth category, also conveys a sense of trouble
and conflict. There are only two such incidents in *War*—the Galilaean–
Samaritan dispute and the trouble in Caesarea that began while Felix
was governor. Both incidents originate in rivalry between ethnic
groups, they are not Jewish–Roman disputes at the outset. The Samaritans are held responsible for initiating the conflict that was finally
resolved in Rome by Claudius. Samaritans attack Galilaean pilgrims
travelling to Jerusalem, killing one of them (*War* 2.232). Responsibility
for the other incident, the dispute over who should have precedence at

Caesarea, is not delegated. Josephus outlines the arguments of the Caesarean Jews and the Caesarean Syrians for why their respective rights should be upheld. After several skirmishes the governor, Felix, decided to send delegates to Rome so that the case could be resolved by the emperor.[26]

The final category to consider is the activities of individuals or certain groups. This category constitutes the vast bulk of the subject matter for the pre-war narrative. Some of the activities are associated with two Roman governors—Pilate and Florus—and with auxiliary soldiers while on duty. All the other incidents pertain to actions certain Jews undertake. Irrespective of whether the incident is initiated by a Roman official or by Jews they are, with a few minor exceptions, examples of conflict. We commence with the activities of Roman officials. Pilate decided to fund the construction of an aqueduct by using money from the Corbonas (*War* 2.175-77). How Pilate acquired the funds is not explained but the action is presented as the cause of a protest by some Jews when Pilate visits Jerusalem. The decision of Pilate to use force to resolve the protest reinforces the level of tension and conflict. The other Roman governor whose exploits are narrated is Florus. After responding to the deteriorating situation in Caesarea, Florus travelled to Jerusalem in 66 CE, and demanded the payment of 17 talents.[27] This initiative was greeted with a mock collection made by some unnamed Jews. What follows is the description of an escalation of conflict in which Florus demanded that the culprits be handed over for punishment, allowed his troops to sack the agora, crucified many Jews (including those of equestrian rank), developed a plan to rouse Jewish anger by ordering troops to ignore the Jewish welcome and then left the city in the control of the chief priests and boule with a cohort of troops (*War* 2.331-32).

26. What we do not know is why the dispute at Caesarea began when it did nor what was happening there prior to the dispute. See D.R. Schwartz, 'Felix and *Isopoliteia*, Josephus and Tacitus', *Zion* 58 (1993), pp. 265-86, and L.I. Levine, 'The Jewish–Greek Conflict in First Century Caesarea', *JJS* 25 (1974), pp. 381-97; cf. A. Kasher, 'The *Isopoliteia* Question in Caesarea Maritima', *JQR* 68 (1977), pp. 16-27. In a similar vein, it is not explained whether this particular festival was the only occasion that Samaritans attacked Galilaeans or why they chose to do so when they did.

27. The relationship between this action and the 'census' ordered by Cestius (*War* 6.422) is not explained by Josephus. It is part of a study being prepared by the author.

Two incidents are related to the actions of soldiers. In one, the action of a soldier exposing himself to the crowd while he was patrolling the temple precinct at a Passover festival was the cause of a large protest by the Jews (*War* 2.224-27). The other incident involving a soldier was not instigated by his action. Instead, the soldier exacerbated a situation when he destroyed a copy of the law while fulfilling orders to punish the villages that failed to capture the 'brigands' which had attacked Stephen (*War* 2.228-31).

The other incidents narrated all pertain to actions carried out by Jews, either individuals or groups. A few actions undertaken by Herodian rulers are briefly cited by Josephus. Philip and Herod Antipas constructed cities within their respective tetrarchies (*War* 2.168) and, with regard to Agrippa I's reign over Judaea, reference is made only to his decision to build a wall around Jerusalem (*War* 2.218). All the other actions are the work of 'rogue' Jews. They include Judas the Galilaean, Eleazar the 'brigand chief', the sicarii, the 'insurgents' active under Albinus, the 'brigands' who attacked Stephen, the Egyptian and other 'deceivers', 'impostors' and 'charlatans' such as Jesus b. Ananias.[28] These people are the instigators of trouble, destabilizing the situation in Judaea. They attack the populace and try to lead them into performing actions that would amount to insurrection against Rome.

The subject matter of *War* prior to the revolt amounts to a bleak picture, with trouble being the prominent characteristic of what is narrated. It is extremely difficult to compare any of the pre-war narrative to the declared interests of Josephus in writing *War*. Josephus was silent regarding the material he would include when he summarized the contents of the text. He simply stated that he would be brief in his description of the subject matter from before his lifetime. Presumably Josephus believed the material he narrated to be relevant to the description of the war, providing a context in which to place the events of 66–70 CE.

Of the second part—subject matter regarding the actual revolt—the level of conflict and disorder only intensifies. All five categories of subject matter are contained in the account of events associated with the war, with the bulk of the material pertaining to the categories of

---

28. An exception is John, the tax collector, and 'the powerful men' of Caesarea. Their protest, however, was a response to an existing situation, they were not initiating a change.

leadership and the activities of certain individuals and groups. The
first category to consider is the information regarding the leadership
of the Jews.[29] Josephus describes several occasions when there is a
change in the leadership. The first occurs after Eleazar b. Ananias and
his associates ceased accepting the offerings on behalf of foreigners in
the summer of 66 CE. Jerusalem is divided between those in favour of
armed conflict with the Romans and those seeking a peaceful resolution to the trouble that had flared up during Florus's visit. The
'powerful men and the chief priests' lead the pro-peace faction (*War*
2.422). They were supported by Agrippa II and among their rank are
such individuals as Ananias, Ezechias, Saul, Antipas and Costobar
(*War* 2.418, 429, 441). Those named as being associated with the faction seeking war are Eleazar b. Ananias, Menahem and his followers
and, presumably, Simon b. Gioras and Eleazar b. Simon (*War* 2.434,
437, 443, 521, 564).[30] The resolution to this dispute and the one
which developed between Eleazar b. Ananias and Menahem was via
armed conflict (*War* 2.422-41, 442-48).

After this initial conflict regarding the leadership, Josephus mentions the appointment of 'additional' generals (*War* 2.562-68). These
people are appointed after the defeat of Cestius and they are given the
responsibility for overseeing the war effort in designated regions of
the country. Of those listed by Josephus three are identified as priests,
one as an Essene, one a Peraean and four simply by the name of their
father (*War* 2.563-64, 566-68). On this occasion the change in leadership takes place within the temple precinct in the confines of a public
gathering.

The next reference to the leadership of the Jews is the description of
a change that is the result of armed conflict.[31] The existing leadership
in Jerusalem of Ananus b. Ananus and Jesus b. Gamalas is ousted by a
coalition of 'zealots' and Idumaeans (*War* 4.121-365).[32] Among this

---

29. Information regarding the three emperors (*War* 2.168, 181, 204) will not be
discussed.

30. Gorion b. Nicomedes, Ananias b. Sadok, Judas b. Jonathan, who are named
as envoys during the attack on the Roman garrison, are probably associated with
Eleazar b. Ananias.

31. The failed attempt to remove Josephus from his command in Galilee (*War*
2.626-31) will not be considered here.

32. There are several 'gaps' associated with the make up of the leadership in this
early period of the war. For example, in *War* 2.562-68 Josephus does not explain

coalition are the Idumaean generals John, James b. Sosas, Simon b. Thaceas and Phineas b. Clusoth (*War* 4.235); John of Gischala; and those named as being prominent among the 'zealots' are Eleazar b. Simon and Zacharias b. Amphicalleus (*War* 4.225). It is a change that involved the death of Ananus b. Ananus and Jesus b. Gamalas (*War* 4.314-17).

Finally, Josephus describes the changes that take place in the make up of the 'new' coalition leadership. Simon b. Gioras entered the city to form his own faction with the result that three separate groups operated under the leadership of Eleazar b. Simon, John of Gischala and Simon b. Gioras (*War* 4.389-97, 556-84; 5.1-38). After more fighting the 'zealots' associated with Eleazar align themselves with John and there are two leaders, John and Simon, who control the war effort during the siege of 70 CE (*War* 5.98-105, 248-57). Of the changes Josephus includes in his narrative, most describe trouble and open hostilities between Jewish groups. With the exception of the appointment of the 'additional' generals, they are narrated in some detail, especially the changes associated with the death of Ananus and Jesus and within the subsequent 'coalition'.

The territorial arrangements described by Josephus all pertain to the campaigning of the revolt. Although Josephus does not outline the extent of territory controlled by the forces fighting against the Romans, he does narrate some of the stages by which the Romans regained control of certain areas. The recapture of several parts of Galilee is described, including Gabara (*War* 3.132-43) Jotapata (*War* 3.135-288, 316-39), Japhna (*War* 3.289-306), Tarichaeae (*War* 3.462-542), Gamala (*War* 4.11-53, 62-83) and Gischala (*War* 4.84-120). Other regions restored to Roman authority of which there is an account given include Peraea (*War* 4.410-39) and Idumaea (*War* 4.550-55). Finally, the siege and subsequent re-conquest of Jerusalem is narrated in detail (*War* 5.39–6.434).

The next category of subject matter is the description of changes to certain practices. The two examples are of initiatives by Jews, which are presented by Josephus as causing a significant level of protest by other Jews, and consequently an escalation in conflict. The first change is the decision of Eleazar b. Ananias and his supporters to stop

the standing of Symeon b. Gamaliel or Gorion b. Joseph (presuming he is different from the Joseph b. Gorion of *War* 2.563), or the rise of Jesus b. Gamalas, who appears to hold a greater standing than Joseph b. Gorion (*War* 4.160, 238, 322-25).

accepting the sacrifices offered on behalf of foreigners. Despite the opposition of 'the powerful men, the chief priests and the most notable of the Pharisees' and the alleged uniqueness of the decision, the practice was not reinstated (*War* 2.417). The other change which Josephus describes is the election of the high priest by lot, replacing the existing practice of appointment by a Herodian ruler. According to Josephus the process and choice of a relatively unknown figure was championed by the 'zealots' (*War* 4.147-50, 153-54). It was an action that was opposed by Ananus b. Ananus, Jesus b. Gamalas, Symeon b. Gamaliel, Joseph b. Gorion and their followers (*War* 4.158-61). No information is provided as to how the change was achieved nor what happened to the previous incumbent.[33]

The fourth category is the narration of relations between communities residing in Judaea. The one substantial reference is to the continuation of a dispute in Caesarea, which began while Felix was governor. The decision of Nero to favour the case of the Syrian inhabitants did not resolve the situation. During Florus's term of office trouble between the Jewish and Syrian residents flared up when news of Nero's decision was received. The flash point for conflict which resulted in the Jewish community leaving the city centred around the site of the synagogue (*War* 2.285, 289). Conflict is evident in the other brief references to interaction between Jewish and Syrian occupants of cities in Judaea. The outbreak of hostilities in Jerusalem marks the point in Josephus's narrative for the citation of several ethnic attacks.[34] There are attacks by the Syrians on the Jews at Caesarea (*War* 2.457) and on the Jews at Scythopolis (*War* 2.466) while the Jews attacked the Syrian villages of the Decapolis and the coastal settlements (*War* 2.458-60). The attack on Ascalon by rebel forces led by Niger is also possibly related to an ethnic dispute (*War* 3.10).

The final category of subject matter is the description of the activities

---

33. Although Josephus refers to other actions they are not initiatives designed to change existing practices. See *War* 4.334-44; 5.36-38, 562.

34. The exact timing of these attacks is not indicated. It is apparent that Josephus appears to be seeking to push a theme at this point in the text—the massacre of the Roman garrison is mirrored by the massacre of Jews and Syrians, with disorder throughout the territory. See A. Kasher, *Jews and Hellenistic Cities in Eretz-Israel: Relations of the Jews in Eretz-Israel with the Hellenistic Cities during the Second Temple Period (332 BCE–70 CE)* (TSAJ, 21; Tübingen: J.C.B. Mohr [Paul Siebeck], 1990), pp. 268-87.

of some Jewish and Roman individuals and groups. The efforts of Vespasian, Titus and Cestius to restore order in Judaea are narrated by Josephus. Cestius marched through Galilee and on towards Jerusalem in 66 CE in an attempt to re-establish Roman control of the province. His 'failed' attack on Jerusalem and the disastrous retreat is described (*War* 2.499-555). Josephus also presents the various military endeavours of Vespasian and Titus. Among the events described are the capturing of cities and regions that rebelled, providing assistance to those cities which remained loyal to Rome and using their personal prowess to avert disaster (*War* 3.29-34, 414-27, 488-90; 4.92; 5.52-66, 291-95, 486-90). Titus's command of the siege of Jerusalem is also described in detail; the various efforts taken by him to prevent the complete destruction of Jerusalem are reported, including a war council meeting at which Roman policy regarding the temple was decided (*War* 6.236-43). Of the events narrated, it is only in the attempt to save the temple and city that Titus was unsuccessful. Josephus also refers to numerous engagements between Jewish and Roman forces in which the individual feats of soldiers on both sides are noted (*War* 3.229-33; 5.474-76; 6.54-67, 81-92, 148, 169-76).

Of the Jews whose activities are described, most relate to individuals. Josephus's command of Galilee and his involvement in the siege of Jerusalem feature in *War*. Regarding the campaigning of Josephus in Galilee, reference is made to his preparations for the Roman assault, several minor skirmishes with Roman troops, the intrigue of John of Gischala in opposing his command and, in some detail, the siege of Jotapata and the circumstances of Josephus's capture and subsequent prophecy regarding the rise of Vespasian (*War* 2.569-646; 3.110-14, 135-288, 316-408). During the siege of Jerusalem Josephus is active on several occasions, trying to persuade the rebels to sue for terms with the Romans (*War* 5.541-47; 6.96-110).

On several occasions Josephus refers to the actions of Jews who appear to reject either the decision to rebel or to continue the fighting against the Romans. Ananus b. Jonathan encouraged 'many of the notable citizens' to open the city gates for the advancing troops of Cesitus, only to be thwarted by the 'insurgents' (*War* 2.533-34). Many of the 'distinguished Jews', including Saul, Philip b. Jacimus and Costobar, flee Jerusalem after the defeat of Cestius (*War* 2.556-58). During the siege of Jerusalem, after the cessation of the daily sacrifice, more prominent Jews escape from the city (*War* 6.111-17).[35] Among their number are the 'chief priests' Joseph and Jesus, several of the sons of the 'high priests' Ishmael, Matthias and another Matthias.

A few other isolated incidents are described by Josephus. Ananus b. Ananus and the 'powerful' began preparations for the defence of Jerusalem (*War* 2.647-48). Ananus and the 'magistrates' sent troops to attack Simon b. Gioras, who was active in Acrabatene (*War* 2.652-53). Josephus also mentions the story of Mary, the daughter of Eleazar, who ate her son during the famine that engulfed Jerusalem (*War* 6.201-13), and the people who gathered in Jerusalem after the destruction of Antonia in expectation that certain oracles would be fulfilled (*War* 6.311-15).[36]

The other Jews mentioned constitute the majority of the subject matter pertaining to the activities of people. Josephus provides information regarding the wartime career of John of Gischala, Simon b. Gioras, Eleazar b. Simon and their followers. The Idumaeans also make a brief, but important, appearance in the narrative of events in Jerusalem. Josephus describes the activities of John and Simon before they became prominent in Jerusalem. With the exception of the final action by the Idumaeans, Josephus describes activities that heighten the level of conflict and disorder. John disrupts the campaign in Galilee (*War* 2.585-94, 614-31) and eventually flees from Gischala under the cover of night, having tricked Titus into respecting the rights associated with the Sabbath (*War* 4.97-105). Simon engaged in brigand activity in Acrabatene and also while based at Masada, until he eventually gained control of the entire region of Idumaea (*War* 2.652-54; 4.398-409, 503-44).

Once in Jerusalem the three 'tyrants'—John, Simon and Eleazar—were responsible for numerous 'criminal' activities. They carried out attacks on prominent Jews on several occasions, including the use of 'mock trials' (*War* 4.138-46, 326-44, 358-63; 5.527-33). They burnt the grain supplies of the city, used resources dedicated for use in the temple and attacked the people of Jerusalem and one another repeatedly (*War* 5.1-38, 98-105, 424-45, 562-66). In the wake of the

---

35. Although Josephus places this desertion immediately after one of his speeches (*War* 6.96-110), the crucial event—even for the timing of the speech—appears to be the end of the daily sacrifice (*War* 6.94).

36. Josephus also mentions that Matthias, the high priest, invited Simon to enter Jerusalem (*War* 4.574).

murder of Ananus b. Ananus and Jesus b. Gamalas, the Idumaeans pillaged the city in league with the 'zealots' (*War* 4.314-15, 326-27). Later, after a change of heart, the Idumaeans freed many prominent Jews that had been imprisoned by the 'zealots' and then apparently left Jerusalem (*War* 4.353).[37]

The subject matter of the revolt presented by Josephus matches the summary list provided in the introduction of *War*. It also clearly complies with the declared aim of narrating events associated with the revolt. The balance of events that describe successful, organized actions as opposed to destructive and disruptive ones is significant. Not one activity performed by the three tyrants could be considered to be anything other than an expression of a destructive nature. In sharp contrast, what Josephus or Titus undertakes is ordered and, in most cases, at least partially successful. The actions of the participants are testimony in themselves.

The nature of the subject matter acts as the proof of the various reflective comments. However, caution is required regarding the use of the subject matter as it stands. The content is selective in the details included and in the stories chosen. A few examples will suffice as an explanation. One is the account of John of Gischala's flight to Jerusalem. Instead of simply noting that John left Gischala before its fall, Josephus gives a colourful description of the flight, where he leaves the weak to fend for themselves (*War* 4.106-11). The contents of the story, and the alleged speech of John, are graphic. The narration of the story does little to honour the character of John. It implicitly provides a contrast to how Josephus responded to the impending capture of Jotapata. Josephus thought of flight but his desire to care for those who trusted him prevented him from doing so (*War* 3.197-204).

A second example is associated with the siege of Jerusalem. Instead of simply summarizing the situation, Josephus narrates a story which he introduces as one of great horror (*War* 6.199-200): the account of Mary, daughter of Eleazar (*War* 6.201-13). Josephus claims the story is narrated because there were other witnesses to its existence (*War* 6.200). However, its imagery helps convey far more than any summary could achieve. Presumably there were other stories that could be told regarding the effect of the famine, but maybe none that could

---

37. There are, however, numerous references to Idumaeans in Jerusalem at a later date (*War* 4.566-70; 5.249-50, 290, 358; 6.92, 148, 378).

parallel the graphic horror of the example of Mary.

A third example is the positioning of the oracles in *War* 6.288-315. Josephus introduces the oracles as he narrates the destruction of the temple, the occasion when some Jews gathered together in the belief that divine intervention was imminent. Most of the content of the section, however, pertains to the years prior to 66 CE. Josephus has deliberately chosen to mention them only when it is appropriate to his interests; he is manipulating his material. The subject matter which is narrated in *War* regarding the first century CE is clearly the result of Josephus making choices about what to include in his narrative.

The bulk of Josephus's reflective comments are linked with the situation in Judaea and the revolt, particularly the theme that the city was doomed. In turn, these comments mirror explicit statements of Josephus in the introduction about the way events unfolded. It is evident that the commentary and subject matter work together. The events narrated reflect the change and trouble of the pre-war period. During the revolt, the content is chosen and recounted to focus the possible outcomes of the war in one direction only. Josephus constructs a tragedy which hones in on 70 CE.

2.2.5 *Commentary within the narrative of events.* The final element—the commentary within the narrative of events—indicates the totality of the tragedy of 70 CE, so displaying an interpretative framework that functions in all levels of the text. These comments are an ever present aspect of *War*. Not one of the incidents narrated is without some form of comment as it is presented in the text. There are three broad categories: the description of the participants; the motivation of the participants; and explanations within the narrative of an event that show how and why it unfolds as it does. There is an overlap between the second and third categories, making the division somewhat arbitrary on occasions. Placing the comments within these categories, however, does help to provide a sense of the nature and direction of how incidents are being narrated.

Josephus's description of Jewish participants consistently incorporates the use of labels by which he displays either a negative or positive view regarding the identity of that person or group. If Josephus wants to state an opinion regarding a Roman official it is done by adding information regarding that person's character, motivation and actions. The following discussion of the way Josephus describes the participants is divided chronologically between the period before 66 CE and then the narrative of the revolt.

In the years prior to the revolt Josephus is critical of Jews engaged in two types of activity. One is the reference to Jews wanting to take up arms in an attempt to resolve a dispute. Those who start the fighting after the soldiers' insult during the Passover festival are the 'more hot-headed young men and seditious people' (*War* 2.225). The people who attack the Samaritans are 'insurgents' (*War* 2.235) and 'the more reckless' roamed the countryside carrying out raids (*War* 2.238) rather than heeding the advice of the 'magistrates of Jerusalem' (*War* 2.237). These actions are performed in league with 'brigands' (*War* 2.235, 238), with Eleazar b. Deinaeus and Alexander being named as leaders (*War* 2.235). At Caesarea, it is the 'insurgents' among the Jews who engage in fighting with the Syrian Caesareans (*War* 2.267).

Various attacks, either physical or psychological, constitute the other type of activity where Josephus employs negative descriptions. The people who attempt to persuade fellow Jews to become their followers are 'deceivers and impostors' (*War* 2.259, 264), 'false prophets' (*War* 2.261) and 'charlatans' (*War* 2.261, 288). Those who initiate physical assaults are 'brigands' (*War* 2.271), as in the attack on Stephen (*War* 2.228, 229), or a specific type of 'brigand', the sicarii (*War* 2.254). Eleazar b. Deinaeus's activities are also characterized by the labelling of him as a 'brigand chief' (*War* 2.253), while 'the revolutionaries in Jerusalem' (*War* 2.274) engage in 'seditious practices' gathering together bands of followers who attack the peaceful citizens.

In sharp contrast, the Jews depicted in positive or neutral terms in the years before the revolt are all working for maintaining peace and upholding just causes. The people who protest against the actions of Pilate are presented in neutral terms—they are 'the townspeople and country folk' (*War* 2.170), 'the Jews' (*War* 2.172, 174) and 'the populace' (*War* 2.175). Those who protest against Gaius's order are 'the Jews' (*War* 2.192, 195), 'the powerful' and 'the populace' (*War* 2.199). The protest against the soldier who exposed himself is undertaken by 'the populace' (*War* 2.225), while it was 'the Jews' who called on Cumanus to punish the soldier who had destroyed the copy of the law (*War* 2.230).[38] In the Galilaean–Samaritan affair 'the notable'

---

38. *War* 2.234 is an exception. Here the 'people' of Jerusalem depart for Samaria, despite the guidance offered by the 'magistrates'.

Galilaeans lodge a protest with Cumanus (*War* 2.233), the 'magistrates' of Jerusalem (*War* 2.237) try to persuade those taking up arms to stop and the Jewish 'notables', including Jonathan b. Ananus, petition Quadratus (*War* 2.240). When the case is sent to Rome it is the 'chief priests', Jonathan, Ananus b. Jonathan, two of 'the most powerful people' and other 'notable' Jews who are despatched by Quadratus (*War* 2.243). It is 'all the people' who join Felix in attacking the Egyptian false prophet (*War* 2.263) and in the incident at Caesarea the 'older' Jews (*War* 2.267) try to persuade their compatriots that fighting is inappropriate. A clear division is being made by Josephus in the way he describes the Jewish participants. The Jews who caused trouble were not representative of the majority of the community. They were a 'rogue' element. Rarely are actual participants named by Josephus. Instead, the divide is effectively created by the use of descriptive labels.

The narrative of events from 66–70 CE reinforces the division that Josephus presents through his description of the Jewish participants. The account is dominated by those Jews for whom Josephus has no time—the people who strive for armed conflict and then try to continue the war effort rather than negotiate a peaceful resolution to the revolt. During 66 CE in the dispute at Caesarea the Jews who wanted to take direct action are labelled as the 'hot-headed youths' (*War* 2.286), 'the insurgents and passionate youth' (*War* 2.290). When the focus of attention shifted to Jerusalem it is some of the 'insurgents' (*War* 2.295) who make the mock collection.[39] Then, in *War* 2.320, the 'insurgents' refuse to accept the advice of welcoming the troops sent from Caesarea, preferring a 'bolder policy'. Eventually, however, these 'insurgents' were persuaded to desist (*War* 2.325). When Florus's troops attack, these 'insurgents' destroy the porticoes (*War* 2.330). The 'insurgents' then throw stones at Agrippa II (*War* 2.406) as he is banished from Jerusalem.[40] The 'most ardent promoters of hostilities' capture Masada and 'the most vigorous of the revolutionary party' support Eleazar b. Ananias and his associates who had ceased to accept the offerings on behalf of foreigners (*War* 2.410). The

39. Elsewhere, in 2.302-303, they are described as 'foolish youths' and 'delinquents'. That this type of person is a minority within the community is implied in *War* 2.302, 325.

40. Note that these 'insurgents' (*War* 2.406) are described as 'revolutionaries' in *War* 2.407.

'insurgents' refuse to buckle under (*War* 2.411, 417), despite the appeals of other Jews. It is the 'insurgents' who attack the Jews in the upper city (*War* 2.423), enclose fellow Jews in the royal palace (*War* 2.429) and proceed to besiege them (*War* 2.432). They are joined by sicarii (*War* 2.425) and Menahem (*War* 2.434). The 'brigands' under the leadership of Menahem murder Ananias and Ezechias (*War* 2.441) and it is the 'insurgents' who massacre the Roman garrison (*War* 2.452).[41] At every possible juncture where negotiation or direct action could be taken these 'insurgents' and 'brigands' chose the latter option.[42] Exactly who these people are is not stated by Josephus. The only individuals linked to the 'insurgents' are Eleazar b. Ananias, Gorion b. Nicomedes, Ananias b. Sadok and Judas b. Jonathan. Of the 'brigands' Josephus mentions Menahem, Eleazar b. Jairus and Absalom.[43]

There is a shift in the way Josephus describes those Jews he is critical of once the campaign of Cestius has ended. Several prominent figures are named and the terminology employed by Josephus is altered. Eleazar b. Simon, Simon b. Gioras and John of Gischala are described as 'tyrants' and their associates are normally labelled as either 'zealots' or 'brigands'. These Jews actively promote the fighting, whether it be against one another or the Romans. It is these Jews who are presented as 'controlling' the war effort once Ananus b. Ananus and Jesus b. Gamalas are murdered. They are the Jews in the narrative who continue to instigate actions that ensure the revolt is not peacefully resolved.

In contrast there are numerous Jews described in a positive manner with the common dominator being their desire for peace. For example, in the dispute at Caesarea it is the Jewish 'notables', of which the tax collector John is named, who negotiate with Florus in an effort to

41. A distinction between the 'insurgents' and the 'brigands' appears also to be made in *War* 2.511 in relation to the situation at Sepphoris.

42. The 'insurgents' are also responsible for the capture of Cypros (*War* 2.484) and the removal of Ananus b. Jonathan and his 'notable' associates from the city wall (*War* 2.534).

43. In *War* 2.444 Menahem's associates are described as 'zealots'. For discussion of the meaning of this term compare M. Hengel, *The Zealots: Investigations into the Jewish Freedom Movements in the Period from Herod I until 70 AD* (trans. D. Smith; Edinburgh: T. & T. Clark, 1989), pp. 64-66, with D.M. Rhoads, *Israel in Revolution: 6–74 CE: A Political History Based on the Writings of Josephus* (Philadelphia: Fortress Press, 1976), pp. 144-47.

find a peaceful solution (*War* 2.287). When trouble flares again, the peaceful Jews try to call for calm (*War* 2.290). When that fails, 12 of 'the powerful', including John, go to see Florus to protest at his lack of assistance (*War* 2.292). Florus's following action in Jerusalem is a further occasion for Josephus to describe those Jews seeking peace in neutral or positive terms, with only a few individuals being named. The citizens of Jerusalem, although angered at the situation, continually work for peace (*War* 2.293-94, 297, 306). Leading these law-abiding people in an effort to prevent armed hostilities are the 'chief priests' (*War* 2.320, 322, 336), 'the powerful' (*War* 2.336), 'the most notable citizens' (*War* 2.301, 316), Bernice (*War* 2.310-12), 'the boule' (*War* 2.336) and Agrippa II (*War* 2.345-404). The 'chief priests' (*War* 2.410-11), 'the notable' (*War* 2.410), 'the powerful' (*War* 2.411) and 'the most notable Pharisees' (*War* 2.411) try to persuade Eleazar b. Ananias and his associates to reinstate the sacrifices offered on behalf of foreigners. When that action fails, it is the 'powerful men, chief priests' and those people in favour of peace (*War* 2.422) who occupy the upper city. Included in this number was Ananias, Ezechias, Saul and Costobar (*War* 2.429). When Cestius had been defeated, 'many distinguished' Jews, including Saul and Costobar, left Jerusalem (*War* 2.556). Later, during the war, other eminent Jews such as Antipas, Levias, Syphas b. Aregetes (*War* 4.140-42) and then Matthias, Ananias b. Masbalus and Aristeus of Emmaus (*War* 5.530-32), are murdered by the 'tyrants' and 'brigands', while some decide to flee Jerusalem (*War* 6.111-17) as did many of the populace (*War* 5.420-23, 548).

One further group of Jews is described in neutral or positive terms. They are some of the Jews who are portrayed as actively participating in the war, siding with the rebels up until the murder of Ananus and Jesus. Similarly, the generals of the rebel forces appointed after the defeat of Cestius are simply named. Some are identified as priests, one as an Essene (*War* 2.562-68). The people who attack Ascalon are also simply presented as 'the Jews' (*War* 3.9, 22). A similar situation exists in the case of those who fought with Josephus at Jotapata: they were 'the Jews' (*War* 3.150, 151, 157, 161, 165, 170, 189, 207).[44] In

---

44. The difference in how Josephus depicts those in favour of peace and those in favour of war is clearly evident in the description of Gischala (*War* 4.84). Note that Jotapata finally fell because of the act of betrayal by one person (*War* 3.317), not because of a division among those who occupied the city.

Jerusalem, the leading figures are named as Ananus (*War* 2.648, 651; 4.160), Jesus b. Gamalas (*War* 4.160), Joseph b. Gorion and Symeon b. Gamaliel (*War* 4.159). They are described as the 'most eminent' of the high priests (*War* 4.160) and the leaders of 'outstanding reputation' of the people (*War* 4.159) respectively.

In the labels used by Josephus a contrast is clearly established. Those in favour of peace are described in positive terms while those favouring armed conflict are labelled with a critical description. This description of the participants in *War* suggests a black-and-white situation. The war was the work of 'insurgents', 'revolutionaries', 'brigands' and the 'tyrants', while prominent Jews and law-abiding people were opposed to the conflict.

The second category of the comments—the motivation of people involved in events—mirrors the contrast made in the description of the participants. Josephus uses the motivation to declare good and bad behaviour in a sparing manner. The pre-war narrative is distinctive because of the lack of references to the motivation of many participants. However, the actions of several Roman officials are explained. Pilate removed the military standards because of the 'intense religious zeal' expressed by the Jews who had protested against the governor's initial action (*War* 2.174). Petronius is described as deciding not to follow through with Gaius's order because of his piety (*War* 2.201), while Cumanus is concerned to maintain peace (*War* 2.226, 231). On the negative ledger, Gaius was motivated by a desire to be a god (*War* 2.184). The one Roman official, and the only person whose motivation is often explained, is Florus. Josephus continually maligns the governor through reference to the reasons why he acts as he does. In the course of describing Cestius's visit to Jerusalem, Josephus states that Florus was 'already contemplating the prospect of war with the nation [Jews]' (*War* 2.282). He accepted the bribe offered by the Caesarean Jews only because he wanted the money (*War* 2.287), and demanded 17 talents on the pretext of 'imperial service' (*War* 2.293). Florus's avarice was further provoked by the mock collection and he set about the task of trying to 'fleece the city' (*War* 2.296). He then concocted a plan to 'relight the flames' by demanding that the Jews greet the troops travelling from Caesarea but also ordered those troops to ignore the salutations (*War* 2.318). Florus's decision to send a report to Cestius is explained by a desire to foster the hostilities (*War* 2.333), as was his decision to ignore the requests for aid by the loyal citizens in Jerusalem (*War* 2.420). Everything Florus did was controlled by a desire to steal from the Jews and to force them into war.[45]

The paucity of references to motivation in the context of narrating events prior to the war is also evident in the limited number of references to the motives of Jews. The Egyptian false prophet wanted to occupy Jerusalem and set himself up as a 'tyrant' (*War* 2.262). The other references are to the events of 66 CE and contrast sharply with Florus. The people want to shame Florus (*War* 2.297) and 'the powerful' sent deputations to Agrippa II and Florus in an effort to protect themselves from blame for the revolt (*War* 2.418). In stark contrast to Florus, Agrippa II responded positively to the request for aid because he was concerned about what the Jews and the Romans would lose as a result of a war (*War* 2.421).

There are a few references to the motivation of the participants in the narrative of events from during the war. Josephus's statements that pertain to the activities of the 'tyrants' and 'brigands' are negative. The 'brigands' decide to kill their captives rather than imprisoning them because they feared revenge (*War* 4.143-45). The 'tyrants' are also marked by their desire for despotic power (*War* 4.85, 208-209, 508, 576; 5.6).

In contrast, some actions of Josephus and Titus are explained in terms of positive motivation. Josephus issued orders to help prevent civil war beginning at Tiberias (*War* 2.620) and declared that he wanted to employ diplomacy rather than force to overcome John (*War* 2.623-24). At Jotapata, Josephus declares that he was motivated by a commitment to be God's servant (*War* 3.351-54, 361).[46] Josephus also justifies a number of Titus's actions. Josephus explains Titus's decision to allow prisoners to be crucified as a desire to 'induce the Jews to surrender' (*War* 5.450). The temple was allowed to be destroyed because the Roman soldiers were being killed as they tried to save the complex (*War* 6.228). Titus even parleyed with Simon and John in an effort to save the upper city (*War* 6.324).[47]

---

45. For further expressions of Florus's corrupt motivation see *War* 2.303, 311.

46. In *War* 3.137 Josephus claims he was committed to the task of fulfilling God's command.

47. A further example of trying to save the city and temple is the activities associated with Ananus b. Ananus and his supporters (*War* 4.198-99, 205, 215). Josephus also draws a sharp contrast in the motivation and attitude of the tyrants and

The motivation and description contained in the narrative of events display Josephus's concern to draw comparisons between the participants. It is a one-dimensional portrayal that is far from subtle. There are numerous overt comparisons made in the text, such as between Florus and Agrippa II in *War* 2.420-21 and between the tyrants and Titus regarding the fate of the temple and city in *War* 6.318, 325. There are, however, many less obvious examples of the comparisons being made where a level of sophistication is evident. The reader is continually drawn to make comparisons, often to promote Josephus. For example, Josephus is unwilling to abandon his command, so he seeks direction from Jerusalem (*War* 3.137-38). John of Gischala, on the other hand, fled Gischala at night without consulting anyone (*War* 4.106-11). Furthermore, the whole population of Jotapata are helping Josephus in the siege, they are not 'insurgents' or 'brigands'. At no other city is there such unity of opinion to be found. The insertion of the Japhna campaign during the description of the siege of Jotapata also works to imply the 'success' at the latter (*War* 3.289-306). Whereas there was a rash attack made at Japhna by some of the Galilaeans who were then shut out of the city by their friends, at Jotapata all were united and fought with some success against Vespasian behind the walls of the city.

The final category of comments contained within the narration of an event are the occasions where Josephus explains why a situation unfolds as it does. There are two common themes that Josephus uses here. One is the involvement of God and the other relates to the actions of the 'insurgents' and 'tyrants'. Divine providence is associated with several turns of event. It explains why the Galilaeans were shut out of Japhna by their fellow citizens (*War* 3.293), the survival of Josephus in the suicide pact (*War* 3.387, 391) and the decision of the men of Gamala to attack the Romans (*War* 4.26).[48]

On numerous occasions Josephus explains what happened in terms of the actions of 'rogue' Jews. Menahem's responsibility for the murder of Ananias and Ezechias resulted in the people joining with Eleazar b. Ananias to remove Menahem and his supporters (*War* 2.442). The decision of such cities as Tiberias (*War* 3.448) and Gischala (*War* 4.84-85, 97) to rebel is also portrayed as the work of 'rogue' Jews. In

---

Romans to changing circumstances. For example, see *War* 5.121-22, 306, 309-11, 344-46, 442-45.

48. Further examples include *War* 4.297; 5.39.

Jerusalem, it was John who was instrumental in the overthrow of Ananus b. Ananus and Jesus b. Gamalas when he betrayed them to the 'zealots' and Idumaeans (*War* 4.126, 208-209). John's treachery continues to have a negative effect during the Passover of 70 CE (*War* 5.98-105) with Josephus even deeming the rejection by John and Simon of Titus's offer to be the reason why the Roman general allowed his troops to burn the city (*War* 6.352-53).

On several other occasions explanations are offered by Josephus as to why a particular event unfolds, displaying a concern to analyse what was happening. Josephus stopped his attack on Sepphoris because of the strength of the fortifications (*War* 3.61). The harsh treatment of Gabara is linked with the memory of what happened to Cestius (*War* 3.133). The centurion Antonius is killed because of the treachery of a Jewish fugitive at Jotapata (*War* 3.334), while the initial defeat of the Romans at Gamala is explained by Vespasian as a lack of due caution (*War* 4.44). Lack of judgment also explains why the outer wall of Jerusalem was not defended (*War* 5.300), while daring explained the success of Jews in their attack on the Roman camp (*War* 5.485).[49]

The first century CE is portrayed in *War* as a period of increasing

---

49. It is notable that the main speeches of *War* clearly echo the reflections on events narrated, alluded to and those on the general situation. For example, the speeches of Agrippa II (*War* 2.345-404), Josephus (*War* 5.362-419) and Titus (*War* 6.323-50) proclaim themes declared elsewhere by Josephus: namely, that most of the Jews wanted peace, that the war was the work of only a few, that the time to rebel had long passed, that God now sided with the Romans, that the decision to fight was not based on a legitimate cause and that the Romans were lenient, wanting to preserve Jerusalem. The speeches of Ananus (*War* 4.162-92) and Jesus (*War* 4.239-69), which focus on the threat of the 'zealots', reinforce the view that 'rogue' Jews were bringing destruction upon Jerusalem. Ananus and Jesus are motivated by noble, righteous concerns, calling on the people to fight for God. Here responsibility for the destruction is implicitly linked with the 'brigands'. Titus's shorter speech (*War* 6.124-28) simply reinforces the guilt of the 'brigands' and 'tyrants'. Through these speeches Josephus is able to reiterate that what happens in 70 CE is not the work of all Jews, nor is it what all Jews wanted. Here Josephus is following the established principle of employing the main characters to voice his own interpretation of the situation. See F.W. Walbank, *Selected Papers, Studies in Greek and Roman Historiography* (Cambridge: Cambridge University Press, 1985), pp. 242-61; cf. O. Michel, 'Die Rettung Israels und die Rolle Roms nach den Reden im "Bellum Judaicum": Analysen und Perspektiven', *ANRW* 2.21.2 (1984), pp. 945-76 (965-66).

turmoil. The two levels of the interpretative framework are woven together by Josephus. The subject matter and the various forms of commentary point the reader in the same direction. The constant feature of the content is the description of various forms of trouble and instability. The nature of the subject matter is reiterated in the way it is narrated, ranging from the description of the participants to the summary reflections on the general situation in Judaea.

3. *Antiquities*

Our attention turns to *Ant*. I will follow the same structure as with *War*, dividing the examination into three sections. Through this discussion it will become evident that Josephus's interpretative framework presents a picture of Judaea as a society in turmoil which moved towards open hostility, particularly from the middle of the first century CE onwards.

3.1 *Declared Aim(s) of the Text*
The reader is provided with an introduction and epilogue, to which can be added comments in *Apion* regarding the subject matter of *Ant*. Josephus uses *Ant*. to present a narrative of Jewish history, from the beginning of time until the outbreak of the revolt in 66 CE (*Ant*. 1.5-9, 20.259-61; *Apion* 1.1-5). The antiquity of the Jews will be explained, drawing on the Jewish Scriptures (*Ant*. 1.17; *Apion* 1.47-56). Although Josephus boldly claims that his account provides the 'whole story in full and accurate detail', the subject matter that is presented in the text is selective. The treatment of the Jews by other nations is included (*Ant*. 20.259) and the focus of the text is on the succession of leaders, the kings, high priests, judges, their achievements and policies (*Ant*. 20.259) and the political constitution (*Ant*. 1.5-9). Some material, however, is deemed to be inappropriate. Jewish thinking about the existence of God and exploration of the laws—particularly the types of things permitted and prohibited—lie outside the boundaries of *Ant*.[50]

The decision to present the narrative of Jewish history, its leaders and relations with other kingdoms, is deliberate. Although Josephus indicates he was interested in the topic when he wrote *War* (*Ant*. 1.5-

---

50. Compare *Ant*. 20.267 and *Apion* 2.287 regarding the laws.

9), the decision to write *Ant.* is expressed in terms of a concern 'to instruct' the Greek-speaking world about Jewish history (*Ant.* 1.5-9; *Apion* 1.1-5). The sponsorship of Epiphroditus may have made the exercise possible but Josephus claims the task was not simply for his own benefit. As a result, it is plausible to expect that the narrative is controlled, one that contains messages that the reader is meant to receive. Indeed, Josephus openly admits that this is the case. The general desire 'to instruct' the Greek-speaking world has a distinctive edge to it, according to the comments in *Ant.* 16.174-78. Explaining the inclusion of decrees regarding the respect shown to Jews, Josephus states that they are appropriate because they indicate a lesson for his audience—the Jews deserve to be credited as a legitimate group in society and to be treated with justice. The comments of Josephus suggest he is concerned to address a real threat to the Jews: denigration of them as a people.[51]

A further general lesson declared by Josephus is the importance of obeying God's will to maintain good fortune (*Ant.* 1.14). This moral is reiterated on several occasions throughout the text, justifying the inclusion of certain stories such as the death of Archelaus and his wife, Glaphyra (*Ant.* 17.354), the family tree of Herod (*Ant.* 18.127) and the death of Gaius (*Ant.* 19.16). What is notable is that the stories all relate to leaders, whether Jews or Romans. Josephus selects material that is associated with themes he wishes to develop and they also relate to the primary subject matter of the text, the leaders.

3.2 *The Two Levels of the Interpretative Framework*

3.2.1 *Reflections on the general situation.* There are only two reflections on the general situation and they present different aspects of a theme of disorder. One is that the activities of the 'brigands' acted like a plague in Judaea (*Ant.* 20.185). A new governor, Festus, was

---

51. This concern is repeated in more blatant terms by Josephus in *Apion*. See Bilde, *Flavius Josephus*, pp. 80-103, 113-21; cf. Rajak, *Josephus*, pp. 120-22. Although these two views reflect different starting points they effectively arrive at the same result, a text written for a Graeco-Roman audience. Note also the approach of D.R. Schwartz, 'Josephus on the Jewish Constitutions and Community', *SCI* 7 (1983–84), pp. 30-52, who argues that the sense of community identity portrayed in *Ant.* can be directly related to apologetical issues associated with the post-70 CE situation. Regarding the possible thematic interests of Josephus in *Ant.* see also Attridge, 'Josephus', pp. 217-26, and Mason, *Flavius Josephus*, pp. 181-93.

greeted with the entire land being 'devastated' by the 'brigands', who attacked villages and plundered whatever they could. The other theme relates to Josephus identifying the causes and effects of war:

> When wars are set afoot that are bound to rage beyond control, and when friends are done away with who might have alleviated the suffering, when raids are made by great hordes of brigands and men of the highest standing are assassinated, it is supposed to be the common welfare that is upheld, but the truth is that in such cases the motive is private gain. They sowed the seed from which sprang strife between factions and the slaughter of fellow citizens. Some were slain in civil strife, for these men madly had recourse to butchery of each other and of themselves from a longing not to be outdone by their opponents; others were slain by the enemy in war. Then came famine, reserved to exhibit the last degree of shamelessness, followed by the storming and razing of cities until at last the very temple of God was ravaged by the enemy's fire through this revolt (*Ant.* 18.7-8).

What is notable from this summary is the close parallel of the circumstances described, the causes and the effects, with the situation as narrated in Judaea by Josephus in *Ant.* 'Hordes of brigands' are active, 'men of the highest standing are assassinated', all apparently for private gain. These activities 'sow the seed' for factional strife in which Judaeans die, famine follows and then the temple is destroyed by fire (*Ant.* 18.8). Both this theme and that of the brigand plague present a very bleak picture. Turmoil and social disorder are evident in these reflections on the general situation.

Although few in number, the location of these reflections suggests they are of some significance for the author in portraying a picture of the state of the society. The plague of brigandage is situated in the period after the return of Judaea to direct Roman rule, at the beginning of Festus's tenure as governor. It does not restore order to the narrative, instead it accentuates the tenor of the surrounding narrative. The reflection on the causes and effect of war is located at a significant turning point in the administrative organization of Judaea, appearing as it does within the discussion of the fourth philosophy, as part of the commentary on the introduction of direct Roman rule in 6 CE. Implicitly, Josephus appears to be drawing a direct link between 6 CE and the revolt of 66–70 CE. The key for explaining the timing is the fourth philosophy and the census, but the underlying suggestion is that the events of 66–70 CE were not at all surprising; they were the fulfilment of 'seeds sown' in 6 CE.

3.2.2 *Comments on events alluded to in the narrative.* Josephus's reflections and commentary on events alluded to but not narrated are more numerous. With one exception, *Ant.* 20.204, they present a very negative picture of what was happening in Judaea. The events can be grouped into three categories. The first relates to the activities of the 'brigands' and 'impostors' (*Ant.* 20.160, 167, 172, 185, 187, 204). In one instance (*Ant.* 20.204) the message is positive. Josephus commends Albinus for his activities designed to rid Judaea of the sicarii. Underlying even this view, however, is the idea that brigandage was at plague proportions. All the other references to the activities of 'brigands' and 'impostors' emphasize their increasing numbers and their negative impact, with the infestation continually spreading as the 'impostors' tried to deceive the populace. For example:

> In Judaea matters were constantly going from bad to worse. For the country was again infested with bands of brigands and impostors who deceived the people (20.160).

> With such pollution did the deeds of the brigands infect the city. Moreover, impostors and deceivers called upon the people to follow them into the desert (20.167).

> ...it happened that Judaea was being devastated by the brigands, for the villages one and all were being set on fire and plundered (20.185).

> They [sicarii] would also frequently appear with arms in the villages of their foes and would plunder and set them on fire (20.187).

These 'brigands' even extended their activities to inciting the populace to rebel, with threats of violent retribution for those who refused (*Ant.* 20.172). Although governors such as Felix and Albinus tried to control the situation a social disease was attacking the Jewish people. Here the reflection of Josephus matches the picture presented in the two reflections on the general situation.

   The second category echoes the atmosphere of the first but relates to the activities of prominent members of the community. In *Ant.* 20.180 Josephus refers to conflict that took place among the elite of Jewish society. The 'chief priests', priests and 'leaders of the people' gathered together bands of 'reckless revolutionaries'. To Josephus this was a grave situation, in which justice was suppressed and disorder dominated (*Ant.* 20.181). It was 'as if no one was in charge of the city'.

   The third category—activities of Roman officials—does little to reduce the sense of strife evident in the two other categories. Here Josephus's focus is the governorship of Florus.[52] Although only alluded to by Josephus, Florus's term of office is summarized by an emotive reflection and commentary on its nature and consequences. The impact of Florus was flagged as early as *Ant.* 18.25, the occasion in Josephus's narrative where he describes the events of 6 CE. It was Florus who caused the revolt to begin when it did, through 'his overbearing and lawless actions'. This 'lawless' behaviour is not articulated in terms of specific actions or events in *Ant.* 18 or in *Ant.* 20 where Florus is again mentioned. At the end of his chronological narrative Josephus merely alludes to Florus's governorship. Through the example of Florus, most Jews were engaged in brigandage (*Ant.* 20.255). Whereas Albinus had 'filled the cup of the Jews with many misfortunes' (*Ant.* 20.252), he was praised 'as a benefactor' in comparison to Florus (*Ant.* 20.253). Florus 'ostentatiously paraded his lawless treatment of our nation and omitted no form of pillage or unjust punishment' (*Ant.* 20.254). He was in partnership with the 'brigands' (*Ant.* 20.255) and the loyal Jews were forced to flee their homeland (*Ant.* 20.256). Josephus concludes by stating that it 'was Florus who constrained us to take up war with the Romans, for we preferred to perish together rather than by degrees' (*Ant.* 20.257). At no stage does Josephus deem it necessary to provide any detail to this bleak survey.

All the events alluded to fall in the period of the second phase of direct Roman rule, 44–66 CE. They combine to present a picture of increasing unrest in Judaea. Certain rogue Jews, the 'brigands' and 'impostors', deal a heavy blow to Judaea, pushing the community to the brink of war. To this problem Josephus adds the conflict among the Jewish aristocracy and the criminal behaviour of the last governor, Florus. Even the end result—the revolt—was signalled as early as *Ant.* 18.25, when Josephus is describing the fourth philosophy in association with the introduction of direct Roman rule in 6 CE.

3.2.3 *Comments on events narrated.* The other form of reflective comment is associated with events which Josephus narrates. There are two basic types of these comments. By far the most prevalent is the attempt to provide an insight into the significance of what is described.

---

52. In relation to Albinus, Josephus declares that the governor's decision to clear the prisons resulted in the land being 'infested with brigands' (*Ant.* 20.215).

There are several themes linked with this type of reflective commentary. They include a concern regarding the trouble caused because of an incident (*Ant.* 18.6, 9, 10; 19.366; 20.102, 124, 184, 210, 214, 215), the emotional response of the Jews to certain situations (*Ant.* 20.112), the effect of events on the relationship between the Jews and their God (*Ant.* 20.166, 218) and the stability that follows certain actions (*Ant.* 20.5, 117). The latter stand out as the exception. Two governors, Fadus and Cumanus, are credited with quelling trouble as a result of their action. Fadus 'purged' Judaea of 'brigands' because of his 'prudent concern' (*Ant.* 20.5). In contrast, Cumanus's achievement in bringing about stability was the result of fear. Concerned that 'another revolution of the multitude' would break out if he ignored the offence of the soldier in destroying a copy of the law, the governor ordered that the soldier be executed. The effect of such an action was the prevention of 'sedition' occurring on a second occasion (*Ant.* 20.117). Even underlying these two 'peaceful' resolutions lies a picture of a place troubled with tension. All other reflections on the significance of narrated events create a rather bleak picture of affairs in Judaea.

Josephus is careful to identify that his concern for the level of trouble is derived from numerous incidents. In 6 CE the call of Judas and Saddok that the people not conform to the demands of the census had such success that these men 'sowed the seed of every kind of misery, which so afflicted the nation that words are inadequate' (*Ant.* 18.6).[53] Summarizing the events associated with the death of Agrippa I, Josephus laments on the negative consequences of Claudius's order that Sebastean and Caesarean levied troops were not removed from the province. According to Josephus, the reversal of Claudius's decision effectively resulted in the troops proving 'to be a source of the greatest disasters to the Jews by sowing the seed of the war in Florus's time' (*Ant.* 19.366). Later, during the dispute that arose when Samaritans attacked Galilaean pilgrims, Josephus describes the significance of the trouble that broke out because Cumanus failed to act. Although the 'first men of rank and birth in Jerusalem' succeeded in persuading the people and 'brigands' to cease their attacks on the Samaritans, 'from that time the whole of Judaea was infested with bands of brigands'

---

53. *Ant.* 18.7-8 appears to be a very brief description of the siege of Jerusalem in 70 CE in line with *War*, further implying the link between the events of 6 and 66–70 CE.

(*Ant.* 20.124). To Josephus, the news of Nero's decision in the Caesarean dispute 'provided the basis that led to subsequent misfortunes
that befell our nation' (*Ant.* 20.184). The basis for such a conclusion,
according to Josephus, was that the Caesarean Jews 'carried their
quarrel with the Syrians further and further until at last they kindled
the flames of war' (*Ant.* 20.184). Finally, in the light of the rivalry
among some of the 'chief priests' and prominent Herodians (*Ant.*
20.213-14), Josephus describes the situation as very dire. From that
point particularly, 'sickness fell upon the city and everything went
steadily from bad to worse' (*Ant.* 20.214).

More often than not the events that took place are viewed by Josephus as drawing Judaea further into a situation of crisis, where 66–70
CE appears to act as a climax. Such a view is confirmed by the reflections that pertain to the relationship between God and the Jews. The
consequence of the people being misled by 'impostors and deceivers'
was punishment from God in the form of Felix (*Ant.* 20.168). Then,
when Agrippa II and the synedrion gave Levites permission to wear
the same linen robes as the priests, Josephus regarded such an action
as 'bound to make us liable to punishment' (*Ant.* 20.218).[54]

The second type of reflective comment on events narrated pertains
directly to the role of God in human affairs. Josephus explains many
events unfolding as they do because of divine providence (*Ant.*
18.119, 239; 20.48, 73, 89-91). With one exception, the statue of Gaius
(*Ant.* 18.286-308), these events are connected with individuals, particularly with the timing of their death. In the example of the statue of
Gaius, divine providence assists the Jews and Petronius.[55] The decision
of the legate not to follow Gaius's order is immediately affirmed by
an unexpected downpour of rain, 'unmistakable evidence that God's
providence was over the Jews' (*Ant.* 18.286). Then, the timing of the
letters that reached Petronius, with the news of Gaius's death arriving
first, is viewed as further evidence of God's providence, the 'reward
for showing honour to the temple' (*Ant.* 18.309).

In contrast, the timing of the deaths of Gaius and Herod Antipas

54. Josephus makes the sense of an intensification explicit in *Ant.* 20.113 when
he links the mourning associated with the festival incident with the trouble that
resulted from the attack on the emperor's slave.

55. The providence of God favouring the Jews and Petronius is most likely
associated with their piety. See the example of positive divine involvement in the
protection of Izates (*Ant.* 20.48, 73, 89-91).

indicate the consequences of failing to honour God. To Josephus, the description of Gaius's death is important for his history but it also 'provides good evidence of God's power' (*Ant.* 19.16). In a similar vein, narrating the history of Herod's family is 'proof of God's providence, showing how neither numbers nor any other worldly advantage can avail aught without acts of piety toward the Divine power' (*Ant.* 18.127). These reflections echo what Josephus declared to be a major lesson of *Ant.*, the importance of obeying God's will (*Ant.* 1.14). It is, however, puzzling that Josephus does not employ this type of reflective comment more often in an explicit manner. The bold statement in *Ant.* 20.166 that the destruction of Jerusalem was the result of the impiety of the 'brigands' and that the Romans were God's agents indicates that Josephus was willing to make the connection. The implication of this notion of God punishing the Jews is that what happened in 70 CE was an inevitable consequence of crimes committed by some Jews. It was part of a cosmic equation.

The various reflective comments of Josephus combine to present Judaea as a place burdened by trouble. The people were infested by 'brigands' and 'impostors', 'rogue' Jews whose impiety God decided to punish. The situation grew worse, especially in the second period of direct Roman rule, but the 'seeds' were present at a much earlier date. Josephus appears to have 70 CE in mind throughout his reflections. The reader is continually provided with explanations for what happened: some are of long-standing origins, such as the fourth philosophy, the Syrian soldiers, the impiety of the 'brigands' and their increased activity; and others are of more immediate significance, such as the dispute in Caesarea and the lawless behaviour of Florus. The 'flames of war' are, therefore, a significant factor in Josephus's reflections of *Ant.* 18–20.

3.2.4 *Choice of subject matter.* With these observations in mind we turn to the first level of the interpretative framework: the nature of the content of *Ant.* 18–20. The subject matter falls into seven separate categories. They are references to: the leadership of Judaea and Rome; territorial arrangements; the personal affairs of the Herodians and foreign rulers; the affairs of Jews outside Judaea; expressions of rivalry between communities in Judaea; the activities of certain Jews; and changes to practice instituted by Jews and Romans and the associated response, often regarding the administration.[56] Several comments are necessary regarding these categories in terms of how they relate to the stated and implied thematic concerns of *Ant.*

The first category refers to the leadership of Judaea and Rome. With few exceptions these references do not incorporate any level of overt comment or extra information. Josephus remarks on the death of several rulers such as Agrippa I, Herod Antipas, Philip and Gaius, but generally only lists the leadership. The inclusion of this material, whether it be naming the rulers of Judaea, Jewish kings and Roman governors or the Roman emperors, is a means by which Josephus can structure his entire narrative. What is notable is that although there are a large number of changes in personnel included, Josephus does not always provide information about what happened during that period of rule. Philip, for example, has comments briefly made regarding the nature of his tenure of office (*Ant.* 18.106-108) but, apart from work he ordered for the building of certain cities, there is no further discussion of his leadership (*Ant.* 18.27-28). Even with Herod Antipas, Josephus provides little detail. Reference is made to the war against Aretas (*Ant.* 18.113-19), to several encounters between Vitellius and Herod (*Ant.* 18.102, 104-105) and to his building activity (*Ant.* 18.27, 36-38).[57] The result, whatever its possible explanation, is that the narrative is unbalanced. Changes are noted, yet there is no counterbalance. This point is particularly apparent in the naming of the various high priests. Some serve less than a year but are named. Actions, if any are undertaken by specific incumbents, are very rarely described.[58]

The second category of subject matter—territorial changes—mirrors the situation with the first. Josephus is careful to list numerous changes to the territory controlled by various Jewish leaders, particularly

56. Due to the uncertainty regarding the originality of the existing narrative pertaining to Jesus (*Ant.* 18.63-64), it will not be included in the following discussion.

57. The fall of Herod is also mentioned (*Ant.* 18.240-51). The paucity of detail is hinted at by the off-hand reference to John the Baptist within the context of Josephus's description of the war against Aretas (*Ant.* 18.116-19).

58. Exceptions include Ishmael b. Phabi (*Ant.* 20.194-95), Ananus b. Ananus (*Ant* 20.197-203) and Ananias b. Nedebaeus (*Ant.* 20.206-207, 209-10, 213-14). Presumably Jonathan b. Ananus (*Ant.* 20.162) was also active during the governorship of Felix. Given that Ananias and Jonathan were not the serving high priest when Josephus describes their activities, there are, therefore, only two incumbents for which information is provided regarding what they did.

regarding the Herodians. Generally the alterations, the work of the Roman emperor, are presented without overt comment or additional information. Furthermore, internal changes in the territory controlled by the Jewish leader are occasionally cited, such as Antipas's rebuilding of Tiberias (*Ant.* 18.36-38). Clearly, Josephus felt that noting some changes was relevant. The reference to the conclusion of the repairs to the temple (*Ant.* 20.219) acts as a warning that what is included may be primarily dependent on Josephus's interest. In this instance it is the consequence of the work being completed that was important to Josephus (*Ant.* 20.219-22). In the other cases we have no clear basis on which to assert why some material has been deemed relevant for inclusion other than that they mirror Josephus's stated interests of focusing on the activities of rulers.

The next two categories of subject matter also appear to conform to Josephus's stated interests. The personal affairs of the Herodians and foreign rulers and the affairs of Jews outside Judaea echo the claim of *Ant.* 20.259-61. When discussing the activities of rulers, it is notable that, apart from Agrippa I (*Ant.* 19.293-96, 331), who is upheld for his piety before God, the references are of a negative nature.[59] For example, the fate of Herodians (*Ant.* 18.127-42), Herod Antipas (*Ant.* 18.245-56) and Gaius (*Ant.* 19.17-113) are described as a consequence of their impiety. The dream of Archelaus and his wife also confirm that their fate related to impious actions they performed (*Ant.* 17.345-53). The affairs of Jews outside Judaea is part of Josephus's concern to promote the status of the Jewish community in the Roman empire.[60]

The other categories of subject matter incorporate the vast bulk of the narrative. In particular, in *Ant.* 20 there is a substantial increase in the number of events described from the fifth and sixth categories in proportion to all the others. We begin with the fifth category: namely,

59. Izates (*Ant.* 20.48-91) is a further example of a ruler upheld for his devotion and piety.

60. See, for example, *Ant.* 19.278-91, regarding the Alexandrian community. The purpose of the relatively lengthy account of some Jews residing in Parthia (*Ant.* 19.310-79) is puzzling. Presuming that *Ant.* is primarily directed to a Graeco-Roman audience it is possible that the 'moral' of the narrative is an attempt to explain what appears to be a tale of disruptive behaviour by a Jewish community. On Josephus's narrative of Parthian affairs see M. Pucci, 'Jewish-Parthian Relations in Josephus', in L.I. Levine (ed.), *The Jerusalem Cathedra: Studies in the History, Archaeology, Geography and Ethnography of the Land of Israel* (Jerusalem: Yad Izhak Ben Zvi Institute, 1983), III, pp. 13-25.

the expression of rivalry between communities located in Judaea. The incidents Josephus narrates are all expressions of conflict: the Peraeans–Philadelphians (*Ant.* 20.3-4), Samaritans–Jews (*Ant.* 18.29-30), Samaritans–Galilaeans (*Ant.* 20.117-36) and Jews–Syrians at Caesarea (*Ant.* 20.173-78, 183-84).[61]

There is an overall pattern regarding who instigated these conflicts: the Jews are not deemed to be the aggressors. The Jewish–Samaritan conflicts are the work of the Samaritans. In *Ant.* 18.29 it is the Samaritans who enter the temple to disrupt the activities of the festival. In the other conflict, despite the claims of the Samaritans and the actions of Cumanus and Longinus, Claudius affirms that it was the Samaritans who instigated the trouble with their attack on the Galilaean pilgrims during the governorship of Cumanus (*Ant.* 20.117). The origins of the conflict between the Peraean Jews and the Philadelphians is not explicitly narrated, although Josephus does claim Fadus acknowledged that the Peraeans had been wronged in the first instance (*Ant.* 20.3).

The other case is more complex. Josephus does not explain who instigated the dispute at Caesarea. The claims of the Caesarean Jews and Syrians are outlined (*Ant.* 20.173), but no reference is made to who began the proceedings that required the 'prefects' to intervene (*Ant.* 20.174). It is suggested in *Ant.* 20.175 that the Jews provoked the second round of trouble. However, that the Caesarean Syrians were 'trouble makers' had already been indicated by Josephus in his reference to their rejoicing at the death of Agrippa I and Claudius's subsequent displeasure at their 'base' behaviour (*Ant.* 19.361-64).

By implication, although these incidents display conflict, Josephus seeks to clarify that the Jews were not the aggressors or, if they were, to make such a conclusion difficult to reach, as possibly in the case of the Caesarean dispute. As a result, these incidents may help confirm what the various decrees of *Ant.* 16 were intended to do: namely, to proclaim that the Jews were legitimate law-abiding people when they cohabited with other ethnic groups.

The sixth category to consider is the description of the activities of certain Jews. The majority of these events are accounts of people seeking either to assert influence and/or authority, or to attack the

61. The one 'exception' is the gift of Helena and Izates during the famine (*Ant.* 20.51-53, 101). However, it should be noted that these people were not residents of the territory.

populace or specific groups in the community. This is one of the main areas of subject matter and it forms an increasingly large proportion of the narrative from 44 CE onwards. On some occasions an individual is named, while in others Josephus refers to types of people. There are several examples of Jews seeking to influence or control affairs. Ananus b. Ananus asserts his authority when he organizes the death of James and certain others (*Ant.* 20.197-203). Ananias b. Nedebaeus, the high priest, used his wealth to gain influence among the populace and with the governor (*Ant.* 20.205-206), while 'the first Galilaeans' (*Ant.* 20.119) and 'the leading men' (*Ant.* 20.121) seek to persuade the populace not to attack the Samaritans after the murder of Galilaean pilgrims. All the other Jews whose activity is narrated and who attempt to influence people are associated with non-establishment figures. John the Baptist was active in Herod Antipas's tetrarchy, apparently trying to persuade the populace to adopt certain practices (*Ant.* 18.116-19). The Samaritan 'prophet' succeeded in calling some of his compatriots to gather at Mt Gerizim (*Ant.* 18.85-87). Theudas (*Ant.* 20.97-99), an Egyptian (*Ant.* 20.169-72) and other 'impostors and deceivers' (*Ant.* 20.167) all call on sections of the populace to adhere to their instruction. To Josephus these activities prey on the community and are dealt with harshly by the ruler.[62] In other words, these activities bring trouble to the community.

The other group of activities consists of direct attacks on the populace or rival groups. Here Josephus refers to Eleazar b. Deinaeus (*Ant.* 20.161), James and John b. Judas (*Ant.* 20.102), Tholomaeus (*Ant.* 20.5) and the sicarii (*Ant.* 20.186, 208-10). The brigands were pillaging the countryside, murdering people in Jerusalem and forcing the Jews to oppose Roman rule (*Ant.* 20.172). The response of the authorities was generally one of trying to restore order. Exceptions to these examples are the references to factional fighting that took place in Jerusalem (*Ant.* 20.179-81, 206-207, 213-14). Here, it is prominent members of the Jewish community who attack one another and any others who are in their way, with no check on their behaviour.[63]

The final category is that of the changes instituted, all of which

---

62. John the Baptist (*Ant.* 18.116-19) is a possible exception to this situation. Herod Antipas interprets John as a potential cause of 'sedition' but Josephus does not necessarily express an opinion (*Ant.* 18.119) in favour of such a view.

63. One further type of exception is the cooperation between some governors and 'sicarii'/'brigands' (*Ant.* 20.163, 255).

pertain, in some manner or another, to the administration of a particular practice. They are instigated by Jews and Romans. All the changes relate to customs or practices centred in Jerusalem, particularly in terms of the temple. Roman-initiated changes include Pilate's decision to bring military standards bearing images into Jerusalem (*Ant.* 18.55), Gaius's order that statues of him be erected in the city (*Ant.* 18.261) and Fadus's demand that the high priest's robes be returned to Roman custody (*Ant.* 20.6). In each instance the Jews respond with protests, petitioning that the order be either rescinded or not carried out (*Ant.* 18.57, 263, 273; 20.7). Several requests are made by the Jews. Levites successfully request that practices within the temple be altered (*Ant.* 20.216-18), while the wall which was heightened to block Agrippa II's vantage point overlooking the temple was allowed to stand, despite the protest of the king and the governor (*Ant.* 20.189-96). Vitellius responded positively to separate requests. One was that he not bring image bearing standards through Judaea and the other, that the high priest's robes be placed under the care of the Jews (*Ant.* 18.90, 121).[64] Not one of these incidents is left unresolved. However, by their very nature they all relate to the notion of change in the society, whether it was imposed or requested and, as such, raise the issue of the possible lasting impact they may have had on the community.

Central to all the subject matter is the theme of change, whether it be attempted or actual. The historical veracity of this account is not at issue here. What is relevant is the impression the subject matter creates. Clearly for Josephus, events pertaining to change were a priority. Change is not necessarily a reason for concern. However, as the bulk of the subject matter derives from the fifth, sixth and seventh categories, the nature of the subject matter is very important. The subject matter may express such stated themes as a concern to describe events associated with the leadership. But it is a particular type of event that is being narrated: namely, change which carries the connotation of instability and conflict. Irrespective of how these incidents are resolved, they convey a sense of trouble. Their location in the text ensures that the trouble intensifies from the mid-first century

64. Regarding the high priest's robes see *Ant.* 15.405. It is not indicated whether or not the removal of taxes on agricultural produce sold in Jerusalem is linked to a request (see *Ant.* 18.90; cf. 17.205).

CE onwards. The subject matter, therefore, mirrors what Josephus expresses in his reflective comments.

3.2.5 *Commentary within the narrative of events*. The final element of the interpretative framework, and the final section of *Ant.* to consider, is the commentary contained within the narrative of events. Here there are two main types of comments made by Josephus: a description of the participants, occasionally in terms of their ability; and the motivation of various participants in an action. Josephus draws a clear divide, with those people whom he believes cause trouble being described in a derogatory manner. At the other end of the spectrum, the Jews who represent the good of the community as a whole, according to Josephus, are portrayed in a positive manner.

Ant. 20.122-24 effectively displays the contrast. In the context of the Samaritan attack on the Galilaeans, the men who are 'first in rank and birth of Jerusalem' try to bring order to the situation, advising against attacking the Samaritans, pleading that Roman justice be allowed to work. These men talk with the people who want to take direct action, who Josephus then describes as 'brigands' (*Ant.* 20.124). The event is narrated with Josephus's labelling of the participants expressing a clear preference regarding which Jews are to be respected and which are to be condemned. In Caesarea the Jews that head the protest to defend their rights are the 'moderate and eminent' (*Ant.* 20.178), while in the protest against Agrippa II's action of increasing the height of the temple, it is 'the eminent' of Jerusalem that lead the cause of justice (*Ant.* 20.191). These protests are deemed legitimate by Josephus and the participants are, therefore, portrayed in a positive manner. In contrast, those who attack Stephen are 'some of the seditious revolutionaries' (*Ant.* 20.113), Theudas is nothing more than an 'impostor' who wanted 'to deceive' the people (*Ant.* 20.97), claiming to be a prophet, and Eleazar b. Deinaeus is a 'brigand' (*Ant.* 20.121). The contrast is also clearly drawn by Josephus in his description of the Jewish participants in the death of James. The incident is, according to Josephus, an example of Sadducean cruelty in criminal cases. Ananus is portrayed in the negative light— 'rash in his temper, unusually daring' (*Ant.* 20.199). In contrast, those who protest are 'the most fair minded and accurate in observance of the law' (*Ant.* 20.201). Here Josephus presents the reader with bad and good examples of human behaviour.

Reference to the motivation of certain participants is a further type of comment occasionally included by Josephus in his narration of an incident. More often than not, the motivation of a participant is linked with an estimation of the existing situation. Furthermore, they are often linked with officials in situations where trouble is either present or seen to be imminent. There are several examples to consider, most of which are located in the period after 44 CE. The one Jewish official mentioned is Herod Antipas. His action against John is explained by Josephus as reflecting a concern that John's large and devoted following could lead to 'sedition'. As a result, the tetrarch decided to act before a 'sedition' began (*Ant.* 18.118). The other examples relate to the motivation of Roman officials. In one instance, Felix's decision to act against Jonathan is for personal gain and is negative in nature. Felix's desire to have Jonathan murdered is explained because the former high priest was a loud and frequent critic of the governor (*Ant.* 20.162). In turn, Jonathan's criticism of Felix is explained as deriving from his concern that he had originally canvassed for Felix's appointment to the governorship of Judaea (*Ant.* 20.162).

The other examples display the concern of a Roman official to prevent the outbreak of conflict or contain the level of trouble in certain situations. Longinus travels to Jerusalem because he feared Fadus's order would result in a 'revolution' by the Jews (*Ant.* 20.7). Cumanus's decision to post sentries around the temple precinct during Passover is explained as a concern to prevent a 'revolution' (*Ant.* 20.106). Finally, Quadratus decided to visit Jerusalem on the occasion of a festival because he was concerned that a further 'revolution' might commence in the wake of the Galilaean–Samaritan dispute (*Ant.* 20.133). Notably, with the exception of Felix, the motivation is always linked with a desire to prevent trouble beginning or worsening. Implied here is the idea that trouble was either already present or close to the surface.

There is a significant correlation between the comments included in the narrative of events and particular categories of subject matter. Most of the comments are associated with the events that describe changes to certain practices and the activities of certain Jews. The events to which the bulk of the narrative is devoted are understandably also those subject to the most comment in their narration. This, however, is not the end of the matter. The overlap between particular categories of subject matter and comments in the narration of those incidents is magnified by the three types of reflective commentary. The general picture drawn, of turmoil and increasing instability associated with the brigandage in which matters were drawing towards a crisis point, balances the presentation of subject matter and the nature of the subject matter included.

4. *Summary*

With the preceding analysis of Josephus's interpretative framework in mind we turn to the final section of this chapter. Here the focus shifts from the identification of individual elements to the final product: the overall picture and its possible implications for the use of Josephus's narrative in historical inquiry. In the first chapter I outlined what Josephus understood to be relevant in portraying the situation in first-century CE Judaea, a place where conflict intensified to such a level that a crescendo was reached in the revolt of 66–70 CE. Josephus narrates incident after incident where trouble is the main characteristic. This presentation of Judaea is deliberate and controlled. It is Josephus's interpretation.

Although the framework is made up of several different elements, it is not haphazard, nor piecemeal. *War*, *Ant.* and *Life* are crafted texts— deliberate attempts by Josephus to address concerns that were of immediate relevance to his lifetime. The interpretative framework is an intrinsic part of the complete package, not just found in isolated accounts.[65] In *War* only the geographical digressions and information regarding the territorial arrangements are devoid of any form of comment.[66] All other subject matter is commented on in some manner

---

65. This framework is a combination of personal interest and a genuine desire to write history. It is not driven by an amateur who is only playing around with a new-found hobby. In this sense, the activity of Thucydides and Josephus is paralleled. As Hunter, *Thucydides*, p. 177, points out, Thucydides selects and narrates material 'in such a way that events themselves would conform to and so demonstrate' Thucydides's 'pattern of history'. Josephus has undertaken the same basic task—selecting and narrating material that relates to his central theme of explaining 70 CE. On the basis that the term 'objective' pertains to avoiding the imposition of 'one's own outlook' on the narrative of events, then Hunter's negative assessment of Thucydides as 'the least objective of historians' should also be applied to Josephus (*Thucydides*, p. 183).

66. The description of Roman military operations is concluded with a comment (*War* 3.70-109).

or another by Josephus. A similar situation applies to *Ant.* Apart from three incidents—the Samaritan intrusion into the temple (*Ant.* 18.29-30), Pilate's use of money from the sacred treasury (*Ant.* 18.60-62) and Vitellius's actions after the removal of Pilate (*Ant.* 18.90-95)—all other subject matter in *Ant.* is narrated with some form of commentary. Of the types of commentary, it is the reflections on events narrated and comments within the narration of an incident, especially in terms of the description of the participants and their motivation, that Josephus employs on the majority of occasions.

War and *Ant.* do not simply repeat the same comments, nor do they necessarily place the emphasis on the same incidents. For example, in *Ant.* the census of 6 CE is given significant billing. It marks the beginning of a new philosophy which Josephus comments on in terms of its significance for the revolt of 66–70 CE. In *War*, however, the census is not actually mentioned as the cause of Judas's activities, nor is any link made between 6 and 66 CE. A further example of the differing focus is the portrayal of Florus. In *War*, Josephus provides a substantial account of the governor's motivation in the few incidents that are narrated. *Ant.*, however, only includes a brief summary of the significance of Florus's governorship. Despite these differences, *War* and *Ant.* work to the same end, presenting a picture of Judaea where trouble is bound to escalate to the point of war.

Individually, each element of the framework points to the same conclusion. The vast majority of the subject matter pertains to incidents of conflict and instability. Without exception, the incidents that are instigated by Jews who were not the official leaders of the community bring about trouble. The changes instituted are, with a few exceptions, also the cause of some form of disturbance. To reinforce the nature of the subject matter Josephus uses his commentary within the narration of the incidents to highlight the 'reality' of the situation in Judaea. These people associated with trouble, whether they be Roman officials or Jews, were motivated by a desire to act in an unjust manner and they are described in a derogatory manner. This is especially the case among the Jews named: that is, people like the 'brigands', the 'tyrants', the 'insurgents' and the 'revolutionaries'. The reflective comments on the events narrated ensure that the sense of turmoil is evident, particularly by locating these comments at the beginning of the event that is being narrated. To cover all options Josephus employs two other types of commentary. The events alluded to convey a sense of continuity in the presence of trouble and disorder. Finally, although a relatively minor element of the texts, the other type of commentary—the reflections on the general situation—are also focused on conveying the image of Judaea as a place of turmoil.

Probably the best example of how the framework is put together comes in the narrative of the governorships from Cumanus to Florus. Here Judaea is rocked from one crisis to another. Josephus glosses over the presumably 'uneventful' period of Festus's governorship and focuses on narrating, or referring to, occasions of trouble under Cumanus, Felix, Albinus and Florus. We are left, therefore, with a situation where Josephus's notion of objective 'truth' in relation to writing history should be rejected. It is not possible to extract the commentary of Josephus and to assume that we possess a bare description of historical facts.

The sense in which a distinction between 'facts' and 'commentary' is artificial is apparent from the issue of timing within the interpretative framework. The obvious starting point for Josephus's work was actual events. The text is the final step in a process which began with historical situations. The discussion of *Life*, *War* and *Ant.* indicates that the transfer from event to text was constructed from a model in which hindsight was the starting point in the process. A concern to understand and come to terms with the ramifications of the war and the destruction of the temple dictates Josephus's process of writing. As a result, it is the first level of the framework—the manner in which the subject matter is narrated—that controls the texts.

Josephus selects material and determines how best to narrate it from the perspective of someone who is dominated by a desire to understand events from his recent past. There is, however, a degree of flexibility and looseness in the process by which Josephus constructs his texts. Hindsight dictates the process, but it does not necessarily result in a tight, controlled and consistent narrative. In other words, Josephus does not always provide one specific line of interpretation. For example, hindsight ensures that Josephus views events which had consequences in terms of the revolt. In this context, Josephus is willing to speculate that a number of individual incidents were the cause of great turmoil, such as, the failure of Claudius's order to be carried out regarding the auxiliary troops, the dispute at Caesarea, the decision regarding the request of the Levites and the burning of the grain supplies of Jerusalem. The significance of each of these events is cast in terms of the 66–70 CE revolt. The key perception by which Josephus strived to achieve understanding was that conflict and instability were central features of the situation. In other words, in *War* and *Ant.*, Josephus created a context for the war and its ramifications.[67]

These observations regarding the functioning of the interpretative framework have important consequences, especially in terms of how Josephus is employed as a source for a historical investigation into the situation in first-century CE Judaea. Three points stand out for their significance. First, it is not possible to distinguish between the subject matter and commentary of Josephus. The two are integral to the picture Josephus constructs. The texts, therefore, are animate; they are an interpretation of what happened in Judaea and of the possible significance and relationship of certain events. It is plausible to claim that Josephus is narrating historical events, but because what he provides is an interpretation this means several issues must be addressed. For example, how complete is the narrative of the events? How representative are the events he describes of what was happening in Judaea? For these and other related issues there are the related fundamental problems of how it is possible to determine whether Josephus's narratives are accurate accounts of what happened and how the significance of events should be interpreted.

The second point pertains to the structuring of the texts. For Josephus, 66–70 CE is the all important controlling agent. It is as though all events lead to 70 CE. *War* was devoted to the task of narrating the revolt. Even *War* 7 does not go beyond narrating events that are part of the aftermath of the Roman victory. *Ant.* deliberately concludes at 66 CE; no effort is made to extend the narrative beyond the revolt. Even in *Life*, where reference is made to some aspects of Josephus's post-70 CE career, the focus is on events associated with part of the actual revolt. After the revolt Josephus appears to have spent the rest of his life trying to make sense of what happened in 66–70 CE, a task he undertook with the 'gift' of hindsight.

The third point pertains to the relationship between the two levels of the interpretative framework. Because the commentary and the subject matter are two levels of the one process, it is not possible

---

67. Josephus wrote with a blueprint in mind. He wanted to explain the disaster of 70 CE and he did so by looking back into what had happened to his community. This dissection of Josephus's texts, however, does not necessarily mean Josephus was conscious of all the elements of the framework he was using.

simply to compare one against the other. The content and comments deliberately echo one another. To use one to validate the other would be simply to reinforce what Josephus has already decided to be accurate. Alternatively, to criticize the comments and yet uphold the subject matter without explanation would be to assume an independence that does not exist.

Life, *War* and *Ant.* are an interpretation of the situation in first-century CE Judaea. We are dealing with animate texts in their entirety, not merely in selective elements of their comments. The challenge is to establish a means by which these texts can be used as an effective resource for a historical investigation of the period. At the very least, it is crucial to establish whether or not the picture of Josephus, especially his two pillars, actually constitutes an accurate record of the historical situation in Judaea. With this goal in mind, our attention turns to explore how scholarship has employed Josephus as it addresses the issue of the state of affairs in Judaea during the first century CE.

Chapter 4

SCHOLARSHIP'S JUDAEA

We have established that Josephus's picture of the situation in Judaea is the product of his interpretative framework. It is one person's view of what was happening and is, therefore, not necessarily an accurate account of how to understand the period. Such factors as the need for a sense of 'balance' and perspective come to the foreground in what is essentially an issue of historical methodology. Our attention turns to the conclusions drawn by contemporary scholarship as to how first-century CE Judaea should be portrayed.

Discussion of the first century CE has attracted attention from a range of scholarly perspectives. Classical historians have occasionally entered the fray, particularly in terms of Judaea as an example of a province within the Roman empire for which there is an extensive narrative source. For Jewish studies the importance of exploring this period is obvious. The end of Hasmonaean involvement in the governing of the Jewish people, the introduction of direct Roman rule and a major rebellion against the Romans during which Jerusalem was sacked and the temple destroyed are some of the headlines that have ensured the period is of significance for any account of the history of the Jewish people in Judaea. Studies that explore the beginning of Christianity have also devoted attention to the situation during this period. Of particular interest is the desire to develop an understanding of the socio-political context in which Jesus's ministry took place and in which the nascent movement arose. This broadly based interest in the first century CE has been given voice in general survey texts and in single issue books and articles.

The following survey is deliberately descriptive in an effort to ensure that the overwhelming sense of unity in what is presented across the breadth of the scholarly accounts is evident. In turn, we will be then in a position to point to the close parallel that exists between Josephus and scholarship in their reconstruction of what happened in Judaea. Whether the focus is classical, Jewish or Christian studies, Judaea is almost exclusively portrayed as being a place of intensifying turmoil throughout the first century CE. Conflict between Jews and Romans, among Jews and between Jews and Syrian-Greeks continued to escalate until the inevitable explosion came in 66 CE with the Jewish revolt. There is variation only in whether this is an explicitly held view or one that is strongly implied through the scholar's choice of subject matter.

What follows is a survey of contemporary scholarship that either refers to or describes the state of affairs in first-century CE Judaea. I make no claims to have incorporated all the statements regarding the situation in Judaea during this period. The survey is intentionally selective and representative. Three controlling agents have been employed. The first is that I have sought to include a cross-section of the views expressed within the different scholarly orientations, classical, Jewish and Christian studies. The second agent is that the examples are taken from the different types of scholarly contributions: namely, a mixture of general, survey texts and the single issue, thematic studies. The third controlling agent is chronological in nature. The discussion deliberately takes 1973 as the starting point. 1973 marks the date in which the first volume of the revised English translation of Schürer was published. Since then there has been a significant growth in late-second-temple-period studies, indicating the popularity of the subject area. As such, the choice reflects a desire to control the extent of the historiographical element of the study rather than the origin of a particular line of investigation.[1]

---

1.   It is important to state that I am not trying to imply that all the comments and views post-1973 are new or that the scholarship before 1973 is now redundant. A few examples of the important contribution of pre-1973 work to current scholarly discussion regarding Josephus and the first century CE include S.G.F. Brandon, *Jesus and the Zealots* (Manchester: Manchester University Press, 1967), W.R. Farmer, *Maccabees, Zealots and Josephus* (New York: Columbia University Press, 1956), Laqueur, *Der jüdische Historiker*, Smith, 'Palestinian Judaism', V.A. Tcherikover, *Hellenistic Civilization and the Jews* (trans. S. Applebaum; Philadelphia: Jewish Publication Society of America, 1959) and H.St.J. Thackeray, *Josephus the Man and the Historian* (New York: Jewish Institute of Religion Press, 1929). As stated above, the dividing line of 1973 primarily relates to a desire to find a means of containing the breadth of the survey to ensure that the detail of the views presented can be appropriately discussed.

These three controlling agents allow the survey to be manageable, especially in chronological terms, and to ensure it is diverse in the type and style of text that is discussed. For convenience, the discussion is divided into two sections. The first will incorporate an account of the views contained in the general survey texts. In the second section I will examine the description of the situation in Judaea within the specialized, single issue texts. Despite this diversity in type and the increasingly large body of literature from differing perspectives, it is striking that the picture we derive from the survey is so 'complete'. The Judaea of scholarship is to be lamented over, a society doomed to being ripped apart by war. From the description of events provided by scholarship one could be excused for thinking that the adage, 'the war we had to have', applies to Judaea in the first century CE.

1. *General Survey Texts*

The views contained in five general survey texts will be outlined. The description is structured to help identify three points: the perspective from which the survey is presented and the time frame used; the overview of the situation in Judaea, particularly in terms of the subject matter which is narrated; and any comments that are made regarding the causes of the 66–70 CE revolt.

In 1973 the first volume of the revised English translation of Schürer's *The History of the Jewish People in the Age of Jesus Christ* was published.[2] The work was undertaken to revise but not rewrite the 1886 edition of Schürer (p. vi). Any changes that were made to the text were determined by the discovery of new data, or were made in terms of revising the bibliography (p. vi): 'the work remains, as far as the evidence now available allows, that of Emil Schürer' (p. vii). Furthermore, the revision is presented as 'material for historical research, but is not intended as an interpretative synthesis, or as a summary of contemporary interpretations' (p. vii). The arguments, therefore, essentially remain the ones that Schürer presented to the reader in the latter part of the nineteenth century. The work covers the period 175 BCE to 135 CE, primarily in a chronological rather than thematic structure in the first volume.[3] The organization of

---

2.   The publication of volume 2 followed in 1979.
3.   The only exceptions to this lineal approach in volume 1 are the three excursus devoted to specific topics. The layout of volume 2 is thematic.

material is determined on two levels by various key events. The large-scale division is made according to military conflicts, such as the period 63 BCE to 135 CE. Sub-divisions within this broad time frame are normally made according to changes in the leadership of the region, such as 6–41, 41–44 and 44–66 CE.

The text is written from the perspective of seeking to provide an explanation of the context in which Christianity developed (p. 1). Through the 'political' history, Schürer argues that the 'chief characteristic of this period was the growing importance of Pharisaism'. Furthermore, it was the era of Jewish political independence, its rise under the Maccabaeans and its downfall with the Bar Kokhba revolt in 135 CE (pp. 1-2).

Schürer provides an extensive account of the situation in Judaea through his introductory comments and the description of events. In the course of this description it is evident that Schürer constantly has in mind the revolt of 66–70 CE and how it relates to events that pre-date 66 CE. According to Schürer, Judaea is in a steady decline towards open war. Conflict and disorder are dominant. The scene was set from the beginning of the first century. Archelaus 'was brutal and tyrannical' and his misgovernment meant Roman rule was introduced in a climate of trouble (p. 354).

Schürer declares his hand when he begins to describe the change-over in 6 CE. Conflict between Rome and Judaea was inevitable, because of Jewish attitudes and the inability of Roman rulers:

> The Jews saw in the simplest administration rulings, such as the initial census, an encroachment on their most sacred rights and came increasingly to believe that direct Roman rule, which they had desired at Herod's death, was incompatible with the principles of theocracy. Even with the best of intentions on both sides tension and hostility were therefore inevitable (p. 356).

Even those emperors with 'good intentions were always failed by the ineptitude of the governors and not infrequently also by gross miscarriages of justice on their part' (pp. 356-57). Furthermore, 'through their [governors'] infringements they in the end so aggravated the people that in wild despair they plunged into a war of self-annihilation' (p. 357). Here, at the outset of the period in question, Schürer displays an awareness of the revolt and a concern to show the sense in which it is linked with the years of Roman rule. Schürer declares the climate of Judaea as one of instability, in which conflict appears to be bound to occur. From this perspective of hindsight Schürer proceeds to narrate the trouble-filled events of the first century CE.

The first element of Schürer's narrative is the outline of the administration employed in Judaea by the Romans. Roman administration per se is not condemned. Deference is displayed to the Jewish religion. Furthermore, of the 'institutions and principles of government, the Jews had no cause to complain'. The Romans had not established a system designed to attack the Jews (pp. 379-81). Where Schürer lays some responsibility for the revolt is with the individuals delegated the task of governing the province. These men failed to display the necessary ability to determine between 'right and wrong' (p. 381). Added to this was the Jewish attitude to the imposition of foreign rule and the payment of tribute. It was an insult to a community who believed they should be the rulers of the world. Here Schürer cites the first action of direct Roman rule—the census—as evidence of the problems the Romans were continually to face (p. 381). Although unsuccessful in this instance, Judas established a group whose activities ensured that 'the spark of rebellion continued to smoulder for sixty years, when it finally burst into flames' (p. 382).

The survey of events prior to 44 CE focuses on the governorship of Pilate, the statue of Gaius incident and the reign of Agrippa I. According to Schürer, Pilate displayed contempt for the Jewish customs, Gaius's order regarding the statues is narrated with little comment, while Agrippa I displayed a level of piety that made him popular among his Jewish subjects. Pilate is of special interest because he is discussed in some detail in Philo and Josephus. Agrippa's 'testimony' regarding the 'unbending and callously hard by nature' character of Pilate's personality is expressed in the description of his activities as a governor—the bringing of standards bearing images into Jerusalem, the use of money from the sacred treasury to build an aqueduct, his probable execution of Galilaeans, the placing of shields in Jerusalem and then his attack on the Samaritans (pp. 384-87).

It is in the second period of direct Roman rule that Schürer lays emphasis on the description of the situation in Judaea. At the outset Schürer states that the level of trouble intensified with the Roman administration being deliberately provocative to the extent that 'it might be thought, from the record of the Roman procurators to whom, from now on, public affairs in Palestine were entrusted, that they all, as if by secret arrangement, systematically and deliberately set out to

drive the people to revolt' (p. 455). Insensitivity to the Jewish religious customs was a common trait of the governors. What follows in
Schürer is the narrative of a deteriorating situation, especially from
Felix's governorship onwards. Although the term of office of Fadus
and Tiberius Alexander 'did not pass without disturbances they were
totally insignificant in comparison with what followed' (p. 458). The
trouble under Cumanus, due to Jewish and Roman actions, was on a
much larger scale. It was, however, the governorship of Felix that
'manifestly institutes the turning point in the drama which started in
AD 44 and reached its bloody climax in AD 70' (p. 460). From being a
'comparatively peaceful' situation to 'more serious uprisings' under
Cumanus, with Felix 'rebellion became permanent' (p. 460).[4] Opposition to Rome intensified with 'the Zealots' obtaining an increased
level of practical support (p. 462). The 'perverse severity and cruelty'
of Felix 'provoked further lawlessness' (p. 461), in the form of the
sicarii and other 'political fanatics'. At the same time, conflict
developed among the priesthood. By the end of Felix's governorship
'the preaching of resistance against Rome continued incessantly and
the agitation to take up arms never stopped until that objective was
reached' (p. 464). Festus was unable to undo the damage despite his
'honest intentions' (p. 467).

The final two governors followed the tradition established by Felix:
they did 'everything in their power to inflame the situation and bring
on the final conflagration' (p. 468). The 'anarchy' was evident in
Jerusalem before the arrival of Albinus, when Ananus had James executed. Schürer highlights Albinus's desire for money, claiming that
his 'venality knew no limits' (p. 468). The lack of control meant it
'was a free for all', the procurator and 'the insurrectionists' free to
attack the people at will (pp. 468-69). Florus was 'the worst'. His
'malevolence was beyond endurance, so inflammable was the situation
that it now needed but one spark. And the explosion followed with
elemental force' (p. 470). It was Florus who provoked the revolt
through his insensitive demand for 17 talents from the temple treasury. The inevitable had happened: the Jews finally broke the shackles
and the 'long threatened' revolt began.

The years that follow the revolt are described in a chapter that
explores the period up to the defeat of Bar Kokhba. After identifying

---

4. Citing Tacitus (*Hist.* 9), Schürer claims that the social background of Felix
helps explain the governor's failure: 'Felix was true to his origin' (p. 461).

the various governors, Schürer explores the situation as it existed between the reigns of Vespasian and Domitian. The defeat of the Jews had brought about two dramatic changes that 'resulted in a violent upheaval in the inner life of the Jewish people' (p. 521). These changes were the 'dissolution of the Sanhedrin and the suspension of sacrificial worship' (p. 523). As a result, political independence and the power of the Sadducean high priesthood was lost. It was the Pharisees who filled the void. After two centuries of seeking control they were 'at one stroke' able to claim 'sole supremacy' (p. 524). Although the potential for trouble was ever present, 'there seem to have been no serious conflicts' up to the end of Domitian's reign (p. 528). One factor, however, that had been prominent in the 66–70 CE war—'messianic hope'—continued to be important. In fact, according to Schürer, it 'drew new nourishment, new strength' and its political connotations 'contained the seeds of further catastrophes' (p. 528). Again, Schürer appears to have a view fixed towards later events: namely, the last two sections of the chronological narrative, the 115–117 and 132–135 CE rebellions.

Published within a year of Schürer's *The History of the Jewish People*, the first volume of CRINT presents an overview of Jewish history as part of a series designed to explore the historical relationship between Judaism and Christianity.[5] The declared focus of the text is Judaism in the first and second centuries CE (p. ix). Given these stated interests it is somewhat surprising that the chronological time frame used in the discussion of affairs in Judaea does not include any reference to the 66–70 CE revolt, its causes, or of the period after 70 CE, other than minor references to changes in the administrative structure of the territory (p. 315).

The survey of events associated with the governing of Judaea, written by Stern, forms only a portion of a thematically orientated text.[6] Although there are no general statements regarding the state of affairs in Judaea, it is apparent that trouble was prominent. The administrative

5. M. Stern, 'The Province of Judaea', in S. Safrai and M. Stern, *The Jewish People in the First Century: Historical Geography, Political History, Social, Cultural and Religious Life and Institutions* (CRINT, 1.1; Assen: Van Gorcum, 1974), pp. 308-76.

6. In line with the stated purpose to provide an 'overview' of the existing knowledge on such topics as the political history, social, cultural and religious life and institutions (p. xi) the chapters are all thematic in nature.

structure of the province is outlined in some detail (pp. 310-46), in which the use of auxiliary troops and the social background of the governors are deemed to be factors that made stability a difficult objective to achieve (pp. 313-15). In terms of responsibility for how events unfolded, Stern identifies as important factors the burden of heavy taxation in association with the Jews' sense of feeling alienation and the harsh character of the governors, who played 'their part in deepening the hostility of the Jewish population towards Roman rule' (p. 347).

The description of events that follows also presents a picture where conflict is a key feature, especially in the period after 44 CE. Of the early period, Pilate is singled out as exacerbating the trouble between the Roman government and the Jewish people (pp. 349-53).[7] In fact, Pilate's governorship marked the time from when 'there is frequent mention of messianic excitement of disorder and of the gradual disillusionment of all the hopes placed in Roman rule' (p. 346). While Judas created an 'ideology' which proclaimed open opposition to Roman rule, it was Pilate's 'strong arm' tactics that created open resistance (p. 353). In narrating the incident of Gaius's order to place a statue in Jerusalem, Stern claims that the death of the emperor 'prevented' what would have ended in a revolt (p. 359). The crucial consequence of the incident was the lasting memory of the order—the awareness that the Jews were subject to the whims of the Roman officials (p. 359).[8]

The years that follow, 44–66 CE, reflect the decline of Roman rule, with relations between the Romans and the Jews becoming increasingly tense. Stern presents the entire period as one of growing conflict with the focus being on the actions of the governors. With Fadus the friction returned with 'more intensity than ever'. Theudas presented a 'grave danger of conflagration', possibly through the 'messianic ferment' that was evident (p. 361). Cumanus's governorship is 'marked

---

7.   The governors before Pilate are very briefly mentioned (pp. 348-49).

8.   In the preceding chapter, Stern also states that although Agrippa I provided a respite by his attempt to provide a 'compromise between Roman rule and the Jewish people', his reign came to an end too soon to have any lasting impact. See M. Stern, 'The Reign of Herod and the Herodian Dynasty', in S. Safrai and M. Stern, *The Jewish People in the First Century: Historical Geography, Political History, Social, Cultural and Religious Life and Institutions* (CRINT, 1.1; Assen: Van Gorcum, 1974), pp. 216-307 (299).

by grave clashes and disorders'. Because of the prevailing attitude of revolt, the soldier who tore up the copy of the law was executed, while the conflict between the Galilaeans and Samaritans meant the 'disorder reached its peak' (p. 363). Although Felix's rule began 'on friendly terms' it 'ended with a crisis'. Felix developed links with Herodians and such figures as Ananias, while others, including Jonathan, became his victims (p. 366). It is during Felix's term that the 'extreme nationalist movement' became 'a permanent factor in the life of Judaea' (p. 366). The suppression of the Egyptian merely resulted in further anger. In Jerusalem, rivalry among the priesthood meant that 'normal life had almost been brought to a standstill' (p. 367). For Festus there was 'almost anarchy' with the extremist movement growing and messianic pretenders promising signs of salvation (p. 368). Regarding the governorships of Albinus and Florus, Stern provides less detail. Although initially Albinus tried to control the sicarii, 'their activity in Judaea increased'. The governor used his appointment to acquire money via ransoms while the rivalry of the priesthood in Jerusalem was intensified by the involvement of Herodians, with the result that the level of 'anarchy' increased (p. 370). Stern is especially brief in his discussion of Florus and the events that preceded the revolt. He simply notes that the struggles within the Jewish community increased in number and the gulf between the Romans and the Jews widened even further (p. 371).

In 1976, Smallwood's *The Jews under Roman Rule* was published.[9] As indicated by the subtitle, the text covered the years from Pompey's capture of Jerusalem in 63 BCE until the reign of Diocletian (284–305 CE). Smallwood discusses affairs in Judaea and the diaspora. The subject matter is arranged chronologically and geographically, with the chapters framed around such key events as changes in leadership. All of the first century is covered by Smallwood. Boundaries for chapters are drawn between 6–41, 41–44, 44–66, 66–70 and 70–115 CE. It is apparent that 66–70 CE acts as a significant focal point in the two chapters devoted to Judaea as a province in the years 6–41 and 44–66 CE (pp. 144, 256-57). Although Smallwood draws attention to the role of individuals in determining how situations unfolded, thus allowing room for an element of unpredictability in the outcome of events, she also implies that there was a sense in which this early period of Roman

---

9. E.M. Smallwood, *The Jews under Roman Rule: From Pompey to Diocletian* (repr.; SJLA, 20; Leiden: E.J. Brill, 1981 [1976]).

rule was doomed because of the 'intransigence' of 'Jewish nationalism'.

Smallwood's primary focus is on the interaction between the Jews and Romans; it is not essentially a Jewish or Roman history. Her concern is to trace the nature of the 'political' interaction, charting the various successes and failings that feature, with a view towards identifying where responsibility for the relative successes or failures should be apportioned. Such a focus helps explain her comments in the conclusion of the book where she places the interaction of the first century in the context of formal contact between Rome and Judaea. There Smallwood recognizes the unpeaceful nature of Jewish–Roman relations between 6–135 CE but claims that it was not the result of any formal or deliberate policy of repression enacted by the Romans (p. 541). Instead, Jews and Romans, together, were responsible for creating 'chronic unrest' which 'culminated in two major revolts' (p. 542).

Smallwood describes the events in Judaea in some detail. The period is presented as one of great instability, with the revolt of 66–70 CE placed in a context that indicated its explanation lay in long-term causes. While discussing what happened in the first century, therefore, Smallwood appears to be revolving around the war of 66–70. At the outset Smallwood declares that although Roman policy in principle should not be blamed, conflict between the Jews and Romans was to be viewed as inevitable. The rule of Archelaus was one of 'brutality and tyranny' and by 6 CE, when he was exiled, 'the subjects [Jews] had reached the end of the tether' (p. 117).

Smallwood begins her discussion of the first period of the direct Roman rule (6–41 CE) with an outline of the administrative structure of the province. Here Smallwood identifies a fault within the system— the presence of only six or seven auxiliary cohorts that the governor could call upon. Such a small military force meant the governor would be unable to control widespread disturbances. Hence, during the 50s and 60s the 'rising turbulence' could not be checked, irrespective of whether the governor wanted to or not (pp. 247, 256).[10]

Clearly with an eye on later events, Smallwood discusses the repercussion of the protest of Judas in 6 CE. Josephus's claims regarding the impact of the fourth philosophy (*Ant.* 18.7-10, 23-25) are revised. It is not possible to identify a single zealot party that existed from 6 CE.

---

10. Here, and at the beginning of her discussion of 44–66 CE, Smallwood is looking forward to the events associated with the revolt, and back, from the perspective of trying to explain why the war took place.

What was founded in 6 CE, however, was a dream of independence. The protest became the spiritual foundation for the later brigand activity. Here Smallwood implies a sense of continuity and inevitability in which 66–70 CE acts as a frame for viewing the events from 6 CE onwards. For Smallwood

> [the] hardening of Jewish nationalist feeling into a militant resistance movement at the very start of the period of Roman rule was the fundamental cause of the recurrent disturbances of the next sixty years and of the revolt which was their climax, in the sense that it created or sharpened the dilemma facing the Romans in attempting to govern Judaea as a province (p. 155).

The last phrase of this quote is all important. The inability of the Romans selected to administer the province was to become the trigger for the Jewish 'intransigence'. Rome protected Jewish 'religious liberty' but could not tolerate any nationalist aspirations. Added to this, a series of governors was unable to display the required diplomatic skills, hampered by limited military support, with the end result that 'the story of the years 6–66 is largely the story of how the occupying power and the nationalists reacted on one another, each provoking the other to further excesses until the final explosion came' (p. 155).

After these introductory comments, Smallwood's discussion of events in Judaea in the years between 6–44 CE focuses on the governorship of Pilate and the order of Gaius that a statue of him be erected in Jerusalem. The years prior to Pilate's governorship are dealt with briefly. The paucity of information before 16 CE could indicate that the situation was quite peaceful (p. 156). For the next decade, however, Smallwood views the short term of office for governors as possibly indicating that trouble was increasing (p. 160). The focus on Pilate and the order of Gaius probably can be explained by the amount of detail available in the sources. The comments of Smallwood suggest that her interest in the governor and Petronius, the legate sent by Gaius to carry out his order, is the result of authorial concern. These men are held up as examples of bad and good administrators. Pilate is described as being 'tactless or deliberately provocative' in deciding to take military standards bearing images into Jerusalem at night-time. Pilate did not act in ignorance and it is 'difficult to exonerate him of conscious provocation' (p. 161). Later, the speed by which Vitellius acted in removing Pilate after the Samaritan incident is interpreted as meaning that he was aware of the general tenor of the governor's character (p. 171). Not content just to compare Pilate and Vitellius, Smallwood then includes Petronius to argue that 'if the province of Judaea had been under the direct rule of men of their calibre [Vitellius and Petronius], its history during the first century AD might well have been very different' (p. 174). The account of Gaius's order emphasizes the importance Smallwood places on the role of individuals. To Petronius and Agrippa I belonged the credit for what was a narrow escape from a revolt.[11]

Smallwood's second chapter on the situation in Judaea, covering the years 44–66, is also introduced with a general overview. These 22 years are viewed as ones of 'progressive breakdown of law and order throughout the province' (p. 257). Under each governor the level of trouble intensified 'until by the late 50s the terrorists had secured such a hold on the province that it was drifting irretrievably into the anarchy from which the revolt of 66 was born' (p. 257). Smallwood marks Cumanus's term of office as the 'turning-point'; by the end of his governorship terrorism had became 'endemic' (p. 263). Although Smallwood views the personality of the governor as a contributing factor to the problems, the situation had deteriorated beyond the point of control (p. 269). Quoting Josephus, Smallwood then states (*Ant.* 20.124), 'the attack of Stephen marked the time when all of Judaea was infested with brigands' (p. 266). Added to this situation was Florus, who, despite Josephus's 'rhetorical exaggeration', was such a failure that 'it [the situation] became irretrievable and the tragedy of the province reached the terrible climax of its last act' (p. 272). The use of the words 'last act' suggests that 66–70 CE was to be viewed as a conclusion. Such a decision is puzzling, given that Smallwood goes on to discuss the revolts of 115–117 and 132–135 CE.

The various impostors, messianic movements and the sicarii adopting 'insidious tactics' characterize the period (pp. 274-75). Terrorism was 'rampant' and 'the religious and political fanatics now joined hands to terrorise the country' (p. 274). People were incited to rebel, the wealthy were attacked, as were those who collaborated with the Romans. Even the high priests began openly to oppose the Romans from the late 50s (pp. 277-78). In this context Smallwood cites the

---

11. Individual personalities are given a prominent place in the way Smallwood explains these incidents. However, as declared at the outset of her discussion of direct Roman rule, there was a prominent 'permanent' feature of this period: 'Jewish nationalism'.

action of Ananus in trying James while the new governor was in transit as evidence of the shift among the high priests (pp. 279-80). Furthermore, the high priests failed to act responsibly on an internal level, gathering rival gangs to grab the tithes, all 'highly detrimental to the peace of Jerusalem' (p. 281). The situation had grown so bad that 'many Jews found emigration the only remedy against terrorism' by 64 CE (p. 283). Within this context the 'most serious aspect of the internal affairs of the province after 52 was the alarmingly steady growth of the extreme nationalist movement' (p. 274).

The trouble in Caesarea between the Jews and Syrian-Greeks was the 'spark which lit the tinder' (p. 288). However, the revolt had its origin in much 'deeper' causes; it 'would have occurred inevitably sooner or later' (p. 288). The Roman administration had failed; it was tactless, deliberately provocative and hampered by a lack of military resources. These circumstances were matched by a 'political and religious fanaticism', with an 'exceptionably truculent and intractable' attitude that was fostered among the Jews (p. 284). The patience of Jews and Romans alike had reached its end. War could not be avoided; the events of 64–66 brought to a head what had long been set in motion in 6 CE.

Smallwood also provides a detailed narrative of the 66–70 CE war. The various campaigns are described through to the capture of Jerusalem in 70 CE. A further chapter is then devoted to the period that follows the revolt.[12] Here Smallwood describes the changes introduced by the Romans, changes to Jewish practices caused by the destruction of the temple and a brief summary of the events up to 115 CE. Smallwood views 70 CE as the 'end of one epoch' (p. 331). The key changes introduced by the Romans—the appointment of a legate to govern the territory and a legion to provide military security— were designed to 'remedy' the problems of the previous period of Roman rule (pp. 331-33). In the years that followed 70 CE, the Romans were cautious regarding the possibility of further trouble (pp. 352-54). Smallwood also views the period between 70–115 CE as the time when the Rabbinic movement became crucial 'in the post-war reconstruction'.

The fourth general survey is Murphy's *The Religious World of*

---

12. The title of the chapter, 'The New Dispensation in Judaea', implies what occurs after 70 CE is different to the period before the war.

Jesus.[13] The text is written as an introduction to the cultural and historical context in which Jesus' ministry took place. As part of this explanation of the origins of Christianity, Murphy includes a survey of the history of Judaea in the first century CE. The focus of Murphy's description is the political situation in Judaea, especially the attitude of various groups to the existing administrative structure. The account is prefaced by a theoretical framework by which to understand what happens in Judaea. Here Murphy draws on the work of Horsley, using his model of a 'spiral of violence' to explain how a colonial power—Rome—interacted with subject people—Jews (p. 282). Although the various stages of the spiral were not always distinguishable, Murphy claims that 'frequently there is a definite progression over time' and that first-century CE Judaea is one such example (p. 283). In effect, the description of the situation in Judaea is one that has a fixed structure, a progression to the inevitable outcome, the revolt. This is reflected in the layout of the narrative. Murphy's survey, entitled 'Jewish Palestine under Rome', terminates with the beginning of the 66–70 CE war, no reference is made to the years that follow the revolt.[14]

Murphy views the years between 6–48 CE and 48–66 CE as forming two distinct phases. The first period of direct Roman rule and the governorships of Fadus and Tiberius Alexander 'were marked by a sustained effort, by all segments of the population to live in peace with the Roman occupiers' (p. 308). Direct Roman rule had replaced the 'tyrannical' period of Archelaus's ethnarchy. It began with a tax revolt which was not widespread nor violent. Furthermore, Josephus exaggerated the role of the fourth philosophy in *Ant.* 18.3-10 (pp. 290-93). During the trouble associated with Pilate and Gaius the response of the Jews was to engage in non-violent protest. Murphy concludes that

> between 4 BCE and 44 CE there is no evidence for sustained, organised Jewish resistance to Roman rule. On the contrary, except for the incident involving the tax revolt of Judas the Galilaean evidence indicates a willingness to accept Roman rule. The people would not do so, however, at the price of gross violation of divine laws (p. 299).

As a result, it is inappropriate to claim that 'the picture in Josephus

---

13. F.J. Murphy, *The Religious World of Jesus: An Introduction to Second Temple Palestinian Judaism* (Nashville: Abingdon Press, 1991).

14. Murphy does devote Chapter 12 to a discussion of the 66–70 CE revolt.

contrasts starkly with what has been common view that the Jews were "nationalistic", and were spoiling for a fight with the Romans so as to place an end to Roman rule' (p. 299). Here Murphy displays his concern to establish the context for Jesus and his support for the interpretation of Horsley that Jesus was not the foil to a violent 'nationalistic' response to Roman rule.

Although trouble was evident in the years 44–48 CE, Murphy views the governorship of Felix as the turning point in Jewish and Roman relations.[15] Cumanus had aggravated the situation but there was as yet 'no revolutionary intent' (p. 302). Under Felix, however, organized, politically aware resistance emerged in the sicarii movement (p. 303). The sicarii targeted the local elite as collaborators in an effort to destabilize the ruling structure of Jerusalem. Popular prophets and bandits also became increasingly active under Felix. As Josephus states in *Ant.* 20.160-61, the situation was rapidly deteriorating (p. 304). Further disorder was evident in the conflict between priests and between the Jews and Greeks at Caesarea (pp. 305-306). The last two governors, Albinus and Florus, far from trying to re-establish order actually contributed to the trouble. Eventually 'Florus's ruthless reparations finally causes the eruption of open revolt' (p. 309). According to Murphy the spiral of violence was evident in Judaea. From

> the broad sweep of the events of the first century, one can discern the fourfold pattern of injustice, protest, repression and revolt. As injustices multiplied, so did protests, at first non-violent, then violent. As protests grew stronger, so did repression. As repression reached its peak under Florus, the people finally restored to complete renunciation of Roman rule and violent revolt (p. 309).

By implication, the revolt is the dominant factor in the survey of first-century CE Judaea, and should be seen as an inevitable consequence of Roman rule.

The long-standing nature of the origins of the revolt are clearly reinforced in Murphy's discussion of the 66–70 CE revolt. Although the question of inevitability is not explicitly discussed, Murphy commences with a brief survey of the 'central factors' that caused the war. He cites Roman maladministration, Roman oppression, Judaism as a religion, hope and expectation of renewal, class conflict, tensions between Jews

---

15. This view is made explicit by the subtitle used by Murphy, 'War Approaches' (p. 302) in Chapter 10.

and Greeks and factionalism within the ruling class as causes (pp. 345-46). Murphy does not try to claim that one particular factor was more significant than the others. What is notable regarding these factors is that they all shift the focus away from explaining the revolt as the result of a short-term, immediate problem. All the factors listed can be traced back over the first century CE and even earlier in some instances. They are compatible with the 'spiral of violence' model, factors that allow for an intensification and escalation as the first century CE unfolded.

Grabbe's two-volume work, *Judaism from Cyrus to Hadrian*, is the most recent and the final example of a general survey I will examine.[16] Although it stands within the classification of a general survey, Grabbe's work is quite distinctive. The focus is on the Jews of Judaea, and chronology provides the means of arranging the bulk of the chapters in the text.[17] Where Grabbe offers a valuable departure from the existing survey tradition is in his concern to identify key issues within a given period, and to examine the relevant sources and scholarly opinions on those issues. As a result Grabbe's narrative incorporates two distinct levels. One is the 'synthesis', in which a brief wholistic narrative of a defined period is presented in line with the existing tradition. The second level incorporates the various 'historical studies' which explore key issues within a given period, as identified by Grabbe. This dual approach is a witness to the boom in specialized, thematic studies that has taken place in the last 20 years. The narrative of events is present, as in the other surveys, but it is structured very much in the light of the various question marks that exist in many issues.

Grabbe's discussion of the first century CE is divided chronologically. A line is drawn at 74 CE, the end of the first revolt. The events before the revolt are discussed in a chapter that culminates in the revolt, while the events from after 70 CE are linked with a chapter

16. L.L. Grabbe, *Judaism from Cyrus to Hadrian* (2 vols.; Minneapolis: Fortress Press, 1992). The relevant sections are located in volume 2, entitled *The Roman Period*. As with all the general survey texts, Grabbe's study addresses a subject area much broader than the examination of the situation in first-century CE Judaea.

17. Exceptions to this chronological structure are Chapter 3 ('The Jews and Hellenization') and Chapter 8 ('Sects and Violence: Religious Pluralism from the Maccabees to Yavneh').

that concludes with the 132–135 CE revolt.[18] In line with the proportion of extant ancient sources and related secondary literature, the
period prior to 70 CE is discussed in much greater detail than the
years that follow 70 CE.

The historical studies and the synthesis present a picture of Judaea in
the period leading up to 74 CE as a place where conflict was a dominant feature. The underlying approach is made evident in the synthesis
of the period 6–74 CE. According to Grabbe:

> Economic, social and political trends all converged towards revolt, espe-
> cially accelerating after the death of Agrippa I in 44, evidenced by a
> dramatic increase in the growth of banditry and revolutionary and terrorist
> groups; an accumulation of uninvested wealth in the temple, parallelled by
> growth in borrowing by the less well off; exacerbation of the gap between
> rich and poor, including between the upper and lower echelons of the
> priesthood; and increasing discontent with both the Roman governors and
> their collaborators among the Jews (pp. 419-20).

For Grabbe, the Herodian rulers after Archelaus were 'bright spots',
with Agrippa I even being put forward as possibly having sufficient
influence to prevent the war if he had lived longer (p. 614). However,
as the Roman governors were 'an insensitive lot and frequently
incompetent', it is implied that the revolt was the obvious outcome of
Roman rule, especially in the period after 44 CE (p. 419). Jewish
society was breaking up as a result of these internal and external
pressures.

The selection of subject matter for the historical studies is most
interesting. Although Grabbe emphasizes the period after 44 CE as a
time of increased trouble, not one of the studies relates specifically to
that period.[19] The studies either refer to the entire period—6–74 CE—
or to the years 6–41 CE.[20] One study, '7.3.9, Causes of the War with

18. What is slightly puzzling is that this chapter dealing with the period after the
revolt is described as an 'epilogue'. Although the focus of the text may be the second
temple period, the title of the text implies that the agenda is events between Cyrus and
Hadrian.

19. Given the nature of the historical studies, to discuss issues that are the subject
of some debate, it could be implied that the events of the period after 44 CE are characterized by a lack of dispute in how they are to be understood.

20. Those covering the entire period include: 'Administration as a Roman
Province'; 'The High Priests and the Sanhedrin'; 'Anti-Semitism and Religious Tolerance'; and 'Expulsions of the Jews from Rome'. Historical studies referring to
6–41 CE include: 'Governorship of Pilate'; 'Troubles of the Alexandrian Community';

Rome', warrants specific comment. Here Grabbe outlines an approach that will be developed in the synthesis of the period 44–66 CE. Furthermore, it implies the importance of understanding the revolt in the context of the first century CE as a whole. The revolt should not be viewed as the result of 'one specific problem'. Instead, Grabbe identifies six explanations that have been championed by scholars. They all indicate that the revolt was the result of long-standing causes. Grabbe lists 'historical memory of an independent Israel', 'Roman misrule' (especially after 44 CE), 'socio-economic pressures', a 'religious ideology' that incorporated an 'expectation of divine intervention', conflict between Jews and the Hellenistic cities and the 'failure of the Jewish upper class' as causes (pp. 412-13).[21] He acknowledges that 'good arguments' exist for claiming the revolt was 'inevitable' but appears to stay on the fence by stating that this 'will naturally remain a moot point' (p. 412).

In Grabbe's synthesis of the years 6–41 CE and 44–66 CE it is trouble that dominates the picture. The census of 6 CE was greeted with 'some sort of rebellion' (p. 423). Pilate's actions while governor display 'stupidity or deliberate provocation' as he managed to offend the local inhabitants on several occasions (pp. 423-24). The tetrarchs and then the reign of Agrippa I provide an important contrast. For Grabbe, the positive presentation of Agrippa I in ancient literature indicates that 'his reign was probably a high point for the Jews as a nation' (p. 434). Such a situation, however, marked a significant contrast to the following 22 years. Grabbe also takes up the theme raised in his discussion of the causes of the war (7.3.9). The return of direct Roman rule resulted in 'a gradual slide into war' (p. 437). The majority of governors displayed a 'lack of personal integrity' (p. 437). Grabbe, however, appears to go even further in his overview of the years 44–66 CE. No longer is the inevitability of the revolt a 'moot point'. Instead, the appointment of governors with noble characters 'might only have postponed the inevitable. Given their own history and religious assumptions, the Jews were bound in time to test themselves militarily against the Roman might' (p. 438). Here Grabbe sheds

and 'Caligula's Attempt to Place His Statue in the Temple'. The last two studies, 'Causes of the War with Rome' and 'Socioeconomic factors' are focused on the later period of Roman rule but refer to issues relevant for the whole period.

21. Grabbe even goes so far as to state that the 'failure of the Jewish upper class... may be the decisive factor contributing to the outbreak of the war' (p. 413).

all caution. A Jewish rebellion would take place; what remained to be determined was the timing of the revolt. The years of direct rule between 44–66 CE provide the appropriate context. In this vein Grabbe goes on to state that 'although there had been rebellions and unruly elements at various times since Pompey, these seemed to crescendo under the procurators: various bandit groups, spasmodic appearances of prophets, the rise of terrorist gangs. Sociologically, these represent a complex set of responses to the general situation...' (p. 438).

Grabbe summarizes the events associated with each governor after 44 CE (pp. 438-44). Fadus and Tiberius Alexander pass by without major incident. With Cumanus, however, there is a 'succession of incidents' (p. 440). Then with Felix, 'allowing for a deal of rhetorical exaggeration' in Josephus's summary of the situation, Grabbe states that there was an increase in 'action of popular sentiment against Roman rule' (p. 442). After Festus's brief attempts to restore order, Albinus and then Florus act as the culmination of a long line of rule, and Grabbe states that 'some sort of explosion' was on the way (pp. 443-44).[22]

Narrating the beginning of the revolt, Grabbe returns to the issue of inevitability. Here, Grabbe follows the caution presented in the historical study (7.3.9), with the issue of the inevitability of the revolt being 'debatable' (p. 446). The revolt did not really begin with one single clear-cut event. Instead 'events of twenty years or more pushed the prospect continually closer...' (p. 446). Again, without explicitly stating as such, Grabbe implies the long-term nature of the causes and a leaning towards the revolt being inevitable by referring to 'the long tradition of Israelite independence as a monarchy; the belief that the Jews were God's chosen people; Roman misrule; socio-economic forces; and the general discrediting of the upper class in the eyes of the Jewish people' (p. 446) as factors integral in the revolt taking place.

Grabbe deals with the years after 70 CE in the final chapter of his text. Here, as suggested by the title 'Epilogue: To Bar Kokhba', the focus is on the culmination of this chronological period, 132–135 CE. The fallout of 70 CE is discussed briefly in the historical study, '9.3.1,

---

22. To these problems could be added a significant internal problem: the level of activity of the revolutionaries and popular movement began 'to crescendo' in the 40s and 50s (p. 513).

Administration of Judea', and in the overview of the synthesis. The scarcity of information is reflected in the abruptness of the narrative. The issue of leadership is raised, particularly in terms of the impact of the destruction of the temple. Then, in discussion of the causes of the 132–135 CE revolt, Grabbe states that many of the pre-70 CE factors, such as economic pressures, nationalism, antagonism against Roman rule and messianic expectations, remained important in the years after 70 CE (p. 574). Grabbe presents 70 CE as a point of change, an important moment in the restructuring of Jewish society. The new leadership 'was a synthesis, a new creation', and the 'period between 70 and 130—the Yavneh period in Rabbinic literature—was a watershed in the history of Judaism' (p. 616).[23]

The five examples of general survey texts display the various perspectives of scholarly interest in the examination of first-century CE Judaea. Smallwood focuses on the Jewish–Roman relations, particularly the extent to which any conflict was the result of a deliberate Roman policy or the consequence of other factors. Schürer, Stern and Murphy share a similar perspective, seeking to identify the context in which Christianity arose. Stern uses the most restrictive framework, outlining the history of the administration of Judaea under Roman rule. Schürer concentrates on exploring the fate of the Jewish people in what is described as an era of 'nationalism'. The most recent survey, that of Grabbe, is less concerned with presenting a continuous narrative of the period than the other texts. For Grabbe, the focus is on providing a resource on issues associated with the study of Judaea in the second temple period.

Despite the overt diversity in terms of the agenda behind each text, there is a consistency in the insights they provide. With varying degrees of emphasis there is general agreement regarding the presentation of

---

23. E. Paltiel, *Vassals and Rebels in the Roman Empire* (Brussels: Latomus, 1991) offers a slight variation in the agenda and conclusions drawn to the approach of other general survey texts. Paltiel focuses on establishing the impact of Roman imperialism on Judaea and other territories that came under direct Roman rule in the first century CE. The deterioration in relations between the Jews and Romans was gradual. The period between 6–26 CE was the 'most peaceful period in the last 200 hundred years of the second temple' (p. 81). Between 26–44 changes, especially the loss of direct contact with the Senate, resulted in a deterioration of the relationship. After 44 CE Claudius's desire to impose imperial universalism, combined with incompetent administration, helps to explain why the war occurred (p. 319).

the state of affairs in Judaea. The chronological framework revolves around 70 CE. In this context Judaea is portrayed as a place where conflict was the chief characteristic. The revolt, if not explicitly deemed inevitable, was definitely to be explained in the context of long-standing factors that featured throughout the first century. There is overt attention given to describing events from the first century CE which convey a society embroiled in turmoil. This concern merely reflects the attitude of the general surveys regarding the situation in Judaea as a society in crisis. The conflict has an internal dimension, whether it be rivalry within the priesthood or fighting between the rich and poor, and an external element, Jewish–Roman and Jewish–Greek antagonism. What remains a matter of debate is the exact nature, extent and timing of the conflict. All the surveys indicate that Jewish–Roman conflict can be linked to the introduction of direct Roman rule in 6 CE. How the trouble develops from there, however, is open to interpretation. For Stern, Pilate's governorship marks the beginning of consistent conflict, with a clear intensification evident from the time of Fadus onwards. Smallwood also accepts that trouble may have resurfaced on an increased level from an early date. However, it was after 44 CE, especially from Cumanus onwards, that the trouble is generally viewed as intensifying to an extent that could no longer be controlled. Schürer views Felix's governorship as the turning point, the time from when the trouble became coordinated and no longer controllable in any sense. A similar view is adopted by Murphy. Grabbe suggests that it might have been possible to contain the trouble within Judaea if Agrippa I had lived longer. The return of procuratorial rule, however, provided the context for the 'trouble' to expand rapidly.

In this context of a society impaled by conflict, the revolt is taken for granted in all texts. While Murphy and Grabbe specifically discuss the causes of the revolt as a separate topic, the revolt is an ever present factor in the discussion of the situation in Judaea. Schürer, Smallwood and Stern begin their discussion of events in Judaea in the first century CE with an overview that looks forward and, at the same time, is a reflection. From 6 CE they project forward to comment on the consequence of the introduction of direct Roman rule, the revolt of 66–70 CE. It is apparent, however, that this overview is dictated by the way events unfolded—the fact that there was a rebellion in 66–70 CE. As their texts project forward, therefore, they do so with the

knowledge of hindsight.[24] Even Murphy, who has deliberately separated his discussion of the revolt from his review of the first century,
lists causes that are all long-term factors. At first glance, Grabbe's
view may appear to be slightly different. The issue of whether the
revolt was inevitable is explicitly raised. Although he does not consistently declare his hand, it is apparent in the nature of subject matter
presented and the causes cited that the revolt was bound to take place
at some point in time.[25] There is an overwhelming sense of unity in
the general surveys. Judaea was a place of turmoil with military
conflict between the Jews and the Romans bound to occur. The revolt
is to be viewed within a context of increased conflict on various levels.

In all the texts, 70 CE acts as a *terminus ad quem*. For Stern and
Murphy the cut-off point is 66 CE, the start of the revolt. Smallwood,
Schürer and Grabbe continue their narrative beyond 70 CE but do so
by using the revolt as a chronological divider in their discussion.
What may appear to be a convenient point at which to conclude a
chapter is in fact of far more significance. The location of material
carries an implicit connotation regarding the appropriate context in
which to understand other events. The actual revolt is often narrated
as a separate chapter but it is, with the exception of Smallwood, placed
within a section that unites the first-century CE events prior to the
revolt with the actual war. The period that follows 70 CE is, if narrated, related to later events.[26] Obviously changes take place as a
result of the way the revolt was resolved. What is notable, though, is
the implicit tendency to relate what happens after 70 CE only to the
years that follow, normally in connection with the revolt of 132–135
CE. There is little or no emphasis on the possible sense in which 70 CE

24. One of the clearest examples of this hindsight is Smallwood's concern to
establish whether or not the system of Roman rule was the cause of conflict between
the Jews and Romans.

25. Although beyond the scope of this study it is interesting to note the differences in how these survey texts explain the revolt of 66–70 and 132–135 CE. For
example, Schürer, *History*, Smallwood, *Jews*, and Grabbe, *Judaism*, identify long-
standing causes as responsible for 66–70 and they trace them in the history of first-
century CE Judaea. In relation to 132–135 CE, however, they all emphasize immediate causes, especially the importance of Hadrian's tour of the East.

26. To a certain extent Grabbe, *Judaism*, pp. 584-86, 595, seeks to show a link
between what happened before and after 70 CE when looking at the possible aftermath of the defeat, particularly in terms of the economic and religious consequences
of the war.

should be viewed as part of the first century CE as a whole or as the catalyst. 70 CE, therefore, is a chronological and thematic divider. Little attention is paid to how issues associated with the period prior to the revolt may impact on what happens after 70 CE. Hence, the revolt is a crescendo, a 'final chapter' that tends to negate discussion of the last 30 years of the first century CE.

2. *Single Issue Studies*

Our attention shifts from the general survey texts to those that are devoted to exploring one particular issue associated with the late second temple period of Judaean society. The same general criteria apply: work published from 1973 onwards that reflects either a classical, Jewish or Christian orientation and which incorporates a discussion of the state of affairs in first-century CE Judaea.[27] There are seven themes from which a selection of scholarly views will be drawn. They are: the causes of the 66–70 CE revolt; discussion of the various popular movements in Jewish society; studies pertaining to the 'historical' Jesus; histories of Galilee; the study of Josephus; an analysis of the 66–70 CE revolt; and Judaea after 70 CE. Not all of these themes are the subject of the same level of scholarly investigation, and the consistency in layout evident in the general surveys does not apply to these thematic texts. They are, however, united in the fact that reference is made to the situation in Judaea in the context of their particular topic of interest. Hence the guiding principle in the following discussion will be identifying the perspective presented on how the first century CE should be viewed. Where possible, attention will be paid to the observations provided regarding the chronological framework employed, the overall situation that is depicted and the explanations offered regarding the cause(s) of the revolt.

27. As a result, such topics as the status of the Pharisees and other groups in Jewish society and the nature of administrative institutions operative in Judaea are not, in themselves, relevant. Although debate continues regarding the importance of the Pharisees, inclusion of this, or any other, specialized topic in this survey is determined by the criteria of providing information regarding the state of affairs in Judaea. On the relative status of the Pharisees and institutions see Mason, 'Chief Priests', pp. 174-77, for a recent example that defends the traditional view; cf. Sanders, *Judaism*, pp. 458-90, and McLaren, *Power*, pp. 199-222.

2.1 *Causes of the 66–70 CE Revolt*

We commence with the topic that has generated the most discussion—specific studies devoted to the examination of the causes of the 66–70 CE revolt. Despite the diversity in the explanations that are provided for why the revolt took place, there is an underlying level of agreement. To explain the revolt it is necessary to locate it within the context of first-century CE events. All the studies trace the origins of the revolt in long-term factors which had been present well before 66 CE.

Brunt's article, 'Josephus on Social Conflicts in Roman Judaea' is the first study to consider.[28] Brunt addresses the issue of trying to explain the Jewish revolt, with a particular concern to establish the attitude of the Jewish aristocracy to the outbreak of the revolt. This concern was derived from his understanding that the Roman approach to provincial government involved the active cooperation of the local aristocracy (p. 149).

The revolt is explained as a social conflict in which the local Jewish aristocracy were opposed to taking up arms against the Romans (p. 149). In other words, the Jewish 'leaders' who had worked with the Roman officials continued to favour Roman rule. It was a rebellion of the populace, not the aristocracy. Although religious fanaticism and the desire for freedom may have been contributing factors, prominence is given to conflict between the Jewish people and aristocracy. Brunt concludes that 'the general social complexion of war and peace parties is quite clear in Josephus's account' (p. 153). Drawing on the account of Josephus's commission in *Life*, Brunt views Ananus's control of the war effort as one designed to contain the outbreak of fighting. The brigands and sicarii, 'the scum of the earth', proclaimed rebellion while the rulers advocated submission to Roman rule (p. 150). The brigands and sicarii attacked the wealthy and destroyed their property. According to Brunt, this conflict between the aristocracy and the masses was evident from as early as 6 CE. The aristocracy perceived Roman rule as a means to prosper: to rebel would only bring ruin to their interests. For the masses, however, Roman rule allowed the aristocracy to oppress them. Most of the conflict prior to the revolt, therefore, was an expression of popular protest

---

28. P.A. Brunt, 'Josephus on Social Conflicts in Roman Judaea', *Klio* 59 (1977), pp. 149-53.

against the aristocracy. In this context, the burning of the public records office in 66 CE was a deliberate ploy by the rebels to win the support of the poor people, the ones who had suffered the most under Roman rule (p. 152).

In a collection of essays published in 1990, Brunt's original article is reprinted with an addenda.[29] The primary purpose of this addenda is to provide a response to the arguments put forward by Goodman (pp. 517, 521). Although Brunt finds Goodman's thesis of blaming the ruling class as 'perverse', he believes the question of causation requires further comment. The addenda, however, is not simply an attempt to restate the line of argument presented in 1977. Brunt begins by claiming that the focus on social conflict in his original article was 'overstated' (p. 517). The province of Judaea was not the only territory subject to such conflict and that a further explanation is necessary to explain why the Jews chose to rebel when they did (p. 517). Brunt also acknowledges that the timing of the revolt is puzzling, describing the delay of some two generations after the introduction of direct Roman rule as a 'unique' feature of the situation in Judaea (pp. 518-19).

Rejecting Goodman's interpretation of the aristocracy as 'zealous activists' in 66 CE, Brunt restates the view that the 'revolt was essentially a popular movement' (p. 527). Most of the aristocracy opposed the revolt and those who did support the cause were not representative of 'their class' (p. 527). Given the uniqueness of the situation in Judaea and, at the same time, the lack of distinctiveness in terms of how the Romans treated the Jews in comparison to other provinces, Brunt accepts that a 'peculiar factor' must have existed in Judaea (p. 528). Here Brunt departs from his earlier approach by arguing that the Jewish religion provides the missing link. Religion was 'the key' that enabled the oppressed populace of Judaea to unite against Rome and the Jewish aristocracy in the revolt (p. 531). The memory of Maccabaean rulers, in particular, the 'independence' attained under their rule and a belief that God would come to their aid, encouraged the Jews to take up arms against the Romans. Although Brunt does not address the issue of inevitability, an implication of the approach taken is that because Jewish religion was the fundamental cause, conflict between Rome and Judaea could not be avoided if Rome continued to

29. P.A. Brunt, *Roman Imperial Themes* (Oxford: Oxford University Press, 1990).

employ direct rule in the province. The specific timing, although not explicitly stated, appears to be determined by such factors as the incompetence of Florus. At the base was the ever present social conflict between the pro-Roman Jewish aristocracy and the anti-Roman Jewish populace (p. 531).

The second author to consider is Bilde, in his article 'The Causes of the Jewish War According to Josephus'.[30] Bilde's approach to the topic is unique. He focuses specifically on identifying Josephus's attempt to explain the revolt rather than providing a modern scholarly interpretation of why the revolt began. Bilde argues that Josephus was 'absorbed' by a concern to explain the revolt, not only in *War* but also in *Ant.* (p. 197). Despite some varying emphases, *War* and *Ant.* present a united approach. By implication, although writing after the revolt, the events of 66–70 CE dominated Josephus's thinking—he was engaged in a 'crusade' to make sense of what had happened.

Bilde argues that Josephus explains the revolt on three different levels: the 'immediate releasing causes'; the 'more fundamental causes'; and the 'abstract level'. The first level, the 'immediate releasing causes', and the associated accelerating process were events connected with the year 66 CE. The dispute in Caesarea, the response of Florus—particularly his demand for funds from the temple and the cessation of the daily sacrifice—were the various 'immediate releasing causes' for the revolt (pp. 184-85). They were the specific events that explain the timing of the revolt. That these events developed into a full-blown rebellion when they did are explained by an accelerating process, which included the murder of the Roman garrison at Jerusalem and the defeat of the legate Cestius (p. 186).

The 'more fundamental causes' explain why the 'immediate releasing causes' and accelerating process were able to become a revolt. Here Bilde argues that Josephus establishes a context for the revolt. Bilde identifies five 'fundamental causes' within Josephus's narrative. They are: the activities of the Jewish war 'party', the fourth philosophy; the Roman administration; a combination of these first two factors; the Jewish–Greek conflicts; and internal division among the Jews (pp. 187-90). Rogue Jews in the form of the fourth philosophy actively promoted the cause of rebellion, bringing disruption and conflict wherever possible. The ineffectiveness and, in some cases,

30. P. Bilde, 'The Causes of the Jewish War According to Josephus', *JSJ* 10 (1979), pp. 179-202.

deliberate provocation of Roman administrators also created an environment ripe for revolt. For Josephus, under the governorship of Albinus these two factors combined—government and rogue Jews together pushed the people towards revolt (p. 188). Further constant factors were the conflicts between Jewish and Greek residents in Judaea and civil strife among the Jews. The trouble in Caesarea during 66 CE merely echoed a long-standing hatred between the Jewish and Greek residents in the city (p. 190). Added to this constant tension was the increasing level of internal division within the Jewish population. This conflict, which reached its zenith during the revolt, was evident between classes and within class groups prior to the revolt (p. 191). These explanations made the revolt a predictable event, with conditions integral to the existence of first-century CE Judaea pointing to an explosion at some point in time.

A sense in which the revolt is inevitable, according to Bilde's view of Josephus's interpretation, is obvious in the third level of explanation—the 'abstract level'. Here Josephus places the 'immediate' and 'more fundamental causes' in a cosmic context, a theological explanation for how the Jews would suffer defeat, especially the loss of the temple. The civil strife, the transgressions of the rebels, the populace and the aristocracy should all be viewed as actions that required a response from God (p. 193). The defeat of the Jews and the destruction of the temple became that response. They were, therefore, God's punishment of Israel. The lack of unity within the Jewish community and the various transgressions of the law, although explainable in human terms, were of more profound significance (pp. 196, 198). They were part of the divine will; they were an expression of God's plan (p. 199). Here Josephus has removed the events from human control. What took place was inevitable, and it had to be accepted and incorporated in the psyche of post-70 CE existence. Although Bilde does not try to suggest that any particular level is given precedence by Josephus in a consistent manner, his interpretation does impart to Josephus a desire to explain what had happened in Jewish terms (pp. 201-202). Furthermore, this was done in a deliberate manner in a belief that what occurred was not entirely 'out of the blue'.

The third example is Rappaport's explanation of the revolt in 'Jewish-Pagan Relations and the Revolt Against Rome in 66–70 CE'.[31]

31. U. Rappaport, 'Jewish–Pagan Relations and the Revolt Against Rome in 66–70 CE', in L.I. Levine (ed.), *The Jerusalem Cathedra: Studies in the History,*

Rappaport boldly asserts that the revolt was inevitable; all that needs
to be determined is the exact basis by which this was the case (p. 81).
In this context, Rappaport declares his intention is to argue that there
is one fundamental cause: namely, the conflict between Jews and
Greeks residing in Judaea. Surveying the various opinions regarding
the origin of the revolt, Rappaport claims that they assume there was a
complex chain of events which worked together over an extended
period of time (p. 81). The debate is simply over an attempt to
'distinguish between the primary and secondary factors'. Rappaport,
however, begins from the premise that even among the so-called primary causes a distinction can, and should, be made. For Rappaport, all
but one factor could be resolved in a manner that would not end in
revolt (p. 84). Therefore, the only factor that made 'the rebellion
inevitable' was the ongoing conflict between the Jews and Greeks in
Judaea.

Rappaport acknowledges that the so-called primary causes were
important. The 'desire for national freedom', which was closely bound
up with Jewish religious sentiment, particularly the focus on messianism, agrarian conflict and the inadequacy of the Roman provincial
government, were all causes of instability (pp. 82-83). These factors,
however, could not individually or in combination result in revolt
(p. 85). The Jews had 'tasted political freedom' under the Hasmonaeans
and opposition to foreign rule was presumably an important element
in the agenda of such groups as the fourth philosophy (p. 82). The
national and religious motives, however, had to be nurtured by other
components. Rappaport also acknowledges one such contributing
factor could be the growing level of 'agrarian conflict'. The concen-
tration of land ownership in the hands of an ever dwindling group
caused 'tremendous social changes' and the landless populace became
'easy prey' for those 'proclaiming justice' through a messianic
kingdom (p. 83). To these circumstances could be added corruption and
incompetence on the part of the Roman procurators. Many examples of
occasions where the governors offended 'Jewish sensibilities' can be
cited. All these factors, however, were at best 'contributory factors'.
The Jews were not alone in suffering from poor government and they
could bear this irritation (p. 84). In a similar manner they could show
restraint regarding the thwarting of their desire for independence, and

Archaeology, Geography and Ethnography of the Land of Israel (Jerusalem: Yad
Izhak Ben Zvi Institute, 1981), I, pp. 81-95.

their religious tradition could adopt to foreign rule (p. 84). The various agrarian changes could also be controlled and the effects contained. Furthermore, in times of oppression and distress, messianic expectation could act as a potent catalyst but not as 'a primary cause' of revolt (p. 84). All these factors 'were not by themselves the source of the revolt; they did not institute an insoluble problem for both the Roman government and the local Jewish leadership' (p. 85).

From such an apparent dead end Rappaport turns to what he argues should be viewed as the factor of inevitability. Jewish–pagan relations in Judaea was the 'issue, apparently that confronted Rome with a dilemma it could not resolve; hence the "inevitability" of the revolt' (p. 84). These relations were a 'constant source of tension', which meant the Jews could not 'reconcile themselves to Roman rule'. Rappaport outlines the nature of Jewish–pagan contact in Judaea, through the Hasmonaean period and into the first century CE. Rome, through Herod, and then during the period of direct rule, tried to maintain an 'equilibrium', protecting both Jews and Greeks. Such an approach, however, was not feasible. According to Rappaport, 'the problem underlying this situation [Roman desire for co-existence] was that Jews and pagans lived side by side amidst the fraction and animosity of their struggle for existence and their mutual refusal to recognize the rights of the other side' (p. 91). Although Rome tried to maintain peace, increasingly the governors were drawn into supporting the pagans in the various ethnic conflicts that broke out. The revolt was waiting to happen, the territory was a time bomb. In this context of confrontation the 'nationalist feeling, religious sensibility and messianic fervour' simply intensified the seriousness of the situation (p. 93). Therefore, for Rappaport, it is no accident that it was a dispute in Caesarea between the Jews and pagans that instigated the revolt and that the most intense fighting of 66 CE was between pagans and Jews in cities throughout the region.[32]

The final contribution to consider on the debate regarding the revolt

---

32. Kasher, *Jews and Hellenistic Cities*, p. 315, also highlights the conflict between Jews and Greeks as making the revolt inevitable. D. Mendels, *The Rise and Fall of Jewish Nationalism* (ABRL; New York: Doubleday, 1992) promotes the idea of conflict between the Jews and Greeks as being inevitable because of a clash of ideologies (pp. 7-8, 23, 194). In terms of explaining the revolt, however, Mendels lays emphasis on the idea that the loss of the temple as a national symbol after 44 CE was the crucial factor (pp. 251-52, 280, 302, 356).

is Goodman's *The Ruling Class of Judaea.*[33] Goodman's central thesis is that the revolt took place because the group who functioned as the ruling class in Judaea during the first century CE failed to act as effective rulers. They were not a 'natural elite' and they were unable to find acceptance among the Jewish community as a whole. As their own internal bickering intensified in the 50s CE so too did the 'fact' that the ruling class was not 'equipped with the local prestige' necessary to govern. The 'ambitions and divisions of the Judaean ruling class thus brought war onto their country'. By implication the revolt was inevitable. The system failed because one of the key components of the administration, the local ruling class, was incapable of fulfilling its function.

Goodman begins by acknowledging the range of explanations for the revolt offered by scholarship. Five explanations are outlined: 'the incompetence of the Roman governors'; 'the oppressiveness of Roman rule'; 'Jewish religious susceptibilities'; 'class tensions'; and 'quarrels with local gentiles' (pp. 5-14). Although these factors may be viewed as making the revolt 'seem inevitable', he does not believe they 'inevitably led to revolt against Rome' (p. 14). Nor does Goodman accept that 'an amalgam of all these causes was responsible' for the revolt in itself (p. 19). Instead, he argues that it is a cause not overtly identified by Josephus in his narrative that acts as the fundamental cause. The 'power struggle within the Jewish ruling class', to which Josephus only makes passing reference, acts as 'a crucial link'.

The ruling class of Judaea that emerged in 6 CE failed to provide the effective type of leadership required to keep the peace in the province. Rome followed its normal practice, identifying a wealthy elite in whom responsibility for helping maintain order would be delegated. It was an elite, however, that did not have the support of the local population. The eventual outbreak of the revolt was, according to Goodman, evident even in 6 CE (p. 23). The removal of Joazar from the high priesthood was an early sign of the impending failure. The census was completed but the high priest was hated to such an extent because of

---

33. M. Goodman, *The Ruling Class of Judaea: The Origins of the Jewish Revolt Against Rome AD 66–70* (Cambridge: Cambridge University Press, 1987). See also M. Goodman, 'The First Jewish Revolt: Social Conflict and the Problem of Debt', *JJS* 33 (1982), pp. 417-27, where the general socio-economic context in Judaea is presented as one in which an uneven distribution of money is a dominant background factor.

his involvement in the process that he had to be replaced. At no stage could the ruling class prove they had the appropriate credentials to the community (p. 124). By implication, what happened in 66 CE was the direct result of decisions taken at the beginning of the first century CE. In fact, the 'leadership [of the ruling class] turned popular discontent into full-scale revolt against Rome' (p. 231). The reality of this situation was acknowledged by the Romans in the actions they took after the revolt, the destruction of the Judaean ruling class (pp. 233-35).

The exact timing of the revolt can be also primarily associated with the activities of the ruling class. Judaea had been beset with many problems throughout the first century CE, such as the social ramifications of the various economic changes and those due to matters of 'religious ideology' (pp. 51-108). It was, therefore, 'almost inevitable' that the ruling class would fail once the community was confronted with a major 'crisis' (p. 50). Such a crisis took place in 66 CE and the end result was the revolt. The events associated with Florus's visit to Jerusalem, in particular, and the activities of Eleazar b. Ananias and the other aristocrats, were the catalyst for the trouble that had been built into the system in 6 CE. Factions within the ruling class developed in the 50s, with rival groups actively trying to assert prominence. This internal division—in part, a reflection of the failure of the ruling class to win popular support from the outset—eventually became such a 'public' battle that it explained why the revolt began in 66 CE (pp. 137-51). One faction, led by Eleazar b. Ananias, made a bold bid to win popular support by ceasing to offer sacrifices on behalf of foreigners (p. 154). Here the revolt comes as the final scene in a 'tragedy': 'the ambitions and divisions of the Judaean ruling class then brought war into their country' (p. 231).[34]

Those studies specifically devoted to explaining the cause(s) of the

34. In his review of Sanders, *Judaism*, M. Goodman states that he had exaggerated the extent to which the ruling class were rejected by the remainder of the Jewish community in *The Ruling Class* (*SJT* 47 [1994], p. 91). For other approaches to the Jewish revolt see S. Applebaum, 'Josephus and the Economic Causes of the Jewish War', in L.H. Feldman and G. Hata (eds.), *Josephus, the Bible and History* (Detroit: Wayne State University Press, 1989), pp. 237-64, and H. Kreissig, 'A Marxist View of Josephus' Account of the Jewish War', in L.H. Feldman and G. Hata (eds.), *Josephus, the Bible and History* (Detroit: Wayne State University Press, 1989), pp. 265-77.

revolt display a diversity in the solutions offered. This apparent diversity is, however, merely a mask under which there exists a uniformly held premise. The revolt is explained in terms of long-standing causes that impact upon the key fabric of the functioning of Jewish society. Whether it be the nature of Jewish–pagan relations, the inability of the 'ruling class' to offer effective leadership, or a class conflict fuelled by religious sentiment, they all have their origins well before 66 CE. Hence what is held in common between the approaches of such scholars as Brunt and Goodman far outweighs the apparent conflict in how to understand the role of the 'ruling class'. The timing of the revolt may lie in the events of 66 CE but the revolt as an event was a forgone conclusion, a scene waiting for the play to unfold.

2.2 *The Popular Movements*

A prominent issue in contemporary scholarship is the debate regarding the possible existence of one or more groups who opposed the Roman administrative structure. While much of the discussion has centred around the theory of the zealot party, several scholars do incorporate a consideration of the situation in Judaea. It is from this group that the following three examples are drawn.

Probably the most important exponent of the case for the existence of an organized resistance party is Hengel's *The Zealots*. According to Hengel, 63 BCE–135 CE is an era marked by the struggle of the Jews to establish religious and political freedom (p. 1). Hengel believes that Josephus has only partially described this movement. The main focus of the study, therefore, is to outline the central role played by the revolutionary movement in the cause of freedom, providing a history of the movement and identifying the religious principles that lay at its core (pp. xiv-xv, 16). In the context of explaining the history of the zealots Hengel makes several comments regarding the state of affairs in Judaea, especially why the war of 66–70 occurred.[35]

The zealots, the revolutionary party founded by Judas in 6 CE, were dedicated to the goal of establishing the rule of God in Judaea by force (p. 143). In other words, the zealots continually worked towards the objective of starting a war. They came close to achieving their aim in the dispute over the statue of Gaius and the dispute between the Galilaeans and Samaritans during the procuratorship of Cumanus

---

35. Although Hengel believes the struggle for freedom continues until 135 CE his survey of the zealot movement concludes with 70 CE.

(p. 384). The machinations of the zealots alone, however, was not enough to bring about war. According to Hengel, the revolt only became a reality when the majority of the populace had decided to adopt the ideas of the zealots (p. 266). The revolt, therefore, became a fight to remove Roman rule and establish the sole rule of God.

The process that culminated with the revolt was set in place in 6 CE when Judas provided an effective structure for the desire for freedom. He created an organization which included a dynastic form of leadership (p. 86). This revolutionary movement was eventually able to marshall the popular opposition to Roman rule after the situation in Judaea gradually deteriorated (pp. 351, 358). The Jewish upper class was unable to prevent the war, in part because of the maladministration of the procurators (p. 283). In this context, the period from 44 CE onwards is highlighted as a 'steady gravitation in the direction of an insurrection of the Jewish people in 66 AD' (p. 343). The order of Fadus that the high priest's robes be handed over to Roman control marked the beginning of a continual series of complaints against Roman rule (p. 345). Eventually the situation became so grave that Albinus ceased trying to control and contain the activities of the zealots (pp. 384-85). For Hengel, 66 CE acts as an inevitable climax to a long process which had begun with the dream of Judas in 6 CE.[36]

Rhoads's *Israel in Revolution* seeks to explore the history of the revolutionary group(s) in Judaea during the period 6–74 CE. A particular concern for Rhoads is to establish the nature of the link between those who actively called for armed resistance to Roman rule and the revolt of 66–74 CE (p. 1). In this context, Rhoads makes several references to the state of affairs.

In principle, Roman rule was not a cause for protest. For some, Roman control was tolerated, and for others it may have provided the opportunity for greater involvement in government than had been possible under Herodian rule (pp. 28-31). What happens in Judaea is that there is a gradual deterioration in the situation, a progression from law and order to disorder (p. 47). This process, however, was not constant. In fact, in the period prior to 44 CE the few protests undertaken by the Jews are spontaneous outbreaks against perceived injustices (pp. 63-64). Given the claim of Josephus (*Ant.* 18.8-10)

---

36. According to Hengel, *Zealots*, the 'tragedy' was that as soon as the war began the zealot movement lost its sense of unity and it splintered after the death of Menahem (p. 404).

Rhoads finds it striking that there is an absence of any revolutionary activity in the period between 6–41 CE (p. 59).[37] Furthermore, Rhoads can identify only one example of brigandage in this period, the threat of what would happen if the strike over the statue of Gaius was to continue (p. 64).

The picture of Roman rule being tolerated is reinforced by the lack of protest associated with the reintroduction of direct rule in 44 CE. According to Rhoads, it is not until the term of Cumanus that the situation changed. In particular, the dispute between the Galilaeans and Samaritans in 51 CE acted as the turning point (p. 72). The failure and incompetence of Cumanus marked the beginning of the breakdown in order. With Felix, Albinus and then Florus the situation further deteriorated (pp. 73-77). Brigandage became common, even if it was localized and lacked a united front. Various economic, social, political and religious factors also combined to encourage the call for armed resistance to Roman rule (pp. 80-84).

In a sense, the outbreak of war became an inevitable consequence of the breakdown of law and order that marked the 50s and early 60s. According to Rhoads, 'the tide was turned in favour of open rebellion against Rome. It is difficult to know what might have been able to remove that tide, for our analysis shows that some form or another of resistance against the Romans came to characterise almost every segment of Jewish society' (p. 92).[38]

Horsley and Hanson's *Bandits, Prophets, and Messiahs* seeks to present a comprehensive account of the various movements and leaders among the populace and their interaction with the established social system.[39] They begin by declaring that the 'zealot theory' is not historically accurate. Instead of lumping all possible peasant, popular protests under

37. Contrary to Hengel, *Zealots*, Rhoads, *Israel*, pp. 54-58, does not accept that Judas founded a single, organized revolutionary sect that was actively engaged in armed resistance to Roman rule. At best, there is a genealogical and ideological link between Judas and *one* group that was active from the late 40s onwards—the sicarii (p. 55).

38. Even in the war, however, it is not appropriate to view the cause of resistance as being controlled by a single revolutionary sect (p. 96). Prior to the revolt one group, the sicarii, appears to have been active but during the revolt it was several different groups that had a prominent role in the fight against the Romans (p. 97).

39. R.A. Horsley and J.S. Hanson, *Bandits, Prophets, and Messiahs: Popular Movements at the Time of Jesus* (New Voices in Biblical Studies; Minneapolis: Winston Press, 1985; repr. San Francisco: Harper & Row, 1988). Horsley has also

the banner of 'the zealots', it is important to explore the diversity of these groups.[40] They attempt to give voice to the peasantry of Judaea, people who did not leave a literary record of their activities and attitudes.

As a backdrop to defining the different groups, Horsley and Hanson provide a brief outline of the historical situation. The first century CE is presented as a period that is noted for being framed by major peasant uprisings in 4 BCE, 66–60 CE and then 132–135 CE.[41] In fact 'the whole period of direct Roman rule from 6 to 66 CE was marked by widespread discontent and periodic turbulence in Palestinian Jewish society' (p. 35). Furthermore, it is possible to sketch this popular discontent in a series of peasant-based protests against the Roman governors and priestly aristocracy. Although the Romans tried to avoid interfering with Jewish religious traditions 'as was virtually inevitable in a situation of imperial domination (occupying troops, intercultural misunderstandings, etc.), they blundered into occasional provocations that further inflamed the situation' (p. 35). In effect, the system of government not only failed to maintain peace and order it actively brought about conflict.

The protests and appeals of the peasantry were rarely heeded by the Roman officials 'until the cycle escalated into the great revolt of 66'. Some protests were spontaneous, while others were deliberate. Pilate and Gaius are cited as examples of Romans provoking trouble (pp. 38-40). It is with Cumanus, however, that the 'governors became increasingly callous and intransigent' (p. 41). For Horsley and Hanson the escalation towards revolt was also accentuated by the priestly aristocracy and Herodians. They were 'engaged in mutually beneficial collaboration with the Roman imperial system', to which they added their own internal rivalry (p. 42). As a result, when the war began in 66 CE it was a peasant revolt, fuelled by apocalyptic hopes. The climax was

---

written numerous articles associated with the various so-called popular movements active in the first century CE.

40. The different categories identified include social banditry, royal pretenders, messianic figures, prophets, the sicarii and zealots. See R.A. Horsley, 'The Zealots: Their Origin, Relationships and Importance in the Jewish Revolt', *NovT* 28 (1986), pp. 159-92, for a detailed discussion of how Horsley suggests that the zealots should be understood.

41. Although brief reference is made to 132–135 CE (p. 45), the historical overview commences with the Exodus and concludes with the 66–70 CE revolt.

prompted by the 'devious Florus, who dared, even forced, the Jewish people into outright rebellion, [so that] the people continued to appeal and protest their condition and treatment, while their ostensible leaders, high priests and nobility alike, sat idly by or collaborated in their oppression' (pp. 42-43). The system of government failed; the leaders, Jewish and Roman, did not work with the peasantry. The various protests by such popular movements as bandits, prophets, royal pretenders, sicarii and messianic figures had gone unheeded.[42]

Obvious differences exist regarding the identification, number and agenda of the groups that express opposition in the opinion of Hengel, Rhoads, and Horsley and Hanson. There is also, however, a significant level of underlying unity. They all employ the same basic chronological boundaries, focusing on the period between the introduction of direct Roman rule and the suppression of the first revolt. Furthermore, they all accept and promote the notion of Judaea as a place embroiled in turmoil and conflict. Hengel gives centre stage to the zealots as active promoters of trouble.[43] Although Rhoads and Horsley and Hanson reject the notion of a single group and portray most of the various popular movements as non-violent protest groups, they do accept that these groups were active in a climate of conflict and oppression. Furthermore, the level of turmoil is viewed by the three texts as escalating during the period leading up to the revolt.

2.3 *Historical Jesus and Early Christianity*
Two monographs and one article that express the concern to establish the historical context in which Christianity emerged will be discussed. Common to the three examples is that whether the agenda is dictated by a desire to identify the 'character' of Jewish society or the nature of how the 'historical' Jesus interacted with various groups in Judaea,

42. D.R. Schwartz, 'Temple and Desert: On Religion and State in Second Temple Period Judaea', in D.R. Schwartz, *Studies in the Jewish Background of Christianity* (WUNT, 60; Tübingen: J.C.B. Mohr [Paul Siebeck], 1992), pp. 29-43, provides a variation on the discussion of the popular movements and the state of affairs. Schwartz indicates that conflict between Jews and Romans was inevitable (p. 42) because of the way such groups as the zealots and desert prophets interpreted the function of the temple.

43. V. Nikiprowetzky, 'Josephus and the Revolutionary Parties', in L.H. Feldman and G. Hata (eds.), *Josephus, the Bible and History* (Detroit: Wayne State University Press, 1989), pp. 216-36, also portrays the shared 'mentality' of the various revolutionaries as explaining their continual effort to promote conflict.

reference is made to the situation in Judaea during the first century CE. More often than not this is undertaken in terms of trying to reconstruct a picture of the distinctive features of the state of affairs.

Barnett briefly outlines the political situation in Judaea during the years 6–73 CE.[44] The impetus for this survey was a desire to ensure that Brandon's 'false' presentation of 6–73 CE be corrected.[45] According to Barnett, Brandon's portrayal of the entire period as 'politically unstable and revolutionary in character' is wrong. Barnett argues that there is a clear division in the first century. 44–66 CE can be characterized as a period of 'revolutionary' activity while the earlier period, 6–44 CE, was basically free from 'revolutionary' activity (p. 564).

According to Barnett, 'by the sixties' Judaean affairs were chaotic and an intensely revolutionary spirit was evident' (p. 566). Many examples of disorder can be identified from the narrative of Josephus. Among the Jews there are a number of named revolutionaries, such as Eleazar b. Deinaeus, the sons of Judas the Galilaean, the development of the sicarii, and the prophetic movement (p. 564). To this climate was added the actions of Agrippa II, who was, with his 'evident paganism and philo-Romanism', possibly motivated by 'malice or greed' in his appointment of the high priests (p. 565). Furthermore, factionalism between the wealthy high priests and the poorer priests brought trouble. Into this potent cocktail was also placed the incompetence of the governors, especially as displayed by Felix and Florus. In combination, these factors ensured that 44–66 CE was a period 'of escalating revolution and violence' (p. 566).

In stark contrast, 6–44 CE was a time of relative stability. There are very few examples of 'disorder'. After the initial uprising against the census, the next recorded disturbance takes place in 26 CE with the arrival of Pilate. Although 'potentially revolutionary' the early period is characterized by stability. Barnett highlights the link between Pilate and Sejanus as the cause of the trouble in Judaea (p. 568). With the fall of Sejanus and then the removal of Pilate the potential for trouble dissipated. The third 'disturbance' discussed by Barnett is the order of Gaius in 40 CE. The non-violent protest by the Jews is taken to be evidence of 'how relatively stable were the public affairs of Judaea at that

44. P.W. Barnett, 'Under Tiberius All Was Quiet', *NTS* 21 (1974–75), pp. 564-71.

45. Barnett's concern to counter Brandon's arguments (*Jesus*) is shared by others. See, for example, E. Bammel and C.F.D. Moule (eds.), *Jesus and the Politics of his Day* (Cambridge: Cambridge University Press, 1984).

time' (p. 569). According to Barnett, much of this stability is the direct result of the attitude of Augustus and Tiberius in Rome and the dominance of the family of Ananus in Jerusalem, which 'must have consistently displayed the ability to keep the peace in Judaea' (p. 569). Although the potential for trouble existed in the early period, good government helped ensure that it was a period of relative quiet (Tacitus, *Hist.* 9) (p. 571). The difference between 6–44 and 44–66 CE, according to Barnett, was the ability of the administrators, from emperors down to the high priest, to determine whether peace or disorder would prevail. By implication, therefore, it would appear that conflict between Judaea and Rome was not a forgone conclusion.

The second example to consider is Horsley's *Jesus and the Spiral of Violence*.[46] Drawing on a sociological methodology, Horsley explores the character of Jesus' ministry and the society in which he operated, especially in terms of the notion of 'violence'. Horsley begins by identifying the need to explain the nature of Jesus' ministry in a context devoid of a long-standing scholarly 'myth'—a picture of Jewish society in which there was a single zealot group active from 6 CE that advocated armed violent resistance (p. x). It is not a case of being able to contrast Jesus, as a non-violent teacher, against the politically active and violent zealots. With the removal of the zealot paradigm Horsley also claims that it is 'necessary to re-examine the view that Jewish Palestine was a hotbed of violent resistance during the time of Jesus' (p. xi). With such an agenda it is not surprising that Horsley devotes a significant proportion of his study to describing the situation in Judaea and identifying the political machinations of the first century CE.

Horsley establishes the model by which the period should be understood, what he labels the spiral of violence. There are four stages in this spiral (pp. 24-25).[47] They are: structural violence; protest and resistance; repression; and revolt. According to Horsley the relationship between the four stages is not always linear, nor clear cut, as there may often be an overlap in the spiral.

Fundamental to the spiral is a recognition that the Jews lived within

46. R.A. Horsley, *Jesus and the Spiral of Violence: Popular Jewish Resistance in Roman Palestine* (San Francisco: Harper & Row, 1987).

47. The model, the spiral of violence, is adopted by one developed in the 1960s by Dom Helder Camara with three stages (1: injustice; 2: revolt; 3: force used to re-establish public order). See Horsley, *Spiral*, pp. 22-24, who refers to H. Camara, *Spiral of Violence* (London: Sheed and Ward, 1971), pp. 29-31.

an imperial system of government. For Horsley this system created a particular environment in which 'we must consider the antagonism and conflicts resulting from the prolonged forcible subjugation of a proud people by the dominant imperial regimes' (p. 4). In turn, this fostered a situation where the Jewish community found themselves 'almost continually in circumstances of crisis'. Horsley cites 168–167 BCE, 66–70 CE and 132–135 CE as key markers of the 'crisis', to which could be added 'continuing tensions and conflicts'. Crucial to the functioning of the imperial system were the local elite and their various channels of authority which then became 'compromised by collaborating with the imperial regime' (p. 17). Hence in Judaea the priestly aristocracy and the temple became symbols of oppression rather than Jewish symbols.[48] Rather than stability, Judaea was beset by 'terrorism and conflict' while under this Roman imperial rule.

Horsley locates various events within their appropriate stage of the spiral. Among the expressions of structural violence, Horsley cites the demands placed on the peasantry, in particular, the priestly tithes and temple dues (p. 30). For Horsley, the temple was at the very centre of the repressive, unjust system. Examples of the second stage—protest and resistance—are dotted throughout the first century CE. The majority of these protests are in the form of non-violent action and various renewal movements. Examples of violent protest are rare. Horsley lists the social banditry as an expression of resistance against various injustices, attempts to 'right wrongs' (pp. 33-39). The popular prophetic movements tried to realize their 'fantasy of liberation' but the only protest group which was 'politically conscious and violent in form' was the sicarii (p. 39). The main target was the high priestly aristocracy (p. 40). According to Horsley, the decision of the sicarii to take violent action reflects the extent to which the situation had deteriorated after 44 CE. In turn all these expressions of protest helped invoke the third stage—repression by the officials. With a few exceptions, the Jewish protests were greeted with a 'brutal military response' (p. 46). A more subtle form of repression was the Roman tolerance of Jewish 'traditional rites and beliefs'. This tolerance, however, 'was repressive in its effect'. What had been 'comprehensive or total (social—economic—political—religious) in its scope and operation'

48. For a detailed discussion of Horsley's view regarding the role of the high priests and aristocracy in bringing about conflict see R.A. Horsley, 'High Priests and the Politics of Roman Palestine', *JSJ* 17 (1986), pp. 23-55 (23, 49-53).

was forced to become spiritual and internal. Cultic celebrations were allowed as long as there were no political overtones. The temple and the cult, therefore, became agents not only of institutional injustice but also of repression (p. 45).

Of the fourth stage—the revolt—Horsley cites three examples, 4 BCE, 66–70 CE and 132–135 CE. The 66–70 CE revolt was 'deeply rooted in the long-range spiral of oppression, resistance and repression' (p. 54). At the same time, it was the result of 'an intensified spiral of violence in the immediately preceding months or years' through the governorship of Florus and the failings of the high priestly aristocracy (p. 54). In other words, there were two spirals in operation at the same time—66 CE—within a spiral that consumed the first century CE as a whole and a smaller spiral set in motion in the years just prior to the revolt. As a result, although the actual timing of the war may have been a matter of chance, the likelihood of war between Jews and Rome was a consequence of the system of government.

Horsley further explores the state of affairs in his examination of particular elements of the imperial situation as it functioned in Judaea. Horsley is especially interested in various examples of protest, whether it be popular or intellectual in origin, and in the possible significance of apocalyptic aspirations as a motivating force for the protests. The majority of the protests are viewed as being popular demonstrations, not led by the priestly aristocracy or the intellectuals. They were non-violent peasant protests that were not always simply spontaneous attempts to defend the ancestral laws of the Jews but deliberate, controlled anti-Roman demonstrations (p. 117). This is particularly the case prior to 41 CE, to the extent that Horsley claims we 'can put behind us the picture of Jewish society at the time of Jesus as a hotbed of violent rebellion' (p. 116). It is only with the sicarii that the normal channel of activity becomes physical violence. Prior to the sicarii all other protests were 'fundamentally non-violent'.

Horsley views the response of the Jews to the imperial system as 'pivotal' in determining what happened in Judaea. The response—popular, non-violent protest—was undertaken by a 'people who still remembered and celebrated their ancestors' liberation from Pharaoh's bondage' (p. 120). For Horsley, the memory of the Exodus event was all the more pertinent because apocalyptic vision provided a contemporary means of viewing the present as the setting for 'God's imminent redemptive action' (p. 144). The distinctive edge of the protest came from the hope associated with apocalyptic vision; the 'creative envisionary' of the future, making direct action against the 'imperial situation' not only legitimate but appropriate (p. 145). It was a society embroiled in an unfolding spiral of violence.

The third and final study in relation to early Christianity is Crossan's *The Historical Jesus*.[49] Crossan's reconstruction is based on a tripartite approach that seeks to locate Jesus in first-century CE Judaea, within the larger context of the Mediterranean world and—on an even broader scale—socio-cultural theoretical structures. As part of this approach Crossan's comments regarding the situation in Judaea are dispersed throughout his work rather than confined to one or two specific sections.[50] Much of what Crossan outlines is in close agreement with the situation as presented by Horsley. Judaea was a province bound up in an imperial situation in which the peasantry encountered oppression in most aspects of daily existence (p. 100). For Crossan, the Roman 'peace' was based on this oppression—the exploitation of the provinces.[51] The spiral of violence is also adapted as the appropriate model for understanding the dynamic of relations between the Jews, as subject people, and the Romans, as imperial overlords. The initiative lies primarily with the Romans, who instigate the spiral through the institutional structural violence. The spiral was in operation in the early part of the first century CE, but not to the point of verging on the third- or, more particularly, fourth-stage, revolt.[52] Crossan views the first century CE primarily as a period of social unrest, in which the peasantry engaged in various protests as reactions to imperial rule. Much of the task for scholarship is to map out accurately the 'evidence of social unrest' expressed by a section of society that left little or no literary account of their activity (p. 100).

Crossan argues that the majority of protests, such as the popular millennial prophets, were peasant movements of a non-violent nature (p. 161). It was only the 'bandits', in their various forms, who used

49. J.D. Crossan, *The Historical Jesus: The Life of a Mediterranean Peasant* (San Francisco: Harper & Row, 1991).

50. For example, see Crossan, *Historical Jesus*, Chapters 2, 5, 8, 9 and 10.

51. Crossan claims that Tacitus's statement 'all was quiet' (*Hist.* 9) must be understood as expressing a Roman perspective on the situation. What Tacitus actually meant was that there was no trouble in Judaea which required the intervention of the Syrian legate (pp. 101-102).

52. Crossan, *Historical Jesus*, pp. 124-25, refers to Horsley, *Spiral*, pp. 24-26.

physical violence (p. 168). Even here, these were protests, responses to an initiative from the imperial system via the Roman governors or the local ruling class centred around the temple. For example, Judas the Galilaean was simply responding to the census, which was an expression of institutional violence (p. 116). The actual protest was insignificant and although it may be possible to draw an 'ideological/genealogical continuity' between Judas and such figures as Menahem, Josephus is incorrect to view Judas as instituting a sect that was actively opposed to Roman rule (pp. 115, 123). For Crossan, the various protests were disparate in nature. Any pattern or consistency that can be identified is simply because the spiral allows various incidents to be grouped according to specific categories.[53]

The trajectories of protesters, prophets, bandits and messiahs evident throughout the first century CE 'all come to a first climax in the mid sixties CE' (pp. 207, 218). Drawing on Gurr's terminology, Palestine moved from a country of 'turmoil' to one of 'conspiracy' in the mid-50s CE with the terrorist activity of the sicarii and then to 'internal war' by 65 CE.[54] The entire first century was a canvas filled with popular turmoil. The revolt—the final stage of the spiral—was the culmination of the 'decremental deprivation' of the peasantry as indicated by the 'massive peasant involvement' in the fighting. Crossan believes that the key to explaining the revolt was the increased financial burden, particularly through the use of the prosbul form of loan, which made the situation under Roman rule worse than under any previous foreign rule (pp. 222-23). Crossan is careful to avoid claiming that the revolt of 66–70 CE was inevitable, 'as if one had to move from one level of unrest inexorably to the next'. However, he does go on to accept that the 'events of 66 CE cast their shadow back over the entire preceding century' (p. 218). Furthermore, Crossan believes that the conditions for revolt already existed in 4 BCE and 52 CE (p. 184). The difference between 66 CE and these two previous occasions was the relative competence of the legate to control the situation. Apparently, if Varus was as 'inept' as Cestius, then 4 BCE may have been the occasion of the first revolt (p. 218).

The characterization of Judaea among the studies devoted specifically to the origins of Christianity and the historical figure of

53. See, for example, Crossan, *Historical Jesus*, Chapters 7 and 9.
54. Crossan, *Historical Jesus*, pp. 218-20, refers to T.R. Gurr, *Why Men Rebel* (Princeton, NJ: Princeton University Press, 1970).

Jesus share a concern to counter existing paradigms. Barnett rejects Brandon's portrait of how the first century CE should be understood, while Horsley commences from the perspective of dismissing the view that 'zealots' were a definable, active, militant opposition to Roman rule from 6 to 73 CE. Working within these confines, a significant degree of unity is evident in the picture of Judaea that is developed. Turmoil and tension are the common denominators of the entire first century CE, which is defined as the years up to the first revolt. The distinctive features are in terms of the detail of the reconstruction. Barnett believes that the period prior to 44 CE was relatively stable but does accept that the potential for trouble was always present. For Horsley and Crossan the turmoil was nuanced. On occasions it was violent, especially when originating from the Romans, but more often than not the Jewish protest should be recognized as non-violent actions with a popular leadership.

The question of why the revolt occurred is not directly addressed by Barnett. The other examples, Horsley and Crossan, present a view of Judaea that carries the expectation that open, armed conflict would occur at some point in time. If anything, this view is built into the mechanism for understanding the situation in Judaea, the spiral model. In effect, war was an inevitable consequence of the administrative system.

2.4 *Galilee*

Within the increasing interest regarding the history of Galilee there are two examples pertinent to this survey. The first is Freyne's *Galilee*.[55] Concerned to explore the nature of Galilaean Judaism, Freyne's study provides a detailed discussion of the political, social and religious aspects of life in the region. As part of this survey Freyne makes brief reference to the state of affairs in the geographical regions of Galilee and Judaea.

It is accepted that Judaea was burdened by a general breakdown in law and order, especially after 44 CE. Banditry, corruption, poor administration and a rise in conflicts between Jews and Greeks are cited as indicators of the deteriorating situation (pp. 73-74). Furthermore, prior to the revolt a significant increase in apocalyptic fervour is evident in Judaea (pp. 230-35). Within this context Freyne poses the

---

55. S. Freyne, *Galilee: from Alexander the Great to Hadrian, 323 BCE to 135 CE: A Study of Second Temple Judaism* (Wilmington, DE: Michael Glazier, 1980).

question of whether Galilee echoes the state of affairs that existed in Judaea. Although Freyne notes the paucity of information from which to resolve the issue he does conclude that Galilee differed quite markedly from Judaea (p. 208). In general, Galilee was not as severely effected by the breakdown in law and order. As a result, when the war began Cestius encountered a region more concerned with such practical issues as tending to crops rather than raising the standard of revolution (p. 247). Galilee did not present a united front of opposition to the Roman forces. Such a situation became apparent to the Romans, who quickly changed from their heavy-handed approach to a more discerning attack on only those people that offered resistance (p. 208). Although some of the social and economic tensions that adversely effected Judaea were evident in Galilee they did not have the same impact (p. 245). As such, Freyne concludes that Galilee is not to be viewed as a seed-bed for revolutionary activity (p. 216).[56]

The second example is Horsley's *Galilee*.[57] Beginning from the premise that many existing paradigms used to portray Galilee are invalid, Horsley declares the agenda of his study to be one of establishing the 'historical realities' of the situation in Galilee (pp. 6, 12). This task is undertaken within the paradigm that the relationship between the rulers in the cities and the people on the land was all one-way traffic, where the people gave to the rulers but received nothing in return (p. 9).

Within the historical survey Horsley views Galilee as a distinct region to Judaea. Drawing on the developments during the Hasmonaean and Herodian periods, he argues that Galilee never fully adopted the features of Judaean society—the temple aristocracy and priestly traditions (pp. 60-68). Instead, it retained a sense of independence.[58] The one aspect of agreement that Horsley identifies between Galilee and Judaea is the prominence of banditry. Especially after 44 CE, banditry is on the increase in both regions to the extent that it was 'epidemic'. Inconsistent rule, high taxation and drought all worked together to provide

56. The focus of this discussion is indicated by the title of Chapter 6, 'How Revolutionary was Galilee?'; cf. F. Loftus, 'The Anti-Roman Revolts of the Jews and the Galilaeans', *JQR* 68 (1977–78), pp. 78-98.

57. R.A. Horsley, *Galilee: History, Politics, People* (Valley Forge, PA: Trinity Press International, 1995).

58. This independence is clearly evident in 66–67 CE when Josephus, a Jerusalem appointee, failed to win over the local population (pp. 87-88).

the right climate for the expansion of banditry from endemic to epidemic proportions (p. 70). Galilee, however, suffered from none of the other problems that were present in Judaea prior to the revolt, where 'Jerusalem had been slipping into increasing anarchy for several years' (p. 73).[59] Freyne and Horsley portray the situation in Galilee as being less severe than in Judaea. In this context they accept that Judaea was plagued by trouble in the years prior to the revolt.

2.5 *Josephus*

Despite the large number of studies devoted to an examination of Josephus, there are only two that fall within the parameters of the present survey. Rajak and Bilde briefly refer to the situation in Judaea.

As part of her concern to explore the figure of Josephus within his cultural setting—namely, first-century CE Jerusalem—Rajak makes reference to the state of affairs in Judaea.[60] In particular, Rajak addresses Josephus's account and understanding of events prior to 66 CE in relation to the oncoming revolt. Little attention is paid to events before 44 CE as it is claimed that the silence of Josephus probably meant that order prevailed (pp. 66-68). After 44 CE, however, the situation changed dramatically. Although Rajak does not view Fadus or Tiberius Alexander as 'crucial', the next five governors are deemed to be prominent in how the situation unfolds (p. 69). Rajak acknowledges Josephus's desire to lay blame on these governors, especially on Felix, Albinus and Florus (p. 72). According to Josephus, these governors failed to promote the necessary support for the Jewish ruling class to prevent war. In an attempt to restore 'balance', Rajak argues that Josephus ignores the negative role of his own class and their responsibility for what happened (pp. 77, 108).

Rajak identifies three factors that helped bring about the revolt. They are: the inadequacy of the Roman administrators; the activities of the Jewish militants; and the inadequacy of the local aristocracy to control internal division within the Jewish community (p. 107). Finally, Rajak concludes that messianism should not be viewed as a

59. The view that brigandage was a significant problem in Galilee is used by S. Schwartz, 'Josephus in Galilee: Rural Patronage and Social Breakdown', in F. Parente and J. Sievers (eds.), *Josephus and the History of the Greco-Roman Period* (SPB, 41; Leiden: E.J. Brill, 1994), pp. 290-306, as a fundamental factor in explaining the revolt in Galilee (pp. 297-300).

60. Rajak, *Josephus*.

significant factor in the outbreak of the revolt (p. 140).

Bilde briefly outlines the situation in Judaea, drawing heavily on
Josephus's narrative in his desire to sketch the 'developments leading
up to the revolt'.[61] According to Bilde the relationship between the
Jews and Romans had been tense from 63 BCE, but the situation began
to deteriorate particularly from the time of Cumanus onwards (p. 34).
Bilde cites conflicts between Greeks and Jews, the activity of false
prophets and the sicarii, the governorship of Felix and the reign of
Nero as examples of the trouble (p. 34). The final governor, Florus, is
described as striking 'mercilessly against the Jewish population'.
There is a continual intensification of the tension with the end result
that the Jews eager for war became 'increasingly strong' (p. 35). The
Jews were divided into two groups: the upper class faction that openly
accepted Roman rule, and the people's party, who desired the immediate removal of the Romans (p. 34). Those wanting peace could do
nothing, 'the movement was so far advanced that it was impossible
to avert disaster' (p. 35). For Bilde, the revolt 'must be looked upon
as the result of a long and complex process in which the failure of
the Romans to take account of the specific traditions and customs
of the Palestinian Jews seems to have played a decisive role' (p. 36).
Although the issue of inevitability is not explicitly discussed, Rajak
and Bilde convey a picture in which the revolt did not come as a
surprise.

2.6 *The Revolt*

For the sixth thematic area of study—the history of the revolt—only
the work of Price is relevant.[62] Seeking to analyse in detail the events
in Jerusalem during the war, from the outbreak of conflict in 66 CE to
the culmination—the defeat of the rebels in 70 CE—Price's central
argument is that stasis was the constant feature throughout the course
of the revolt. Factionalism helps to explain the defeat of the Jews and
to indicate that even from the start the revolt was doomed to fail

61. Bilde, *Flavius Josephus*. This approach is an expression of Bilde applying
the method he outlines as essential to understand Josephus (p. 24). Note also that
M. Hadas-Lebel, *Flavius Josephus: Eyewitness to Rome's First Century Conquest
of Judea* (trans. R. Miller; New York: Macmillan, 1993), pp. 19-20, 62, views the
period before the revolt as one of 'endemic unrest'.

62. J.J. Price, *Jerusalem under Siege: The Collapse of the Jewish State, 66–70
CE* (BSJS, 3; Leiden: E.J. Brill, 1992).

(pp. xii, 48-50). Furthermore, the factionalism evident during the war was not new to Judaea in 66 CE. For Price, stasis marked the entire period that preceded the revolt (p. xii).

Rather than launching directly into a discussion of affairs in 66 CE, Price deems it appropriate to commence by plotting an outline of the situation in Judaea prior to the revolt and identifying the key players in what was to unfold between 66–70 CE. The picture presented in this sketch is one of a society facing an ever increasing level of trouble in which the revolt was inevitable. What happened in 66 CE 'was the explosive culmination', the origins of which go as far back as 63 BCE (p. 2). In the intervening century, Price believes 'disorder and defiance were more frequent than peace, internal divisions and struggles constant' (p. 2). Conflict between Judaea and Rome was bound to occur, not so much because of any policy enacted by the Romans, but because of an unwillingness by the Jews to accept foreign rule. Indeed, 'rebellion against the Romans had become entrenched, even respected by 66 CE...' (p. 3). Furthermore, the Jews were beset with internal divisions, factionalism that was intensifying between 63 BCE and 66 CE.

From these general remarks Price proceeds to describe some of the events that give evidence to such a picture of the situation in Judaea. The lack of stability in the first century CE is evident. Archelaus was 'deposed after an ill-remembered reign' and Roman rule was greeted with a rebellion. Despite the lack of information for the early period of direct Roman rule there are five incidents during Pilate's term of office and Gratus found it necessary to replace no less than four high priests. In 40 CE, 'full-scale rebellion' because of Gaius's order was only prevented by the murder of the emperor (p. 6).

Although the reign of Agrippa I marks a time of 'peace' the return of procuratorial rule in 44 CE brought about an escalation in the trouble. 'Abuses' by the governors gave 'the ideological opposition to Roman rule urgency and practical cause'. Price then comments on what he sees as an excessive emphasis given to the claims of Tacitus in scholarship, by its willingness to lay responsibility for the revolt at the feet of the procurators (p. 7). Certainly the procurators did not help contain the extent of trouble. For example, Cumanus's actions merely contributed to the deterioration of order in the province (p. 8). For Felix, Albinus and Florus, Price calls upon Josephus's own words to display the inadequacy of procuratorial rule. Clearly, Jerusalem's fate was sealed well before 70 CE. What Florus did was play out his part and Judaea was plunged into war when Eleazar b. Ananias ceased offering sacrifices on behalf of foreigners. However, it is also important to acknowledge 'the near tradition of rebellion began in 63 BCE...' The present world order was a cause for much agitation and hope for the advent of a re-ordering. The activities of such people as Theudas, the sons of Judas, Eleazar b. Deinaeus, the false prophets and the sicarii express the willingness to rebel.

That the revolt took place is not at all surprising. According to Price, 'what is true is that insurrection began from the moment Roman rule was imposed and did not cease before the full-scale rebellion broke out...' (p. 49). The Roman governors may have added to the burden of the Jews but they alone do not explain what happened in 66 CE. The conflict could not be avoided primarily because the Jews were predisposed to a rejection of foreign rule. In 66 CE the debate among the Jews was not whether they should fight—that had long been 'outmoded'. At issue in 66 CE was who should control the rebellion (p. 50). The context for the debate was that before the war those who opposed Roman rule did not constitute a single united group. In fact, they 'tended to compete with each other' (p. 13) with bad governors stimulating their activity. Price argues that the zealots, prominent during the revolt, were related to one of the main pre-war revolutionary groups, the sicarii (p. 24). They and other revolutionaries passionately argued for the freedom of Judaea as rhetoric around which to draw a following. Alongside the revolutionary groups Price places some of the aristocracy as competing for leadership in the anti-Roman crusade as 'the crisis approached...'. Yet even among the aristocracy there was no unity, as some argued for and some against the revolt. The coalition that was formed in the closing months of 66 CE was a marked contrast to the situation before the revolt. It was, however, a coalition that could not last long and by the end of 67 CE the factionalism of the pre-war years would reassert itself. For Price, Judaea was moving on a path that had only one outcome: armed conflict on a large scale between the Jews and Romans and, even more significantly, within the Jewish community.

2.7 *Judaea after 70 CE*
The other theme where there is only one relevant example is the concern to understand what was happening in Judaea in the years immediately following 70 CE. S. Schwartz focuses attention directly on

'recovering the history of the three or four decades after 70'.[63] As such it is a distinctive study.[64] S. Schwartz does not try to go beyond the end of the first century CE and the work is based on the premise that Josephus's narrative provides a means by which it is possible to reconstruct the post-70 political machinations among the Jewish community in Judaea (p. 3). Comparing *War* with *Ant.* and *Life*, S. Schwartz argues that changes in the way Josephus portrays people and themes in these texts can be viewed as evidence of the shifts in the political make up of Judaea.[65]

S. Schwartz argues that Josephus was an apologist for the 'old regime' of the pre-war leadership of the high priestly aristocracy and the Herodians in *War* (pp. 87-88, 137-38). In the mid-70s CE, therefore, groups who had been prominent prior to the revolt continued to claim a major role in the community. They were trying to regain leadership in the wake of the revolt and found a willing ally in Josephus. In *Ant.* and *Life*, however, Josephus shifts his allegiances. Although the 'upper priests', including himself, were praised, the high priests are the subject of open criticism (pp. 92-96). Furthermore, there is a distinct lack of support for the Herodians in *Ant.* (pp. 152-54), while the Pharisees are portrayed in a more sympathetic light. Consequently, Josephus is promoting a new group as the appropriate leaders for the Jewish community. This group is an amalgam of remnants of priestly, aristocratic and Pharisaic elements and it was not directly linked with any specific pre-66 CE group (pp. 214-16).

On a general level S. Schwartz suggests that the state of affairs was far from peaceful after 70 CE. In the years that followed the revolt there was no smooth transition nor a continuation in leadership. The groups prominent and active prior to the revolt tried to reassert their claims but it was a new amalgam that managed to succeed by the 90s CE.

---

63. S. Schwartz, *Judaean Politics*.

64. B. Issac, 'Judaea after AD 70', *JJS* 35 (1984), pp. 44-50, a further study directly relevant to the years that immediately follow 70 CE, is primarily concerned with exploring the meaning of *War* 7.216 regarding Vespasian's settlement of affairs in Judaea.

65. This line of argument has featured within the debate regarding the status of the Pharisees. See, for example, Smith, 'Palestinian Judaism', and Cohen, *Josephus*; cf. Williams, 'Morton Smith'.

3. *Summary*

The preceding survey displays the diversity of scholarly interest that seeks to present a picture of what was happening in Judaea during the first century CE. It is a topic that has drawn the interest of general survey texts and specialized, thematic studies. Diversity is also evident in the perspective from which many of the texts are written, whether it be concerned with Jewish, Christian or classical history. Despite the diversity, the most striking feature of the picture that scholarship constructs is the overwhelming level of consensus in three key areas.

The first area is in the depiction of the overall situation. Judaea was a society racked by conflict and turmoil. Furthermore, this turmoil was escalating. The people were oppressed, suffering at the hands of the wealthy and the Romans. Within this broad outline two related issues remain the cause of significant debate. One is the concern to clarify the nature of the escalating turmoil, particularly its practical expression and underlying causes. Emphasis is placed on such factors as rivalry within the aristocracy, the Jews as a whole being in conflict with the Romans, and with the Greek residents in the cities of Judaea. The second issue pertains to the exact timing of this turmoil. For some, the turmoil was prominent throughout the first century and its origins may even go back as far as 63 BCE. Others view the turmoil escalating primarily after 44 CE when direct Roman rule was reinstated.

The second key area of consensus is that the revolt of 66–70 CE was not a surprise. If anything, the war was a forgone conclusion—the natural climax of what had happened in the preceding 60 years. Few scholars actually openly question whether the revolt was inevitable. For most, it is implied simply by the nature of the causes listed. Among those who do broach the issue, the conflict is deemed as an event that could not be avoided. Although the personalities involved in Roman rule play a prominent part in discussion of the revolt, what tends to ensure that it is seen as inevitable is the sense of turmoil present in the society. As to the actual cause(s) of the revolt, most scholars present a combination of factors being at work. The timing of the revolt may be a matter of 'chance' but the causes are all of a long-standing nature and they tend to be crucial to the actual fabric of the society and the functioning of the administrative system.

The third key area of consensus is in terms of the chronological limits of the work undertaken, in which there is an overwhelming emphasis on 66–70 CE. The revolt acts as a magnet and a landmark. The attempts to construct a picture of the situation in Judaea generally conclude with the revolt. Furthermore, there is a close overlap between the description of events from during the first century and the revolt. What happens before 66 CE is cast as a background from which to approach an understanding of the revolt. The period after 70 CE is only briefly discussed and mainly in the general surveys. Furthermore, any discussion of post-70 CE that occurs is done in terms of later events, especially the revolt of 132–135 CE. In effect, the first century CE could be defined as 6–70 (or 66) CE. The one exception here is S. Schwartz's study. By focusing specifically on the last 30 years of the first century CE he provides a sharp contrast to all the other texts cited. He alone displays an explicit willingness to investigate a 'silent' part of the first century CE in terms of how it relates to the events from prior to the revolt rather than only in relation to events of the second century CE.

The pervasive nature of the consensus is even evident in the one text that appears to go against the tide, E.P. Sanders's *Judaism: Practice and Belief 63 BCE to 66 CE*. In his study of Judaism as a way of life and its associated underlying beliefs, Sanders presents a brief historical overview of the period.[66] Noting Josephus's intention to present the first century CE in Palestine as moving from 'war to war, riot to riot', Sanders actually views it as a period of 'peace and tranquillity'—a time of strong and stable government (p. 35). In fact, the war took everyone by surprise. In terms of the situation in 66 CE, the Jewish leaders—the chief priests—could have 'coped if the problems they faced had been less severe' (p. 36) and there was 'less expectation of war' in 66 CE than there had been in 41 CE (p. 41). Furthermore, 44–66 CE was not a period where the system of government was more likely to cause trouble than what had operated prior to 41 CE (p. 492).

Here Sanders is unique. His comments stand in stark contrast to the steady stream of texts that continually paint Judaea as a place wrecked by turmoil. Even the apparent boldness of this brief overview, however, is tempered by elements of the consensus of scholarship's Judaea. For example, 'we may and should doubt that the total quantity of violence was remarkable and that there was a steady escalation of revolutionary zeal, but we should accept the view that insurrection

66. Apart from the overview in Sanders, *Judaism*, Chapters 3–4, also see Chapters 21–22.

was never very far from the surface' (p. 36). Sanders then briefly outlines 'the major' examples of conflict between the years 63 BCE and 66 CE (pp. 36-40). There were protests, normally passive in nature, and when there was a hiatus in government, factionalism became prominent (p. 42). Then in the context of summing up his study, Sanders comments on the outbreak of war, stating, 'all things considered, I think that there were bound to be uprisings and I am not in the least surprised that one of these led to full revolt' (p. 492). This is particularly the case because the Roman empire, with its military occupation, 'impinged' on the Jewish community more than any previous foreign ruler. With the success of the Hasmonaeans, the 'ideal of national natural sovereignty lived...from 175 CE to 135 CE' and directly impacted on what happened in the first century CE (p. 493). Jewish rebels did want freedom and the two major disturbances, according to Sanders— Pilate's order regarding the standards and Gaius's order regarding the statue—helped create the perception that the sanctity of the temple and Jerusalem were threatened by the Roman presence (p. 40). Even the clearly distinctive comments of Sanders, therefore, accommodate aspects of scholarship's willingness to view Judaea as a place of unrest and conflict.

The picture constructed by modern scholarship is a juggernaut of consensus. In literary terms it is a 'tragedy'. Judaea of the first century CE is a place of gloom and crisis. Conflict is evident in almost every aspect of existence. This is a picture that begs several questions. Of central importance, particularly because of the overwhelming level of agreement, is the origin of this picture. Other important issues also require clarification. For example, what is the function of Josephus in the construction of these separate yet uniform portraits? Furthermore, what is the nature of the relationship between scholarship and Josephus?

These questions are all the more relevant because of the apparent parallel between what Josephus and scholars present—Judaea in turmoil that escalates to the point of open war, with 70 CE viewed as a climactic end-point. It is towards these issues that our study turns in the following chapter with a particular concern to identify the nature of the relationship. The importance of providing such clarification is all the more urgent because Josephus's picture should be regarded as *an* account, rather than *the* account, from which to construct an interpretation of the first century CE.

Chapter 5

THE GIFT OF JOSEPHUS

A very clear and close parallel exists between Josephus and contemporary scholarship in the picture they present of the situation in first-century CE Judaea. The two crucial pillars of Josephus's construction—namely, Judaea as a place dominated by turmoil and a revolt which should be viewed as the inevitable crescendo of the escalating turmoil—are also central to the scholarly reconstructions. It is a parallel that makes the following analysis of how scholarship has employed the narrative of Josephus in its attempt to describe what happened in Judaea a necessary task. What will become evident is that the parallel is not a coincidence. Rather, it is the expression of a relationship in which scholarship is dependent upon Josephus on two levels. The first, a material dependency, is more often than not readily acknowledged. The second level, a conceptual dependency, however, is rarely given due recognition. Irrespective of how much Josephus's interpretation of events may be criticized, he remains the architect of the Judaea constructed by scholarship. As such, existing reconstructions of Judaea are flawed. Scholarship has received a 'gift': Josephus's narrative of events. It is, however, a gift wrapped in his interpretative framework.

We commence with the first level of the dependency—the reliance on Josephus for information regarding what happened in Judaea. Here we can be brief. There is little, if any, dispute regarding the central role of Josephus as the most substantial source for this period of Judaean history. Probably the clearest sign of Josephus's importance, in material terms, is that not one reconstruction of the situation in Judaea is based upon the narrative of any other source. General surveys and specific single issue studies are dependent on Josephus for information. A few examples of this dependency are warranted. Here the general surveys stand out because of their desire to provide a broad descriptive outline of events. Smallwood and Schürer are clear examples of this approach. Both texts make extensive use of *War* 2 and *Ant.* 18–20 as the basis of their account of affairs in Judaea during the first century CE. Josephus's narrative provides the structure for the account. Individual incidents recorded by Josephus are normally paraphrased, with occasional direct quotations used. Where other sources narrate the same incidents their details are added to the narrative and where they describe separate incidents they are inserted into the narrative according to their appropriate location in the chronological sequence.[1]

Within the common approach there are two interesting differences between Schürer and Smallwood. The first pertains to the introductory comments of the scholars. Schürer provides the reader with an introduction to Josephus, especially his military and literary career. In this context the material dependency on Josephus is openly acknowledged. Josephus's 'works provide the main source for the history studied here' and it is stated that without them, 'the present history could not have been written'.[2] In contrast, Smallwood does not provide an overview of the sources used to help construct her narrative. Passing reference is made to the one-sided nature of the sources: that is, Josephus presents a Jewish world-view. It is also noted that Philo and isolated accounts of events in the New Testament will be used to supplement Josephus (p. 144). There is, however, no attempt to familiarize the reader with the main source for the history, or to acknowledge the material dependency on Josephus.

The second difference relates to the way Schürer and Smallwood employ Josephus in their description of affairs. In the light of the preceding observation the comparison is somewhat contradictory to what might be expected. Schürer's narrative of events ignores problems in the sources, whether between Josephus and other extant accounts or between Josephus's own accounts. Hence, the description of Gaius's order for a statue to be placed in Jerusalem makes no mention of problems in the chronology of the event. All such discussion of possible differences in the sources is reserved for the footnotes. Smallwood, on the other hand, explicitly discusses several differences in the

1. See, for example, Murphy, *Religious World*, pp. 296-98, Schürer, *History*, I, p. 465, and Smallwood, *Jews*, pp. 166, 277.
2. The reliance on Josephus rather than such sources as Philo is indicated by the lack of any introductory remarks regarding the latter.

process of describing certain events. For example, Smallwood notes the differences between Josephus and Philo in the account of Gaius's order in an effort to establish which should be regarded as the more accurate account.[3]

Although few of the single issue studies provide the same comprehensive description of events as those located in the general surveys, the material dependence is still evident. Where a general overview is used as a backdrop to their particular investigation Josephus's account takes centre stage. For example, Price, Horsley and Hanson provide a brief historical outline which is based on *War* 2 and *Ant.* 18–20. Josephus's narratives are paraphrased and occasionally quoted in a chronologically arranged account.

A second, more common, approach adopted by the single issue studies clearly displays the material dependency on Josephus. It is the employment of Josephus as the main source of evidence for the particular issue being explored. Three examples will be sufficient. The first is Rappaport.[4] To substantiate his view that the 'root' cause of the revolt was Jewish–Greek conflict Rappaport draws heavily on the relevant passages in Josephus's description of events. Second, Goodman declares that he will 'make extensive use of four often neglected passages in Josephus's AJ' regarding faction fighting among the ruling elite.[5] These passages act as a crucial element for Goodman's analysis of the causes of the 66–70 CE war. In turn, Goodman draws

---

3. Smallwood's decision to favour Philo over Josephus where there are differences in the details of their accounts of the statue incident raises an important issue that she does not address (*Jews*, p. 174). She displays an obvious reliance on Josephus's account but in the one instance where a different version has survived she prefers the details of the alternative account. It would seem most appropriate, therefore, that the remainder of Josephus's narrative should not be taken at face value as an accurate account of events. For a defence of Josephus regarding this incident see D.R. Schwartz, 'On Drama and Authenticity', pp. 113-29. On the comparative value of Josephus and Philo as sources for historical inquiry also see E.M. Smallwood, 'Philo and Josephus as Historians of the Same Events', in L.H. Feldman and G. Hata (eds.), *Josephus, Judaism and Christianity* (Detroit: Wayne State University Press, 1987), pp. 114-28, and D.R. Schwartz, 'Josephus and Philo on Pontius Pilate', in L.I. Levine, *The Jerusalem Cathedra: Studies in the History, Archaeology, Geography and Ethnography of the Land of Israel* (Jerusalem: Yad Izhak Ben Zvi Institute, 1983), III, pp. 26-45.

4. Rappaport, 'Jewish–Pagan Relations'.

5. Goodman, *Ruling Class*, p. 20.

extensively on the remainder of Josephus's narrative to clarify the exact nature of his interpretation of the situation in Judaea. Finally, Horsley relies primarily on Josephus's narrative of various distur- bances to help explain the function of the spiral of violence.[6] Thus, the protest over the standards and the aqueduct under Pilate feature as examples of 'popular protest' while the response to the action of the Roman soldier at Passover during Cumanus's governorship is cate- gorized under the heading 'Jerusalem crowd protests'. Although other sources are used, they are always in a supplementary role.[7]

We need not prolong discussion of the material dependency on Josephus any longer. It is self-evident that all reconstructions of the situation in Judaea rely first and foremost on the narrative of Jose- phus. There is nothing significant or unusual in acknowledging the material dependency. Historical inquiry is reliant on the availability of sources. Material remains are important but the existence of literary records is an obvious bonus. What can potentially be significant, how- ever, is that the reconstruction is dependent on only one particular source of information. Where more than one literary source is extant, historians have the benefit of making comparisons between different perspectives. Apart from obvious complications with the reading of any text, extra difficulties are encountered when the material depen- dency is on one particular source. Unfortunately the reconstruction of the situation in first-century CE Judaea is one such example of the latter category.[8] As a result, great care is required to ensure that the material dependency—that is, the subject matter—does not also become a conceptual dependency. It is my contention that existing schol- arship has not been able to avoid this trap. The conceptual framework from which scholarly accounts of the situation in first-century CE Judaea are constructed is controlled by Josephus's interpretative frame- work. In other words, the parallel that exists between Josephus and scholarship is explained by this conceptual dependency. It has resulted in a re-hashing of *an* interpretation as *the* perspective from which to view the first century CE. Despite anything to the contrary claimed by scholarship, Josephus continues to control the discussion. He is the

6.   Horsley, *Spiral*.

7.   This dependence on Josephus is also explicitly acknowledged by, among others, Horsley, *Galilee*, p. 3, Hengel, *Zealots*, p. 16, and Rhoads, *Israel*, p. 1.

8.   These observations echo the points raised in the introduction regarding the various sources that can be drawn upon.

architect of all that is done. Josephus crafted his own narrative within his interpretative framework and scholarship reinforces that framework by continuing to view the first century CE within the parameters established by Josephus.

Given the extent of scholarly debate regarding the use of Josephus as a source, such a conclusion may seem puzzling.[9] In the remainder of this chapter we will explore how this conceptual dependency is evident in the reconstructions of the situation in Judaea. Our starting-point is an outline of the four basic approaches adopted by scholars as they employ Josephus in their reconstructions. The first takes Josephus's narrative at face value with little or no comment. The second accepts that the account of Josephus needs to be critically evaluated. Such an evaluation may result in aspects of his narrative being adjusted or refined but also essentially concludes that what Josephus describes accurately reflects how the period should be understood. The third approach is critical of Josephus's narrative, particularly of the polemical nature of Josephus's bias. In practical terms, the reader needs to identify the bias and remove it from the narrative of events where possible in order to establish what actually happened in Judaea. The final approach is also critical of Josephus's bias. Here the distinctive means of controlling that bias is the use of a theoretical paradigm that is 'independent' of Josephus.[10]

The exponents of the third and fourth approaches, representing the majority of scholarship, are of most concern. Despite the claims of independence they continue to undertake their reconstructions of Judaea within the interpretative framework established by Josephus. It is a subtle conceptual dependency, but it is a reality. The gift of Josephus's narrative has been allowed to determine the nature in which the first century CE is understood, irrespective of how critical and discerning scholars claim they may be in their treatment of Josephus's narrative.

9.   There is an important distinction to note at this juncture. The following discussion pertains to the comments made by those scholars who have explicitly devoted attention to a discussion of the situation in first-century CE Judaea and have actively used Josephus. Discussion of general issues regarding the use of Josephus will be reserved until Chapter 6.

10.   Compare with Bilde, *Flavius Josephus*, pp. 123-71, who divides scholarly opinion regarding Josephus into two major categories: 'the classical conception' and 'the modern conception'.

The role given to Josephus as a source of information for late-second-temple-period history has been the subject of a significant amount of discussion in the last two decades. In the context of that discussion, probably the least favoured approach now is to accept Josephus's account as being historically reliable without any debate. Despite Josephus's personal and professional interests, his account is accepted as having integrity as a historical record. This first approach is a rather rudimentary and naive manner of employing Josephus. There is no stated or implied methodology used to explain why Josephus's account warrants such open acceptance. In effect, Josephus's account is cited in the style of 'proof texting'. A simple listing and re-narration of incidents is deemed as evidence of the historical situation, irrespective of any other considerations.

Probably the best examples of this approach are the general surveys of Schürer and Smallwood. Schürer acknowledges the existence of 'imperfections' within Josephus's narrative. He presents a 'distorted picture', ignoring such factors as messianic expectation and he places a halo over the Jews in terms of their involvement in factors that brought about the revolt of 66–70 CE. Comparison is even made between *War* and *Ant.*, with Schürer declaring a high level of confidence in *War*, where Josephus 'provides an account of reliability of which there is no reason to doubt'.[11] Such confidence is clearly evident in the text of Schürer. The account of Josephus's biographical details takes verbatim the information provided in *Life* regarding his education. In describing events during the first century CE Schürer occasionally quotes directly from Josephus, particularly in relation to trouble during the governorship of Felix (pp. 463-64). More often than not, the approach of Schürer is to paraphrase the text of Josephus, as in the description of the three conflicts during Cumanus's term of office (pp. 458-59). This paraphrase makes no acknowledgment of where *Ant.* or *War* is being used, nor of differences that may exist between the texts (p. 459).[12] Furthermore, Schürer uses the

---

11. Note, however, that in the account of the death of Jonathan, Schürer, *History*, I, p. 463, relies on the *Ant.* account.

12. The dependence, and therefore, acceptance of Josephus's account and interpretation even extends to the use of his symbolism. Schürer uses the image of fire on several occasions to portray the revolt and to indicate its long-term origins, referring to 'spark', 'smoulder', 'burst into flame' (p. 382), 'inflammable', 'one spark' and 'explosion' (p. 470).

summary statements of Josephus regarding the motivation of such Roman officials as Petronius (p. 395), Albinus (pp. 468-69) and Florus (p. 470). As a result, the comments and flavour of Schürer's narrative are dependent on Josephus: war was inevitable in a community where conflict escalated throughout the period.

The other major example of the first approach, Josephus's account being taken at face value, is Smallwood. Her conceptual dependency is curious. Despite his 'defection' to the Romans during the revolt (p. 144), Josephus is identified as a partisan source (p. 257) giving a Jewish perspective of the events. Smallwood is also aware that Josephus is not always consistent in the details he provides in *Ant.* and *War*. Furthermore, where there is another major account of the same incident, such as Philo's description of the statue of Gaius, Smallwood expresses a preference for the alternative account. She states that chronological problems and fairy tale elements in Josephus's narrative mean that where the two sources, Josephus and Philo, contradict one another, then Philo should be given precedence (p. 174). In a similar vein, clarification of details is openly discussed in such incidents as the Samaritan intrusion into the temple while Coponius was governor and the reason for Ishmael being detained in Rome after the petition regarding the temple wall. Despite these apparent expressions of scepticism, Smallwood displays a conceptual dependency on Josephus's account of affairs, allowing it to stand as an accurate historical record for how to understand what happened in Judaea.

The dominant feature of Smallwood's narrative is the paraphrasing of Josephus, with occasional use of direct quotes (pp. 274-75). Descriptions of incidents are drawn from *Ant.* or *War*, almost implying that no distinction needs to be made between the two texts. Minor events and their explanation are taken at face value, such as the statement that Jews left Judaea because the terrorism had become so prevalent (p. 283). In other, more significant ways, what Josephus describes stands as the historical description of what happened. For example, the narrative of events during 66 CE is a paraphrased version of what is located in *War* 2 without any alteration.

Among the single issue studies a further example of the first approach to the reading of Josephus is Brunt's argument regarding the causes of the 66–70 CE revolt.[13] Brunt draws on statements in Josephus

13. Brunt, 'Social Conflicts'.

to portray a society divided, with the aristocracy eager to preserve peace while the brigands tried to bring about open conflict. Although Brunt acknowledges that Josephus may have heightened the focus on social conflict in his account because of apologetic interests, he claims 'it seems unlikely that his [Josephus's] interpretation had no basis in the facts' (p. 153). These 'facts' are, essentially, the listing of numerous passages which show the upper class as opposed to war and the rebels attacking those opposed to the war. Brunt cites examples of the upper class advocating submission to Roman rule and being motivated by a concern to protect their property (p. 149). The rebels, on the other hand, had greed as a motive (p. 151), attacking the property of the wealthy and those who initially did not join them (p. 150). This process of 'proof texting' is a reading of Josephus that takes his comments and narrative at face value. It is an approach that Brunt reinforces in his 1990 addenda.[14] Commenting on Goodman's interpretation of 66 CE Brunt argues that the weight of evidence favours the view that the aristocracy actively tried to maintain peace. This weight of evidence is the citing of numerous passages from Josephus's account (p. 525).[15]

The first approach to dealing with Josephus as a source displays a rather simple, one-dimensional 'trusting' outlook. Josephus wrote an accurate account of historical events. Material is quoted from the texts with the implicit understanding that it is factual. There is an assumed separation between the author and the narrative. Josephus may have written his texts with particular interests, but what is described stands as an accurate account of events during the first century CE. In other words, as an author Josephus was able to curtail his bias; he is objective. This process of proof texting, taking the narrative on a literal level, is fraught with problems. By far the most serious problem is the failure to give due attention to the nature of Josephus's interpretative framework. As such, there is no consideration given to the way Josephus functions as an author, to how he goes about the task of constructing a picture of first-century CE Judaea. The literary text is viewed as the window which exposes the period without distortion or any blind spots. By implication, it is an approach that is conceptually

14. Brunt, *Roman Imperial Themes*, pp. 282-87, 517-31.

15. A further expression of Brunt's willingness to rely on Josephus is that no attempt is made to explore the actual identity of the 'revolutionaries' and 'insurgents'. They are allowed to remain faceless 'rebels' in Brunt's discussion.

dependent on Josephus, as his world-view becomes that of the scholar without any discussion.

The second approach to the reading of Josephus is best expressed in the work of Rajak.[16] It requires more substantial comment than the first approach. As in the first approach, Josephus is regarded as an accurate recorder of historical events whose description and interpretation are, in essence, valid. The distinctive element of the second approach is that this view is not merely assumed, it is explicitly asserted after Josephus's writings have been subjected to a detailed analysis. In other words, a critical reading of Josephus confirms that what he describes is essentially an accurate account and interpretation of what happened in Judaea. Where the first approach fails to address the issue of how the source may have distorted the narrative of events, the second approach consciously explores the issue of authorial bias and reaches the same conclusion: Josephus's account should be taken as it stands.

Within her concern to locate Josephus in his cultural context, Rajak analyses the account of events during the first century CE, especially in relation to the revolt. Rajak is well aware of criticism that scholars have levelled at the account of Josephus, particularly the interpretation of the revolt. In general terms it is acknowledged that one must distinguish between bias and accurate information. Josephus's account is subjective and it is important to ensure that what is being read is not simply one person's 'highly personal, eccentric opinions' (p. 105). Furthermore, Rajak recognizes that the narrative is the product of hindsight. What we read, therefore, are the opinions of Josephus that he held after the revolt, not necessarily before or during the war (p. 66). For Rajak, recognition and discussion of the author's social and historical context are crucial to the assessment of his narrative as an accurate record of events. Rajak even accepts that Josephus is not an objective writer (p. 185).[17] However, she also claims that it is not a stark alternative with which the reader is faced. It is not necessary to either

16. Rajak, *Josephus*. Another example of this approach is Bilde, *Flavius Josephus*. The narrative of Josephus needs to be read in a critical manner but the end result of this process will be an affirmation of historical accuracy regarding what is described. See, for example, Bilde's discussion of the *War* and *Life* descriptions of Josephus's commission in Galilee, pp. 45-46, 176-79.

17. Rajak, *Josephus*, p. 79, claims that Josephus often expresses his opinions in a bold and over-zealous manner.

adopt the entire gambit of Josephus's account or reject everything he has to say (p. 106).[18] There is a means by which the reader is able to discern what elements in Josephus's narrative are accurate.

The methodology which Rajak adopts is extremely positive in outlook. On several occasions Rajak indicates that the onus of proof is on establishing Josephus's inability to correctly interpret what is happening in Judaea. For example, in the context of discussing the claims Josephus makes regarding his family, Rajak states 'while there are some features which are improbable, there are none which are impossible; and, as long as what Josephus tells us is possible we have no right to correct it' (p. 16). Such a view may appear valid and harmless in relation to personal biographical details but it is a principle that is echoed elsewhere in Rajak's reading of Josephus's account of events. Thus, in connection with her discussion of Josephus's analysis of how the revolt unfolded, Rajak states 'if we find no internal grounds for impugning the historian's story, then, in the absence of evidence from outside, it must have a prima face claim on our belief' (p. 127). Such a view assumes not only that the intention of the author is to be accurate in the description of what happened, but that the author was also able to narrate an accurate representation of what took place.

Part of Rajak's critical reading of Josephus accepts that there are aspects of his account which display apologetic interests. The narrative may require clarification or refinement at certain points, particularly in relation to the main characters. Hence the presentation of the brigands fails to display an adequate understanding of their motivation and concerns (p. 85). Of the Jewish aristocracy, a 'corrective' is necessary: their inability to control the situation needs to be highlighted (pp. 77, 108), while the comments regarding such governors as Florus may have been exaggerated (p. 73).

What is significant about these revisions is that they do not point toward possible 'internal grounds for impugning' the account. Instead, the tinkering with the details of the narrative are used to help confirm the core elements of Josephus's interpretation. For example, the 'failings' of the Jewish aristocracy are apparent within the narrative (p. 77). Probably the best example of this process of 'revision' is the

18. These comments are made, in part, as a response to the work of Cohen, *Josephus*. Further detailed discussion of the approaches outlined by Rajak, *Josephus*, Cohen, *Josephus*, and others regarding the use of Josephus will be made in Chapter 6.

description of the role adopted by the aristocracy before the revolt and during its early stages. As Josephus claims, they were eagerly seeking a peaceful resolution. Josephus's trip to Rome before the war was part of 'an anxious search for remedies' to the trouble (p. 40). When war broke out the move by the aristocracy to claim leadership was a further example of their concern to achieve a negotiated settlement. Here Rajak clarifies the account by employing Brinton's model for explaining the process of European revolutions. The moderates, the aristocracy, stepped in once the war had begun, asserting their natural desire to promote the cause of peace, playing their trump card as a last resort. All of this points to the conclusion that the way Josephus documents the final stages before the revolt 'cannot be faulted' (p. 75). It is intriguing that Rajak calls on a modern theoretical model to explain what, on the surface, stands as an internal inconsistency—the apparent dramatic turn around in the attitude of the aristocracy. It is, however, entirely in line with the positive nature of the underlying methodology. The idea that Josephus's intimacy with the events he describes is an asset is a further expression of a positive critical reading. Josephus's closeness meant that he was 'bound to see things very clearly' (p. 105). It is an approach which *assumes* a positive response to the question posed at the conclusion of the third chapter of this study: Josephus does present an accurate account of the situation.

In this second approach Josephus is subjected to a test through which he passes with flying colours. Josephus is an objective writer of historical events. Much of his narrative, especially in the years before and during the revolt, is paraphrased. The parallel, therefore, is not accidental—it is an assertion of the ability of Josephus to accurately analyse the situation in first-century CE Judaea. As such, this approach fails to recognize the implications of how Josephus's interpretative framework operates. What is disturbing about this critical reading is that the conclusion is reached after Josephus's narrative and the socio-political context have been explored.

The two other approaches to the use of Josephus begin from the premise that the reader needs to be sceptical of his interpretation. The need for a discerning and critical mindset apparently results in the rejection of how Josephus presents the situation, and conceptual inde-pendence is strongly asserted. Examples of these two approaches will be outlined and then their limitations will be discussed together.

In the third approach Josephus's bias must be identified and siphoned out of the narrative of events through various internal criteria. Only when this 'bias' has been removed will a historical reconstruction be possible. That there is an account of historical events buried within Josephus's narrative is not disputed. What is rejected in this third approach is the involvement of Josephus in the guise of his possible apologetical and polemical interests. In other words, the narrative is inflicted with a disease. The task of the scholar is to identify correctly the nature of the disease and then provide the cure, restoring the historical core of the narrative by reconstructing what happened in Judaea. This is by far the most common approach and what follows is an outline of some of the remedies put forward by the 'medical fraternity'.

The first example is Grabbe's general survey. Grabbe's approach to the use of Josephus is one of the significant features that distinguishes it from the other survey texts. Aware of the divergent opinions expressed by such scholars as Cohen and Rajak regarding the value of Josephus's narrative, Grabbe presents the reader with an introduction to Josephus as a source.[19] Grabbe declares the need for caution on the part of the reader when they engage Josephus's narrative. Generalizations must be avoided. In this cause Grabbe identifies five principles that should be in continuous use to ensure that Josephus's bias is distinguished from the narrative. They are: the 'parallel accounts should be compared and their differences carefully evaluated'; the importance of always considering the sources used by Josephus; the need for an awareness of the principles of ancient historiography; the need for care with those passages where Josephus has apologetical interests; and the need to incorporate all other available source material. Of these principles the first and fourth are particularly relevant. Grabbe repeats the caution of Moehring: 'every single sentence of Josephus is determined and coloured by his aims and tendencies'.[20] It is not possible to read the narrative without questioning the way Josephus may have edited what happened. Hence Grabbe is particularly concerned that the reader display the 'special care' required to understand correctly 'the passages clearly intended' for Josephus's 'apologetic purposes or which lead themselves to this use'. Furthermore, Grabbe states that 'Josephus's aims and biases in each case must be carefully

19. In fact, Grabbe provides a general introduction to all the major sources and then specific comments at the commencement of each chapter.

20. Grabbe, *Judaism*, pp. 10-11, quoting H.R. Moehring, review of Cohen, *Josephus*, in *JJS* 31 (1980), p. 241.

examined'. The warning signs have been posted. The reader must stand apart from Josephus; not all of his narrative is historically objective.

In practical terms Grabbe displays the need for conceptual independence most clearly in the account of events leading up to the outbreak of the revolt. He warns that there is 'rhetorical exaggeration' (pp. 442, 444), 'hyperbole' and a distinct lack of detail to substantiate some of Josephus's claims (p. 444). Furthermore, there are problems with the description of what happened in Jerusalem because the 'account sounds rather one-sided' (p. 447). The bias also makes it difficult to determine 'how far to accept Josephus's picture' (p. 448). Probably the best example of where Grabbe seeks to depart from Josephus is in the analysis of why the revolt began. Emphasis is placed on the argument developed by Goodman, which is based on a rejection of the overt interpretation provided by Josephus.[21]

This third approach is prevalent among the single issue studies. Four such examples will be discussed. The first and the clearest example is Price, who declares that Josephus's bias must be detected and removed to ensure conceptual independence and allow an accurate reconstruction of what happened in Judaea.[22] In his first appendix Price deals with the issue of how *War* is to be treated as a historical source and, in the process, provides a detailed description of the methodological basis on which Josephus's interpretation can be removed. Price starts by declaring that the narrative of Josephus is based on historical events. However, into this narrative has been woven Josephus's apologetic in which several themes have 'guided the writer'. As such, Price's task is one of detecting the disease and effectively removing it so that the description of the historical situation can be reconstructed by the historian. Maintaining a distinction between the writer (Josephus) and the events narrated (the situation in Judaea), the problem is seen

---

21. Murphy, *Religious World*, provides a slightly different focus. The description of events in Judaea is dictated by a dual concern: to give voice to the brigands and to dismiss the scholarly theory of the 'zealots' (pp. 282-83). Murphy upholds the relevance of Josephus as a valuable source of information regarding what happened in Judaea. Contained in his texts is the description of historical events. What needs to be done is to cut through the dual layer of bias, that of Josephus and scholarship. When this is done some of the insights derived include that the fourth philosophy did not mark the beginning of a permanent armed resistance movement (pp. 291-92) and that Josephus fails to give voice to the diversity of groups that existed in Jewish society (p. 281).

22. Price, *Jerusalem*, pp. 180-93.

to be finding the means of defining where the distinction exists. To achieve this goal and thus establish conceptual independence from Josephus's interpretation, Price outlines a methodology which has nine stated elements. The nine elements are: 'the incorporation of incidental details'; 'contradictions'; 'unnoticed patterns'; 'events separable from interpretation'; 'arbitrary emphases'; 'polemics'; 'The Romans'; 'thematic manipulation'; and 'siege τόποι' (pp. 183-93). The key elements in the methodology are the 'contradictions' within the account, inconsistencies through 'unnoticed patterns' and 'incidental details' and 'events separable from interpretation'. They allow the reader to cut through the apologetic and reclaim the historical situation. In other words, contained within Josephus's narrative are the means of establishing the antidote required.

In practical terms, Price cuts through the 'thick fog' of Josephus's interpretation in the analysis of the role played by the aristocracy in the revolt. Josephus tries to present the aristocracy as united against the war. A close reading of the description of events in Jerusalem allows Price to conclude that the opposite applies. In particular, the 'contradictions' and 'incidental details' help show that elements of the aristocracy were actively involved in bringing about the revolt and then eagerly took on the task of running the war effort at the end of 66 CE. By implication, Price indicates that Josephus had deliberately tried to suppress the reality of the historical situation. Josephus actually knew the 'truth' but had attempted to construct a narrative that diverted responsibility away from the aristocracy, playing down the real nature of their involvement.

Rappaport's discussion of the causes of the revolt is the second example of a single issue study that adopts the approach of asserting conceptual independence by rejecting Josephus's interpretation.[23] Here the rejection is expressed in subtle terms. Rappaport's starting-point is the established parameters of scholarly debate regarding the so-called primary and secondary factors associated with the outbreak of war in 66 CE. No attempt is made to explain the value and limitations of Josephus as a source of information. Instead, Rappaport briefly discusses and then dismisses the various factors which scholarship promote, all of which are a development of issues highlighted by Josephus. Although dismissing Josephus's interpretation, Rappaport does not

23. Rappaport, 'Jewish–Pagan Relations', pp. 81-95.

believe that all is lost in the search for understanding. In fact, Rappaport turns to the narrative of events presented by Josephus to further his search. It is asserted that buried within Josephus's account are the indicators of the real cause of the war: namely, Jewish–Greek conflict. In other words, Josephus has preserved the essential elements of what happened, all that is required is a reinterpretation of that narrative in which it is located, within its proper historical context. Hence Rappaport uses Josephus but in a manner that allows him to claim conceptual independence.[24]

The next example of the third approach is Crossan's examination of certain events in Judaea for their relevance to understanding the historical Jesus. Crossan acknowledges the bias of Josephus as being an active ingredient in the narrative. Writing from the perspective of the aristocracy, Josephus displays a bias against the populace (p. 99). For example, Josephus is deliberately derogatory of the brigands which results in the ignoring of any possible socio-political agenda they may have proclaimed. For Crossan, this socio-economic bias of Josephus means that he must be read 'against himself'. The interpretation of Josephus must be distinguished from the narrative of events if the latter are to be properly understood in historical terms.

The modern reader must stand conceptually independent of Josephus in order to properly understand what happened in Judaea. The key for Crossan is to identify Josephus's bias. There are numerous examples of this re-reading, taking into account Josephus's polemical interests (pp. 165, 186). They include: being able to clarify the exact nature of the diverse prophetic movements and bandit groups in Judaea; the conclusion that the claim Judas was the 'seed-bed of all that was to follow' is 'pure narrative speculation' (p. 115); that the rebels active under Festus (*War* 2.254-57) are not simply one united group but three distinct movements—the sicarii, brigands and millennial prophets; the deliberate playing down of the role of millennial and apocalyptic expectations by Josephus (p. 111); and the sicarii and probably the fourth philosophy were actually 'activist manifestations of apocalypticism or messianism' (p. 112). In these, and other instances, the historical reality can be established, but only when Josephus's narrative is stripped of its disease—the author's interpretation. It is the healing hand of the scholar, in this case Crossan, which allows

24. It is notable that this context allows Rappaport to assert that the inevitability of the revolt can be assumed from the outset.

the true significance of what is described to be revealed.

The final example of the third approach to the reading of Josephus is evident in the work of Horsley and Hanson. They openly reject Josephus's interpretation of the social situation in first-century CE Judaea and attempt to correct Josephus's distorted picture.[25] Josephus is biased against the 'common people'. His apologetic protects and defends the elite. As a result, anyone expressing an attitude that questioned or criticized the status quo is portrayed in a negative and summary fashion. Josephus's narrative, however, is not beyond repair. The 'voiceless' peasantry can speak on the basis that the bias of Josephus makes him a 'hostile' source. In other words, what Josephus claims about a given situation, especially in terms of the non-establishment participants of an incident, needs to be read as the view of the opposition. A further ingredient used by Horsley and Hanson is a 'historical critical analysis of social history'. Josephus's narrative, therefore, can be read outside the bias of his social group. From this context, Horsley and Hanson are able to identify four major types of popular movements, all of which are deemed to be attempts by the common people to deal with the oppression in their daily existence. In effect, by using Josephus against himself, Horsley and Hanson claim to bring to the forefront the 'dynamic force' in Judaea: namely, the 'movements among the peasantry'. The bias of an opponent of the peasantry is corrected to show the movement of protest that was becoming increasingly vocal and active during the first century CE.[26]

An interesting offshoot to the use of the third approach is the attitude of Hengel. Josephus is described as a 'tendentious writer and apologist' whose work needs to be carefully interpreted. Rather than removing Josephus's bias, however, Hengel claims it is necessary to

---

25. At the same time, Horsley and Hanson also seek to counter the scholarly theory of an ever present national armed resistance movement known as the zealots.

26. Rhoads, *Israel*, pp. 11-13, also portrays Josephus as a source that needs to be read with caution. Josephus's pro-Roman bias must be taken into account when trying to establish the reliability of the narrative. For example, the war was the work of many groups, not just one sect, as Josephus claims in *Ant.* 18.6-8. Rhoads effectively sums up the agenda of the third approach. Despite 'Josephus's ancient claim to objectivity, his descriptions of the events of the war and his depictions of the revolutionaries are shot through with his subjective bias, his distinctive perspective and his purpose for writing. Anyone who reads Josephus's work in order to reconstruct historical events must persistently keep in mind the person of the author and the point of view from which those events are described' (p. 14).

fill in the gaps, identifying the elements that Josephus has failed to describe in sufficient detail. Here the bias of Josephus is deemed to have curtailed the narrative, and Hengel views his task as one of completing the picture. In particular, by examining the language used and the religious motivation of the zealots, Hengel argues that Josephus's silence can be overcome.[27]

The fourth approach adopted by some scholars also begins from the premise of questioning Josephus's interpretation of what happened in Judaea. This approach asserts that the bias of Josephus results in a distorted picture and it must be identified to allow the historical situation to be properly explained. The distinctive feature of this approach is the means by which the text is liberated from the shackles of Josephus's bias. The mechanism employed is the examination of Josephus's narrative within an external theoretical paradigm. In other words, external aid is deemed necessary in an effort to heal the narrative of disease.[28] A distinction is upheld between Josephus and the events he narrates, with the focus of attention being centred on explaining the latter, outside the themes stated through Josephus, by the use of 'new' paradigms. Implicit in this approach is the notion that Josephus understood what was happening but deliberately tried to cover up the truth of the situation. The two prominent examples of this approach are Goodman and Horsley.

We commence with the model developed by Goodman.[29] He accepts that Josephus tries to analyse the revolt and that the account of events Josephus presents is essentially accurate (p. 5). What Goodman does not accept is Josephus's interpretation of those events (p. 5). Goodman identifies a number of problems associated with explaining the revolt through the use of Josephus's comments. For example, readers are required to make subjective decisions as to what factors are accepted as causes of the war. Furthermore, Josephus's summary apologetical comments require caution on the part of the reader. As such 'it is

27. There is a parallel between Hengel, *Zealots*, and Horsley, *Spiral*. Both assume that Josephus is silent about certain characters in the narrative. Where Hengel and Horsley differ is that the latter views this 'silence' as a reason to portray Josephus in negative terms.

28. The key distinction between the third and fourth approach is that the latter begins by claiming a theoretical conceptual framework is required to effectively view Josephus's narrative for the purposes of establishing what happened in Judaea.

29. Goodman, *Ruling Class*.

unwise to assume the accuracy of any of his analyses of the events through which he lived' (p. 6).

Goodman is eager 'to break away from the straitjacket of Josephus's point of view'. Having rejected the explanations of the revolt given by Josephus, Goodman develops a theoretical model by which to read Josephus in order to identify the historical reality. Models based on the study of modern European revolutions or Marxist theories are deemed inappropriate (pp. 24-25). For Goodman, the valid model is located in the world of Josephus, within the Roman imperial situation. In particular, he draws on the type of provincial administration employed by the Romans to help explain the revolt, thereby correctly interpreting the information contained in Josephus's narrative. Goodman acknowledges that his framework may be 'purely theoretical' but deems it valid as it originates from a reading of Josephus placed in the context of an understanding of the provincial system of the Roman empire. In such a context it is possible to explore the Judaean situation of how the local ruling class failed to fulfil their role in the system, and the implication of that failure. To argue this case Goodman relies heavily on contradictions in Josephus's narrative and what he describes as a number of neglected summary comments in *Ant.* It is implied that Josephus was aware of the actual situation, the failure of the ruling class, but actively tried to shift attention to other factors.[30]

Using the model constructed, Goodman's thesis is then based on the accounts of Josephus, especially the material that 'contradicts the main thrust of his apologetic'. Josephus's own evidence is used 'to break through his reticence' and it is 'fully exploited' to display the extent of faction fighting and inability of the ruling elite to effectively fulfil their task within the imperial system. Essentially what Goodman argues is that the correct framework from which to explain the narrative of Josephus is the crucial ingredient. Once Josephus's interpretation has been dismissed the way forward is to rely on the historical context of the political situation to explain what happened.

The other major exponent of employing a new paradigm to make sense of the historical situation in Judaea is Horsley.[31] Although

---

30. This was a task for which Josephus is given a back-handed compliment (pp. 20-21). The majority of scholarly discussion prior to Goodman had focused on a reshaping of the explanations provided by Josephus.

31. Horsley, *Spiral.*

Horsley does not present an explicit analysis of Josephus, nor of how he views the way various sources should be employed, his discussion of popular Jewish non-violent resistance draws heavily on the narrative of Josephus.[32] However, Horsley clearly tries to avoid relying on Josephus's understanding of the situation. Horsley claims to achieve his goal by releasing the historical events that are located within the depths of Josephus's narrative by employing a theoretical model which is derived from modern socio-historical political study. The fundamental element to this model is the 'colonial situation': that is, viewing Judaea as part of the Roman empire. Drawing on examples of modern colonial empires, Horsley claims that 'relations between the dominant empire and the subject people are full of tension and conflict...'. Hence, Judaea was 'continually in circumstances of crises' and the gulf between the rulers—Roman and Jewish—and the peasantry widened throughout the first century CE. Although the Jewish aristocracy happily cooperated with their Roman overlords, the peasantry desired a return to the 'traditional way of life'.

The 'colonial situation' forms the context within which Horsley places a further theoretical framework. It is what Horsley describes as the 'spiral of violence'. In turn, the spiral provides the mechanism for understanding the socio-political interaction in Judaea, measuring the 'colonial situation' in practical terms. What Horsley does is locate the various individuals, groups and incidents described in Josephus's narrative in relation to the various stages of the spiral. Events are located in their proper historical context.[33] For Horsley, the reality of the actual situation can be retrieved from Josephus's narrative, but only after radical surgery in the form of placing the narrative in a new theoretical paradigm.

32. A further agenda is to discuss the period on the basis of rejecting the scholarly view which supports the existence of a zealot party from 6 CE that actively opposed Roman rule through the use of violence. In relation to the order of Gaius, Horsley states a preference for Josephus over Philo (*Spiral*, p. 111).

33. For example, Horsley, *Spiral*, pp. 100, 113-15, presents the protest against Gaius's order and Pilate's action regarding the standards as 'protest' and 'resistance', the second stage of the spiral. They are not 'religious' protests as such. Instead, they reflect deeper tensions—a 'conflict between Roman imperial rule and the subject Jewish people...'. What makes them 'pivotal' events is not the provocation of Pilate or Gaius but recognition of their function within the spiral. They are responses of the common people, their 'extensive and prolonged resistance' to the oppressive system of imperial Roman rule.

An exception to the four individual approaches outlined is Horsley's *Galilee*, where he presents a curious mix of the second, third and fourth approaches to the reading of Josephus. From the general standpoint that it is important Josephus's narrative be employed in a critical manner, most of Horsley's statements proclaim the third approach: that is, identifying and removing biased material.[34] For example, in many ways Josephus should be viewed as a 'hostile witness'. He provides a highly distorted picture of the peasantry, including them in his narrative only when they come to the attention of the 'literate elite': that is, in protests that are perceived as threatening the established order. As a result, it is necessary to 'sort through the arrogance and polemics' to determine the 'historical realities of Galilee'. Here Horsley argues for the siphoning out of Josephus's bias from the existing narrative. Josephus remains a valuable eyewitness source of such events as the revolt of 66–70 CE but his narrative is apologetic, 'self-glorifying and self-serving in the extreme'. Thus, a careful reading of Josephus is required to establish what actually happened in a given situation (p. 55), where only those elements 'that cannot be reduced to or explained away as his own rhetoric' (p. 84) can stand as evidence.

The fourth approach is also employed. The 'hostility' of Josephus to much of his subject matter and his self-interest require Horsley to go beyond the approach of siphoning out Josephus's bias. According to Horsley it is necessary to provide a theoretical framework in which to analyse Josephus's narrative. As a result, Horsley deems it appropriate to view Josephus within 'the fundamental structure and dynamic of the imperial situation' in order to 'critically assess' the narrative (p. 73). In a similar vein, the extreme bias against the peasantry necessitates the use of such sociological theories as those advanced by E.J. Hobsbawm regarding ancient banditry in order to understand the dynamic of the situation in Galilee (p. 258).

The need for extreme care evident in the preceding statements is juxtaposed by Horsley's use of the second approach when it comes to explaining the beginning of the revolt and the level of banditry. At no stage does Horsley query the description of banditry. Given the view that Josephus is biased against the peasantry, Horsley does not question whether the references to banditry could be exaggerated. Even more

---

34. Horsley, *Galilee*, p. 13 n. 28, refers to the work of Cohen, *Josephus*, Rajak, *Josephus*, and Bilde, *Flavius Josephus*. It is notable that Horsley sees Cohen as being 'balanced' by the work of Rajak and Bilde.

significant is the attitude of Horsley regarding the narrative of events in 66 CE. What is required, he asserts, is to read between the lines.[35] Such an approach allows Horsley to paraphrase Josephus's account, accepting that the moderate aristocratic leaders of the community wrestled control of the war away from the revolutionaries (p. 75). In effect, the narrative of *War* 2 is affirmed by drawing on the motivation associated with Josephus's appointment as general, as described in *Life*. In this one text Horsley has managed to employ the gambit of approaches used by contemporary scholarship in single issue studies in an effort to read Josephus in a critical manner.

A small proportion of scholars favour the positive reading of Josephus adopted in the first and second approaches. Josephus's entire account—that is, the description and interpretation of events—is accepted as valid. Scholarship is blessed not just with a detailed account but also with a perceptive and accurate picture of how the situation should be understood. Conceptual independence is not necessary, he was an accurate historian. However, the majority of scholars who comment on the situation in Judaea reject such a positive approach to Josephus's narrative. Conceptual independence is deemed to be crucial. Most concentrate on what amounts to a siphoning out of Josephus's bias, while a few believe that it is necessary to go even further to read his account within the parameters of an entirely 'new' paradigm. Ironically, many of the scholars who adopt the third or fourth approaches actually credit Josephus with a substantial level of analytical skill. In commenting on the bias of Josephus, it is often lamented that he deliberately tried to cover up the reality of the situation. In other words, Josephus knew exactly what was happening in Judaea. There is, therefore, a level of agreement in the assessment of Josephus by all the approaches. The positive reading of the first and second approaches accepts that Josephus narrated the situation accurately while the critical, negative base of the third and fourth approaches claims that Josephus deliberately tried to lead the reader astray while he still held full knowledge of the real situation.[36]

35. Horsley, *Galilee*, p. 75 n. 24, refers to Rajak, *Josephus*, Chapters 4, 6 and Bilde, *Flavius Josephus*, Chapters 2, 5, as support for his line of interpretation over against that provided by Cohen, *Josephus*, pp. 153-60.

36. Here the 'failure' of Josephus to complete his task is matched by the 'success' of scholarship to unearth the exact nature of the cover-up.

The following discussion focuses on the claim of conceptual independence that makes the 'negative' aspect of the third and fourth approaches appear to be distinctive from the 'positive' reading of Josephus. Caution acts as the catch-phrase of these scholars. It is deemed inappropriate to use Josephus at face value. According to these scholars, there is no doubt that Josephus described actual events and that he is an extremely valuable source of information for any discussion of the situation during the first century CE. Lurking within Josephus's texts lies a healthy, vibrant description of events. What prevents the reader from gaining ready access to this information is the disease of Josephus's bias, his polemic and apologetic. Therefore, what Josephus presents must be used selectively and with extreme care. The task of scholarship is to isolate the disease and remove it from the text. Where there are differences among the scholarly fraternity is in terms of how to apply the appropriate remedy. Most scholars adopt an internal approach, reading Josephus against himself. Some, however, consider that the disease can only be removed by also employing an external remedy, a theoretical model through which to view Josephus. In effect, both the third and fourth approaches work at siphoning out Josephus's comments and interpretation so that the historical events remain unscathed. Scholars are then free to re-arrange the raw data to establish the means of correctly analysing the dynamic of what was happening, and why events unfolded as they did. Throughout the process of cleansing the narrative, conceptual independence from Josephus is jealousy proclaimed. The narrative of Josephus is used but the interpretation is rejected. In other words, there may be a material dependency but that is where the relationship ends. The belief is that, conceptually, the reader is independent of Josephus as the resultant interpretation adopted by scholars has stripped the narrative of Josephus's polemical and apologetical input. These two approaches work from the perspective that 'historical fact' and interpretation can be readily separated. The task of the scholar is to establish clearly the division between these two entities so that the 'facts' may be properly understood.

The assertion that the subject matter and the interpretation of Josephus are distinct entities fails to recognize a fundamental aspect of how Josephus's interpretative framework functions. The subject matter is an intrinsic part of Josephus's interpretation of the situation in Judaea. The two are not simply intertwined, they are integral to one another. To question or reject the interpretation, therefore, should also result in the questioning or rejecting of the subject matter.

The supposed division between 'interpretation' and 'subject matter' reveals a fundamental flaw in the two critical negative approaches. Irrespective of any claims made by scholars, the use of the third and fourth approaches means the reader remains conceptually dependent on Josephus. Whereas those adopting a positive reading readily display this dependency on Josephus for understanding the situation in Judaea, those who adopt one of the two negative approaches do so unwittingly. Although such a conclusion may seem puzzling, to reject this view would be to fail to recognize that the subject matter of Josephus's narrative and the way in which it is all recorded is a manifestation of his interpretative framework. There are no half measures here—everything Josephus records is the result of his choice to include the material.

It is now clear that the parallel between Josephus and scholarship in the picture they construct of Judaea is no coincidence. This parallel is a clear expression of the way Josephus's interpretative framework continues to control how the situation in first-century CE Judaea is understood. Josephus's two pillars—a society racked by conflict and escalating turmoil, and a belief that the revolt was to be explained as an inevitable climax to the escalation of conflict—are borrowed by scholarship primarily because they have not been recognized as expressions of his interpretation. In other words, the most fundamental element of Josephus's narrative has become the framework for all contemporary discussion of the first century CE. There are five key indicators that the parallel between Josephus and scholarship is far more than a mere coincidence. They are: the use of Josephus's reflective comments; structuring the narrative in the same manner as Josephus; comments regarding the completeness of Josephus's account; 70 CE acting as the controlling factor in the reconstruction of the situation in Judaea; and the failure to question Josephus's underlying assumptions. Each indicator warrants detailed discussion. Not all indicators are evident in the work of every scholar who outwardly rejects Josephus's interpretation, nor is there a priority among these indicators. In combination they are examples of the way critical scholarship, despite its best intentions, remains conceptually dependent on Josephus. They help show that scholarship's Judaea is a reorganization of Josephus's interpretation and that it is not the result of 'independent' analysis.

The first of the indicators to consider is the frequent use of Josephus's reflective comments in the course of describing the situation in Judaea. What is important here is to recognize that this is not an example of scholarship being dependent on Josephus simply for information. Instead, the appearance of numerous summary comments displays the willingness of scholars to employ an obvious element of Josephus's interpretation. In other words, scholars are employing material that is part of the second level of the interpretative framework, the various types of overt commentary. In effect, despite the declared aim of isolating and removing the bias of Josephus from the narrative, scholars are using the same 'apologetic' features in their description of events.

Reflections on the general situation, on events alluded to and on events narrated, are often included. A few examples will suffice. Price's brief outline of events in Judaea prior to the revolt is littered with the summary comments of Josephus, especially in relation to the governorship of Albinus and Florus.[37] Albinus 'neglected no form of evildoing' (*War* 2.272) and, paraphrasing Josephus, Price states: 'At this time the historian tells us, the seeds of the city's future destruction were sown (BJ 2.276)'. Although Josephus displays 'excess' in his account of Florus, Price takes the narrative at face value. Apparently Florus 'exploited and grossly mishandled the Jewish Greek conflict at Caesarea' and 'Josephus's judgement' where Florus is compared with Albinus in *War* 2.277 is quoted without further comment. By implication, it is a comment that is deemed historically valid.

A further example of rejecting Josephus's interpretation but also adopting his reflective comments is Horsley and Hanson. In particular, their discussion of the problem of banditry is dependent on Josephus's comments. For example, they state that the 'direct effect of this inconsistent administrative policy [Albinus's actions] did not escape Josephus: "Thus the prison was cleared of inmates, but the land then became infested with brigands" (*Ant.* 20.215)' (p. 69). Furthermore, describing the spread of banditry Horsley and Hanson quote the reflective comment on the event in *War* 2.238 as evidence of the historical situation (p. 68). They also adopt Josephus's reflection on his account of the Galilaean–Samaritan dispute—'from then on the whole of Judea was infested with brigands' (*Ant.* 20.124)—as a significant observation regarding the actual situation (p. 68).[38]

---

37. Price, *Jerusalem*, pp. 2-11.
38. For his detailed criticism of the aristocracy see Horsley, 'High Priests',

In a similar vein Murphy openly employs the comments of Josephus. Murphy's description of events in Judaea, especially after 44 CE, draws heavily on Josephus's reflective comments. The reflection on the general situation in *Ant.* 20.160-61 is quoted as an accurate summary of the state of affairs during Felix's term of office. Then, in connection with Albinus, his act of clearing the prisons resulted in Judaea being 'infested with brigands' (*Ant.* 20.215). The various reflections on the events alluded to during Albinus's governorship allow Murphy to claim that 'Albinus' corruption pushed the country further toward war'.[39]

Hengel also readily adopts Josephus's summary statements at face value on several occasions. For example, while discussing the nature of the relationship between the zealots and the false prophets Hengel quotes the summary of *War* 2.264-65, simply stating that this 'explicitly confirms the link between' the two groups. During the governorship of Albinus the statement of *Ant.* 20.215, that the release of prisoners resulted in the countryside being full of robbers, is quoted as factual.[40]

Rhoads also makes extensive use of Josephus's comments, especially in the context of revising the situation during the 60s. Florus's 'wicked extremities' are 'amply described by Josephus', as Rhoads contends by quoting *War* 2.278 without any further comment. The situation under Albinus and Florus is aptly stated by Josephus according to Rhoads,

pp. 23-55. Note the way Horsley cites information derived from Josephus at face value, such as the criticism levelled at Florus (p. 48) and the comments on Ananus (p. 53).

39. The dependence even extends to the point of using the imagery of Josephus, referring to 'fanning the flames of rebellion' (p. 293). An even more blatant expression of drawing on Josephus's imagery is located in N.T. Wright's very brief summary of the situation in Judaea: 'the embers of potential rebellion smouldered on, ready to be fanned into flames of expectation and aspiration' (*The New Testament and the People of God* [Minneapolis: Fortress Press, 1992], p. 161).

40. Possibly most illuminating of the manner in which Hengel, *Zealots*, readily employs Josephus's comments and narrative is his interpretation of the events of 66 CE. Hengel states that it was 'very remarkable that... the radical party lost its decisive influence in the leadership of the war' after the defeat of Cestius (p. 269). Here Hengel encounters the problem of matching his interpretation with Josephus's description of events. Rather than question the existing account, let alone his own interpretation, Hengel postulates that 'the moderates had skilfully adapted themselves to the changed circumstances and had decided—at least outwardly—to support the cause of the war' (p. 370). What Hengel does is resolve an apparent inconsistency by drawing upon other elements of Josephus's narrative (*Life*) to affirm his account.

when he quotes *War* 2.276 and *Ant.* 20.257 respectively as evidence of the extent to which matters had deteriorated.[41]

A final example of the use of Josephus's reflective comments is the work of Grabbe. Within the synthesis of events in Judaea, Grabbe occasionally cites Josephus's various types of reflections as evidence of the historical situation. Under Felix the reflections on events alluded to in *War* 2.264-65 are used to indicate the effect of the combined work of brigands and impostors. Despite the lack of reference to any named groups or individuals, and Grabbe's acknowledgment that they include 'rhetorical exaggeration', he still views the comments as an indication of 'an increase in the translation into action of popular sentiment against Roman rule' (p. 442). In reference to Florus, Grabbe states that the governor 'supposedly did nothing about brigandage because he was in league with the brigands and concerned only with getting his share'. Grabbe accepts that such a view is based on statements in Josephus that are 'exaggerated and sweeping'. However, he also claims that they 'may be true' and thus these reflections on events are allowed to stand as expressions of the historical situation (p. 444).[42]

Numerous reflective comments of Josephus feature in the description of affairs by those scholars who seek to resist the influence of Josephus's bias. All the comments used, however, are part of the interpretative framework of Josephus. They are an expression of Josephus's opinion of the situation and yet they appear in the work of scholars as evidence of the historical situation. At one and the same time the bias of Josephus is seen as a drawback that needs to be removed and is also used as historical data. Significantly, the reflective comments employed convey Josephus's picture of a deterioration in the state of affairs, an escalation in the level of turmoil. In effect, by

41. Note the extent of paraphrasing of Josephus's description of 66–70 CE employed by Rhoads, *Israel*, pp. 100-107. Note also the way he uses *Ant.* 20.205-207 and *War* 2.275 as sequential elements in the picture of Albinus's governorship (p. 77). Here Rhoads uses the two texts as though they form two parts of a single narrative that displays how Albinus undermined stability.

42. A further example of this willing use of Josephus's comments is ably expressed by Kasher, *Jews and Hellenistic Cities*. Having stated that Josephus was biased and needed to be used with care (pp. 12-13, 19) Kasher then borrows Josephus's imagery and language regarding the impact of several events (pp. 253-54, 315).

employing Josephus's reflective comments scholars are drawing on an established mindset that defines the boundaries in which the situation in Judaea is to be understood.

The second indicator of the conceptual dependence is the way the description of events in Judaea is structured. It is apparent that the order in which events are narrated is dictated by the manner in which Josephus presents his account of affairs in *War* 2 and *Ant.* 18–20. It is understandable that scholarship adopts a chronological framework for the presentation of events.[43] What appears to be puzzling, however, is the absence of certain events from the account of contemporary scholarship that is critical of Josephus. There are three events of note: Josephus's trip to Rome to defend several priests sent there for trial; the activities of Jesus b. Ananias; and the population count taken in either 65 or 66 CE. These three events act as a test case. They are all associated with the final years before the revolt, a period subject to a significant amount of discussion among scholarship. They are, however, not part of Josephus's chronological narrative of *War* 2 or *Ant.* 18–20. Their presence, or absence, therefore, from the description of events by scholars becomes an important 'test' for defining the extent and nature of the parallel between Josephus and scholarship. What is striking about the comparison test is that, with two exceptions regarding the career of Jesus b. Ananias and one regarding the trip to Rome, the incidents are not mentioned. In effect, scholarship parallels the structure used by Josephus in *War* 2 and *Ant.* 18–20. We will consider each incident in turn.

The first event is Josephus's account of the trip he made to Rome to defend several priests sent there for trial. The absence of this event from the thematically orientated elements of such single issue studies as those of Price and Horsley may appear understandable because it does not pertain to the specific aspects of Judaean history being explored. What is not understandable is the absence of this incident from the brief outline of events in Judaea provided by such scholars as Price, Horsley and Hanson, Murphy and Grabbe. In defence of this absence it could possibly be claimed that because the story is only described in *Life* it was not deemed relevant. However, its incorporation in the biography of Josephus by such scholars as Grabbe (p. 5) and Rhoads

---

43. A partial exception to this approach is Horsley, *Spiral*, pp. 28-58, who seeks to identify incidents within their appropriate category. Within each category, however, Horsley does present the incidents in a chronological sequence.

(p. 6) suggests the explanation lies more in terms of the conceptual orientation of scholarship. The story is recorded in *Life* and in the view of Josephus it pertains to his personal affairs. It does not pertain to the history of Judaea, which Josephus deliberately described mainly in *War* and *Ant.* The narrative of *Life* is deemed relevant for scholarship exploring the historical situation, however, when Josephus describes his generalship in Galilee.

Even if the absence of the trip to Rome continues to be explained, in part, because it is located in *Life* rather than *War* or *Ant.* no such hesitation can be held regarding the two other 'test cases'. The career of Jesus b. Ananias and the reference to the population count are part of *War* 6. The story of Jesus' activities in Jerusalem is cited by Goodman and Horsley and Hanson. For Goodman it is mentioned simply in terms of an example of how the Romans responded to certain situations in Judaea (p. 174) and as evidence that there were prophecies regarding the fate of the Jews.[44] Horsley and Hanson include Jesus b. Ananias in their discussion of the oracular prophets active in Judaea prior to the revolt (p. 174). At no stage do Goodman or Horsley and Hanson try to relate the story of Jesus to the general state of affairs in Judaea. Furthermore, not one of the brief outlines of events or any of the thematic discussions in the single issue studies make any reference to Jesus b. Ananias.

Possibly even more significant is the third test case—the population count mentioned in *War* 6. Not one scholar who argues for the need to stand independent of Josephus's interpretation refers to the 'census' in their analysis of the situation. Its absence is most puzzling.[45] For example, Horsley actively highlights the importance of Jewish protest regarding the payment of tribute in 6 CE and 66 CE.[46] Reference to the 'census' in *War* 6 would presumably add weight to his line of argument in relation to the visit of Florus. In a similar vein, the demand of Florus for the payment of 17 talents features in the accounts of events from 66 CE in Price, Grabbe, Goodman and Murphy, to

44. Goodman, *Ruling Class*. He also briefly refers to Josephus's trip to Rome (p. 139). Note also that Hadas-Lebel, *Flavius*, p. 64, refers to the various signs (*War* 6.288-310), including Jesus b. Ananias, in the context of depicting the instability of the years before the revolt.

45. Hengel, *Zealots*, pp. 130, 356, does refer to the population count but only to note the sensitivity of the Jews to such practices.

46. Horsley, *Spiral*, pp. 77-89.

name but a few. Generally, it is accepted that the payment is linked to arrears in tribute (*War* 2.408).[47] There is, however, no discussion of how the population count may relate to what happened in Jerusalem in 66 CE. Openings for the inclusion of the 'census' are evident, but it is a notable absentee from the discussions.

The absence of these test cases is very significant. Scholars may claim they are undertaking an examination into the situation in Judaea independent of Josephus. This supposedly 'independent' study, however, does not avail itself of all the possible information provided by Josephus. The significance of these absentees is all the more noticeable because those scholars who claim their conceptual independence from Josephus portray Judaea as a place of increasing turmoil. Their failure to include one or more examples pertinent to this apparent 'turmoil' appears, on the surface, to be puzzling. There is, however, a plausible and simple explanation. Scholars have constructed their accounts entirely within the boundaries set by Josephus in *War* 2 and *Ant.* 18–20. As such, they reinforce the extent to which scholarship, allegedly critical of Josephus and conceptually independent, parallels the description of affairs provided by him.[48]

The third indicator to consider is the supposed level of completeness of Josephus's narrative. At issue here is the attitude of scholarship towards the representativeness of what Josephus has narrated. A prominent aspect of this expression of dependency is a common trait displayed by such scholars as Crossan, Horsley and Hanson and Horsley. There is no examination of the criteria by which Josephus selected the subject matter he included. What is especially significant regarding this silence in relation to the three scholars mentioned is that they all make assertions about the content left out by Josephus. In other words, what Josephus includes is, apparently, taken for granted, while what he fails to include is a matter of overt interest. Here the bias of Josephus is taken to task, with Josephus's aristocratic interests being deemed as an explanation for what is left out of the narrative. For example, Crossan declares that the level of banditry far exceeds what Josephus describes (p. 160). For Horsley, Josephus deliberately played down the extent to which it was the common people who

47. See, for example, Grabbe, *Judaism*, p. 447, and Hengel, *Zealots*, p. 356.
48. Ironically, Smallwood, *Jews*, an example of the first approach to the use of Josephus, includes all three incidents in her narrative of events in Judaea.

inspired the various non-violent protests against the Romans.[49] Horsley and Hanson argue that 'Josephus's incidental comments' help plot out the features of the expanding banditry of the mid-first century CE (p. 67).[50]

Underlying these claims is a belief that the narrative, whether of actual bandit activities or summaries of the extent of banditry, pertains to the historical situation. It is assumed that Josephus has not given the full picture, leaving out details that point towards even more upheaval and turmoil than is narrated. Thus, Josephus's narrative under-represents the nature of the turmoil and the extent of conflict in Jewish society. By adopting this stance these scholars work within the boundaries established by Josephus. The starting point is to affirm the accuracy of one of Josephus's pillars—it was a period of turmoil. Scholars then claim that, if anything, Josephus's bias has resulted in him dismissing details relevant to understanding the nature and extent of banditry. No attempt is made to question whether Josephus's interpretative framework accurately reflects the state of affairs, nor whether he plays down or accentuates the level of turmoil. The 'complete' picture, it is assumed, is based on the principle of conflict being played down by Josephus.[51]

A second aspect of the assumptions made by scholarship in relation to the subject matter included in Josephus's narrative pertains to the impact of his bias. Josephus is almost universally accepted by those who reject his interpretations as a voice of the ruling class, probably with overt sympathy for his Flavian benefactors. It is even possible, as Horsley, Crossan and Horsley and Hanson claim, that Josephus was an open opponent of the 'common people'. This aristocratic bias translates

49. Horsley, *Spiral*, pp. 116-20.

50. An alternative view is expressed by Rhoads, *Israel*, pp. 55-59. He argues that Josephus was eager to highlight any possible signs of turmoil and revolution. The failure to mention more than he does indicates that a single organized party was not active in the period of Roman rule up to at least 41 CE. Going even further, Paltiel, *Vassals*, p. 269, claims that Josephus actually exaggerates the level of conflict that existed in the years between 44–66 CE. What is at issue here is the completeness of Josephus's narrative and the means by which any perceived 'silence' on the part of him should be understood.

51. Grabbe, *Judaism*, p. 523, raises a similar point to the one made here when he comments on Horsley's apparent inability to pay due attention to 'the incompleteness of the data'. Note also the comments of S. Schwartz, 'Josephus in Galilee', p. 290, regarding some of the biases of Josephus.

into a distorted picture of the situation in Judaea.[52] For example, Murphy and Horsley and Hanson raise suspicion regarding the critical description of the brigands. In particular, it is argued that Josephus ignored their social and political agenda. This criteria of exploring the bias of Josephus is not, however, applied with consistency. There is, for example, no attempt to consider how Josephus's aristocratic background may have influenced his presentation of other Jews and Romans involved in various incidents.[53]

A similar problem is apparent in the approach of Horsley and Hanson. Because of Josephus's bias it is assumed that he has continually covered up the true nature of the protests, especially the extent to which they originated among the 'common people'. The same concern regarding any other possible authorial interests is not considered in relation to the way other groups or individuals may have been depicted by Josephus. In terms of the supposed completeness of Josephus, the nature of the questions posed by scholars is extremely one-sided. Josephus is challenged on the information he has left out that relates to further conflict or the motivation of some participants.[54] In effect, the turmoil that acts as a pillar for Josephus automatically acts as a pillar for scholarship that is concerned to siphon out his bias.

The fourth indicator of the conceptual dependency is the central role given to 70 CE in the reconstruction of the situation in Judaea. The dependency is expressed primarily in two distinct ways that make 70 CE alternate book-ends: one is that 70 CE is the end-point of many discussions; the second has 70 CE as the starting-point, where events are examined to establish an appropriate context in which to understand 70 CE. The majority of studies adopt the first path. They culminate with 70 CE, to the extent that one could almost be forgiven for thinking that the first century CE ends with the destruction of Jerusalem. Probably the most prominent example of 70 CE acting as the end-point is Horsley's *Spiral*. Horsley develops the spiral model to

52. Hengel, *Zealots*, pp. 15-16, and Rhoads, *Israel*, p. 86, also claim that the bias has resulted in the suppression of the religious motivation associated with the revolutionaries. Cohen, *Josephus*, p. 28, views the silence of Josephus in leaving out incidents as an attempt to ensure that the people he was associated with could not be held responsible for anything that went wrong.

53. For example, see Murphy's depiction of Pilate (*Religious World*, p. 296).

54. Sanders, *Judaism*, pp. 35-36, is an exception, noting the tendency of Josephus to focus only on matters of instability and change.

plot the escalation in the type and level of conflict. Although not always reaching the final stage, the model culminates with 'revolt'. Horsley does make mention of 135 CE but his examples of the various stages in the spiral are all derived from the period prior to 70 CE. There is no attempt to apply the model after 70 CE, nor to explain how the model is applicable once the revolt stage has concluded. The model may help explain what Josephus has narrated, but it is artificial. It does not allow for continuity in history and the model appears to be working backwards with a known end-point acting as the guiding principle for how to reconstruct the years that precede the revolt.[55]

The other aspect of the prominence given to 70 CE is that it has become the context from which to view the events of the first century CE. Just as Josephus tried to explain 70 CE by establishing a narrative context in which to view what happened as the culmination of various factors, scholarship has also used 70 CE as the starting point of its investigation. Much energy is devoted towards constructing a context in which to explain 70 CE, particularly among some of the single issue studies.

The works of Price and Murphy display the pivotal role given to 70 CE. Although Price is particularly concerned to explain the situation in Jerusalem between 66–70 CE, he does consider it pertinent to out-line the context in which those years should be explored.[56] The context favoured involves a serious of clashes and conflicts that culminate in 66 CE. The factionalism that looms large in the years prior to 66 CE and then dictates the course of the revolt, however, is not fol-lowed through. The agenda is to explain 66–70 CE and the events that follow are not deemed relevant in any sense. On an even more explicit and detailed level, Murphy displays the contextual approach. Murphy describes his narrative of the years prior to 66 CE as a 'History of First Century Jewish Palestine'. The revolt of 66–70 CE and the years 74–135 CE are described in a later chapter. The years prior to the revolt, and those that follow it, are part of a different type of discus-sion. In effect, an artificial boundary is established with the first century CE being cast in the shadow of the 66–70 CE revolt. What

55. The dominance of 70 CE is evident by the chronological boundaries used. For example, Rhoads, *Israel*, covers 6–74 CE, Hengel, *Zealots*, refers to 63 BCE–135 CE but focuses mainly on 6–66 CE, Horsley, *Galilee*, divides his discussion explor-ing 4 BCE–67 CE and Murphy, *Religious World*, uses 6–66 CE.

56. Price, *Jerusalem*, pp. 2-11.

follows 70 CE pertains to a later period of Jewish history.

In part, Goodman is an exception to the division of the first century around 70 CE.[57] Although Goodman's focus is explaining the 66–70 CE revolt, he goes beyond 70 CE to survey the Roman response. He does so in an attempt to confirm his interpretation of the causes of the revolt. He traces the Roman reaction and, using the example of Gaul, argues that the decision not to return leadership to those responsible prior to 66 CE supports the notion they had been viewed as responsible for the breakdown in affairs (pp. 247-50). Here Goodman tries to explore the pre-70 CE factors in the years that immediately follow the revolt.[58] It is, however, important to recognize that 66–70 CE dominates Goodman's discussion of the first century. 70 CE acts as the perspective from which to explore other events of the period, whether from before or after the revolt.[59]

The close parallel between scholarship and Josephus in the prominence given to 70 CE is a further expression of scholarship, supposedly independent of Josephus's interpretation, borrowing from his interpretative framework. This aspect of the dependency raises two important issues. One is the possible implication of hindsight for the type of investigation undertaken. In particular, the concern is whether the hindsight results in a tendency to view events from a tunnel perspective, assuming that they are, in some manner or another, related to a later event that was viewed as the end-point in a process. The other issue pertains to the possible importance dates have in dictating the nature of the investigation that is undertaken. With the exception of S. Schwartz, not one study into the situation in first-century CE Judaea culminates with 100 CE; they all end with 70 CE. Linked with the issue of hindsight, it raises the question of the way the end-point effects the type of investigation being undertaken. Does 70 CE beg an

---

57. Goodman, *Ruling Class*.

58. Grabbe's survey of Jewish history in Judaea can be viewed in a similar vein (*Judaism*). The account continues beyond 70 CE, concluding with the Bar Kochba revolt of 132–135 CE. Even here, the focus on 70 CE is implicit. The end of the revolt acts as a chronological boundary for the segmentation of his narrative. Although some attention is paid to the years that follow 70 CE (pp. 583-85, 594) the discussion of that information is generally linked to the events of the early second century CE, especially the Bar Kochba revolt, rather than to the preceding years.

59. The notion that the discussion of the first century CE ends with 70 CE is reinforced by the uniqueness of S. Schwartz's study of the period immediately after the revolt in relation to the situation that preceded the war (*Judaean Politics*).

examination that looks for explanation of conflict and disorder where 100 CE would not? This is an issue to which we will need to return in the following chapter.

The final indicator of the conceptual dependence is the failure to question appropriately the underlying assumptions of Josephus's narrative. In particular, we turn to the starting-point of the entire discussion of the relationship between the Judaea of scholarship and of Josephus, the paralleling of the two pillars. It is the pillars of Josephus that act as the framework for scholarly reconstructions. The crucial factor is that their legitimacy is assumed rather than substantiated. In effect, those who claim to question Josephus's interpretation begin their analysis from an acceptance of the key principles of Josephus's conceptual framework. What is especially significant regarding this indicator is that the conclusions of the major exponents of this supposed rejection, such as Goodman and Horsley, are becoming increasingly popular as an 'orthodoxy' from which to interpret what was happening in Judaea.

Horsley's *Spiral* is an excellent expression of this fifth indicator of the conceptual dependency (pp. 3-28). Arguing that the key to understanding the first century CE is a proper recognition of the 'colonial situation', events are interpreted in the context of conflict, which has its origins in the functioning of Roman imperial rule. In Horsley's model the events recorded by Josephus stand as an account of historical events. What is required is their correct decipherment. At the very base of Horsley's argument is a belief that turmoil is the crucial feature of Jewish society. The theoretical model, the 'colonial situation', explains the central role of turmoil and the spiral then explains how the turmoil escalates. The starting-point of this interpretation, Judaea as a place of turmoil, is in total agreement with the view Josephus depicts. Although the correlation is striking, even more important is that turmoil as the dominant theme is assumed by Horsley but never substantiated. What Horsley 'contributes' is an explanation for the nature of the turmoil that Josephus presents to his reader.[60] As a result, the approach of Horsley effectively legitimizes one of Josephus's key pillars—Judaea in a continual situation of turmoil and conflict.

---

60. Not surprisingly, Horsley and Hanson, *Bandits*, pp. 35-43, display a similar dependency on Josephus. Hence, turmoil was the 'salient characteristic' of the period in which the various events mentioned in Josephus's narrative must be properly located.

Goodman also displays a ready acceptance of Josephus's two pillars.[61] That Judaea was characterized by an escalation in the level of turmoil, and that the revolt is to be explained by long-standing factors, are taken as the starting-point. What Goodman contributes is a means by which the two pillars are to be understood. In other words, although Goodman offers a form of causation that is not proclaimed by Josephus, he continues to work within the boundaries established by Josephus. At no stage are either of the pillars substantiated; they are assumed to be the basis from which the search for and the explanation of their existence is undertaken.

There are several other expressions of the failure to question the underlying parameters of Josephus's interpretation. For example, it is evident in Price's thesis that factionalism was the dominant feature in the years of the revolt and those that precede 66 CE.[62] Price unravels the constant presence of faction fighting that weaves through the narrative of Josephus. Here Price adopts a major feature of the 'turmoil'. Because Josephus's 'most effective distortions are based on truth' it is appropriate to highlight the degree of factionalism located in his account. Price does not subject the mention of factional conflict during the revolt to scrutiny. He does not ask whether Josephus has created, or even exaggerated, it as part of his interpretative framework. In other words, Price accepts the presence of factionalism as historically valid; it is the starting-point of an investigation that seeks to explore its practical expression. To assume that the factionalism is an example of what is normally an 'overreaction to real events rather than malicious flights of fancy' is to construct a study that commences within the interpretative framework of Josephus. The problem of failing to question the underlying parameters is effectively indicated by Price. The observations he makes regarding the 'excesses' of Josephus in portraying the fate of the aristocracy under the post-67 CE administration should have encouraged a total reassessment of the whole description of events between 66–70 CE (pp. 135-40, 166-67). It should have also resulted in a questioning of whether the 'factionalism'

61. Goodman, *Ruling Class*, pp. 109-33.
62. Price, *Jerusalem*, pp. xii-xiii. Rhoads, *Israel*, pp. 96, 108, also displays the willingness to take the extent of factional trouble at face value. Note how Rhoads uses Josephus's description of Idumaean action to verify the comments regarding the terrorism of the zealots (p. 108). Here Josephus is being called upon to act as the witness for his own defence.

among the rebels is historically accurate. At no stage, however, does Price address either of these concerns.

Finally, one further brief example displays the inability to question the framework established by Josephus. Despite statements that indicate the need for caution, Grabbe expresses the control willingly acquiesced to Josephus in the description of the events leading up to the revolt. Grabbe notes that the account of Florus's governorship lacks much in terms of detail. In itself, this is not deemed to be a significant problem, as 'one does not need to know the details to appreciate that things were bad and leading up to some sort of explosion' (p. 444). The narrative structure and the underlying assumption of imminent conflict which controls Josephus's description of Florus's governorship are adopted without debate.

The pervasiveness of Josephus's interpretative framework controlling the existing discussion of the first century has an important bearing on what elements of his narrative are allowed to stand as historically accurate details. Critical scholarship proclaims the need for caution and that the subject matter be separated from the interpretation. However, in the light of the comments just made it is apparent that all existing discussion regarding decisions of when agreement and disagreement between Josephus's bias and subject matter warrant rejection of information are made within the boundaries of Josephus's interpretative framework. The process is circular in nature. It is, by default, Josephus who determines what is valid and what is bias. The problem of what elements of the narrative need to be verified because of the possible colouring by Josephus's bias is directly addressed by Goodman and Price.[63] However, both of these scholars cite incidents mentioned by Josephus in passing, taking them for granted. Probably the best example is Josephus's statement that many Jews had departed from Judaea prior to the revolt because the level of anarchy had become so intense. It is possible that Jews did leave Jerusalem, and that their motivation was a concern about increased turmoil. However, before such statements are narrated at face value they should be weighed up against other comments by Josephus. For example, if the situation was so bad, why did Josephus return to Jerusalem after being in Rome to defend several priests? Furthermore, on what criteria is the claim that Jews departed from Judaea to be measured against the

---

63. Goodman, *Ruling Class*, pp. 19-21; Price, *Jerusalem*, pp. 180-93.

claim in *War* 6.300 that Jerusalem was experiencing a period of relative peace in 62 CE? The crucial issue here is how much of the subject matter is questioned. Suspicion of only selected elements of the narrative is totally inappropriate. To do so simply ensures that the examination remains bound by Josephus's world-view. There can be no half measures. Every element of the narrative needs to be queried, not just certain sections that are perceived to be important.

There is an explicit and deliberate attempt made by those scholars who adopt the third and fourth approaches to go beyond Josephus's interpretation. This concern has been effectively expressed in terms of why the revolt began.[64] Any overt diversity in the conclusion derived from the application of these two approaches, however, masks what is an overwhelming unity in the framework by which scholarship explores the first century CE. This unity is expressed in the parallel between the picture constructed by Josephus and scholarship, especially in the central role played by the two pillars of Josephus. The explanation for this parallel lies in the continued conceptual dependence of all contemporary scholarship on the interpretative framework of Josephus. In the case of those adopting the first and second approaches to the reading of Josephus in relation to the first century CE it is a matter of choice. Despite any claims to the contrary, those who adopt the third and fourth approaches, unintentionally remain conceptually dependent on Josephus. The boundaries established by Josephus clearly remain in place. The revolt was bound to take place and 66–70 CE was the end-point of a period of escalating turmoil.

Attempts to find an explanation for the continued conceptual dependency among those adopting the third and fourth approaches belong to the realm of conjecture. It is unlikely that a universal explanation for this situation exists, other than the obvious need to draw on Josephus as the only significant narrative source for the period and the associated inability to properly understand the all encompassing nature of his interpretative framework. I can offer only one possible practical reason which is probably more appropriate regarding the work of some scholars than others. The explanation relates to an approach to historical inquiry, particularly in terms of the recording of 'historical' events in texts and to several statements of Josephus. It appears that certain claims made by Josephus may have unduly influenced some

---

64. Another prominent area is the level and nature of involvement in the war by the aristocracy.

scholars. In order to defend the legitimacy of his texts Josephus describes what he views as a distinction which exists between the narrative of events (subject matter) and the commentary of the writer (interpretation). According to Josephus, it is possible to separate the facts of history from the views of the person recording those facts. Josephus is only too aware that his narrative contains many personal comments and tries to allay possible criticism by calling on the reader to ignore those comments if they so desire and just focus on the description of events (*War* 1.12; 5.20). The reader, and presumably Josephus, can separate historical facts from personal polemic.[65]

Parallel to, and compounding, the notion of an alleged distinction between interpretation and subject matter is that Josephus was genuinely engaged in trying to write about actual events.[66] Within this context what is required of the historian is to identify the elements of the narrative that are tainted by his bias. Thus, such scholars as Price, Goodman, Horsley and Crossan argue that Josephus uses his polemic to either accentuate or play down various details in the actual situation. It becomes, therefore, as Crossan claims, a case of having to read Josephus against himself.

Although such an approach may appear to display sufficient independence, it does not go far enough. It has resulted in suspicion falling predominantly on the 'foreground' comments of Josephus. Insufficient attention has been paid to the all encompassing nature of Josephus's

65. Grabbe, *Judaism*, provides a good example of how such a division works. The reader needs to be wary of the parts of Josephus's narrative that are an expression of personal apologetics. Although not stated, this is presumably to be done to a greater degree than it is with the elements that narrate events. The subject matter and interpretation appear to stand as separate entities. However, note Grabbe's introductory comment to the description of the events between 67–70 CE, where he calls for caution because of the reliance on Josephus (p. 454).

66. Archaeological findings indicate that Josephus was reasonably accurate in his description of sites, especially the topographical features. Where much debate remains is in terms of his account of what happened at a given location. See B. Mazar, 'Josephus Flavius and the Archaeological Excavations in Jerusalem', in L.H. Feldman and G. Hata (eds.), *Josephus, the Bible and History* (Detroit: Wayne State University Press, 1989), pp. 325-29. Further work at Yodefat, beyond the initial survey, may provide a valuable insight into a site of major importance to Josephus's personal affairs. See D. Adan-Bayewitz, M. Aviam and D.R. Edwards, 'Yodefat, 1992', *IEJ* 45 (1995), pp. 191-97. Regarding the work at Yodefat I am grateful for assistance provided by D.R. Edwards.

bias. As outlined in Chapters 2 and 3, the interpretative framework controls the entire narrative, the selection of contents and the nature of its presentation. Josephus's account may be based on historical events and he may desire to be regarded as an accurate historian (*Life* 339; *Ant.* 14.1-3; 16.187; *War* 7.455). Conceptual independence cannot be achieved, however, while it is assumed that the modern reader simply has to distinguish between Josephus's personal comments and the narrative of facts. In effect, the intrinsic nature of his interpretative framework has not been properly comprehended.

The net result of the four approaches outlined may be that individual elements of Josephus's bias are identified and a reinterpretation of his narrative devoid of that specific expression of bias is constructed. All that is being achieved in such work, however, is a reorganization of information within the same boundary markers that Josephus has set in place. This central point brings to the forefront the need to determine the agenda that is being pursued. If the task is to understand Josephus's interpretation, then much of the existing discussion partially achieves that goal, even if that was not the scholar's intention. If, however, the task is to develop an understanding of the actual historical situation in Judaea, it is not appropriate to continue along the same line of inquiry. The gift of Josephus's narrative has been allowed to be all encompassing because the interpretative framework of Josephus has controlled the approach of scholarship. Historical inquiry into the first century CE has been working from a false premise. Undue influence has been given to hindsight derived from the view of one source.

Ironically Grabbe and Rajak express the nature of the predicament. When discussing the events of 66 CE Grabbe refers to a twofold problem faced by scholarship: there is only one account and it is one-sided (p. 447).[67] The same situation applies to the first century CE as a whole. Rajak is even more telling in her comment that 'almost without thinking, we tend to follow him in his basic point of interpretation: yet usually he is denied the credit for shaping an influential and valuable analysis'.[68] Indeed, Josephus is the architect of scholarly interpretations. Dependence on Josephus for subject matter is openly acknowledged. What the comments of Grabbe and Rajak unwittingly indicate is that the dependence is far more profound and significant

---

67. See also his comment regarding the narrative of 67–70 CE (p. 454).
68. Rajak, *Josephus*, p. 77.

than merely relating to subject matter. The dependency is also in terms of structure and conceptual understanding of the period. One interpretation—namely, Josephus's—stands as the interpretative framework through which to understand the first century CE. For scholars who seek to establish the historical situation this is the crux of the problem.

We are drawn back to the question posed at the end of Chapter 3, whether or not Josephus's picture is an accurate presentation of the historical situation. It is now clear that this question, at its fundamental level, is not explored by scholarship. Without even addressing the question it is assumed that Josephus's interpretative framework is valid. Due recognition is not given to the involvement of Josephus in controlling the entire discussion of the period. With an agenda concerned to understand the actual historical situation there is a need to shift the focus. The challenge is to identify a means of breaking free from the existing boundaries to use Josephus as a source of subject matter but also stand independent of his framework. It is a challenge that points toward a minefield: on what basis does the reader achieve 'objectivity' in deciding exactly how the narrative can stand as 'raw data'?

Chapter 6

CASE STUDIES: A MEANS TO AN END

The vast majority of scholarly interest in first-century CE Judaea is engaged in the pursuit of unearthing a means of working independently of Josephus's interpretation of the situation. The content of Josephus's narrative texts is extensively mined. However, scholars claim to be doing this within a framework that differs from that of Josephus. I have argued that this assertion does not reflect what actually happens. Although elements within the framework have been extensively reshaped, the pillars from which all analysis begins—escalating turmoil and the revolt of 66–70 CE as an inevitable climax—provide the basis from which reconstructions are made. The existing discussion is, in fact, entirely dependent on the interpretative framework of Josephus.

Scholarship's declared interest in establishing the historical situation dictates the agenda for the remainder of this study. My aim is to outline a means by which we can explain the state of affairs in first-century CE Judaea using Josephus's narrative, but in a way that allows us to be independent of his framework. The challenge being faced is significant. What can be suggested that is distinctive from the genuine but flawed existing attempts to make use of Josephus's accounts of events of the first century CE in a conceptually independent manner?

1. *Exploring the Past—Towards What Goal?*

At the outset several important comments need to be made regarding the nature and purpose of historical inquiry. First and foremost, investigations into the past can focus on two dimensions: one pertains to the study of the actual events and situations; the second pertains to the exploration of the various interpretations of events and situations. They are quite distinct and are legitimate fields of inquiry in themselves. The first dimension focuses on what can be ascertained regarding the nature of what actually happened in a given situation. Often the issue of causation features prominently in such a line of inquiry. The other dimension, establishing the various interpretations, focuses on how people perceived and understood what was happening in a given situation and on the way these events were seen to be of significance by various people. The essence of such interpretation can involve a genuine desire for understanding and/or propaganda or polemical motivation to promote a particular line of interpretation.[1]

A further important comment relates to the way we understand the relationship between action and interpretation. In one sense this relationship is best understood as functioning on three distinct chronological time frames. The first is at the level of the actual incident. In terms of how specific events unfold, an initial action may act as the inspiration for interpretations. In turn, these interpretations can help shape the way the incident continues to unfold by supplying the motivating factor for some of the actions following the event. The second time frame is the description of that event in the 'near contemporary' accounts. These are constructed after the event. They are accounts of actual events, written within approximately one or two generations of the main subject matter of the narrative. The final time frame is the examination of events by historians in a later era.

An example of how the relationship between action and interpretation is expressed is the protest over military standards during Pilate's governorship. The first time frame is the actual incident of troops taking images into Jerusalem. Within this time frame action and interpretation appear to work together. Pilate's order that soldiers march into Jerusalem with standards displaying images was an initial action, which was, in turn, greeted with a response among the Jewish community. In turn, the actions of Jews, including the visit to Pilate at Caesarea, triggered a response from the governor. Presumably, each of the actions within this incident was related to how certain people interpreted what had just taken place. The second time frame is represented in the account of Josephus himself, who was presumably interested in describing the actual event. What can become 'blurred' here, therefore, is the nature of the distinction between the actual

---

1.   A further expression of the distinction is the type of discussion associated with each dimension. For the first the focus will be on establishing a single narrative pertaining to what happened, while the second dimension will be characterized by a multiplicity of views regarding the aspects of the incident perceived to be important.

incident and the interpretation of Josephus. From Josephus's perspective there was a clear link between action and interpretation, especially in the way he presents Pilate's final decision on how to resolve the incident. However, there may have also been other actions associated with the order of Pilate. If so, they were not deemed important or relevant according to Josephus, or his source. Hence, without an alternative source, our only way into exploring the order of Pilate as a historical event is Josephus's interpretation, written some 50 years after the event.

Finally, the relationship between action and interpretation also functions on the third time frame, in the scholarly reconstructions. The vast majority of interest here lies in attempts to establish the causation and/or significance of the various actions that constitute the incident. More often than not this is undertaken within the context of a study with interests that extend well beyond simply understanding this one incident. Thus, the elements which are highlighted are determined, first and foremost, by the agenda of the scholar.[2]

It is important to understand the time frame in which the available sources belong. The only literary sources that are part of the first time frame are diaries or reports written at the time of the event. In the ancient world these are extremely rare. Belonging to the second time frame are accounts that have been constructed after the event. These near-contemporary accounts may include eyewitness material and/or they may be constructed by people who participated in the events described, but they are written with the benefit of chronological distance.[3] For example, Josephus may have been particularly concerned to describe actual events and the general situation in Judaea before and during the war, but what he presents is an interpretation of what had occurred.

---

2. This is evident in the variety of conclusions regarding the importance of the event. See, for example, Horsley, *Spiral*, pp. 100-103, and Hengel, *Zealots*, pp. 104-105.

3. It is important to reiterate that eyewitness accounts do not hold a status that liberates them from the notion of bias. For example, a Jewish account of the protest over the standards during Pilate's governorship written by a participant at the time it occurred is not necessarily going to portray the way all Jews responded to the appearance of the images in Jerusalem nor what Pilate believed was the appropriate course of action. The significant benefit of eyewitness accounts lies in the absence of hindsight and that they are the record of at least some of the people directly associated with the incident.

Situated, as we are, in the third time frame, it is important that the line of investigation undertaken is clearly focused on one or another of the dimensions of historical inquiry. This decision determines the type of questions posed and the manner in which the sources are examined. For instance, in an inquiry that focuses on the actual situation, we must not assume that Josephus is a source from the first time frame. The significance of identifying the agenda and time frame of the sources is evident in a hypothetical example from recent history.

Let us for the moment imagine that we are living in the year 4000 CE. As historians we are keen to examine the 'ancient' conflict known as World War II, especially the campaign in the Pacific—its causes, key events and implications. For this task only one substantial account survives—a Japanese description of the war written within some 30 years of the events by an active participant in them. It is an account that is based on actual historical events and it is a genuine attempt to explain why the war took place.[4] In general terms, the war is explained as an attempt by the Japanese to prevent the continued expansion of European colonization in South-East Asia: the Japanese were defending their rights and interests when they attacked Pearl Harbour. Furthermore, the Japanese are portrayed as liberating various South-East Asian countries. We struggle to deal with the problem of breaking through the signs of interpretation evident in this extensive account. We raise doubts regarding the 'objectivity' of the account, noting that the motivation of the various opponents of the Japanese appears to be depicted in a one-sided manner. These opponents are described in very negative terminology; there are numerous inconsistencies regarding the type of actions undertaken by some of the participants, the number of events described are associated with only certain geographical regions and there are periods of silence. It is apparently an account which requires modification. In the resultant reinterpretations, however, the underlying framework that the Japanese were 'liberators' in the fighting is taken for granted.

We return to the 1990s. Here, we still have the benefit of access to many other interpretations. We also have the opportunity to interact with actual participants in some of the events or, at least, to draw upon their records through diaries. We are able to note that the only

4.   For example, there are traces of the war in archaeological findings and allusions to it in the fragments of literature reflecting on the major events associated with the twentieth century.

extant account in 4000 CE has ignored some events, such as the use of 'comfort women' for the Japanese soldiers, or the atrocities associated with the building of the Burma–Thailand railway. The boundaries within which the entire war is being understood, that the Japanese were liberators, may be one perspective on the situation. Furthermore, it may be an account that is genuinely trying to understand and explain what happened in a critical manner. Today, however, we can rightly claim that for a historical inquiry concerned with the actual events it is necessary to consider the perspective held by the other groups who were affected by the events in South-East Asia during the war. The example of the Pacific campaign clearly illustrates the fundamental importance of locating sources in their appropriate time frame. The Japanese account is a near-contemporary interpretation. It is a gold-mine for examining how the war was interpreted by a representative of one of the groups involved. It is not, however, a source of the first time frame. Furthermore, under no circumstances is it *the* framework by which to undertake a reconstruction of the actual situation. To do so would be to give the account a status that is entirely inappropriate.[5]

Applying the same principle to the use of Josephus is vital. To explain how Josephus interpreted what was happening in Judaea is, in itself, a legitimate and important task. A study of this nature is devoted to the second dimension of historical inquiry, examining a near-contemporary interpretation of what was happening. Because of Josephus's proximity to the events he was narrating, we have access to an example of how at least one person was trying to deal with the impact of those events.[6] If, however, the agenda is to examine the actual situation, then what Josephus describes does not necessarily equate with a full picture of what was happening. As with the hypothetical Japanese account,

---

5.   This hypothetical example would be equally valid whether the account was the work of an Australian, American, Malaysian or Papua New Guinean participant. The key principle is that the account of one participant is being allowed to act as the framework for understanding the entire war.

6.   Ironically, this interpretation then becomes the basis of an actual situation. The manner in which certain events are interpreted helps define the means by which people then act in the future. For example, how Josephus understood what happened during the revolt helped determine, or at least confirmed, his view regarding the appropriate course of action to take, especially in relation to continuing to live within the Roman empire.

Josephus's can not be allowed to stand as the framework.

Seeking to understand actual events is legitimate and achievable. Incidents take place and they can be examined. This assertion does not, however, necessarily mean that a complete or 'objective' account of any given event can be constructed. In some instances the amount of detail, or the role and motivation of participants may simply be shrouded in mystery.[7] Possible lack of detail because of the avenue by which actual events are discussed, however, does not negate the value of focusing on them. What we need is a mechanism to undertake such a study.

The obvious starting-point is any source material that is part of the first chronological time frame. Accounts written at the time of the events being narrated give direct access to views of participants or witnesses of what was happening. As already noted, this time frame is rarely represented within the extant material from the ancient world. Rather, most energy is devoted to employing the near-contemporary interpretations. In other words, it is examples of the second time frame that act as the avenue for examining the actual events. Ideally, the study would be accessed through a variety of sources that preserve different perspectives of participants. We would draw upon several

---

7.   Here the issue of 'objectivity' in historical inquiry is drawn into question. The perceived liberation of scholarship from the naive notion of objectivity in the writing of history has tended to result in an overwhelming sense that all history is the study of interpretations. Everything becomes relative and the notion of exploring actual events becomes an anachronism. In this context see the approach to understanding Dionysius of Halicarnassus as a writer by M. Fox, 'History and Rhetoric in Dionysius of Halicarnassus', *JRS* 83 (1993), pp. 31-47. For Fox, Dionysius is a role model of the move away from an 'objective history' that is required by the historian (pp. 32, 39). The downside of the traditional approach to writing history—namely, establishing *the* account of a given period—has been well highlighted by the recent concern of such scholars as Crossan, *Historical Jesus*, and Horsley and Hanson, *Bandits*, to give voice to the silent 'majority' of antiquity—the populace. However, the 'balance', especially for Horsley and Hanson, is to write about the first century CE from the perspective of the populace as though it presents the truth of what happened. The outcome is simply that one perspective is being replaced by another. The line of argument adopted in this study is that 'subjectivity' is ever present in the examination of history. All levels of the chronological time frame are expressions of subjectivity. The presence of this subjectivity, however, does not negate the reality of events. Judaea was attacked by the Romans and Jerusalem was captured and sacked by them. We can, and should, focus on the actual situation, but acknowledging that discussion of such aspects as the who, how and why may never be fully understood.

Jewish, Roman and Greek accounts of what was happening. Such cross-referencing would allow us to explore the events from a broad range of perspectives and ensure that as many of the events as possible were discussed. The situation in relation to first-century CE Judaea, however, is far from this ideal. The 'dream' is shattered by the bleak reality. Furthermore, it places us in rather ironic circumstances. Josephus's account is the only detailed narrative on which we can draw. Instead of multiple perspectives we are limited to one specific interpretation made by one Jewish person who participated in a number of the events he narrates. In other words, the only practical way by which to explore the actual situation is to immerse ourselves in Josephus's narrative, which is an interpretation.

2. *Searching for a Life Raft?*

There are a number of methodological and philosophical issues which the contemporary reader must address when seeking to establish a relationship with the first century CE through the texts of Josephus. The starting point in this process is to step back and acknowledge the irony of where we stand in relation to the interpretative framework of Josephus. We are unable to remove ourselves entirely from Josephus's reconstruction of the situation. On each occasion that we read his texts we are drawn into and encounter the interpretative framework of Josephus.

The predicament is highlighted by Carr in his discussion of historical facts.[8] 'The facts speak only when the historian calls on them: it is he who decides to which facts to give the floor, and in what order or context' (p. 11). Carr's comment is primarily concerned with the way historians engage in the process of selecting and interpreting material for their study of the past. The quote, however, is equally apt for how we should understand the relationship between Josephus and his subject matter. Every element of his text, from the reflections on the general situation to the way specific events are narrated, is an expression of Josephus's interpretative framework. The reality, therefore, is that even though the goal is to break free of Josephus's framework, whenever we read his account of events we will be immersed in that very framework from which we are seeking to distance ourselves.

---

8. E.H. Carr, *What is History?* (Harmondsworth: Penguin Books, 1964), pp. 7-30.

Our focus is on the actual situation, but the point of access is the near-contemporary interpretation of Josephus. It is, as Carr states, a situation in which 'our picture has been preselected and predetermined for us, not so much by accident as by people [in this case, Josephus] who were consciously or unconsciously interested with a particular view and thought the facts which supported the view worth preserving' (p. 13). If this strange irony is not going to signal the end, how can we to respond to this rather bleak situation? Is there a life raft that can be used to rescue the quest for understanding from the predicament with which we are confronted?

Although scholarship has actively engaged in exploring actual events through Josephus's narrative, there is no clear-cut consensus regarding the nature of the life raft. In the discussion of the first century CE, four approaches to the reading of Josephus were identified. For the majority the mechanism used to rescue the narrative requires the corrective of removing Josephus's bias from the description of events. In the following discussion the parameters are broadened to consider what resolutions have been offered in the search for a life raft in general methodological discussion of Josephus as a source of historical information.

The use of Josephus, especially in terms of the appropriate mechanism, has been the inspiration for a significant amount of discussion in the last 25–30 years. As study in the history of the late second temple period has increased, the status of Josephus in such a line of inquiry has become of paramount importance. In many ways Josephus has been his own worst enemy in this concern. Josephus's personal affairs, especially his capture by the Romans and his move to Rome after the war raises questions regarding his possible allegiances. This initial suspicion is reinforced by what appear to be contradictions in *Life* and *War* regarding the way Josephus explains his appointment and commission in Galilee.[9]

The result of the scholarly interest in the value of Josephus for historical inquiry of the first dimension is that three basic approaches can be identified.[10] Although there will be some overlap with the comments made in the previous chapter regarding the use of Josephus in

---

9.   Much of this debate also incorporates rather emotive comments regarding the person of Josephus. For example, see Rappaport, 'Where was Josephus Lying', pp. 279-89, and Schalit, 'Die Erhebung', pp. 208-327.

10.   Compare with Bilde, *Flavius Josephus*, pp. 123-72.

relation to the first century CE situation, it is important to review these three approaches. They reflect the spectrum of scholarly opinion regarding the value of Josephus as a source for historical inquiry of actual events, and the mechanism by which such a task is deemed possible. Each approach mirrors the degree of confidence or scepticism in how Josephus's narrative should be regarded.

At one end of the spectrum is the very positive approach. Josephus is a reliable historian, his account is accurate and perceptive. Furthermore, it deserves to be given the credit for providing scholarship with a framework in which to understand what was happening in Judaea. The approach is best encapsulated in the work of Rajak and Bilde.[11] Josephus's closeness to the events, especially what occurred in Jerusalem at the beginning of the revolt, enables us to reconstruct a thorough description and detailed analysis of the events and situations. He is consistent in his views throughout all his texts. There is no need for concern about languishing in the second dimension of historical inquiry. Josephus's interpretation provides a direct avenue to the actual events and the state of affairs. If anything, there is no distinction to be drawn between what Josephus claims and the reality of what happened.

Rajak focuses on locating Josephus within his cultural context, suggesting that he remained loyal to Judaism as he understood it to operate. Rajak's means of substantiating Josephus's interpretation as an accurate one is to refer to the events he narrates. This is most effectively expressed in terms of how Josephus's view of the beginning of the revolt can be confirmed by reference to the events narrated in *War*. In other words, the mechanism for critiquing Josephus is circular in nature. His interpretation is assessed on the basis of an analysis of the events he describes. Certain elements of the situation may have been overlooked or played down, but the gist of the account provides the reader with the essence of what happened and explanations for how and why events unfolded as they did.

Bilde also proclaims Josephus's narrative should stand as an accurate account of the historical situation. Although Bilde does not argue that

11. A similar approach is evident in the study of the status of the Pharisees. In particular, Mason, *Flavius Josephus*, pp. 372-73, upholds the claims expressed in Josephus's summary statements that the Pharisees were the dominant group. Mason, 'Chief Priests', pp. 158-77, reaffirms this view by examining what Josephus has to say regarding the Pharisees, among other groups, in relation to other available sources in the light of an examination of what each source has to say about the Pharisees.

every statement of Josephus is impartial, he does believe that this was a principle that Josephus genuinely aspired towards fulfilling. In fact, comparison of Josephus's account with known topographical and archaeological material encourages Bilde to conclude 'Josephus's personal involvement—both in many of the events which he describes and in his interpretation and rendering of them—does not result in a historically distorted picture... Generally speaking, his understanding and interpretation of the events and the material are not allowed to obscure and distort his historical accounts' (p. 199). Such confidence in Josephus's narrative is echoed in areas where material remains cannot act as an external witness. Bilde outlines the mechanism by which to employ Josephus as one that seeks the most plausible, simple solution, where the investigation commences with what Josephus has to say and then searches for hypotheses that may help resolve any complications (p. 24). It is within this framework that Bilde argues the alleged differences between *Life* and *War* regarding Josephus's command in Galilee can be explained as two interpretations of the same commission. One was a formal report, the other was a personal recollection. In this positive approach Josephus's narrative is an accurate account of historical situations. The mechanism that enables him to be used as a source for the first dimension of historical inquiry is essentially a close reading of the text.

At the other end of the spectrum stands the second approach. It draws the exact opposite conclusion, viewing the use of Josephus in a negative light. Lamenting the hopelessness of the predicament, scholarship should give up any hope of being able to employ Josephus in the first dimension of historical inquiry. The one prominent expression of this extremely negative prognosis is the work of Moehring.[12] His test case is the depiction of the relations between Judaea and Rome. Although negative regarding the historical situation, Moehring is very positive regarding the second dimension. Josephus's own thesis of how Judaea and Rome should interact needs to be heard on its own merits as the view of one Jewish person deeply concerned about the future of the Jewish people. The narrative of Josephus should be accepted for what it is—an interpretation, full of polemic and apologetic. Criticism of Josephus because he does not stand as an 'objective' historian is unwarranted. Furthermore, Josephus should not be condemned

---

12. Moehring, 'Joseph'.

because he does not provide scholarship with something he never intended to present. In this context, Moehring criticizes Cohen's attempt to reconstruct the situation in Jerusalem in 66 CE because 'he fails to realise that every single sentence of Josephus is determined and coloured by his [Josephus] aims and tendencies'.[13] Moehring's approach to the use of Josephus is summarized by Carr's comment on the relationship between the historian and facts: 'The belief in a hard core of historical facts existing objectively and independently of the interpretation of the historian is a preposterous fallacy, but one which it is very hard to eradicate' (p. 12).

Moehring undertook a personal crusade to 'eradicate' the 'belief in the hard core of historical facts' in relation to the study of Josephus. According to Moehring, 'every word had a purpose'. As such the reader 'can expect no more than a general outline of history underlying the data' because it is impossible to separate the objective from the subjective interpretation of Josephus.[14] Moehring sees a consistency in the outlook of Josephus but rejects the examination of this within a scope other than the second dimension—the examination of an interpretation. Therefore, Moehring's criticism is levelled at scholarship rather than Josephus. There is no way by which Josephus can be used in terms of the first dimension, a study of the actual situation. For Moehring it is time scholarship recognized this 'fact' and concentrated on using Josephus as he is, a near-contemporary interpreter trying to make sense of significant recent events.[15]

Situated between the extremes of these two approaches rests the vast bulk of scholarly discussion of Josephus. In this middle ground lies the third approach, covering a wide range of views regarding how best to employ Josephus's narrative on a practical level. What unites these numerous voices is their use of Josephus with a keen sense of scepticism. Josephus cannot be taken at face value. However, it is legitimate and appropriate to use Josephus in a study of the first dimension of historical inquiry. What is required of the reader is that they must cut

13. See Moehring, review of Cohen, *Josephus*, p. 241. This condemnation is even more forceful because it is levelled at a scholar who is generally viewed as being one of the more critical interpreters of Josephus. Note also the strong criticism of Schalit by Moehring, 'Joseph', pp. 918-44, regarding how the account of Josephus's capture and encounter with Vespasian should be understood.

14. Moehring, 'Joseph', p. 867.

15. Moehring, 'Joseph', pp. 868-69, 917.

through Josephus's bias to identify the historical reality. For most exponents of this approach one of the crucial factors to siphoning out the bias of Josephus is the criterion of comparison.[16] Differences in the detail of what is narrated or, more commonly, in terms of the stated themes and subject matter, generally act as a means of determining the historical accuracy of what is narrated. The underlying concept to this use of 'contradictions' is that they are present in the text against the wishes of Josephus. Although trying to convey a particular line of interpretation, Josephus's inability to completely 'doctor' the text indicates that the content and/or overt comments do not reveal the entire picture of what was happening.[17] Whether Josephus intended to deceive or tried to be loyal to the task of recording actual situations is not really at issue. The reader is not dependent on the honesty of Josephus, but on his narrative of events. Consequently, although the criterion of contradiction is used with varying degrees of scepticism, it is viewed as the key weapon in the effort to cross-examine Josephus. He is read against himself, with the veracity of the narrative being assessed primarily in terms of comparison with perceived bias on the part of Josephus and the way he employs source material. Displaying an underlying faith in the existence of a 'core of historical facts', this is the most popular approach to the quest of employing Josephus in historical inquiry. Four examples will be discussed.[18]

The first is the work of Price. Aware of the approaches adopted by scholars Price expresses the need to find a mechanism that is independent of scholarly subjectivity. For Price, the solution lies within the text of Josephus, particularly within the 'contradictions' and 'incidental details'. At no stage does Price doubt that the first dimension is

16. For such scholars as Goodman and Horsley this process also requires theoretical paradigms to establish the boundaries in which to read Josephus critically against himself.

17. The most popular example of contradiction cited is the commission of Josephus as general in Galilee. More recently, the idea that the aristocracy were only involved in the revolt reluctantly as suggested in *Life* and allegedly implied in *War* has also been questioned on the basis of passages in *War* that indicate a continued presence of at least some aristocrats in Jerusalem during the war. In particular, see Price, *Jerusalem*, pp. 40-45, McLaren, *Power*, pp. 172-84, and Goodman, *Ruling Class*, pp. 152-75.

18. As an alternative, note the emphasis D.R. Schwartz, 'On Drama and Authenticity', pp. 124-25, places on understanding the sources of Josephus for explaining some of the details associated with his narrative.

achievable, nor that Josephus can play a crucial role in such a study. If anything, Josephus was fully aware of the situation in Judaea but deliberately tried to suppress the 'truth'.[19]

The second example, Goodman, adopts a very similar line of argument to Price. Josephus knew the real situation but set about trying to cover up what happened in relation to the war, especially in terms of the role played by the aristocracy. It is an internal mechanism, the contradictions within Josephus's narrative and certain hidden elements of his description of the situation, viewed in the context of an external paradigm, that hold the key for being able to access the first dimension of historical inquiry.[20]

Price and Goodman declare the need for caution. Josephus's bias is evident in the exaggeration and/or suppression of various details. The actual situation is clearly coloured by Josephus in the way he has structured his record of events. The two remaining examples of the third approach reflect views that appear to be extremely sceptical of Josephus's intention. Cohen and, in particular, Rappaport, see personal interests as the paramount factor in determining the make up of Josephus's narrative.

Cohen appears to adopt an extremely sceptical approach towards the

19. Price, *Jerusalem*, comments on existing scholarly approaches to the reading of Josephus, asserting the need for 'balance'. Price is critical of 'unnecessary subjectivity' where because a detail in the text matches one of Josephus's stated themes it results in the rejection of that material. Price is equally critical of allowing the narrative to stand unless it can be clearly discredited. These two extremes apparently depend on a subjective criteria, in which the notion of 'plausibility' is determined by the individual reader (pp. 182-83).

20. See Goodman, *Ruling Class*. This sense of needing to siphon out the bias of Josephus to reveal the actual situation is also clearly expressed in the reconstruction of what happened in Galilee during the war by S. Schwartz, 'Josephus in Galilee', pp. 290-91, and G. Jossa, 'Josephus's Action in Galilee During the Jewish War', in F. Parente and J. Sievers (eds.), *Josephus and the History of the Greco-Roman Period* (SPB, 41; Leiden: E.J. Brill, 1994), pp. 265-78. In his discussion of Josephus's approach to the writing of history Villabla i Varenda, *Historical Method*, also claims that Josephus was biased: 'throughout his works certain moments and viewpoints may be perceived which answer more to the very personal vision of the historian' (p. 278). For Villabla i Varenda this is evident in such elements as the admiration for the Romans, the anti-Samaritan views and the idea that God was on the side of the Romans (pp. 278-79). In other words, elements of the text reflect Josephus while others reflect the actual situation. It is the reader that must make the choice as to which elements belong to whom.

issue of whether Josephus can be used in a historical study of the first dimension.[21] For Cohen, Josephus is far from being a static figure. There is a clear change in his allegiance between the writing of *War* and *Ant./Life*, which helps explain the apparent differences in the polemical aspects of the two texts.[22] Cohen states that the objective is 'to separate historical fact from Josephus's fiction' (p. 84). What Cohen deems to be crucial in the process of employing Josephus's narrative is an internal mechanism. Comparing his different versions of events the criteria that separates the description of actual situations from polemic is how the narrative matches up with the various themes associated with each text. For Cohen, these themes are established first by an analysis of each text. Once the themes are identified the elements of the description of events are compared with the themes. Those elements which clearly agree with the themes are treated with suspicion while the elements that stand out as being contrary to the themes are generally allowed to stand. Even with this process Cohen accepts that although Josephus's narrative can be effectively stripped of its polemic there is still no certainty that understanding of the historical situation is attainable. As his account of events in Jerusalem and Galilee suggests, however, Cohen affirms that a historical inquiry into the actual situation is possible (pp. 181-82).

The final example is the work of Rappaport.[23] The bias of Josephus is openly lamented by Rappaport. Historical inquiry is burdened by a writer who Rappaport believes was deliberately engaged in a continuous process of trying to lie and distort the truth (p. 283). For Rappaport, that the first dimension can be explored using Josephus is primarily the result of chance. His approach is explained in the comparison of *Life* and *War* regarding Josephus's commission. In what is a rather cynical discussion, Rappaport argues that Josephus declares the truth regarding his mission in Galilee in *Life* (p. 283). At no stage was Josephus a revolutionary, nor was he ever fully in charge of affairs in Galilee (p. 283). The change made by Josephus between *War* and *Life*, however, was simply done because it suited Josephus's purposes in *Life*. To defend himself against the accusations of Justus of Tiberias, Josephus deemed it necessary to tell the truth regarding his

21. Cohen, *Josephus*.

22. There is, however, a sense of consistency. Whatever changes in outlook took place between the texts are, in effect, controlled by Josephus's personal opinions.

23. Rappaport, 'Where was Josephus Lying?'.

activities in Galilee. When Justus used *War* to blame Josephus for causing Tiberias to rebel against the Romans, Josephus decided to 'confess' the truth in *Life* (pp. 287-88). He, Ananus and the initial war government, were not trying to promote the war effort, they were hoping to work for peace. For Rappaport caution is required with both texts. In *War* and *Life* the controlling factor for what Josephus includes in his narrative is not an interest in describing the truth but his own personal interests. If revealing the truth happens to comply with Josephus's interests it is by good fortune rather than a professional concern. Again, it is contradiction that features prominently in the mechanism that allows Rappaport to begrudgingly attribute Josephus the function of describing a historical situation.[24]

Of the three basic approaches outlined it is only Moehring who directly queries whether Josephus can be used in relation to a study of the actual situation. Moehring concludes that the answer is in the negative. His open call for a shift in the value placed on the narrative of Josephus is, however, more than matched by the overwhelming agreement of those adopting the two other approaches that Josephus can and should be used. From the respect for Josephus evident in the writing of Bilde to the harsh condemnation in Rappaport, there is agreement that Josephus is a viable source regarding historical study of the first dimension. Where the debate remains—and it is wide ranging—is in how Josephus is to be effectively employed.

Each approach accepts the need to deal with Josephus's bias. The first approach believes the bias is healthy, it is the accurate interpretation of what was happening and should be adopted by scholarship in their search for understanding. The second approach sees the bias as

---

24. The approach advocated by Mason, *Flavius Josephus*, pp. 42-44, in his discussion of the Pharisees as presented by Josephus, warrants brief comment. Mason promotes the notion that reading the accounts within their immediate literary context will help explain the significance of the various references in relation to the historical situation. Such an approach, however, remains bound by Josephus's interpretative framework. Although the approach may help clarify the function of the passages within their immediate context it does not help clarify the actual situation in terms of Pharisaic influence within the community. The discussion remains confined within the 'three philosophical schools' and the associated comments in the summaries of Josephus regarding the status of these groups. Furthermore, to make comments about the status of the Pharisees it is important to place Josephus's references to them within the context of his entire narrative of the period. The use of Josephus in relation to the Pharisees is the subject of a forthcoming study by the author.

an immovable object. There is no way of going beyond Josephus and the appropriate course of action is to give up. The third approach tries to find the middle ground. Josephus's bias must be identified and siphoned out to allow the historian access to the actual situation. A constant feature, therefore, is the concern of scholarship to find a means of effectively dealing with Josephus's bias.

The deficiencies of these three approaches are apparent when they are placed within the context of the sources and in their appropriate chronological time frame, and when an awareness of the all encompassing nature of Josephus's interpretative framework is acknowledged. The positive first approach, as expressed by such scholars as Rajak and Bilde, ignores the nature of the relationship of the source to the actual situation.[25] It also fails to recognize the relationship between ourselves and the text. Using the detail of Josephus's narrative to affirm his interpretation is simply drawing on one part of the framework to affirm another. Given the nature of Josephus's interpretative framework it is not surprising that the two elements, subject matter and interpretation, are in agreement.[26] Even more significant in the light of the different chronological time frames is that the approach fails to acknowledge that Josephus belongs to the second time frame, not the first. In other words, he provides a near-contemporary interpretation but cannot be viewed as an expression of an account written at the time of the actual situation. The hypothetical situation of the Pacific War helps clarify the problem. To view the one surviving account of the Pacific War as an account of the actual situation would

25. The nature of the problem is clearly expressed by Carr, *What is History?*, p. 159, 'the facts of history cannot be purely objective, since they become facts only in virtue of the significance attached to them by the historian [in this case, Josephus]'.

26. There is also no attempt to explore how hindsight has influenced Josephus's texts. Although Rajak, *Josephus*, recognizes that Josephus wrote his narratives after the event the possible implication of this observation is not explored. This is probably most evident in the discussion of Josephus's view regarding the appropriate way to deal with the reality of Roman rule. It is assumed that Josephus's pro-Roman attitude was part of his background as an aristocrat. No assessment is made as to whether this could have been a 'revelation' for Josephus that followed the disaster of 67 and 70 CE. See especially Bilde, *Flavius Josephus*, pp. 179-81, who accepts that because Josephus was pro-Roman in all texts that it was a view he always held. There is no discussion of how the events of the war, particularly his involvement, may have been the inspiration for such a view to be upheld in texts written after the event.

be to turn *an* interpretation into *the* account. This is exactly what the first approach to the use of Josephus achieves. An interpretation, in which turmoil and the revolt as an inevitable event are the cornerstones, sets the boundaries within which the first century is understood.

The second approach is quite different. Josephus is correctly recognized as an example of the second chronological time frame, a near-contemporary interpretation. The problem in this instance is associated with the understanding of historical inquiry. Because Josephus is biased it is argued that there is no possibility of going any further. Even if Josephus was trying to write an account of actual situations he was simply describing his own interpretation. History, therefore, becomes 'trapped' in the realm of simply exploring the second dimension, the interpretations of near contemporaries.

Despite the overt differences, the third approach parallels the first. Those sceptical of Josephus but willing to employ his narrative do not correctly identify his status in the relationship between action and interpretation. Josephus is writing about actual situations but it is always from the level of a near contemporary. The alleged removal of Josephus's bias does not leave the reader with a restored narrative of the actual situation. It is a fallacy to believe that Josephus's bias can be separated from the narrative and that a 'core' of historical events is then left over. To siphon out the bias is to remove the entire narrative. Even though Josephus was a participant in a number of the events he narrates, his account is constructed in hindsight, not as a diary as the events unfold.[27] Again, as with the first approach, Josephus's narrative, however much reduced after extracting the so-called bias, takes on the same status as that given to the Japanese account in the example of the Pacific War. It becomes, in its 'restored' form, the parameter for understanding actual situations. A source that rightly belongs in the second time frame is asserted to fulfil the function of one from the time of the actual event and to be not just one of several possible views but the basis of all understanding.

The search for a life raft among existing scholarship is a lost cause. At this juncture it almost appears that Moehring is right. We should give up on the actual situation and devote our energies to properly understanding the interpretation of a near contemporary, the second dimension of historical inquiry. It appears we require more sources to

27. Even if the latter were the case, it would remain an interpretation. The benefit would be the lack of hindsight as an influence on the type of account presented.

consider exploring the first dimension. Such a conclusion, though, is
unwarranted. There is a way by which we can use Josephus to focus
on the actual situation. We can, and should, explore the first dimension. For this task we are chronologically distanced from the events
and we are almost entirely dependent on Josephus's interpretation. As
a result our avenue into the actual situation will be through an interpretation of that situation. What much of scholarship has been, in effect,
busily trying to siphon out—the 'bias' of Josephus—is the means
through which to proceed. This is our life raft, and the outlook is far
from being 'bleak'. The two key elements are conceptual issues the
reader must address, and a case study approach to the use of the
source.

3. *A Life Raft*

As a precursor to exploring these elements two important observations need to be made. They help establish the direction in which a
study of the first dimension of historical inquiry should proceed. The
first observation is to acknowledge the nature of the interpretation
with which we are working. Rather than lamenting the presence of the
'bias' it should be welcomed as the means of giving life to the text. In
fact, without the interpretation the text would not have been constructed. What is important to establish is the nature of how the bias
acts as the controlling agent of what Josephus narrates. As discussed in
Chapters 2 and 3, attention needs to be paid to identifying and acknowledging the nature of Josephus's interpretative framework, especially
the integral link between commentary and subject matter. In practical
terms regarding the situation in Judaea, it is important to understand
how the two pillars, escalating turmoil and the revolt as the inevitable
culmination of ongoing conflict, are presented by Josephus. Here the
parallel accounts in *War/Ant.* and *War/Life* are a crucial bonus. They
allow us to compare Josephus against himself. Obviously, for much of
the description of the revolt the comparison is entirely internal, in
terms of the account presented in *War*.

A consequence to recognizing and accepting the bias of Josephus is
the issue of what interests combine to constitute the bias. Josephus's
motives have been the subject of much scholarly debate. The identification of his specific polemical concerns have ranged from blatant
propaganda for the Romans, or apologetic for his fellow Jews, to an

overriding desire for self-gratification and aggrandizement. Individually or corporately, these interests may explain why Josephus designed the interpretation that constitutes his narrative. It is unlikely that any one particular interest can be understood as responsible for all that is described by Josephus.[28]

Awareness of the apologetic concerns that lie behind the narrative may help to emphasize the nature of the interpretative framework. It does not, however, act as a criterion by which to accept or reject subject matter that pertains to the actual situation. It is not simply a case of concluding that what clearly relates to a perceived polemical interest should be dismissed because it is part of Josephus's bias. Such an approach carries an implicit connotation that the remaining elements of the text probably preserve the 'hard core of historical facts'. Furthermore, it ignores the all encompassing nature of the interpretative framework. Discussion of the possible influences on Josephus is important for what it can achieve: that is, a heightened awareness that we are dealing with a narrative that is biased. Therefore, it is part of an examination of the second dimension of historical inquiry. For the first dimension, however, its relevance is primarily in terms of reminding us that the avenue toward the actual situation is an interpretation, not simply a biasless description of events. Without this sense of perspective, the majority view of siphoning out the bias would continue, failing to realize that such a process really requires the entire narrative to be siphoned out as it is all an expression of Josephus's bias. The bias is not the rogue enemy which it is often portrayed to be. It is the 'life blood' of the text.

The second observation is that the investigation must commence in an open-ended manner. Preconceived notions of how the first century functioned should be avoided. All existing discussion explores the situation in Judaea framed in terms of the way in which it is appropriate to describe the territory as being in a state of turmoil. In a similar vein, those concerned to explain the revolt do so in terms of seeking to establish the exact nature of the long-standing, fundamental causes in either economic, social, religious and/or political terms. Furthermore, in both areas of interest, 70 CE acts as the focal point, the climax

---

28. Debate also remains regarding the degree of consistency in thought and interest within Josephus's writings. Rather than an 'either or' approach to this issue it is probably more feasible to recognize a degree of consistency and change as characterizing the figure of Josephus.

of all that occurred in the years prior to the revolt. To ensure the study is open ended we need to make a radical departure from the existing approaches, one that does not incorporate any such assumptions regarding what happened in Judaea.[29]

It is essential that the questions posed do not reflect either of Josephus's pillars, but express a concern to undertake an examination of the actual situation. This means that, rather than ask in what sense Judaea was in a state of turmoil, we should commence with a more neutral question, by asking what was the state of affairs in first-century CE Judaea. Although a somewhat minor shift by all appearances, it is a crucial preliminary step if we are going to be able to start the process of staking a claim for conceptual independence from Josephus's interpretation.

These two observations shape the nature of the investigation that needs to be undertaken. They raise the important issue of exploring the nature of the relationship we are seeking to establish with the historical period in question and with the primary source for this study. Following on from this discussion of the conceptual issues the reader must address, our attention turns to the mechanism by which it is possible to examine the actual situation in the first century CE. Such a mechanism is the use of case studies. Two methodological elements are crucial to successfully undertaking the case study approach. The first is conceptual in nature and it relates to the factors the modern reader must deal with on an ongoing basis. The second methodological element deals with effective ways of employing Josephus's narrative and any other relevant source material. In what follows, my intention, especially in relation to the conceptual element for the modern reader, is to raise the various factors that need to be explored. Attention will be paid to some of the possible implications of these factors but this is

29. The underlying concept equally applies to any other topic of historical inquiry where Josephus is employed. For example, exploration into the functioning of 'the sanhedrin' should not be structured around such questions as what was the power of the sanhedrin or could the sanhedrin try to execute people under direct Roman rule. Instead, the questions need to be less specific in the first instance. In other words, what type of administrative structure existed in Judaea and were their formal institutions in Judaea? A further example of the need for open-ended investigation is the status of the Pharisees. Instead of questioning whether the Pharisees were the leading group it is important to structure the study around such questions as what groups existed in Jewish society, what type of role they played and what status the Pharisees held in the community.

not the place where it is appropriate to proclaim a particular line of interpretation. Indeed, rather than being 'prescriptive', the focus should be more in terms of the need to be continually aware of how these factors may impact on the study of what we understand was happening in Judaea. In combination, it is these two elements that provide the means by which we can achieve an appropriate balance. They enable us to reject Moehring's call for a cessation to the study of what actually happened, and yet preserve us from falling into the web of Josephus's interpretative framework with its two colossal pillars casting their shadow over existing scholarly discussion.

3.1 *Issues for the Reader*
We commence with the various factors that relate to the perspective of the modern reader. The factors fall into three broad categories: the role of hindsight; a conceptual understanding of the causes of war; and the theoretical concerns regarding measuring the state of affairs in a society. Each requires detailed comment.[30]

3.1.1 *Hindsight.* On a general level, the role of hindsight in a historical inquiry is a major concern, especially in terms of how it may influence the way events are perceived. Although we cannot avoid the use of hindsight, it is important to consider how it impacts on the nature of investigating the past. For example, at what point in time is it appropriate to deem that an event was inevitable? Even the less predetermined concept of when an event becomes the probable consequence or outcome of certain circumstances needs to be addressed. Because events actually take place it is understandable to think of them in a sense as being 'inevitable'. Once the revolt of 66–70 CE took place it had occurred; to think or speculate in terms of it not taking place is non-sensical and rather esoteric, to say the least. One could be forgiven for thinking, why speculate about something that happened? What is being questioned here is the way the knowledge that a certain event occurred affects the manner in which we talk about its causation and the degree to which it may have been inevitable. For example, are

---

30. Other topics will necessitate their own issues that require the attention of the modern reader. Although the role of hindsight will be common to all areas of investigation, the other factors do not apply to such topics as the status of the Pharisees, where it is more of a concern to establish how influence is to be quantified, the significance of diversity or uniformity and how groups function within a society.

we required to view the revolt as inevitable simply because it took place? Furthermore, is it appropriate to understand that the way the revolt unfolded was also inevitable?

A recent example helps to clarify the impact hindsight can have on the way events are perceived and understood. It is an article discussing the beginning of the war in Bosnia which was written several years after the war had began.[31] Tanner declares that: 'I should have seen it coming the day before, as I watched Mrs Karadzic and their daughter Sonja, dragging suitcases down the steps into a waiting car—Radovan Karadzic having vanished to the ski resort of Poli a day or two previously.' Tanner implies that, despite being at the scene of the conflict, he did not read the signs correctly. Then near the end of the article Tanner displays a perspective that is clearly nestled in the comfort of hindsight. 'For the war in Bosnia was triggered by the war in Croatia, which was triggered by the succession of Slovenica...'. For Tanner, in 1995, the conflict was there to be recognized before it happened. At the time the onset of the war was not recognized but hindsight provides Tanner with the means to understand that certain events were unfolding and were bound to occur. Furthermore, hindsight allows Tanner the opportunity to reflect in leisure in an effort to explain the sequence of events. Here hindsight has a subtle but fundamental impact on the nature of Tanner's inquiry into the immediate past. Because the war occurred, it carries the connotation of inevitability. Although not necessarily stated explicitly, this has been clearly expressed in a desire to explain the war in the context of preceding events or situations. Thus Tanner turns his attention to establishing causation.

The pervasiveness of hindsight is evident by approaching events from the other end of the 'tunnel'. Here, instead of assuming some sort of connection, the intention is to avoid linking events in terms of cause and effect. From this perspective the focus shifts away from the historical context towards exploring events internally. Furthermore, it helps ensure a sense of surprise and openness to the possibility of the unexpected. The strangeness of approaching subject matter in this way is testimony to how intrinsically hindsight is part of historical methodology. Yet hindsight robs the modern reader of these commodities of surprise and openness, making a study of the past 'clinical' and directing such study towards assuming and identifying a cause and effect. The

31. The article by M. Tanner was published in *The Independent* on 15 October 1995.

search undertaken by scholars is not so much as to whether events are linked, which is taken for granted, but more towards which events are linked and in what manner.

Within this context our attention focuses on how hindsight has become the controlling agent in the portrayal of the first century. The control is evident not only in Josephus but also in contemporary scholarly discussion. For Josephus, the dominance of hindsight is expressed in two related ways. The first is the rather basic observation that all of Josephus's narrative based texts were written after the events that they describe. There remains some debate as to whether either *Life* or *War* were based on notes that Josephus or Vespasian made during the revolt.[32] Even if this theory could be substantiated it does not alter the 'fact' that the final form of both texts dates from after the events being narrated. Josephus compiled his account in the luxury of hindsight. He was aware of how the various events unfolded and were resolved. For the narrative he constructed, especially *War* and *Ant.*, he knew the outcome.

Second, the significance of being able to construct the account after the event is given practical expression in the structure and themes of the narrative texts. The events of 70 CE act as both the impetus for Josephus to write an explanation of what happened and they also act as the end-point of the story, the climax of what is narrated. The structure and the contents of *War*, *Life* and *Ant.* 18–20 are controlled by Josephus's desire to explain the events of 66–70 CE. *War* explicitly focuses on describing and explaining the revolt by narrating events from during the war and by providing a sketch of what Josephus perceives to be the appropriate context for these events. *Ant.* 18–20, concerned with describing the events of the first century CE, is deliberately drawn to a close at 66 CE. Written in the 90s CE, Josephus could have provided information regarding events involving the Jews after 70 CE in either Judaea or Rome, where he was resident. It is clear from brief remarks in *Life* and *War* 7 that there was subject matter that could have been included. Instead, Josephus chose to conclude *Ant.* 20 at 66 CE, with a rather brief summary account of the last governor. To help ensure his narrative extended to 20 books, like that of Dionysius of Halicarnassus, Josephus included such material as a detailed description of certain Roman imperial affairs during the

32. See, for example, Cohen, *Josephus*, pp. 67-83.

30–40s CE in *Ant.* 19 and information regarding some Jewish inhabitants in Parthia in *Ant.* 20.[33] It is apparent that Josephus did not want to finish his history of the Jewish people with an account of the revolt or what happened after 70 CE.[34] It would be inappropriate, therefore, to suggest that *Ant.* 18–20 was simply an attempt to provide a full narrative of Jewish history in the first century CE. Constructed after the event, Josephus deliberately chose to close the narrative before the revolt began.

The timing of the other narrative text, *Life*, was probably inspired by concerns regarding Josephus's personal status in the 90s CE. However, the attacks against which Josephus tried to defend himself relate to his activities during the revolt. Brief reference is made to events that follow the revolt, but the primary focus of interest for Josephus was explaining his involvement at the beginning of the revolt, particularly the initial stages of his command in Galilee. What happened in 66–70 CE, therefore, was apparently still very important in the late 80s and early 90s CE for Josephus and his critic, Justus of Tiberias. With the benefit of hindsight the contents of each of the three texts was controlled in the light of known outcomes. There is no sense of open-endedness or uncertainty regarding how a particular situation would unfold.

Apart from the structure, hindsight also controls the themes Josephus presents. This dominance is especially given voice in Josephus's desire to make sense of what had happened. The search for meaning focuses on explaining how and why the disaster of 70 CE occurred. *Ant.* and *War* display a degree of consistency and diversity as Josephus grapples to explain the revolt. Here, hindsight is at work. A context in which the war occurred is constructed. It appears that Josephus is motivated

---

33. For discussion of the extent to which the structure and style of *Ant.* is influenced by the work of Dionysius and the possible reason for any parallel see T. Rajak, 'Josephus and the "Archaeology" of the Jews', *JJS* 33 (1982), pp. 465-77; cf. M.R. Niehoff, 'Two Examples of Josephus' Narrative Technique in His "Rewritten Bible"', *JSJ* 27 (1996), pp. 31-45, and G.E. Sterling, *Historiography and Self-Definition: Josephus, Luke–Acts and Apologetic Historiography* (NovTSup, 64; Leiden: E.J. Brill, 1992), pp. 253-97. The choice of 20 books is not, in my opinion, a mere coincidence. This recognition, however, does not necessarily act as a prologue to viewing the contents of *Ant.* as an adoption of Dionysius's style.

34. A further example of extra material is the long list of people who held the high priesthood (*Ant.* 20.224-51). Whether this, and other additions, are included for a perceived Roman or Jewish audience needs to be considered on an individual basis.

by the belief that events which have a significant climax also require equally significant explanations. With the benefit of hindsight, the final acts of the revolt, the capture of Jerusalem and destruction of the temple, possibly seemed to be out of proportion to the situation when the revolt began in 66 CE. Such a finale required an appropriate explanation. It is apparent that as Josephus searched for answers he raised the stakes, taking what happened beyond the human realm into a cosmic context in *War*. What happened in 70 CE was a form of divine punishment, the consequence of actions undertaken by Jews prior to 70 CE. Irrespective of how genuine Josephus's various attempts to explain 70 CE may have been they are a clear expression of the use of hindsight. The final act dictated the presentation of history.

As with Josephus, existing scholarly discussion of the revolt is directly impacted by hindsight. Scholars search through the description of events from prior to the revolt to explain its origin. The revolt and the serious repercussions of the Jewish defeat are tangible and real. As a result, the concern is to establish how and why such a disaster could take place. To pose the more fundamental question of whether the revolt would take place is not deemed to be relevant. After all, why debate the existence of something that happened? This 'knowledge' of how events unfolded is the heart of the problem. It has resulted in debate centring on explaining why and how the revolt happened. Little, or no attention is given as to whether the events of the revolt must have taken place in the way they did. Discussion of alternative outcomes is deemed implausible as the revolt was bound to happen. It is an approach that ignores the question of when an event should be understood as being inevitable.[35]

Within historical inquiry the role of hindsight needs to be treated with caution. Hindsight provides the obvious benefit of knowing how

---

35. It is somewhat of an irony that there are occasional acknowledgments that events may have turned out differently. The implication of this view is not explored in terms of how the causation of events is portrayed. For example, see Grabbe, *Judaism*, p. 614. An alternative approach to the problem of dealing with the uncertainty of how events unfold is the 'chaostory' approach of writing virtual history as advocated by N. Ferguson (ed.), *Virtual History* (London: Picador, 1997). The problem with such an approach is that it can easily become agenda driven in its attempt to construct what might have happened. What I am arguing for is the constant recognition of our position of hindsight. We need to release the past from the constraints of a sense of order and sequence that soon turns into a sense of inevitability regarding the way situations unfold.

various situations were actually resolved. In this sense it can be an aid. The distance and barrier that come with this knowledge, however, can also encourage us to allow hindsight to become the controlling agent. Subject matter is often approached from a perspective that ignores how hindsight influences the type of questions raised, particularly in terms of the inevitability of events. For example, the revolt of 66–70 CE did take place, with disastrous consequences. Thus the focus shifts away from the circumstances in which the war began and concentrates on the long-standing fundamental issues that brought matters to a head. The revolt is like an iceberg. The revolt is the tip, merely the final stage. The large submerged section of the iceberg is the series of conflicts that had been building up throughout the first century.

It is crucial to call into question what I regard as a compliancy that comes from the comfort zone of hindsight, a 'wisdom' that Tanner so aptly displayed regarding the outbreak of the conflict in Bosnia. Once the war began it became obvious, explainable in terms of long-standing issues. The same situation applies in relation to discussion of the 66–70 CE revolt. What happens to the inquiry if you start from the perspective of claiming that the revolt was not inevitable? In what manner does such a view influence the way events in Judaea prior to 66 CE are to be understood? In particular, to what extent should these events be cast in a shadow of 66–70 CE? In effect, how would an analysis of first-century CE Judaea, especially the revolt, unfold if we were to adopt a philosophical motto whereby 'no event is inevitable until it has happened'?[36]

3.1.2 *Causes of war*. From hindsight our attention turns to the second conceptual factor relevant to the perspective of the modern reader. At issue here is how we are to understand the causes of war. There are

---

36. The extensive impact of this hindsight is evident in Mason, 'Josephus, Daniel', pp. 161-91. Mason relates Josephus's acceptance of Roman rule as expressed in his writings as an interpretation of Daniel on the appropriate response to foreign occupation. Mason's argument is based on the assumption that Josephus grew up with this interpretation. The events of the revolt are reduced to the role of reinforcing what Josephus already knew and believed. It is an approach that also highlights a problem. If Josephus already knew war was the wrong course of action why was he an active participant at its outset? It was a problem Josephus tried to answer in *Life* 28-29 and which many have subsequently eagerly adopted in the search for a solution.

three points that require comment. The first point pertains to how the end of a war relates to its beginning. Of particular concern is the way the outcome of a war influences the nature of the discussion regarding the causes that are identified. Yet again, the influence of hindsight is being brought into question. The 66–70 CE revolt probably began with an action initiated by certain Jews in Jerusalem. Almost all the explanations of the war in Josephus and scholarship, however, are in terms of major, long-standing issues. The trouble in 66 CE simply brings to a head problems that had been intensifying over a long period of time. Whether it is intended or not, the effect of this approach is that an equation is made, profound causes match profound conclusions and consequences. Care is required not to allow the knowledge of what happened in 70 CE to unduly influence the under-standing of what occurred in the lead up to the revolt.[37] Any such equation between the profundity of the cause and the outcome should be the result of a detailed investigation that begins from an open-ended perspective. Simply because the revolt concluded in the destruc-tion of Jerusalem and the temple does not mean that the origins of the conflict were also significant.[38]

The second point relates to the insights that can be derived from 'conflict theory' study. Of particular interest are the possible theoreti-cal frameworks which can be used for explaining why wars occur. Within discussion on establishing criteria to identify and explain the outbreak of armed conflict, there are two basic approaches that may prove to be relevant. The first is the inherent model. It is based on the premise that there are factors contained in the political and social structures and the functioning of those structures that makes conflict a likely consequence. One of the more fundamental expressions of this

37. In a similar vein, it is important that the length of the revolt not be allowed to imply a level of significance beyond what is actually due. Without the crisis in Roman leadership it is conceivable that the war would have been over by the end of 68 CE.

38. The outbreak of World War One acts as an interesting comparison. The assassination of Archduke Ferdinand of Austria is often viewed as the immediate cause of the war. However, in keeping with the length and severity of the conflict the true origins of the war tend to be traced back to such factors as the rise of European nationalism and the growing influence of the arms industry. See D. Kagan, *On the Origins of War and the Preservation of Peace* (New York: Doubleday, 1995), pp. 81-231.

approach is the model of collective action developed by Tilly.[39] According to Tilly, access to decision-making processes is limited to a select few. Conflict arises when those who normally do not have access to the decision-making process actively express their desire to participate. Conflict is inherent because control of the socio-political system of a given society has been kept at a constant, controlled level. It is a problem of demand for access being exceeded by the supply. Simply by the functioning of the society, conflict becomes a likely consequence.

The second approach is contingent on certain circumstances combining to create unusual conditions. Gurr's relative deprivation theory is an example of this approach.[40] The crucial element in Gurr's model is that conflict is dependent on certain factors combining to trigger other factors. For Gurr there is a significant imbalance that exists between what individuals and/or sections of society believe is their due and what they are actually able to gain from the functioning of their society. Conflict occurs when the level of frustration of those who believe they are being deprived of what is rightfully theirs reaches the point of physical aggression. For this explosion to take place a number of different circumstances need to be encountered.

These two approaches may be useful in explaining aspects of the structure of the 66–70 CE revolt. They suggest that unrest and war can lie in the functioning of a society or in the attitudes and expectations of those within society. It is unnecessary and probably even inappropriate to suggest that only one or the other approach should be understood as explaining the situation in first-century CE Judaea. Instead, they open the possibility of viewing the revolt in terms of structural and/or circumstantial factors. Furthermore, these approaches enable us to identify the nature of the existing scholarly explanations. For example, the prominent study by Horsley clearly falls into the category of inherent explanations of the revolt, while Goodman's work combines the two approaches.[41]

---

39. See C. Tilly, *From Mobilization to Revolution* (Reading, MA: Addison Wesley, 1978), pp. 52-97.

40. See Gurr, *Rebel*, pp. 22-58, and H. Eckstein, 'Theoretical Approaches to Explaining Collective Political Violence', in T.R. Gurr (ed.), *Handbook of Political Conflict* (New York: Macmillan, 1980), pp. 135-65.

41. See Horsley, *Spiral*, and Goodman, *Ruling Class*. By implication, the version of the inherent model developed by Horsley, *Spiral*, means that war was inevitable. Such a view is made explicit by another exponent of the inherent model,

The third point regarding how the cause of a war is to be under-stood relates to the possible interplay between short-term and long-standing factors. The discussion here is best expressed in two related questions. First, what makes 'trouble' turn into a war? Secondly, can either long-term or short-term causes turn into a war without the presence of the other? In both instances it is apparent that the answers dictate the nature of the investigation undertaken. Short-term causes are often described as triggers, they help ensure a war begins. The connotation is that these causes alone would not result in a war taking place. Automatically focus shifts from the immediate circumstances to an investigation of long-term causes that had presumably been build-ing to a crescendo. What the triggers do is release the safety switch so that the explosion ensues. This process is already evident in discussion of the 66–70 CE war. The actions of certain Jews in Jerusalem trigger the war, but do not explain why the war occurred. Such an approach fosters what hindsight has already encouraged, namely, a tendency to assume that the revolt needs to be explained within a long-term con-text. As a result, 'tunnel' vision is imposed on the study in which trouble becomes a war because it is the culmination of a long process of conflict.

Consistent with the dominance of long-standing causes being seen as responsible for the outbreak of war, is the common assumption that short-term causes alone do not result in a war. A significant conse-quence of this view is the way the human factor, the sense of the unexpected or the irrational, is minimalized in how events may unfold. Rather than assuming that short-term causes alone could not result in war, it is important to be open to the notion that they could. It may appear appropriate to identify long-term issues within a society that heightened a sense of unrest, allowing tension to reach the point of no return. It is important, however, to be open to viewing situa-tions from the opposite perspective. So-called triggers could act, not as the final straw, but as the beginning of a process. To use the lan-guage of Horsley, there may be a 'spiral', but rather than the revolt being the final act, it could be the prologue.[42]

Rappaport, 'Jewish–Pagan Relations'.

42. An alternative approach to the discussion of the causes of the war would be to begin by focusing on the events associated with the revolt, to establish if they pro-vide any insights regarding what some of the protagonists believed they were fighting for. It is an approach that differs entirely from the one provided by Josephus

3.1.3 *Measuring the state of affairs.* The third and final conceptual factor is the manner in which the state of affairs in a society is to be classified. The fundamental problem here that needs to be considered is the use of boundaries to describe a given situation. The two boundaries that stand out as being integral to 'measuring' the state of affairs are the points of comparison and the chronological limits. The significance of each boundary requires some elaboration.

Concerning the points of comparison which are employed, there are four related observations. The first is the need to identify appropriate labels by which the state of affairs can be described. Blanket statements describing a society as one of peace, turmoil, conflict, instability or any other term is meaningless without an appropriate context. These terms are subjective in how they are defined and as to what proportion of the community held which perspective. Attention needs to be paid to establishing what contributes to the labelling of a period as one of 'stability' or 'turmoil'. Furthermore, it is important to consider whether there are particular aspects of how a society functions that are more fundamental than others, thus carrying a greater level of impact for the community as a whole.[43]

The second observation is that clarification is required as to whether an absolute or relative scale of comparison is the more appropriate to employ. At stake here is whether it is ideals and principles, or the actual situations encountered during other periods of Jewish history, that should be used as a means of comparison. Irrespective of the approach taken, they bring with them several problems. Comparison with an ideal carries such philosophical complications as to whether it is legitimate ever to expect that an ideal can operate as a reality. Individuals may profess an ideal that should be strived for and a community may declare its *raison d'être* to be an attempt to live out a certain ideal or principle. In both instances, it is a concept that is being evoked, a goal to be aimed at. The pertinent issue concerning

who commences with a historical context, leading the reader also to assume that such a context is historically accurate.

43. There are occasional expressions of an attempt to quantify the points of comparison. For example, Rajak, *Josephus*, pp. 91-95, and Price, *Jerusalem*, pp. 177-79, highlight the importance of using and understanding the language of Josephus. A further example is Horsley, *Spiral*. He seeks to define the variety of violence and protest in Jewish society.

the relevance of such an ideal for the measuring of a given state of affairs is whether the ideal was ever looked upon as achievable. It may be appropriate to cite ideal images of Jewish society that were current during the first century, but it should not be assumed that the community, as a whole, was trying to achieve that ideal and was, therefore, assessing their own times according to that ideal.[44]

Alternatively, a relative scale requires decisions to be made regarding what period of Jewish history should act as the appropriate point of comparison. For example, should the choice be based on a thematic parallel—namely, another period of Jewish history or culture that contains similar features to the first century CE—or should the comparison be made with a chronological period from immediately before and/or after the time in question? A further complication for the relative scale is determining when a situation is deemed sufficiently static to be used as a point of comparison.[45]

The third observation is simply to note the importance of determining whose perspective is being sought. Presuming that the focus lies in discussing the attitude of the first-century Jews it is reasonable to expect that several different opinions co-existed at any given point in time within the community. What was deemed as good to some was possibly the cause of concern, consternation, outrage or simply irrelevant to others. As such, identifying the 'Jewish' attitude to such things as Roman rule or a particular incident such as Pilate's use of money from the temple to build an aqueduct, needs careful qualification. It is conceivable that specific incidents evoked a variety of responses and

44. This is particularly important given the rather idealistic context used by Horsley, *Galilee*, pp. 19-33 and Horsley and Hanson, *Bandits*, pp. 5-8, to describe the mindset of certain elements within the community. The notion of a golden era in which a biblical image of 'Israel' as a place of equality, prosperity and harmony is prominent.

45. The recent discussion on the concept of nationalism in the late second temple period by Mendels, *Jewish Nationalism*, is a good example of the importance of establishing appropriate points of comparison. Although Mendels seeks to identify symbols of nationalism from within the cultural context of the ancient Near East it is difficult to determine whether a relative or absolute scale is appropriate in terms of a community-wide attitude. While kingship may have been a symbol of community identity to some, to others it could have been a symbol of oppression. Furthermore, even if the four symbols identified by Mendels are the accepted channels for expressing nationalism in Judaea it is necessary to indicate when they are sufficiently static to act as a point of comparison.

that we need to be open to talking about a majority attitude in some instances and a diversity of opinions regarding others. The same situation could be concurrently understood as a sign of stability and conflict. It is important to avoid assuming that the Jewish attitude is necessarily a single entity.

The final observation regarding the points of comparison is the need to establish the criteria by which to describe individual incidents. Even if turmoil and conflict are defined and, after investigation, they are deemed to be the chief characteristics of a society, it is important to employ criteria that indicate all unrest is not viewed as being exactly the same.[46] There is a need to be specific enough to allow distinctions to be drawn between types of incidents. For example, is the incident a response to the action of another group or individual? Is the incident resolved, and if so, in what manner? Who is involved in the incident and what is their role? These and other questions can help to ensure that individual incidents are not grouped blanketly as expressions of protest or conflict.[47]

The second boundary associated with the classification of the state of affairs is the chronological limit of the study. In a similar vein to hindsight, the time frame employed carries important conceptual connotations. The character of a study, especially the issues explored and the type of incidents discussed, are influenced by the termini chosen. Furthermore, this choice is purely subjective and arbitrary. For example, an investigation which uses wars as its starting- and endpoints attracts attention towards explaining events that may relate to those wars, especially any examples of conflict and turmoil. Such a choice almost begs discussion of how the intervening years relate to those wars and whether a link exists between them. Alternatively, time frames that use changes in leadership or government highlight change and result in a tendency to portray history in terms of epochs. By implication, events in the intervening years are viewed in a tunnel,

46. Such a view is fundamental to Horsley, *Spiral*, pp. 90-120, who seeks to identify violence in a physical and non-physical form. In a similar manner different types of protest are explored.

47. Although not directly relevant to the situation in Judaea, comparison with attempts to define conflict in modern societies indicates the need for caution in the use of terms in an unspecified sense. For example, see M. Stohl, 'The Nexus of Civil and International Conflict', in T.R. Gurr (ed.), *Handbook of Political Conflict* (New York: Macmillan, 1980), pp. 297-330, and Gurr, *Rebel*, pp. 3-21.

how they may or may not relate to the beginning or end of an era.

Essentially the termini act like magnets, attracting the attention of scholars in an effort to link events within the parameters of the chosen dates and their associated themes. The arbitrary nature of the choice is clearly apparent from some of the existing time frames used. For example, 175 BCE–135 CE or 175 BCE–70 CE are often cited as the time frame. They mark major revolts against foreign overlords, occasionally deemed to be displaying a thematic link as revolts of 'nationalism'. Another time frame employed is 6–70 CE. This narrower frame is also thematically linked to a particular period, that of direct Roman rule, from its introduction to the end of the second temple. Within these boundaries events are generally explored in terms of their link to the 'book-ends'. As noted earlier, in existing scholarly discussion the first century CE is almost universally regarded to be defined as the events that culminate in 70 CE. The years that follow the revolt are related to the next magnet adopted by scholarly discussion, the revolt of 132–135 CE.[48]

The crucial role played by the chronological limits is well illustrated by the way the revolt takes centre stage. Where the revolt is the starting-point of the inquiry it is assumed that the events prior to 66 CE should be cast as a backdrop. Where the revolt is portrayed as the climax of the inquiry, bringing an end to an era of Jewish history, it is generally perceived as the final stage in the increasing level of turmoil in the society. An example of the problems derived from such focus on the revolt is the scholarly discussion of the 67–68 CE civil war in Jerusalem. The civil war is viewed as the culmination of factors that were present in Judaea from before the revolt.[49] In effect, it is assumed that the civil war has a pre-history. Such a perspective ignores the possibility that the opposite can apply. Rather than the civil war being the culmination of pre-war circumstances, it may be appropriate to view the civil war as being caused by the revolt.

---

48. The issue of how the chronological boundaries of a study are drawn is raised by S.J.D. Cohen, 'The Political and Social History of the Jews in Greco-Roman Antiquity: The State of the Question', in R.A. Kraft and G.W.E. Nickelsburg (eds.), *Early Judaism and Its Modern Interpreters* (Philadelphia: Fortress Press, 1986), pp. 33-56 (35-36).

49. See, for example, Price, *Jerusalem*, pp. 85-94, Rajak, *Josephus*, pp. 126-35, and Horsley, *Galilee*, pp. 75-77.

The preceding discussion of three central conceptual factors under-lying any history of the state of affairs in first-century CE Judaea highlights the importance of trying to control our subjectivity. Many of the questions arising from this analysis can be only appropriately resolved after all the relevant subject matter has been examined. It is important at the outset, however, that these questions are consciously borne in mind throughout the study. Such an open-ended approach may make controlling the investigation difficult, but it is a fair reflection of the hesitancy with which we proceed. Combined, these questions alert us to the direction the study must take in order to establish conceptual independence from Josephus.[50]

3.2 *Case Study Approach*

Having considered the conceptual issues, our attention turns to the second methodological element of the process, the manner by which Josephus's narrative should be examined in an attempt to undertake a historical inquiry of the actual situation. It is clearly not appropriate simply to weave together events mentioned by Josephus. We have established that his narrative is the direct expression of his interpreta-tive framework and cannot be used without an effective mechanism of control.

The crucial aspect of the life raft which allows the reader to break away from being conceptually dependent on Josephus is a case study approach for the analysis of the source.[51] It incorporates three spe-cific stages of inquiry. The first is identifying and isolating individual

---

50. A further reason for caution is the difficulty associated with measuring the psychological aspect of events. For example, by what mechanism(s) is/are the pos-sible long-term implications of Gaius's order to be understood? What is raised here is the role of hindsight in how people behave in a given situation. In other words, to what extent and in what way are previous events taken into account in the way people act? See T.R. Gurr, 'A Causal Model of Civil Strife', in J.C. Davies (ed.), *When Men Revolt and Why: A Reader in Political Violence and Revolution* (New York: Macmillan, 1971), pp. 293-313 (293-95), and E.N. Muller, 'The Psychology of Political Protest and Violence', in T.R. Gurr (ed.), *Handbook of Political Conflict* (New York: Macmillan, 1980), pp. 69-99.

51. The idea of focusing on actual events through case studies rather than autho-rial summaries is derived from comments and suggestions made by E.P. Sanders. The following discussion is an elaboration and development upon the case study approach I outlined in the examination of Jewish involvement in the administration of the territory during the late second temple period. See McLaren, *Power*, pp. 28-34.

incidents that require investigation. The second stage is the examination of each incident on an individual basis. The final stage is the synthesis, where disparate pieces of information regarding each incident are drawn together. Each of these stages warrants explanation.

The first stage is the identification and isolation of the incidents that are narrated. It is vital that each relevant incident is examined separately. This disparate approach to the subject matter is contrary to the way it is preserved by Josephus, where the incidents are part of a continuous narrative. What may appear to be an 'artificial' distinction between events is deliberately made. The intention is to ensure that the subject matter is not examined within the framework that Josephus provides. We need to break individual incidents out of Josephus's pattern of escalating turmoil, to dismantle the existing paradigm by cutting through one level of his interpretative framework. As a consequence, it is necessary to define the boundaries of individual incidents, even if they appear to be unfolding simultaneously. The primary criterion used to establish these boundaries is the direct relationship of material to central participants and/or actions. A subsidiary factor is that the link to the central participants and/or actions needs to be within a close chronological proximity. Although such a division is subjective in nature and is made from the narrative as it is presented by Josephus, it is of fundamental importance. It is quite possible that some incidents have a direct link to others and that a re-drawing of the boundaries between incidents may be appropriate in the final stage of the approach. However, because Josephus weaves incidents together does not necessarily mean that the events were actually connected. Consequently, we must begin by identifying the incidents that need to be examined on an individual basis in order to dismantle Josephus's sequential narrative. For example, although occurring during the governorship of Cumanus it is important to separate completely the trouble at Passover incident from the attack on Caesar's slave, Stephen.

With the incidents defined and isolated we can turn to the second stage in the approach—the examination of each incident on an individual basis. There is no cross-referencing with other events or sources within the examination of each incident. This principle must be upheld even though there may appear to be, at first glance, obvious parallel incidents that could be used to clarify apparent gaps. It is only after all the individual incidents have been completed that any comments, observations and possible points of clarification can be considered. The primary goal here is to establish, so far as possible, what actually happened. Towards this objective the following elements are explored: the nature of the issue(s) at stake; the identity of those involved; what the various participants claim and do; and the means by which the incident begins, unfolds and concludes. In effect, the how, why, what and when of the event. This process will probably result in the examination of many of the incidents being concluded with a number of elements unresolved and requiring further clarification. Again, the aim is not to take the incident simply as Josephus reports it, but to analyse it carefully out of his context, questioning the placement of different aspects within the account, the language being employed and the roles attributed to various individuals. Here an awareness of how the various components of Josephus's interpretative framework function in the narrative of an incident will also be important. In this way we can work independently of Josephus's interpretation and identify the various elements of the actual event he has used in building his picture. Here open-ended questioning is effective in bringing these elements forward without displaying them from within Josephus's context.[52] For example, rather than ask why Eleazar b. Ananias ceased the practice of accepting gifts from foreigners we should consider who was involved in the decision to cease the practice.

In practical terms the examination of what actually happened in the incidents is governed by the number of extant versions. Where there is more than one version of an incident, each account will be examined separately in the first instance. The various elements of each version will be identified. This principle will apply even though almost all of the multiple accounts come from the hand of Josephus. The surviving accounts will be then compared to identify the differences, gaps, alterations, inconsistencies, contradictions and common elements of the versions. Always the focus is on trying to ascertain as much information as possible regarding the actual event that lies behind the narrative. In this context it is pertinent to consider the possible sources used in the construction of the extant narrative. Whether eyewitness, hearsay or written sources were employed may help clarify the nature of Josephus's particular interests in narrating the event

---

52. At issue is the need to establish the dividing line between using Josephus's narrative and yet not being controlled by that narrative. It is always easy to fall back into the paradigm Josephus has established, hence the importance of needing consciously to question on which side of the dividing line the investigation lies.

as he does. What then follows is a reconstructed outline of the incident, describing the common and irreconcilable elements between the separate versions of the incident, and the various areas of uncertainty as to what happened.

Where there is only one extant version of an incident the process is complex and requires great caution. Again, the goal is to provide an outline of what happened while also identifying areas of uncertainty. The various details of the account as it stands must be closely scrutinized, without assuming that any aspect is necessarily more than an interpretation of the event being described. Furthermore, the lack of any substantial external points of comparison make examination of possible sources used in the account particularly important. This is especially the case in terms of seeking to explain why the incident is described, the amount of detail and the way that it is included. It is important to remember that although the goal is always a description of what happened, the examination of incidents in isolation may often result in focusing on gaps and elements for which more information is required before a comprehensive explanation of the incident is possible. However, identifying these gaps is very important as a check against sliding over them. This 'sliding' leads to being subsumed in Josephus's picture—taking on board his paradigm of how things worked—even if that picture is incomplete, or even if it is manipulated by omissions into suggesting something that is not accurate to the event.

The third and final stage of the approach is the synthesis. This is the most complex part of the approach. It is here that unresolved aspects of the incidents can be explored in detail in a broader context. In the first instance they are placed within the context of other incidents. Through cross-referencing, questions raised within the individual incidents are discussed. The incidents are also placed in two further contexts. One is the material contained in the various non-event based sources, such as archaeology and apocryphal texts, that can be used to clarify aspects of the incidents. The other pertinent context is the broader socio-political environment of the Graeco-Roman and Near Eastern world. It is important to consider how the various terms, concepts, issues and insights associated with the incidents may be understood within a regional context. This principle applies whether it is as a point of comparison, or as part of a concern to identify how a given situation in Judaea can be explained in the context of events occurring across a region.

With the various unresolved aspects examined, it is then appropriate to turn our attention to the other part of the synthesis. Possible themes and patterns across the incidents will be considered. Connections, in terms of the participants, issues, and the way the incidents unfold will be established.[53] In turn, it is appropriate to consider if there are categories and criteria by which the various incidents should be labelled with a view to determining the type of conceptual framework by which to understand the topic of inquiry—the state of affairs in first-century CE Judaea. We will be able to determine whether we need to identify a historical context for the revolt and the general state of affairs that is distinct from the framework of Josephus. In other words, it is in the synthesis that we can address the question posed at the conclusion of Chapter 3 concerning the veracity of Josephus's interpretation, and the scholarly consensus regarding the two pillars of escalating turmoil and the inevitability of the revolt. It is also here that material from non-event based sources, which is not directly relevant to explaining the details of the incidents, and the broader socio-political context, will be an important adjunct to the insights that can be obtained from the comparison of the incidents.

There is nothing within the case study approach that makes its use restrictive or which requires a manual. Its application is simple, if also laborious, in the isolationist investigation of individual incidents. Two related benefits of the approach underpin its effectiveness as a means of allowing us to stand independent of Josephus's interpretation. One is that the approach is not structured to either implicitly confirm, or reject, Josephus's framework. The second significant benefit is that the approach is event based, focusing on examining actual situations. In a topic of inquiry concerned to establish the state of affairs in first-century CE Judaea, comments regarding the general situation can only be made after all the individual incidents have been analysed and then examined in the confines of the synthesis. The starting point of the case study approach, therefore, is not thematic—Josephan or scholarly.

---

53. Here a concern is whether the connections are the result of Josephus's framework or a reflection of what actually happened. The crucial factor to prevent the former occurring is the removal of incidents from Josephus's narrative sequence, and posing questions outside the boundaries established by Josephus: that is, the first two stages of the case study approach.

In a similar vein, using descriptions of events ensures that the inquiry is not based on the authorial summaries of Josephus or the philosophical and conceptual literature of the period.[54] In essence, the case study approach, in conjunction with an awareness of the conceptual factors previously raised—our position of hindsight, the need for open-ended questions, especially in the consideration of the cause(s) of war, and the necessity of broadening the ways we classify and measure the state of affairs—allows the reader to stand outside the existing framework from which the first century CE is viewed. Aware of the framework established by Josephus and adopted by scholarship, we can return to the subject matter without having to display allegiance to that interpretative framework.

There are several explanatory notes regarding the application of the case study approach which require brief comment. They all relate to the expectations we hold in relation to the subject matter contained in Josephus. The first is to acknowledge that the approach is founded on an assumption that we are dealing with accounts of actual events. Although exceptions will be identified, the event-based narrative texts of Josephus are accepted as generally describing events that took place. It is acknowledged that the amount of detail provided will vary greatly. Josephus may be 'economical', whether deliberately or out of a necessity dictated by lack of information. On other occasions he may provide extensive detail. Individual incidents may also be enhanced by the inclusion of detail for which Josephus has no evidence, but which he considers appropriate. Thorough investigation of each incident through the case study approach will help clarify the possible veracity not only of the basic story, but also of the various details. However, the starting-point is not that each incident is fiction until proven otherwise. Instead, a more positive view is adopted: the narrative of incidents is an attempt to record an account of actual events. What is important to remember is that we are always dealing with Josephus's interpretation and that we should not expect to establish a comprehensive account of every event. In a number of instances it will be possible

54. It is accepted that speeches generally reflect the view of Josephus rather than the protagonist in whose name it is placed. The primary value of speeches, therefore, will pertain to revealing the interpretation of Josephus rather than a description of the actual situation.

only to present a broad outline of what occurred with many unresolved questions.[55]

A second point to note is that the approach implies the existence of a hierarchy in the order in which sources are employed. Because it is a description of what actually happened that constitutes the cornerstone of the case study approach, only those texts which provide a description of incidents will be used to provide the individual case studies. Epigraphical, numismatic, archaeological material and texts that are not event based need to be considered in an effort to clarify aspects of the incidents being investigated, but they will not constitute case studies in themselves. This comparison will be undertaken only in the synthesis. It is, however, not to be assumed that these sources are only relevant for how they may clarify aspects of incidents. As a result, to ensure that the study is comprehensive, information from these 'subsidiary' sources, which may be relevant to the topic being explored but not directly relevant to the individual incidents, will be examined in its own right within the synthesis.

The final point of qualification relates to the manner in which we interact with the sources. Of particular significance is how pre-existing knowledge of a source such as Josephus is controlled. This problem focuses our attention directly on the ever present issue of the way the intrinsic link between Josephus's interpretation and narration influences the examination of what actually happened in Judaea. We require a sense of balance. It has been established that a 'prescriptive' approach which seeks to quantify Josephus's apologetic themes, and then determine the historicity of events in relation to these themes, is inappropriate. Instead, it is important to work with and through the interplay of Josephus's interests in each incident on an individual base. In other words, being conscious of Josephus's involvement in shaping and controlling the narrative, whether it be in terms of his personal circumstances, those of his sponsors, friends, allies or fellow Jews, is relevant. We need to be aware of his background and the various features of his life that influence the framework he develops. The incidents are, therefore, not being read in isolation from what we know of the person Josephus. Rather, the narrative of events is used as a practical means of exploring how Josephus expresses his understanding

55. That certain aspects of what happened in Judaea will remain lost because of gaps in information is noted by T. Ilan and J.J. Price, 'Seven Onomastic Problems in Josephus's *Bellum Judaicum*', *JQR* 84 (1993–94), pp. 189-208 (207-208).

of what was happening, while maintaining a focus on the actual situation.

I am arguing for a departure from Josephus's interpretative framework. Although we need to be immersed in the very same subject matter that is used to express the interpretation, it is crucial that our investigation of the first century CE is not undertaken from the assumption that turmoil and conflict were escalating to an inevitable end-point in the revolt of 66–70 CE. The narrative is examined with an awareness of this interpretation, but the appropriate frame of reference, presuming there is one for understanding the first century, must flow from the analysis, not precede it. In effect, the task is to establish what happens when we remove the parameters of Josephus's interpretative framework, and address our own subjectivity as readers who are 'burdened' with hindsight.

In principle, I am not trying to claim that it is invalid to conclude that turmoil and conflict culminating in the revolt is a parameter from which to understand what happened in first–century CE Judaea. Rather, I am arguing that, with a focus on establishing the events that lie behind the interpretations, it is important to explore the subject matter independently of the existing framework. The framework used needs to be the consequence of an examination, rather than a precondition of considering the subject matter. The case study approach is, therefore, an appropriate means to an end. It provides the avenue by which the history of Judaea can be presented, but without the 'gift' of Josephus being the controlling agent.[56] What follows is a brief foray that indicates where this approach can take us in an examination of Josephus's narrative regarding one aspect of first-century CE Judaea.

---

56. How that history should be narrated is another issue that is part of a study in its own right. For the moment it is sufficient to indicate that such a history needs to function on two levels. One is the description of the events and the other outlines the various interpretations of the events by the participants, witnesses and near contemporaries. While the former incorporates a search for a single narrative the latter actively seeks out the diversity of opinions that equates with the variety within the Jewish community.

Chapter 7

THE TRAILER:
A READING OF EVENTS IN JUDAEA DURING 66 CE

There is a certain degree of compulsion to adhere to the motto
'practise what you preach'. To reject existing attempts which claim
conceptual independence from Josephus and then outline another
approach is one thing, but it is an entirely different matter to follow
up by putting that approach into practice. However, I have no intention of extending this particular study into a comprehensive analysis
of the situation in first-century CE Judaea according to the case study
approach. To do justice to such a task warrants a study in its own
right, and that lies in the future. Instead, what will be undertaken here
is a brief example of how the approach functions and where it might
lead by focusing on one aspect of the first century CE. In other words,
what follows is the 'trailer' to a forthcoming 'attraction'.[1]

Our focus will be on 66 CE. After defining and isolating the various
individual incidents associated with 66 I will narrow this focus further, selecting three of the incidents to be studied in detail. Because of
the limited scale of the investigation, the synthesis will be used primarily to indicate some of the issues, questions and themes raised by
the examination of the three incidents. Despite the absence of a 'full
picture', this foray into case study history will identify significant
issues that need to be explored within parameters that do not assume
the validity of Josephus's two pillars.

Before the case study is undertaken it is important to signal that
the narrative of 66 CE is a vibrant expression of Josephus's interpretative framework. There are numerous examples of commentary

1. It is important to reiterate that the concern of this study is the methodological
process derived from a recognition of a short-coming within the existing attempts to
portray the situation in first-century CE Judaea. Putting the process in practice is the
next stage, and it will follow in a separate study.

within descriptions of events. For instance, Josephus identifies the motivation of several participants. Rarely is Florus mentioned without some reference to the reasons underlying his actions. As a direct contrast, the motivation of Agrippa II is also cited. Josephus also comments through the labelling of several participants. Those Jews seeking war are generally described as 'the revolutionaries' and 'the insurgents', while the Jews trying to prevent conflict include 'the chief priests', 'the powerful' and 'the notable'. A further element of the interpretative framework is the prominence of reflective comments on the events that are narrated. These reflections generally pertain to the significance of an event. A 'classic' in this context is the way Josephus sums up the massacre of the Roman garrison that had laid down their arms in return for the promise of freedom:

> To the Romans this injury—the loss of a handful of men out of a bound-less army was slight; but to the Jews it looked like the prelude to their ruin. Seeing the grounds for war to be now beyond remedy, and the city polluted by such a stain of guilt as could not but arouse a dread of some visitation from heaven, if not the vengeance of Rome the people gave themselves up to public mourning... (*War* 2.454-55).

Other incidents for which Josephus provides reflections include the trouble at Caesarea, the decision to cease accepting gifts and sacrifices from foreigners, Florus's actions in Jerusalem and the campaign of Cestius. Not surprisingly, the subject matter all pertains to conflict. Relations between communities residing in the territory and the activities of groups and individuals, which constitute the majority of *War* 2, portray Judaea as a place racked with trouble.

1. *Defining the Incidents*

Aware of Josephus's interpretation, our attention turns to an examination of the state of affairs in Judaea during 66 CE. Having declared these chronological and geographical boundaries, the first step in the application of the case study approach is to determine where individual incidents begin and end. In general, incidents are defined by their association with a central character or characters, or with a central action. The incident is usually specifically located in time and place. This process is subjective and arbitrary in nature. It is essential, however, that events which form part of a sequential narrative text are removed from that context. Although a cursory reading may suggest there is a causational link between certain events, any such relationship is deliberately avoided at this stage in the approach.

Josephus's narrative of 66 CE can be divided into 23 separate incidents.[2] They are as follows:

(1)   Cestius's visit to Jerusalem (2.280-82, 6.422-27);[3]

(2)   the dispute in Caesarea associated with the synagogue (2.285-92);

(3)   Florus's visit to Jerusalem (2.293-332);

(4)   Neapolitanus's visit to Jerusalem (2.333-41);

(5)   Agrippa II's visit to Jerusalem (2.335-407);

(6)   the capture of Masada (2.408);

(7)   the rejection of sacrifices and gifts offered by foreigners (2.409-17);

(8)   the fight for control of Jerusalem among rival Jewish groups (2.418-29; 434-37; 440-49; *Life* 17-23);

(9)   the fighting between Jewish and Roman forces in Jerusalem (2.430-33, 438-39, 450-56);

(10)   Menahem at Masada (2.433-34);

(11)   fighting between Jews and Greeks at Caesarea (2.457);

(12)   fighting between Jews and Greeks in Peraea, Galilee, Judaea (2.458-60, 477-78; *Life* 26, 30, 44, 67);

(13)   fighting in Scythopolis, among Jews and between Jews and Greeks (2.466-76; *Life* 26);

(14)   fighting within Agrippa II's territory (2.481-83; *Life* 48-61);

(15)   capture of Cypros (2.484);

(16)   capture of Machaerus (2.485-86);

(17)   campaign of Cestius Gallus (2.499-555, 558; *Life* 24);

(18)   flight of certain Jews from Jerusalem (2.556);

(19)   appointment of Jewish generals (2.562-68; *Life* 28-29);

(20)   preparations for war in Jerusalem (2.647-51);

(21)   activities of Simon b. Gioras in Arcabatene (2.652-53);

(22)   Jewish attack an Ascalon (3.9-28);

(23)   trouble in Tiberias (*Life* 62-69).

The definition of most incidents requires no comment; they can be directly linked with a central action or character within a set time and

---

2.   Events that take place outside of Judaea and Galilee are not included, such as, the trouble in Alexandria (*War* 2.487-98) and in Damascus (*War* 2.559-61).

3.   Unless otherwise stated, the references in the list are to passages from *War*.

place.[4] Some of the boundaries drawn, however, do require explanation. Several incidents appear to be occurring contemporaneously, such as the visit of Neapolitanus and Agrippa II to Jerusalem. Furthermore, in this instance, they appear to be connected with the same basic issue—assessing the situation in Jerusalem after the departure of Florus. We should draw a distinction between these visits, however, on the basis that the central character is different. If there is a thematic and/or causational link, this can only be considered after each of the incidents has been assessed in isolation.

A similar distinction exists between incidents (8) and (9). The fighting between Jews and Romans and among the Jews appears to have been happening simultaneously. Furthermore, the action taken in relation to one incident may have affected what was happening in the other one. However, they are categorized as individual incidents because one reflects an internal conflict in which the central participants are Jews fighting Jews, while the other relates to external conflict with Jews and Romans as the central characters. In these examples a direct link with the central participants is matched by a link to the location and timing of the actions to provide a narrow definition of the boundaries between incidents.

Alternatively, defining incidents by association with the central participants and their action can also result in what may initially appear to be several different events being labelled as one large-scale incident. One such example is the campaign of Cestius. As part of the campaign there are a number of sub-plots, such as Ananus b. Jonathan's attempt to open the city gates for the Romans (*War* 2.533-34) and the capture of Joppa by Roman troops (*War* 2.507-508). These sub-plots are deemed to be part of a single incident because they all appear to be directly linked with the action initiated by the central character: namely, Cestius Gallus and his decision to march on Jerusalem to suppress the trouble that had broken out in the province.[5]

---

4. For example, incidents defined according to the central action include the capture of Masada (10), Cypros (15), Machaerus (16) and the trouble in Caesarea (2). The criteria used mean that the rejection of sacrifices and gifts offered by foreigners (7) includes not only the action but the subsequent debate regarding what had been done; cf. McLaren, *Power*, pp. 169-72.

5. The crucial issue being raised here is at what point you accept/reject Josephus's narrative structure. What is important to remember is the purpose of making the division, placing the events outside of Josephus's narrative sequence. Criteria are

The other point of clarification pertains to the dating of incidents. Here the arbitrary, subjective nature of the drawing of boundaries is most apparent. The problem originates in the decision to set the chronological boundary tightly to the single year, 66 CE. Josephus rarely provides any means of determining the timing of certain incidents. The most obvious example that requires comment is the visit of Cestius to Jerusalem and the census associated with this visit. The event is clearly linked to Passover, but there is no means of establishing whether this visit should be placed in 65 or 66. The choice is, at this stage, purely arbitrary.[6] The other example relates to the dating of events at the close of 66. Several of the incidents listed are located in Josephus's narrative after the defeat of Cestius in October/November. However, exactly when the Jews attacked Ascalon, or when the activity of Simon in Acrabatene took place is unknown. Even more debatable are the events associated with Galilee. It is possible that some of the incidents listed took place early in 67, while others not listed should be linked with 66. The narrow chronological boundary and Josephus's lack of signposts make the process of selection difficult in this particular example.[7]

The detail in the description of the incidents listed varies greatly: some are brief summary statements, while others include extensive discourses which even describe the motives of individual participants. For the purposes of this study three of the incidents which reflect this diversity will be examined. They are all described in only one text, making the principle of inherent plausibility a crucial factor in explaining what aspects of the account portray historical events. They are: the capture of Masada; the rejection of sacrifices and gifts offered by foreigners; and the capture of Machaerus.

employed to help control the division of material into separate incidents but there is always the flexibility to allow a redrawing of the boundaries within the context of the third stage of the case study approach—the synthesis.

6. There are a few scholars who accept that 66 CE is the appropriate date of the visit. For example, see Smallwood, *Jews*, pp. 284-85, and Hengel, *Zealots*, p. 356.

7. Incidents that have been excluded from the list but cannot be defined in a definitive manner include the Dabarittha affair (*War* 2.595-609; *Life* 126-31), the preparations of Josephus in Galilee (*War* 2.569-82; *Life* 78-79) and the petition sent to Jerusalem by John of Gischala (*War* 2.626-31; *Life* 189-332).

2. *Examination of Individual Incidents*

Initially we must examine the incidents on an individual basis. The primary goal is to explore what actually happened. In other words, we will consider what can be established regarding the nature of the central issues, who was involved, in what way they participated, when various actions were undertaken, how the incident unfolds, and in what manner it is concluded. Furthermore, apparent 'gaps' in knowledge regarding the incident will be identified. For many of these aspects of the incident it is quite possible that we will be left with more questions rather than answers.[8]

2.1 *The Capture of Masada (War 2.408)*

For a description of this incident we are dependent on the narrative contained in Josephus's *War*. Some clarification is required regarding exactly how many versions there are of the incident. The occupation of Masada is referred to on eight occasions in *War* (2.408, 434, 447; 4.400, 516; 7.253, 275, 297). If any of these references to Masada being captured relate to the same incident then it is important that they be examined as separate versions of the one event. Alternatively, if

---

8.   It is important to state that the various observations of existing scholarly discussion of 66 CE, or the three specific incidents, will not be explored in any detail during the examination of the individual incidents. Much of the discussion engages in cross-referencing to other events before they have been examined in their own right. What is important to note at this stage is the general nature of the views expressed. Rather ironically, the most popular approach is to adopt Josephus's account with occasional alterations to provide clarification. For example, see Rajak, *Josephus*, pp. 73-75, 116-18, Horsley, *Galilee*, pp. 73-75, Smallwood, *Jews*, pp. 289-95, Hengel, *Zealots*, pp. 357-65, Rhoads, *Israel*, pp. 100-102, 150-53, and Bilde, *Flavius Josephus*, pp. 34-35. A second approach argues that certain elements of Josephus's account should be queried, particularly in terms of the role played by particular elements of the aristocracy in the beginning of the revolt. See, for example, S. Schwartz, *Judaean Politics*, pp. 84-85, Grabbe, *Judaism*, pp. 446-48, and Goodman, *Ruling Class*, pp. 147-72. The third approach, which is also the least favoured, is the most radical in its dismissal of certain aspects of Josephus's picture regarding 66 CE. See Price, *Jerusalem*, pp. 28-45, and, especially Cohen, *Josephus*, pp. 191-99. Similar to the second approach, the focus here is the role of various groups in the outbreak of the war. Although derived from a different process, several of the conclusions reached by Cohen parallel those arrived at in this examination. The parallel will be discussed in more detail below (n. 28).

they describe different events then no comparison is appropriate at this stage. Caution is the motto here. Unless there is compelling, explicit evidence to conclude that they are multiple accounts of the same event, then the references should be viewed as separate incidents. The detailed investigation of the accounts can then be compared within the synthesis where a re-evaluation of the relationship between them can be made.[9]

A brief, cursory reading of the possible similarities and differences between the eight references indicate that Josephus appears to be describing more than one event.[10] The only obvious common point in all the accounts is the naming of Masada.[11] There are significant overt differences in the identity of those who occupy the fortress and the timing of the occupation.[12] Therefore, although the naming of Masada

9. It is a matter of principle that is raised here. Where there is more than one account it is important to be sure that they refer to the same event before they are used together. Adopting the approach outlined has the added advantage in that through the synthesis it will be possible to draw together accounts that may outwardly appear different but upon detailed investigation refer to the same event. The alternative—accepting a link but then finding there is not one—requires an element of destruction. The approach used is partly based on the premise that it is easier to put something together when all the possible pieces have been properly studied than it is to undo and repair something that has been hastily constructed without all the individual pieces being assessed.

10. Cohen, *Josephus*, p. 193, and R.A. Horsley, 'Menahem in Jerusalem: A Brief Messianic Episode among the Sicarii—Not "Zealot Messianism"', *NovT* 27 (1985), p. 338, also conclude that *War* 2.408 and 434 refer to different events. Horsley, however, does not suggest who it was that actually captured the fortress. Goodman, *Ruling Class*, p. 169, notes that the reference in 2.434 is confusing. For the view that 2.408 and 434 are two accounts of the one event see Hengel, *Zealots*, p. 358, Rhoads, *Israel*, p. 112, and H.M. Cotton and J. Geiger, *Masada II. The Final Report: The Latin and Greek Documents* (Jerusalem: Hebrew University of Jerusalem, 1989), pp. 5-6. H.M. Cotton and J.J. Price, 'Who Captured Masada in 66 CE and Who Lived There until the Fortress Fell?', *Zion* 55 (1990), pp. 449-54, claim that *War* 2.408 refers to the capture of the fortress by Menahem and his associates while *War* 2.434 refers to the occasion when Menahem returned to Masada to obtain arms for his followers.

11. A common element between *War* 2.447, 4.400, 516, 7.253, 275 and 297 is the identity of those who occupy the fortress. A further possible link is the means of occupation mentioned in 2.408 and 7.297.

12. The people are not identified by name in *War* 2.408. In *War* 2.433-34 it is Menahem and his 'notable' associates, while in 2.447, 4.400, 7.253 and 297 it is Eleazar b. Jairus and the sicarii.

acts as an initial magnet, at this stage it is appropriate to treat the account in *War* 2.408 as the only description of this particular capture of the fortress.[13]

The central issue described in *War* 2.408 is the capture of Masada, the fortress-palace situated on the south-western side of the Dead Sea. Josephus's account is extremely brief, with very little detail provided. The fortress had been in the hands of the Romans. There is no detail provided regarding the size of the Roman force or when the garrison was placed in Masada. The Roman guards were apparently killed by the people who captured the fortress, 'some of the most ardent promoters of war'. The description of the incident concludes with the fortress being garrisoned by those who killed the Romans. Nothing appears to happen to the fortress itself: it was captured through 'secrecy'. Whoever it was that managed to acquire Masada was able to enter the fortress, apparently without having to make a major armed assault. Exactly how the fortress was infiltrated, however, is not explained. A question mark remains, therefore, over the exact nature of the secrecy employed. We can suggest such possible explanations as betrayal, either from among the Roman guards themselves or of a 'friendship' that existed between the guards and the assailants. Alternatively, local knowledge may have allowed the attackers secret access not known by the defendants.

Clarification as to how the attackers gained access to Masada may lie, in part, in the identity of the assailants. Unfortunately though, Josephus's narrative is far from helpful in this aspect of the event. Josephus simply states that 'some of the most ardent promoters of war' had 'joined together' to attack the fortress. No actual participants are named. It is possible that Josephus did not know the identity of the assailants, hence the use of what appears to be rather vague terminology. It is also possible, however, that Josephus was being deliberately vague in an effort to protect certain people from being associated with the action. Yet again, a question mark hangs over the incident as to the exact identity of those who captured the fortress.

13. On a cursory reading it would appear that Josephus's references relate to three separate events. One is *War* 2.408, the second is *War* 2.433-34 and the third is mentioned in *War* 2.447, 4.400, 516, 7.253, 275 and 297. Examination of these as separate incidents does not preclude the possibility of concluding that an alternative structure is deemed more appropriate in the context of a synthesis of a study that incorporates 66–70 CE.

One further aspect of the incident that could be relevant to the identity of the assailants is their action after the Romans were killed. These people placed their own garrison in the fortress. By implication, the action of attacking Masada does not appear to have been one of an itinerant group of robbers engaged in a raid. Whoever captured and then occupied the fortress possibly did so as part of a larger plan. Whether this was a desire to find a permanent, supposedly secure, base, or part of a larger scale operation designed to gain control of important strategic sites as a precursor to open war, is a matter of speculation. Further clarification of the method of attack, the aims and identity of the assailants, is dependent on being able to provide more information, which must wait until the synthesis.

Josephus's brief account of the capture of Masada in 66 CE is an intriguing incident. From the extant narrative, we are able to establish that the fortress passed from Roman hands into the control of those who are described as 'some of the most ardent promoters of war', apparently by means of secrecy rather than overwhelming physical assault. Several fundamental questions pertinent to explaining the incident remain unresolved. They include, the identity of the assailants, the exact nature of the secret acquisition of the fortress, and the purpose for which it was captured. Explanations of one or another of these issues will probably help clarify the other problems. These gaps raise further puzzles: why does Josephus actually describe the capture of Masada and what is the nature of the link between the incident and the war? It is a point of curiosity that Josephus mentions the incident, and yet provides so little detail. This is almost an off-hand reference, but presumably it has significant potential for helping to explain the beginning of the war. If this potential is to be harnessed then we must rely on the synthesis to help explain some of the unresolved issues.

2.2 *The Rejection of Sacrifices and Gifts Offered by Foreigners (War 2.409-17)*

For a description of this incident we are entirely dependent on Josephus.[14] The incident pertains to certain practices associated with the temple in Jerusalem. Josephus's account of the incident is most

---

14. The notion of allusions to the event in Rabbinic literature cannot be linked with the incident in question. Note the arguments of Hengel, *Zealots*, p. 359, and C. Roth, 'The Debate on the Loyal Sacrifices, AD 66', *HTR* 53 (1960), pp. 93-97 (p. 93).

intriguing. He provides a substantial amount of detail, yet not in a balanced manner. The account opens with a brief reference to the crucial action, the decision of Eleazar b. Ananias and his associates to stop accepting gifts and sacrifices offered by foreigners. With the action completed, Josephus then provides a reflective comment on the significance of this action. According to Josephus the decision to stop the practice brought profound ramifications in terms of Jewish–Roman relations: the 'action laid the foundations of the war with the Romans' (*War* 2.409).

The bulk of the account focuses on the aftermath of the action. In the ensuing debate concerning the appropriateness of the decision, Josephus provides a significant amount of detail regarding the views of those who were opposed to what had been done. The incident is drawn to a close with the decision to stop accepting the gifts and sacrifices being upheld. By implication, it appears that effective power lay with the people who took the action. Ironically, however, these are the people who are least represented in the description of what occurred.

Despite Josephus's overt interest in the incident and the amount of detail that is provided, the account is far from comprehensive. There are substantial gaps regarding how the incident unfolds. One aspect that is especially difficult to explain is the purpose of the decision.[15] A comparison of the motivation of the two groups, those in favour and those against, also highlights the gaps. No information is provided regarding the intentions of those who make the decision and then refuse to change their minds. No context is provided for the action. It is simply stated that Eleazar b. Ananias managed to persuade certain people to cease accepting the offerings. There is no indication whether this was a response to a Roman action or an initiative of Eleazar. In a similar vein, the timing of the action, undertaken in the middle of 66 CE, is also not explained. In the narrative of the ensuing public debate no attempt is made to provide any justification for what has been done. The actual decision, barring gifts and sacrifices offered by foreigners,

---

15. Note the detailed discussion of D.R. Schwartz, 'On Sacrifices by Gentiles in the Temple of Jerusalem', in D.R. Schwartz, *Studies in the Jewish Background of Christianity* (WUNT, 60; Tübingen: J.C.B. Mohr [Paul Siebeck], 1992), pp. 102-16, regarding the relevance of mentioning gifts and sacrifices in the public gathering. Although the debate may have been primarily concerned with the offering of sacrifices the example of accepting gifts was possibly used to justify the supposed legitimacy of the arguments of both sides in the debate (p. 115).

does not necessarily explain the motive of Eleazar and his associates. It is possible that the end result was a snub to the Romans as Josephus claims. However, that result may have simply been a by-product, not part of Eleazar's intention. When motivation on the part of those instigating the action is sought, we are struck by the silence.

By way of contrast, Josephus's description of the motives of those opposed to the decision is quite extensive. It also appears to provide an explanation for why the action was taken. It is notable that Josephus's sympathy lies with these people. The explicit comments of Josephus regarding the consequence of the decision—that it 'laid the foundation of the war'—parallel the views and concerns of those who opposed what happened at the time of the incident. Josephus ensures that the reader is well versed in the objections with a description of a public forum. Wisdom and understanding are shared between Josephus, the 'chief priests', the 'notable/powerful' and the 'most notable Pharisees'.

The first point to note regarding the motivation of those opposed to the action is that they are presented as being concerned for the 'common good'. There is no sense of personal gain in any of their comments. The protest is based on two lines of argument. One is that the action was an innovation. This concern is flagged in *War* 2.410 where the voice of opposition is first noted and is then expressed in more detail through the summary of what was said at the public gathering (*War* 2.412-14, 417). The second line of argument was concerned with the possible implications of enforcing such an exclusivist regulation (*War* 2.415-16). What is highlighted by these people is the perceived practical consequence of the action 'provoking the arms of the Romans and courting a war with them' (*War* 2.414). This concern regarding the likely Roman response may help clarify the purpose of the action. Indeed, whereas the desire of these people who plead to have the decision reversed may have been to prevent the situation from developing into even further trouble (*War* 2.410), it is possible that such foresight was also shared by those who made the decision. For the latter, the intention may have been to bring about war.[16]

16. There is, however, an important distinction to be drawn. The action may have been targeted directly against the Romans, a deliberate declaration of war. This is the view commonly expressed. For example, see Rajak, *Josephus*, p. 117, and Goodman, *Ruling Class*, p. 152. An alternative approach is that the motivation was primarily to 'cleanse' the temple. As such, the war is a by-product of the action. This approach is implied by Jossa, 'Josephus's Action', p. 265, who portrays Eleazar as

The means by which the protest is registered is significant. As described by Josephus, the debate regarding the legitimacy of the action takes place after the event. The public gathering is instigated by the people who want to reverse the decision. As a result, we are encouraged by Josephus to assume that they had been divorced from the whole process of the action. Josephus conveys the idea that what had taken place was the work of a faction which failed to submit their proposal to proper community discussion. It was those protesting the legitimacy of what was done that sought to restore order. We do not know whether the decision was the result of a process of consultation. Because Josephus makes no reference to a meeting before the action does not necessarily mean there was not one, especially given the apparent weighting of the narrative in favour of those who opposed the cessation.

Even working from the extant narrative and accepting there was a public gathering in the temple complex, there are several further issues that require clarification. The agenda of the gathering is depicted as an attempt to have the action reversed (*War* 2.411). An important question needs to be addressed: why was this approach employed rather than any other? Without explicitly stating as much, it appears the answer relates to where effective power resided. Josephus describes Eleazar as the captain of the temple, presumably a person closely connected with the temple operation. Furthermore, we are told that one of the reasons the supporters of the action were confident was their large numbers (*War* 2.410). Eleazar and his associates were well placed and numerous. They had not closed off access to the temple complex as the meeting was held near the Bronze Gate (*War* 2.411). However, the people opposed to the action could not reverse the decision quietly or by any other means. These people may have had 'wisdom' regarding the ramifications of the action but they had no effective power or influence. The only course open to them was to make a public appeal. Authority and control, therefore, rested with those who ceased the practice of accepting the gifts and sacrifices offered by foreigners. The way the public gathering, and the incident as a whole, concludes, reinforces the point that those complaining about the action were powerless. After making their various appeals the opponents of the action realized they could not alter the situation (*War* 2.417).

a reformer of the temple system. The end result may be the same but the intention could be quite different.

There is a lingering sense of unease regarding the neatness of how the event unfolds, especially in terms of the imbalance in the type of information regarding what happens. Josephus's account of the incident concludes where it begins. Irrespective of the type of protest made, the decision stands. All that is achieved in between is the depiction of a polarization of views. Those who opposed the action are faced with their own important decision. Assuming that the concerns associated with their protests regarding a Roman reaction are genuine, then a significant re-think was urgently required. Those who made the decision had played a 'trump card'. Unless the opponents of the action, whether small or large in number, were willing to relent, there was now a clear division in the community.

Our attention turns to the identity of various participants in the incident. Josephus's narrative is even more vague here than it is in detailing how the event unfolded. We commence with those portrayed as being in favour of the action. Central to this group is the only person named, Eleazar b. Ananias. As Eleazar clearly did not act alone according to Josephus, his appearance as the only named character is most puzzling. The literary effect of naming only Eleazar is obvious. He becomes a maverick figure, persuading others to follow his plan. He is presented as the instrumental figure, instigating the action and as the one in whom many associated with the deed placed their trust. The relevance of this presentation to an analysis of what actually happened, however, is not so apparent. Several personal and professional details are provided regarding Eleazar. Josephus indicates that he was the 'captain', whatever the title means, and the son of Ananias b. Nedebaeus, the high priest. Of his character, Josephus claims that Eleazar was a 'very daring youth' (*War* 2.409). Whether this description is intended as a compliment or criticism is not made explicit. Despite this information it remains unclear why Eleazar alone is named. The details provided by Josephus indicate that he was probably closely connected with the temple. Not only had his father served as high priest at one stage, but also Eleazar now held some form of public office himself. He was not an outsider who burst into Jerusalem to overthrow the existing authorities. If anything, the knowledge we have about Eleazar simply reinforces the extent of the puzzle that he is the only person named.[17]

---

17. In existing scholarly discussion there is no attention paid to why Eleazar is the only person named. It is openly assumed that Eleazar was the leader. See Price,

The people aligned with Eleazar appear to be linked with the temple. They are referred to as the 'ministers who conduct the services' (τὴν λατρείαν λειτουργοῦντας [*War* 2.409]) and 'the ministers' (οἱ λειτουργοὶ [*War* 2.417]). It is important to note that the exact identity of these people is not made clear in Josephus's account. In combination with Eleazar, these people had the means of access to the temple and the power to carry out action. Although Josephus avoids actually stating it as such, these people were most probably either priests and/or Levites. 'The ministers' who sided with Eleazar were large in number and they were willing associates (*War* 2.410). The apparent vagueness of the terminology, however, begs further questioning. Comparison with other possible references to the identity of the people associated with the functioning of the temple is required. If Josephus is vague in other, less 'hostile' contexts, then the term 'ministers' is a curiosity. If, however, Josephus specifically refers to priests and/or Levites elsewhere in relation to the services in the temple, then we have reason to be suspicious that he is seeking to play down the role of the priesthood in support of the action.[18]

At present there is a strange contrast between the naming of the supposed leader Eleazar, who was captain and the son of a high priest, and the general non-identifying terminology used to describe his associates. It is, however, not the end of the complication regarding the participants in favour of the action. According to Josephus, after Eleazar and his associates made the decision they were supported by other Jews. Again, no individuals are named and Josephus simply employs broad descriptive terms. Apparently the 'most vigorous of the revolutionaries' supported the decision (*War* 2.410).[19] Later, at

Jerusalem, p. 9, and S. Schwartz, *Judaean Politics*, p. 84. Where curiosity is occasionally expressed is in terms of why Eleazar disappears from the narrative after he was such a prominent figure in the events during 66 CE according to Josephus's narrative. For example, see Price, *Jerusalem*, p. 79, Ilan and Price, pp. 205-208, and S. Schwartz, *Judaean Politics*, p. 75. A possible influence on the naming of only one person is whether Josephus was particularly interested in writing an account that was people or institution orientated. See B.D. Shaw, 'Tyrants, Bandits and Kings: Personal Power in Josephus', *JJS* 44 (1993), pp. 173-203.

18. Several scholars refer to these people as priests but fail to note the possible significance of Josephus's use of 'ministers'. For example, see Goodman, *Ruling Class*, p. 152, and Cohen, *Josephus*, p. 192.

19. It is curious that the Loeb translation of ἀκμαῖος is 'stalwarts' in relation to

the public gathering, 'the revolutionaries' (οἱ νεωτερίζοντες) and 'the ministers' are present (*War* 2.417). Presumably these two references to 'the revolutionaries' are to the same basic group of people, one to the elite among their number and the other to the group as a whole. Reference is also made to the presence of 'the insurgents' (οἱ στασιασταὶ). This is the group towards which the appeal to reverse the action was directed (*War* 2.411).

It is important to establish to whom Josephus is referring by the use of these descriptive terms. First, 'the revolutionaries' appear to stand as a distinct group from Eleazar and 'the ministers' responsible for the action. Josephus explicitly views 'the revolutionaries' and 'the ministers' as two separate groups in *War* 2.417. This distinction reinforces the idea conveyed in *War* 2.409-10 that the 'most vigorous of the revolutionaries' supported the decision that Eleazar and his associates had made. Other than to say 'the revolutionaries' are not the group led by Eleazar in this incident, we are no closer to a positive identification of them.

Establishing the meaning of the other term used by Josephus, 'the insurgents', is extremely difficult. These 'insurgents' are the people to whom the appeal is being made, presumably in an effort to reverse the action. As such, it would appear that they are Eleazar and his associates. The complication, however, is the possible relationship with 'the revolutionaries'. The latter were at the gathering along with 'the ministers'. If Josephus uses terms with little sense of consistency, then the idea of identifying 'the insurgents' and 'the revolutionaries' is a hopeless cause. If Josephus did use specific terms to describe particular groups, we are left with at least three options regarding the identity of 'the insurgents'. One is that Josephus is using the term to refer to the two groups mentioned individually in *War* 2.417. The second is that 'the insurgents' refers only to the people who are described as 'the revolutionaries'. The third option is that the term refers only to Eleazar and his associates.[20]

---

the revolutionaries, while it is translated as the 'flower' in relation to the Roman infantry in *War* 3.255.

20. The various terms used by Josephus to describe the types of participants should not be assumed to be interchangeable. How Josephus employs the various terms, whether as a reference to a specific group or individual, or more generally and loosely of a type of person, needs to be determined in the light of detailed investigation of the case studies. Until such examination is undertaken it is important to be

An important rider to the discussion of these general terms in this incident, especially 'the revolutionaries', is that they are not important in the way the event unfolds. If anything, it appears that Josephus has tried to promote the involvement of 'the revolutionaries'. They are the focus of Josephus's comment in *War* 2.417, with 'the ministers' being cited in their wake. 'The revolutionaries', as such, is a vague term in this incident. Josephus suggests that they are separate from, and are subsidiary to, Eleazar and his associates. Although Josephus names Eleazar, much of the remainder of the reference to those in favour of the action tries to place the focus on the undefined 'revolutionaries'. To complicate matters even more, Josephus also makes a single reference to 'the insurgents'. Care is required to ensure that attention is placed on those who are known to have played a role in how the incident unfolds—Eleazar and 'the ministers'—not the decoys in the guise of undefined groups.[21]

Josephus employs broad descriptive terms for those who oppose the action. Despite the detail regarding the content of the protest, named individuals are conspicuous by their absence. On two occasions Josephus names a number of groups. Initially, 'the chief priests' and 'the notables' register their opposition and try to reverse the decision (*War* 2.410).[22] After this failure to persuade Eleazar and his associates, the public gathering is presented by Josephus as being instigated by 'the chief priests', 'the powerful' and 'the most notable Pharisees' (*War* 2.411). Later, in the midst of the public gathering, some of those who speak against the action are named as 'priests who were experts in the traditions' (*War* 2.417). Clearly, priests were among those who opposed the action. This openness of Josephus at declaring the presence of the 'chief priests' on both occasions and the 'priests' in

---

aware of the different terminology and employ a consistency in the translation offered.

21. Note the detailed discussion of Rajak, *Josephus*, pp. 86-93, regarding the possible meaning of the descriptive terms. Rajak accepts that Josephus employed the terms deliberately and that the 'revolutionaries' and 'insurgents' should be understood in the context of Greek political terminology. Even with this clarification it is not clear as to who these political opponents actually were.

22. An alternative translation to 'chief priests' is 'high priests'. The appropriateness of one or another translation is dependent on comparison with other incidents in the hope that they can help establish a picture of which people should be associated with the term. Until such a comparison is possible 'chief priests' will continue to be used.

War 2.417 is in stark contrast to the description of Eleazar's associates. It also reinforces the need to explain why Josephus used 'the ministers' to describe one group in this incident.

The exact identity of the 'chief priests' in this incident is not apparent. The term implies they were the leading priests, presumably closely connected with the temple. The references to 'the powerful' and 'the notable' are also not explained in any manner within the narrative of this incident. It is possible that Josephus is referring to the same prominent people, using terms that were interchangeable. It is also possible, however, that he was referring to different groups. They may be associates of the 'chief priests' who also team up with 'the most notable Pharisees'. The latter are not part of the initial protest but become involved in the organization of the public gathering. The grouping identified in *War* 2.411 implies a gathering of like-minded, concerned, prominent Jews, at least within their own group, who were eager to prevent war.

Josephus appears to be leaving the reader in no doubt regarding the groups opposed to the action and, therefore, opposed to provoking conflict with Rome, at least according to the wisdom allocated to them. However, this neat picture is nothing more than a blurred vision. The identity of the 'most notable Pharisees', 'the notable' and 'the powerful' is not defined. The importance of this observation is highlighted by a major problem with the other group mentioned—the 'chief priests'. Although this group is named as being opposed to the action, it must be placed beside the realization that the only person actually named, Eleazar, is the captain and the son of a high priest. Depending on the definition of the term 'chief priests', Eleazar would appear to be a possible candidate as one who could be described by the term. From the evidence in this incident, therefore, it is possible that the 'chief priests' were not completely united, despite what Josephus seeks to convey.[23]

Josephus refers to one further participant in the incident, 'the populace' (δῆμος). Their exact role and attitude cannot be determined. Josephus claims that they were called together to the public gathering as part of the attempt to persuade 'the insurgents' to change their decision. Why the populace should be called upon is not stated. It is

---

23. Even if 'chief priests' refers specifically to people who once held the office of high priest, it is apparent that the incident was primarily a debate within the priesthood.

possible that the people who opposed the action hoped to sway most of
the populace to favour their cause and thus influence Eleazar and his
supporters. In other words, the latter were the primary target, with
the populace being used as an avenue by which to change the balance
of power. If this view is accurate, then the extent to which Eleazar
and his associates controlled the situation is further reinforced.[24] Irrespective of Josephus's intention for referring to the involvement of the
populace, the way the incident concludes implies that they were not
sufficiently opposed to Eleazar and 'the ministers' to take action.

The decision to cease accepting the offerings of foreigners is a significant event. It was a public action, initiated by people from within
the temple, with Eleazar b. Ananias being presented as a key player.
Irrespective of the number and status of the people who opposed the
action, it was not reversed. The action is portrayed as an innovation
that would bring a harsh response from the Romans. Clearly it had
already made an impact among the Jews, drawing a dividing line
between those who approved of what had happened and those who did
not. The extant narrative of the incident is intriguing for what it
leaves out, as much as for what it includes. It is a rather one-sided
account, explicit in describing the arguments of those who tried to
reverse the decision, but totally silent as to why 'the ministers' and
Eleazar believed the action was appropriate. At best, we can speculate
from the protests that it was intended as a rejection of Rome. This,
however, is presented as the view of the people opposed to what had
been done. Furthermore, Josephus appears to have directed the reader
to focus on certain features, such as the role of 'the revolutionaries'
and of an individual with personal influence. In reality, though, this
appears to have been an internal debate among the priesthood in which
effective power lay with a group referred to as 'the ministers' and one
named participant, Eleazar. More information regarding such aspects
as the identity of almost all the participants and the reasons for
initiating the action are required to fill in substantial gaps in the existing narrative.

24. A possible mitigating factor to this interpretation is if public meetings were
the normal process by which decisions were reached. Again, only comparison
with other incidents can help clarify the decision making process that operated
within the Jewish community. According to Goodman, *Ruling Class*, pp. 152-55,
and T. Donaldson, 'Rural Bandits, Urban Mobs and the Zealots', *JSJ* 21 (1990), pp.
19-40 (38-40), the authority of Eleazar was dependent on the populace.

2.3 *The Capture of Machaerus (War 2.485-86)*

Josephus provides a brief account of the capture of Machaerus, a fortress located in Peraea, to the east of the Dead Sea. The fortress was held by a Roman garrison. In the context of describing the incident no information is provided regarding how long a Roman garrison had occupied the fortress or the number of troops in the garrison. In fact, very little detail is provided regarding the entire incident.

There are also a number of elements which are not explained in the way that events unfold. For instance, it is unclear when the incident actually took place. Although Josephus draws a chronological link with the previous event narrated, the capture of Cypros, the timing of the capture of Machaerus cannot be ascertained from within the narrative of *War* 2.485-86. The lack of information regarding the timing is frustrating because a chronological marker may help clarify the purpose of the action. A further puzzle relates to the manner in which the fortress was captured. According to Josephus the garrison was not subject to attack. Instead, it was persuaded to leave the fortress under arranged terms and no assault took place at any stage in the proceedings. The account then concludes with the Jews placing their own garrison in Machaerus. No explanation is offered as to why the Jews wanted to occupy the fortress. Furthermore, nothing is indicated regarding the fate of the Roman garrison after their departure.

There are, however, some details which allow comments to be made regarding the identity of those who initiate the action and the possible motivation of the Roman garrison. The people who offer terms to the Romans and then occupy the fortress are described as being the 'multitude' of Jews of Machaerus (πλῆθος). Josephus appears to be referring to the local population; it is not a military force that had been sent to capture the fortress. As noted above, no information is provided to help explain the possible motivation of the Jews, and no force was used in the actual capture of the fortress.

The other aspect that requires comment is the motivation of the Roman garrison. They are portrayed as being concerned that they might be over run by an 'armed assault'. As a result, the garrison willingly accepted the terms of withdrawal offered to them and departed from the fortress. These two details make it difficult to establish the nature of the threat. According to Josephus, the Roman garrison believed they could 'trust' the promises made by the Jews. At the same time, however, the garrison feared an attack on the fortress. Josephus's account is puzzling in that the Romans were fearful of those from whom they also accepted terms of withdrawal. Further information regarding the motivation of the Jews who occupy the fortress may help clarify the situation. A number of questions are unanswered: did the Jews greatly outnumber the garrison and demand its surrender? If so, did they allow the Romans to escape? Was there a detachment of Jewish troops on their way to Machaerus and did the local Jewish community manage to prevent armed conflict by persuading the Romans to leave? Clearly, there are important aspects of this incident that require further clarification to gain a better understanding of what happened and why it occurred.

Within Josephus's account of 66 CE, this brief aside to the takeover of Machaerus is curious. It is not related to any conflict in the town or region and there is no sense of violence associated with the action in the narrative. It is an incident that raises questions. We must ponder why it ever occurred, and why it has been described by Josephus. In other words, what is the significance of this incident for Josephus and for the way events unfolded in Judaea during 66 CE?

3. *Synthesis*

With only three of the 23 incidents recorded by Josephus examined, it is not possible to present an extensive account of what happened in 66 CE. As a result, the following synthesis is somewhat piecemeal in nature. It is, however, important to indicate the direction that can be undertaken in this final stage of the case study approach. In particular, several areas of overlap between the three incidents need to be explored in an effort to explain some unresolved details. It will be then possible to suggest a framework in which the events of 66 CE may be considered. Therefore, even within the boundaries of this limited discussion there is sufficient means to indicate the value of the case study approach. It is apparent that we are able to achieve the objective of going beyond Josephus's interpretative framework. So doing, we can focus on the actual situation in an attempt to understand what happened in 66 CE.

Each of the three incidents displays some distinctive features. The brief reference to the capture of Masada prompts us to be cautious with regard to those events for which there appear to be multiple accounts. It is important to avoid drawing links before each account is examined on an individual basis. The rejection of gifts and sacrifices offered by foreigners is an example of one of the few incidents described in relative detail by Josephus. However, on a close reading it is apparent that the account is selective in the type of information provided. The third incident, the capture of Machaerus, is simply one of many examples of an event which is cited almost in passing, for which very little detail is provided.

There are a number of ostensible similarities between the three incidents. Two share the same type of action—the capture of a fortress which had been in Roman hands. There also appears to be a chronological link between the capture of Masada and the action undertaken by Eleazar and 'the ministers' (*War* 2.409). It is important to acknowledge, however, that Josephus does not try to suggest that there is any practical link between these two incidents. From the individual examination of the incidents it is also apparent that they share a number of unresolved questions regarding the details associated with what happened. It is in examining these aspects of the incidents that the synthesis can be particularly helpful. The unresolved questions revolve around two central themes: the identity of the participants; and the nature of their motivation for undertaking certain actions.

It is unclear who actually captured Masada, just as it is unclear who was in favour, and who against, the action in which Eleazar is named. With the exception of Eleazar, Josephus describes the type of person in these incidents, but names no one. It is possible that Josephus was unfamiliar with many of the actual people involved. However, it is also possible that Josephus has chosen to use generic group names deliberately, being, in fact, fully aware of at least some of the individuals who participated.[25] It is curious that Eleazar is the only person named in any of the three incidents. Josephus's naming of this one participant is particularly troublesome because Eleazar was probably associated with a group which was apparently opposed to his action,

25. Against the idea of Josephus not knowing who was involved is the admission that he had returned from Rome and was in Jerusalem at the time of the event (*Life* 16-21). Here discussion of other events relating to 66 CE would help highlight how close Josephus appears to have been to what was happening. It is, therefore, unlikely that he lacked information regarding the details of what happened. It would appear that Josephus is being deliberately vague.

the 'chief priests'. Such an anomaly acts as a warning regarding the use of descriptive terms by Josephus when identifying the participants. Why Eleazar alone is named cannot be resolved on the basis of just these three incidents. The fact that Eleazar is identified and clearly located within the social and administrative structure of Judaea, however, must be acknowledged. Furthermore, it is important that his name not become a magnet in the sense of assuming that he was the one and only prominent person in favour of the action. Caution is required to ensure that the nebulous of the descriptive terms and the singleness of naming only Eleazar are not allowed to construct a boundary that has one opposed to the many.[26]

In all three incidents there is also a sense of frustration at the lack of information concerning why events unfolded as they did. We do not know why Machaerus was acquired, why and how Masada was captured, or why the gifts and sacrifices of foreigners were rejected. The isolated naming of Eleazar and the way he is presented as juxtaposed to a group with which he was probably associated reinforces the need to explain why he and 'the ministers' undertook the action they did. Similarly, an explanation of the causation underlying the events at Masada and Machaerus may help clarify the significance of not detailing them. In the following section I will explore some of the possibilities of interpretation offered by the case study approach of these three incidents. The limitations of the material will also then be commented on.

It is possible that the two outstanding questions—those of the identity of the participants and the causation—are related. Moreover, there may be a causational connection between the capture of Masada and the decision taken by Eleazar and 'the ministers'. The chronological parallel between the two events has already been noted. In the discussion of the capture of Masada it was also noted that the means of capture was most probably linked with the identity of the assailants. Furthermore, one possible explanation as to how access to Masada was obtained was that the assailants were known to the defendants and that they tricked their way into the fortress. It is in this context that the account of the temple action becomes relevant. It is possible that Eleazar and his associates were also responsible for the capture of

26. The need for care to avoid following Josephus's direction is reinforced by the use of 'the ministers' in relation to those undertaking the action and 'chief priests' and 'priests' regarding those who oppose the action.

Masada. As the captain and son of a high priest, Eleazar would have been known to the Roman authorities in Judaea. His associates, 'the ministers', are played down in the account. They were, however, clearly linked with the temple, knew Eleazar, and could therefore have also been known to the Romans. At the very least, they were connected with a very prominent public aspect of the Jewish establishment—the temple. It is even possible that 'the ministers' were people who could be described by the term 'chief priests'. Whatever their exact identity, before the action in the temple, Eleazar and some of his associates could have travelled to Masada in an effort to gain control of the fortress. Alternatively, some of Eleazar's companions may have gone to Masada at the same time as Eleazar made his move in the temple.

In favour of such a general line of interpretation is that it helps explain the capture of Masada by secrecy. The garrison either knew, or knew of, the men who sought entry into the fortress and allowed them access, believing they were friendly. Once in the fortress these men turned on the garrison and killed them. The 'most ardent promoters of war', therefore, is a cloak used by Josephus to protect the identity of those who captured Masada.[27] It is no wonder that Josephus is vague regarding the identity of those who attacked the fortress and the link between the two events. They were probably the work of prominent, respected members of the priesthood.[28]

---

27. The one rider to this interpretation is if the description of the people who captured Masada is used elsewhere by Josephus and it can be linked with a specific group of people. For examples of those who believe that the fortress was captured by Menahem and his sicarii associates see Hengel, *Zealots*, p. 358, Smallwood, *Jews*, p. 292, Hadas-Lebel, *Flavius*, p. 63, and Rhoads, *Israel*, p. 80.

28. The conclusion reached here parallels that expressed by Cohen, *Josephus*, p. 193. However, here the parallel ends. Cohen does not consider the identity of who captured Masada—Menahem or Eleazar—as part of the main concern regarding the events of 66 CE. Furthermore, he regards the problem between *War* 2.408 and 2.434 as a sign of 'Josephus's lack of concern for accuracy'. The events are crucial for an understanding of what happened in 66 CE and a more likely explanation for the supposed confusion is that this is a sign of Josephus deliberately trying to cover up the real situation but not quite succeeding in this task. Throughout his discussion of 66 CE Cohen displays a keen concern to be very cautious in the use of Josephus's narrative. Despite this 'care' Cohen continues to work within the boundaries established by Josephus in the way he portrays the machinations among the Jews vying for leadership. For example, it is assumed that because Eleazar is named he was a

The identification of those who captured Masada as the same group responsible for the action in the temple has a further benefit in terms of explaining the question of motivation in each incident. Josephus does not indicate why the fortress was attacked, nor why the offerings ceased to be accepted. If anything, Josephus actually tries to present these incidents as being quite distinct from one another. If the same group of people were responsible for both actions, however, then an entirely new dimension to these incidents would be exposed. They could have been part of a large-scale strategic operation. Knowing the strategic value of Masada and how difficult it would be to take by assault, the fortress may have been captured before trouble began. Having secured the fortress, the cessation of the practice of accepting gifts and sacrifices offered by foreigners could be done in relative 'safety' as a public declaration of liberation.[29] The 'wisdom' of the

prominent figure at the outset but was out-manoeuvred later in the year (p. 198). Caution is required not to allow the naming of Eleazar to overshadow the possible involvement of other prominent people with the initial actions. It is important to ask why Eleazar alone is named, particularly whether it was because Eleazar was the only prominent figure or whether it was because Josephus used him as a 'scapegoat' to pass over the involvement of other well-known people. Apart from Cohen, no other scholarly account of 66 CE explores the possibility of a link between these two incidents. Note also that Cotton and Geiger, 'Who Captured Masada', p. 6, refer to Cohen in their conclusion that the people mentioned in *War* 2.408 were the sicarii. Although Cohen, *Josephus*, p. 193, lists the option favoured by Cotton and Geiger they have not acknowledged that Cohen goes on to accept the alternative choice, that it was Eleazar and 'the ministers' who captured Masada at first. One of the main arguments of Cotton and Geiger, 'Who Captured Masada', p. 6, that *War* 2.408 and 2.433-34 refer to the same event, is that if they describe two separate events then Josephus would have mentioned it as an example of fighting among extremist factions. This approach ignores the key issue of who initially captured Masada and that the visit in *War* 2.433-34 does not refer to an attack on the fortress. At the time of the visit of Menahem he was an ally of the group that occupied the fortress.

29. The rejection of gifts and sacrifices appears to have a distinctive flavour of being an anti-Roman action. Sacrifices were offered daily (*Apion* 2.77), possibly even twice a day (*War* 2.197), in honour of the emperor and Rome. The complication regarding the purpose of the action is that this order pertained to gifts and sacrifices offered by foreigners. In *Apion* 2.77 Josephus claims the Jewish people paid for the daily offering on behalf of the emperor. If so, then the action initiated by Eleazar and 'the ministers' is not directly related with the imperial offerings. According to Philo (*Leg. Gai.* 157) it was the emperor who paid for the offerings. In these circumstances, the rejection of the gifts and sacrifices offered by foreigners would exclude those provided by the emperor. For further discussion see D.R. Schwartz, 'On Sacrifices', pp. 111-15.

opponents of the action in the temple, therefore, may reflect genuine concern by people who recognized the sense of coordination associated with both actions. In this context, the meeting in the temple should be read as a last-ditch effort by a group wanting the recent course of events stopped before the situation got out of control.[30]

One element of the cessation incident to which we are not able to add further insight is the identity of those opposed to the action. In the analysis of the incident it was noted that the descriptive terms used by Josephus should not automatically be assumed to mean that all the 'chief priests', 'notable', 'powerful' and 'most notable Pharisees' were involved. Evidence from other relevant incidents is required to provide sufficient data regarding the use of these terms. At this stage caution is the crucial catch-phrase in the use of these terms to help explain what happened and who was involved in a given situation.[31] A similar situation applies to another complication, the naming of Eleazar. Within the context of the three incidents examined, the uniqueness of naming Eleazar is even more apparent. It is possible that other incidents may help explain Josephus's general practice regarding the naming of participants. In particular, it will be important to consider in what circumstances people are named and what detail is provided regarding their status in society. The specific identification of Eleazar, a person for whom Josephus can outline

30. An alternative explanation for claiming an association—namely, that 'the revolutionaries' mentioned in connection with the actions of Eleazar and 'the ministers' may have been responsible for the capture of Masada—is often proclaimed. See, for example, Hengel, *Zealots*, p. 358, and Rhoads, *Israel*, p. 80. For this link to be viable it must be assumed that 'the most ardent promoters of war' were also 'the revolutionaries'. Far more significant than this hurdle are problems regarding the identity of 'the revolutionaries'. They enter the fray only after the action had been taken. They are a separate entity from 'the ministers' (*War* 2.417) and are promoted by Josephus beyond the actual role given to them in the action. Until further evidence is available, caution is required regarding the notion that 'the revolutionaries' can be associated with any move towards war. They are an unknown group. To link them with the capture of Masada is simply to change one general descriptive term with another one. It also provides no assistance in explaining how the fortress was penetrated by secrecy.

31. In particular, from the immediate historical context the visit of Florus, the fighting between the Jews and Romans, the fighting among the Jews and Cestius's campaign will help clarify the use of these terms. From the literary context it will be important to understand how Josephus employs various terms and his practice regarding the naming of participants.

apparently respectable credentials, suggests his name was well known in relation to the incident.

The capture of Machaerus acts as the wild card amongst these three case studies. It is portrayed as an action instigated by the local Jewish population. If so, explaining why these Jews wanted to acquire the fortress, and why the defendants readily relinquished control is difficult. Sequentially, Josephus separates the action from the two other incidents, placing it much later in the narrative. Whether its location is an accurate reflection of its actual timing in relation to other events is not possible to determine. The whole issue of why the fortress was captured also remains a puzzle. Moving the action chronologically so that it is linked with the capture of Masada is appealing. It would allow the occupation to be viewed as part of a large-scale operation. However, the capture of Machaerus is presented as a localized action. Exactly what, if anything, is to be made of this incident must await the examination of the remaining events associated with 66 CE and the events that follow. This incident is a salutary warning that even some aspects of the actual situation may remain shrouded in uncertainty because of a lack of information. Josephus deemed it to be relevant, but exactly how it relates to other events in 66 CE is not at all clear.

There is a sense of frustration associated with the case study approach. Gaps and problems in the accounts which are not resolved when first raised are highlighted. This is one of the distinctive features of the case study approach. There is an ongoing temptation to automatically look for the 'other' elements in Josephus's narrative that appear to provide the relevant explanation as each incident is explored. It is, however, crucial that the cross-referencing does not take place before the incidents have been individually examined. The level of frustration that might be felt because of the isolationist approach should not be viewed as a hindrance but as a 'healthy' sign. It reflects success at being able to stand outside Josephus's interpretative framework, ensuring that the interpretation of one incident is not explained in the context of another incident that has yet to be examined.[32]

Even on the basis of the limited scale of the preceding investigation,

32. It also helps reinforce the importance of asking why Josephus has included this information. Unless Josephus has narrated everything that took place or has chosen material on a purely random basis—two options that cannot be supported because of the way the interpretative framework functions—then the events mentioned must have been deemed to be important for one reason or another.

it is apparent that the case study approach offers rich pickings. The narrative of Josephus can be used to explore the actual situation independent of the framework established by Josephus and adopted by scholarship. In terms of the incidents examined, there is a significant level of clarification possible, especially in relation to the capture of Masada and the action which involved Eleazar and 'the ministers'. Both incidents were probably the work of priests, of which there is one named person—the captain, Eleazar. Their actions were premeditated, and carefully coordinated. Why elements of the priesthood should take such a course of action, and when they decided to do so, becomes important to consider in relation to other events associated with 66 CE.

Brief comment is also appropriate regarding Josephus's use of terminology. Certain descriptive terms need to be understood with great care. 'The insurgents' and 'the revolutionaries' are not defined. In fact, Josephus draws a distinction between 'the revolutionaries' and the one named participant, Eleazar.[33] There is a suspicion that Josephus has used these terms freely to identify a 'type' of people, but who they actually are needs to be established before their existence and function as a group linked with the war can be determined. Although the 'chief priests' are probably identifiable with the leadership of the temple, the action of Eleazar and 'the ministers' indicates that exact identity of the 'chief priests' is not necessarily clear. Again, reference to other incidents may help clarify their identification. In this instance, the only person named—the one apparently responsible for the entire action—appears to warrant association with the group known as the 'chief priests', yet it is those people who allegedly oppose him.

On a broader level, in terms of the outbreak of the war and the general situation in Judaea, significant insights are derived from the application of the case study approach to the three incidents. The portrayal of the aristocracy and the revolutionary movement at the beginning of the war needs to be reconsidered devoid of the existing parameters of scholarly inquiry. Furthermore, the implications of a direct link between the attack on Masada and the action in the temple need to be explored.[34] The ever present but rarely defined

33. This is where Rajak's discussion of the terminology fails to take the investigation beyond Josephus (*Josephus*, p. 93). If the revolutionaries were innovators and opponents of the established leadership the question still remains: Who are they?

34. This is the case even for those who appear to adopt a more critical stance to

'revolutionaries' in scholarly reconstructions of 66 CE should not be portrayed as the ones responsible for the war. It cannot be assumed that Eleazar was an exception to his class because he is opposed by the 'chief priests', as is commonly acclaimed. Nor should it be assumed that because Eleazar alone is named that he is the only leader. It is important to avoid the bait offered by Josephus. Simply because Eleazar is named does not mean that he is the only prominent person involved in the actions.[35] The attack on Masada and the cessation of accepting gifts and offerings were not actions where an alliance of 'revolutionaries' and some rogue aristocrats joined together. They were the deliberate actions of a group in which one of the leading figures was 'the captain'. In this light a further concept associated with the standing of the aristocracy requires a significant re-examination. The notion that the aristocracy were 'quislings' and active supporters of Roman rule, who always acted in a manner that tried to preserve the status quo, is not an appropriate framework from which to understand the events of 66.[36] Without the actions of Eleazar and his associates, the

the narrative of Josephus, such as Price, *Jerusalem*, and Goodman, *Ruling Class*. Although Cohen, *Josephus*, p. 193, notes the link he does not consider the possible implications.

35. The idea that Eleazar is the key figure is entrenched in existing scholarly discussion. For example, see Rajak, *Josephus*, pp. 118, 129, G. Baumbach, 'The Sadducees in Josephus', in L.H. Feldman and G. Hata (eds.), *Josephus, the Bible and History* (Detroit: Wayne State University Press, 1989), pp. 173-95 (186), and S. Schwartz, *Judaean Politics*, p. 84. Hengel, *Zealots*, pp. 359-60, also seeks to explain why Eleazar would desert 'the Sadducean tradition'. Goodman's approach, *Ruling Class*, pp. 152-55, that Eleazar was making a last ditch effort to win power through popular support, does not give sufficient credit to the extent of planning that had been undertaken. It also implies that Eleazar and his faction were working alone, thereby accepting Josephus's basic division of 'chief priests' being opposed to the 'rogue' faction of Eleazar (p. 153). Note, however, that Goodman implies Eleazar may have entered this supposedly 'last ditched' attempt earlier in 66 on the basis that he was among the people who played the practical joke of making the mock collection after Florus ordered the payment of extra money (pp. 171-72).

36. The principle of viewing the aristocracy as quislings is strongly asserted by Horsley, 'High Priests', pp. 23-55, and has become relevant in other debates, such as the meaning of the action undertaken by Jesus before his arrest. For example, see C.A. Evans, 'Jesus' Action in the Temple: Cleansing or Portent of Destruction?', *CBQ* 51 (1989), pp. 256-64. It raises the issue of whether or not the aristocracy were accepted as leaders by the Jewish community. See McLaren, *Power*, pp. 184, 202-22. Note that in the context of the actual revolt Goodman, *Ruling Class*,

war would not have begun in the time and manner that it did. The real puzzle is why at least some of the people normally cited as having the most to gain from Roman rule had decided to 'bite the hand by which they were fed'.

The exercise of examining the three incidents in this trailer has been most fruitful. Although we are far from constructing a full picture of 66 CE, let alone the first century CE, it is apparent that the actual situation in the three incidents examined differs quite substantially from how Josephus has directed his readers to understand what was happening. It is clear that conceptual independence from Josephus is achievable and that it raises issues and possibilities that have yet to be properly explored by scholarship.

pp. 152-75 and Price, *Jerusalem*, pp. 31-45, also argue that elements of the aristocracy were actively involved in promoting and then controlling the revolt.

CONCLUSION

The two primary goals of historical inquiry are the acquisition of information and the means of understanding that information. Knowledge about relevant data does not automatically result in the ability to explain 'the past'. We may know that there was a war in Judaea during the years 66–70 CE. We may even know that the war culminated in the capture and destruction of Jerusalem in 70 CE and that the main protagonists were Jews of Judaea and Galilee matched against troops of the Roman empire. Awareness of these events, however, does not mean that we understand why the war occurred, nor the possible significance of the war for the various protagonists. These concerns fall within the realm of understanding. As historians, therefore, the simple collection of information is only part of the task. Without the accompanying analysis the data acquired remains a silent record. As such, the relationship between historians and their sources only becomes active when understanding of the data is sought.

Where historians interested in recent events may be burdened by a great abundance of source material, those concerned with the ancient world often lament the paucity of sources they have at their disposal. More often than not ancient historians are left guessing, trying to piece together a picture when many of the pieces in the puzzle are missing. The general paucity of material makes the occasional availability of major narrative texts a 'gold-mine'. Scholars flock to the texts in relief that, at last, there is a source which provides sufficient data to focus on a period in some detail.

Josephus is one such gold-mine. For scholars interested in Roman, Jewish and early Christian history the texts of Josephus provide a substantial body of information. Although Josephus is not the only source for historical inquiry into the late second temple period in Judaea, he stands out. It is only Josephus who provides a narrative of events that covers the entire period. Moreover, he has the added bonus of being a contemporary of the events which mark the end of the period. In fact, in Josephus the historian has a kindred soul. Just as Josephus was interested in preserving information and providing understanding, so too is the historian who reads his texts. We are, therefore, entering into relationship with someone who also wanted to dialogue with others. As historians are interested in understanding Jewish society, so too Josephus was interested in promoting understanding of the society in which he grew up. So far so good. The problems begin when we commence our dialogue with Josephus. Extreme care is required for the relationship to develop into a meaningful exchange. We want to use Josephus in an effort to acquire knowledge and establish understanding. The question we need to resolve is: who is in control? Is it the historian, or Josephus?

This study has focused on the implications of trying to make use of the gold-mine, particularly in terms of the nature of the relationship between Josephus, his narrative of events, and contemporary scholarship, in the reconstruction of first-century CE Judaea. Scholars have increasingly voiced the need to display caution in the application of Josephus's narrative in an effort to understand the dynamic of the society. In fact, reference to Josephus without some introductory words of caution is now extremely rare. With Josephus we are dealing with a biased source. In itself, such a statement should not be a concern. Josephus has provided his own understanding of what happened and scholarship has labelled this his bias.

The gold-mine begins to take on the appearance of a minefield. The one and only substantial narrative of events pertaining to the first century CE is biased. If we are to establish a means of understanding the data it is of fundamental importance that we be able to distinguish between the bias and the narrative of actual events. Where the real problem lies is being able to stop before we become dependent on Josephus's interpretation. It is most appropriate to know how Josephus understands what happened. It may also be that his interpretation of the situation is to be regarded as historically accurate. What is crucial, however, is that Josephus's presentation to the reader is either affirmed, rejected or adjusted after the period in question has been examined independently of Josephus.

The insights obtained regarding the nature of the relationship between Josephus and contemporary scholarship are most disturbing. It is evident that scholarship has failed to draw the line between employing Josephus for the acquisition of data and for understanding the dynamic of the state of affairs in Judaea. Scholarship strongly asserts that it stands conceptually independent of Josephus. Actively declaring a concern to avoid contamination by Josephus's bias, scholars have outlined a variety of ways in which they achieve their goal. This belief, however, does not reflect the actual nature of the relationship. The investigation into the first century CE has been undertaken within the boundaries of Josephus's understanding. In effect, *an* interpretation of the first century has been adopted as *the* interpretation, with scholarship failing to read Josephus independent of his bias. Although individual features within Josephus's picture may be changed, his interpretative framework stands in place. The two pillars central to this framework are that Judaea was a place of escalating turmoil and that the revolt of 66–70 CE was the inevitable climax of long-standing causes. Although refined in a variety of ways, these two pillars act as the boundary markers within which existing scholarly reconstructions of the first century CE are undertaken. Despite all the criticism and words of caution, Josephus's understanding of the data prevails.

Josephus's narrative of events relating to the first century CE is not simply a collection of information. The narrative is crafted with choices made by Josephus regarding the detail provided, the location and the inclusion of subject matter. For Josephus, the crucial points are providing a context for the revolt, which requires the description of events that convey conflict and trouble. Irrespective of his need to use sources for at least part of the narrative, the accounts should be viewed as the fruits of Josephus's own labour. The end result is a product best described as Josephus's interpretative framework. It is all encompassing; not one part of the narrative is devoid of Josephus's controlling hand. The two levels of this interpretative framework are the choice of subject matter and the means of recording the subject matter. Within the second level there are four sub-categories: the reflections on the general situation; the reflective comments on the events that are alluded to but not narrated; the reflective comments on the events that Josephus narrates; and, the various types of comments within the narrative of an event. What Josephus narrates is primarily an expression of his desire for understanding of the disaster of 70 CE. It is a history of flash points which has focused on certain issues and events. That scholarship parallels the account of Josephus by explaining the dynamic of the situation within the two pillars is not a mere coincidence. Because scholarship fails to understand the nature of Josephus's interpretative framework, a line is not drawn between information and understanding.

As a result, the legitimacy of the two pillars is never questioned. Instead, it is assumed that any investigation into the first century CE commences on the understanding that the revolt is to be explained in terms of long-standing causes and that conflict was the common denominator to the period. Significant variation is evident in terms of the type or nature of conflict that is identified, but never is the pillar of escalating conflict doubted. In a similar vein, although many avoid explicit discussion of the revolt as being inevitable, all scholars point to causes that lie in the years long before 66 CE, with some even willing to trace the cause back to 63 BCE. It is almost as though these two pillars are like unwritten canons that cannot be challenged. It is, however, time that the pillars were brought under scrutiny. As yet, the accuracy of Josephus's understanding has not been properly addressed. Scholarship has not established that the two pillars accurately reflect the dynamic of the situation in Judaea, and the history of the first century CE continues to be portrayed in terms of the flash points identified by Josephus.

Given the all encompassing nature of Josephus's interpretation, a rather bleak outcome on the viability of establishing understanding of the first century CE independent of Josephus would appear likely. If other substantial narrative sources were extant it may be possible to view the period from another perspective, but while Josephus acts as the only extensive source it would appear we are bound by his interpretation. We are most certainly confronted by a substantial problem: how do we draw the line between using Josephus's narrative to provide information and being dependent on his interpretation, particularly when the latter is the means by which Josephus conveys the former. All is not lost—there is a lifeline that allows us to enter the first century CE through the perspective of Josephus, but not to be bound by his interpretation.

In terms of reading Josephus within manageable limits that restrict his narrative to the role of information there are two important requirements. The first pertains to the mindset of the reader. In particular, it is the type of questions that are applied to the text and the role of hindsight that must be considered. It is crucial that open-ended questions be posed. We must avoid such questions as, 'In what way was Judaea a place of turmoil?', asking instead, 'What was the situation in Judaea?'. Of similar importance is the need to be cautious of the influence of hindsight in the nature of the investigation undertaken. Here the status of 70 CE is significant, particularly in terms of whether it is appropriate to view events prior to 70 CE primarily within the context of the destruction of Jerusalem.

The second requirement pertains to the manner in which Josephus's narrative is read. It is crucial that the case study approach be employed, not only in relation to the state of affairs in first-century CE Judaea, but in every historical inquiry where an understanding of what actually happened is the primary goal. The approach provides a means of obtaining conceptual independence from Josephus's interpretation. Incidents are removed from their narrative context and examined on an individual basis. Such an arbitrary division is fundamental to the approach being effectively employed. Only when each incident has been examined, dissecting and analysing all the elements of the account, and the various gaps and inconsistencies explored, will the individual case studies be discussed as a whole. The final stage of the process—the synthesis—allows the reconstruction to begin. Such an approach is laborious and it is frustrating. The rewards, however, are extremely fruitful. No longer does Josephus's interpretation have to stand as the boundary markers for the historical inquiry undertaken. The available data, however limited in scope, can be considered independently of the understanding of Josephus.

'Proof of the pudding' in terms of the case study approach is apparent in the redirection required in how the first century CE is to be perceived. Although only hinted at in this stage, we are in a position to call for a major shift in perspective. The questions posed, and the reconstruction that is presented, must avoid the limitations of hindsight. Of particular importance is the need to curtail the influence of 70 CE as the centre point of the first century CE. Hindsight has almost dictated that 70 CE be viewed as the climax of the trouble and that existing discussion of the first century CE is normally defined as 6–70 CE. The framework of an escalating level of turmoil which climaxes with the inevitable revolt is no longer the appropriate starting point for historical inquiry into the period. In a similar vein, it is no longer valid to assume that the level of conflict in the society is greater than what Josephus describes. Furthermore, it is not necessarily only the two pillars relating to the state of affairs in Judaea that should be removed. A domino effect is created. Conceptual dependency on Josephus marks all topics of historical inquiry regarding Jewish society. Such dependency can now be avoided.[1]

Much more groundwork is required. Discussion of the mechanism for measuring the state of affairs in a society is necessary. Alongside such investigation should be placed analysis of the actual revolt, its relationship to the events before and after, and a comparison of the first century CE to the centuries immediately before and after. Possibly the most fundamental issue to consider is the status of 70 CE. Instead of regarding 70 CE as the end-point it may be appropriate to explore 70 CE as the starting-point. The possibility needs to be examined that the years following 70 CE may have been the time in which an ideological focus to Jewish–Roman relations developed. In other words, 70 CE may be most appropriately viewed as the spark, not the culmination. The ramifications of defeat and destruction incorporated the need to restore or re-establish symbols of the Jewish community. The extant narrative may direct our focus towards the pre-70 CE period. However, this narrative needs to be viewed within its own historical and communal context. Josephus and others turned to their immediate past to seek meaning for their current circumstances. The 'dark age' of the first century CE (70–100 CE) may be, in fact, the time of increased turmoil and tension in Jewish–Roman relations, in which the ideological edge to the way Jews related to the Roman overlords was defined.

The first century CE is like an ancient monument. It is a place of interest with riches that the visitor wants to stand among, their ambience to imbibe. Unfortunately access to the site is limited to one point of entry. Most of the sources only provide a mere glimpse of the site. The only point of entry which allows you to view the site from within is the narrative of Josephus. The problem is that, once inside, we are offered an 'official' guided tour of the site. Josephus takes us to

---

1.   Such a move echoes the desire to view the dynamic of leadership within the community outside the Sadducee-Pharisee paradigm and the notion of institutional control encapsulated in the idea of *the* Sanhedrin. See Sanders, *Judaism*, McLaren, *Power*, and D. Goodblatt, *The Monarchic Principle* (TSAJ, 38; Tübingen: J.C.B. Mohr [Paul Siebeck], 1994). Note also the approach outlined by M. Goodman, 'A Note on the Qumran Sectarians, the Essenes and Josephus', *JJS* 46 (1995), pp. 161-66, who cautions against the tendency to view various movements within the limited confines of the three sects named by Josephus.

the various locations that he deems are the highlights. Our excitement at entering the site, therefore, is balanced by the requirement of Josephus that he shows us the official tour. It is time we leave the official tour party. We have been given access to the site by Josephus but to ensure that we are able to explore its contents in detail we must stand apart from him. As such, our visit to the site may take more time than the official tour programme allows. But who wants to stay on a tour that does not let you stop and take your own pictures?

BIBLIOGRAPHY

1. *Texts*

Josephus, *Works* (trans. H.St.J. Thackeray, R. Marcus, A. Wikgren, L.H. Feldman; 10 vols.; LCL; London: Heinemann; Cambridge, MA: Harvard University Press, 1926–65).

Suetonius, *The Twelve Caesars* (trans. R. Graves; Harmondsworth: Penguin Books, 1957).

Tacitus, *Annals* (trans. J. Jackson; LCL; London: Heinemann, 1937).

—*Histories* (trans. C.H. Moore; LCL; London: Heinemann, 1931).

2. *Selected Secondary Works*

Adan-Bayewitz, D., M. Aviam and D.R. Edwards, 'Yodefat, 1992', *IEJ* 45 (1995), pp. 191-97.

Applebaum, S., 'Judaea as a Roman Province: The Countryside as a Political and Economic Factor', *ANRW* 2.8 (1977), pp. 355-96.

—'Josephus and the Economic Causes of the Jewish War', in Feldman and Hata (eds.), *Josephus, the Bible and History*, pp. 237-64.

Attridge, H.W., *The Interpretation of Biblical History in the Antiquitates Judaicae of Flavius Josephus* (HDR, 7; Missoula, MT: Scholars Press, 1976).

—'Josephus and His Works', in M.E. Stone (ed.), *Jewish Writings of the Second Temple Period: Apocrypha, Pseudepigrapha, Qumran Sectarian Writing, Philo, Josephus* (CRINT, 2.2; Assen: Van Gorcum, 1984), pp. 185-232.

Badian, E., 'Thucydides and the Outbreak of the Peloponnesian War: A Historian's Brief', in J.W. Allison (ed.), *Conflict, Antithesis and the Ancient Historian* (Columbus: Ohio State University Press, 1990), pp. 46-91.

Bammel, E., and C.F.D. Moule (eds.), *Jesus and the Politics of his Day* (Cambridge: Cambridge University Press, 1984).

Barnett, P.W., 'Under Tiberius All Was Quiet', *NTS* 21 (1974–75), pp. 564-71.

Baumbach, G., 'The Sadducees in Josephus', in Feldman and Hata (eds.), *Josephus, the Bible and History*, pp. 173-95.

Bilde, P., 'The Causes of the Jewish War according to Josephus', *JSJ* 10 (1979), pp. 179-202.

—*Flavius Josephus between Jerusalem and Rome: His Life, his Works, and their Importance* (JSPSup, 2; Sheffield: JSOT Press, 1988).

Brandon, S.G.F., *Jesus and the Zealots* (Manchester: Manchester University Press, 1967).

Brunt, P.A., 'Josephus on Social Conflicts in Roman Judaea', *Klio* 59 (1977), pp. 149-53.

—*Roman Imperial Themes* (Oxford: Oxford University Press, 1990).

Camara, H., *Spiral of Violence* (London: Sheed and Ward, 1971).

Carr, E.H., *What Is History?* (Harmondsworth: Penguin Books, 1964).

Cohen, S.J.D., *Josephus in Galilee and Rome: His Vita and Development as a Historian* (CSCT, 8; Leiden: E.J. Brill, 1979).

—'The Political and Social History of the Jews in Greco-Roman Antiquity: The State of the Question', in R.A. Kraft, and G.W.E. Nickelsburg (eds.), *Early Judaism and Its Modern Interpreters* (Philadelphia: Fortress Press, 1986), pp. 33-56.

Cotton, H.M., and J. Geiger, *Masada II. Final Reports: The Latin and Greek Documents* (Jerusalem: Hebrew University of Jerusalem, 1989).

Cotton, H.M., and J.J. Price, 'Who Captured Masada in 66 CE and Who Lived There until the Fortress Fell?', *Zion* 55 (1990), pp. 449-54.

Crossan, J.D., *The Historical Jesus: The Life of a Mediterranean Peasant* (San Francisco: Harper & Row, 1991).

Daube, D., 'Typology in Josephus', *JJS* 31 (1980), pp. 18-36.

Donaldson, T., 'Rural Bandits, City Mobs and the Zealots', *JSJ* 21 (1990), pp. 19-40.

Eckstein, H., 'Theoretical Approaches to Explaining Collective Political Violence', in T.R. Gurr (ed.), *Handbook of Political Conflict* (New York: Macmillan, 1980), pp. 135-65.

Evans, C.A., 'Jesus' Action in the Temple: Cleansing or Portent of Destruction?', *CBQ* 51 (1989), pp. 237-70.

Farmer, W.R., *Maccabees, Zealots and Josephus* (New York: Columbia University Press, 1956).

Feldman, L.H., 'Introduction', in Feldman and Hata (eds.), *Josephus, the Bible and History*, pp. 17-49.

—'Josephus' Portrayal of the Hasmoneans Compared with 1 Maccabees', in Parente and Sievers (eds.), *Josephus and the History of the Greco-Roman Period*, pp. 41-68.

Feldman, L.H., and G. Hata (eds.), *Josephus, the Bible and History* (Detroit: Wayne State University Press, 1989).

Ferguson, N. (ed.), *Virtual History* (London: Picador, 1997).

Fox, M., 'History and Rhetoric in Dionysius of Halicarnassus', *JRS* 83 (1993), pp. 31-47.

Freyne, S., *Galilee: from Alexander the Great to Hadrian 323 BCE to 135 CE: A Study of Second Temple Judaism* (Wilmington, DE: Michael Glazier, 1980).

Gafni, I.M., 'Josephus and 1 Maccabees', in Feldman and Hata (eds.), *Josephus, the Bible and History*, pp. 116-31.

Goodblatt, D., 'The Place of the Pharisees in First Century Judaism: The State of the Debate', *JSJ* 20 (1989), pp. 12-30.

—*The Monarchic Principle* (TSAJ, 38; Tübingen: J.C.B. Mohr [Paul Siebeck], 1994).

Goodman, M., 'The First Jewish Revolt: Social Conflict and the Problem of Debt', *JJS* 33 (1982), pp. 417-27.

—*The Ruling Class of Judaea: The Origins of the Jewish Revolt Against Rome, AD 66–70* (Cambridge: Cambridge University Press, 1987).

—review of *Judaism: Practice and Belief, 63 BCE–66 CE* (London: SCM Press, 1992) by E.P. Sanders, *SJT* 47 (1994), pp. 89-95.

—'Josephus as a Roman Citizen', in Parente and Sievers (eds.), *Josephus and the History of the Greco-Roman Period*, pp. 329-38.

—'A Note on the Qumran Sectarians, the Essenes and Josephus', *JJS* 46 (1995), pp. 161-66.

Grabbe, L.L., *Judaism from Cyrus to Hadrian* (2 vols.; Minneapolis: Fortress Press, 1992).

Gurr, T.R., *Why Men Rebel* (Princeton, NJ: Princeton University Press, 1970).

—'A Causal Model of Civil Strife', in J.C. Davies (ed.), *When Men Revolt and Why: A Reader in Political Violence and Revolution* (New York: Macmillan, 1971), pp. 293-313.

Hadas-Lebel, M., *Flavius Josephus: Eyewitness to Rome's First Century Conquest of Judea* (trans. R. Miller; New York: Macmillan, 1993).

Hata, G., 'Imagining Some Dark Periods in Josephus' Life', in Parente and Sievers (eds.), *Josephus and the History of the Greco-Roman Period*, pp. 309-28.

Hengel, M., *The Zealots: Investigations into the Jewish Freedom Movement in the Period from Herod I until 70 AD* (trans. D. Smith; Edinburgh: T. & T. Clark, 1989).

Horsley, R.A., 'Menahem in Jerusalem: A Brief Messianic Episode among the Sicarii— Not "Zealot Messianism"', *NovT* 27 (1985), pp. 334-48.

—'The Zealots: Their Origin, Relationships and Importance in the Jewish Revolt', *NovT* 28 (1986), pp. 159-92.

—'High Priests and the Politics of Roman Palestine', *JSJ* 17 (1986), pp. 23-55.

—*Jesus and the Spiral of Violence: Popular Jewish Resistance in Roman Palestine* (San Francisco: Harper & Row, 1987).

—*Galilee: History, Politics, People* (Valley Forge, PA: Trinity Press International, 1995).

Horsley, R.A., and J.S. Hanson, *Bandits, Prophets, and Messiahs: Popular Movements at the Time of Jesus* (New Voices in Biblical Studies; Minneapolis: Winston Press, 1985; repr. San Francisco: Harper & Row, 1988).

Hunter, V., *Thucydides: The Artful Reporter* (Toronto: Hakkert, 1973).

Ilan, T., and J.J. Price, 'Seven Onomastic Problems in Josephus' *Bellum Judaicum*', *JQR* 84 (1993–94), pp. 189-208.

Issac, B., 'Judaea after AD 70', *JJS* 35 (1984), pp. 44-50.

Jossa, G., 'Josephus' Action in Galilee during the Jewish War', in Parente and Sievers (eds.), *Josephus and the History of the Greco-Roman Period*, pp. 265-78.

Kagan, D., *On the Origins of War and the Preservation of Peace* (New York: Doubleday, 1995).

Kasher, A., 'The *Isopoliteia* Question in Caesarea Maritima', *JQR* 68 (1977), pp. 16-27.

—*Jews and Hellenistic Cities in Eretz-Israel: Relations of the Jews in Eretz-Israel with the Hellenistic Cities during the Second Temple Period (332 BCE–70 CE)* (TSAJ, 21; Tübingen: J.C.B. Mohr [Paul Siebeck], 1990).

Kreissig, H., 'A Marxist View of Josephus' Account of the Jewish War', in Feldman and Hata (eds.), *Josephus, the Bible and History*, pp. 265-77.

Laqueur, R., *Der jüdische Historiker Flavius Josephus: Ein biografischer Versuch auf neuer quellenkritischer Grundlage* (Giessen: Munchow, 1920).

Levine, L.I., 'The Jewish–Greek Conflict in First Century Caesarea', *JJS* 25 (1974), pp. 381-97.

Loftus, F., 'The Anti-Roman Revolts of the Jews and the Galileans', *JQR* 68 (1977–78), pp. 78-98.

Luedemann, G., 'Acts of the Apostles as a Historical Source', in J. Neusner, P. Borgen, E.S. Frerichs and R.A. Horsley (eds.), *The Social World of Formative Christianity and Judaism* (Philadelphia: Fortress Press, 1988), pp. 109-25.

McLaren, J.S., *Power and Politics in Palestine: The Jews and the Governing of their Land 100 BC–AD 70* (JSNTSup, 63; Sheffield: JSOT Press, 1991).

Mason, S.N., 'Was Josephus a Pharisee? A Re-examination of *Life* 10-12', *JJS* 40 (1989), pp. 31-45.

—*Flavius Josephus on the Pharisees: A Composition-Critical Study* (SPB, 39; Leiden: E.J. Brill, 1991).

—'Josephus, Daniel, and the Flavian House', in Parente and Sievers (eds.), *Josephus and the History of the Greco-Roman Period*, pp. 161-91.

—'Chief Priests, Sadducees, Pharisees and Sanhedrin in Acts', in R. Bauckham (ed.), *The Book of Acts in its First Century Setting*. IV. *The Book of Acts in its Palestinian Setting* (Grand Rapids: Eerdmans, 1995), pp. 115-77.

Mazar, B., 'Josephus Flavius and the Archaeological Excavations in Jerusalem', in Feldman and Hata (eds.), *Josephus, the Bible, and History*, pp. 325-29.

Mendels, D., *The Rise and Fall of Jewish Nationalism* (ABRL; New York: Doubleday, 1992).

Michel, O., 'Die Rettung Israels und die Rolle Roms nach den Reden im "Bellum Judaicum": Analysen und Perspektiven', *ANRW* 2.21.2 (1984), pp. 945-76.

Moehring, H.R., review of *Josephus in Galilee and Rome: His Vita and Development as a Historian* (CSCT, 8; Leiden: E.J. Brill, 1979), by S.J.D. Cohen, *JJS* 31 (1980), pp. 240-42.

—'Joseph ben Matthia and Flavius Josephus: The Jewish Prophet and Roman Historian', *ANRW* 2.21.2 (1984), pp. 864-944.

Muller, E.N., 'The Psychology of Political Protest and Violence', in T.R. Gurr (ed.), *Handbook of Political Conflict* (New York: Macmillan, 1980), pp. 69-99.

Murphy, F.J., *The Religious World of Jesus: An Introduction to Second Temple Palestinian Judaism* (Nashville: Abingdon Press, 1991).

Neusner, J., *The Rabbinic Traditions about the Pharisees before 70* (3 vols.; Leiden: E.J. Brill, 1971).

Niehoff, M.R., 'Two Examples of Josephus' Narrative Technique in His "Rewritten Bible"', *JSJ* 27 (1996), pp. 31-45.

Nikiprowetzky, V., 'Josephus and the Revolutionary Parties', in Feldman and Hata (eds.), *Josephus, the Bible and History*, pp. 216-36.

Paltiel, E., *Vassals and Rebels in the Roman Empire* (Brussels: Latomus, 1991).

Parente, F., and J. Sievers (eds.), *Josephus and the History of the Greco-Roman Period* (SPB, 41; Leiden: E.J. Brill, 1994).

Press, G.A., *The Development of the Idea of History in Antiquity* (Montreal: McGill-Queen's University Press, 1982).

Price, J.J., *Jerusalem under Siege: The Collapse of the Jewish State 66–70 CE* (BSJS, 3; Leiden: E.J. Brill, 1992).

Pucci, M., 'Jewish-Parthian Relations in Josephus', in L.I. Levine (ed.), *The Jerusalem Cathedra: Studies in the History, Archaeology, Geography and Ethnography of the Land of Israel* (Jerusalem: Yad Izhak Ben Zvi Institute, 1983), III, pp. 13-25.

Rajak, T., 'Justus of Tiberias', *ClQ* 23 (1973), pp. 345-68.

—'Josephus and the "Archaeology" of the Jews', *JJS* 33 (1982), pp. 465-77.

—*Josephus: The Historian and his Society* (London: Gerald Duckworth, 1983).

—'Josephus and Justus of Tiberias', in L.H. Feldman and G. Hata (eds.), *Josephus, Judaism and Christianity* (Detroit: Wayne State University Press, 1987), pp. 81-94.

—'Ciò che Flavio Giuseppe vide: Josephus and the Essenes', in Parente and Sievers (eds.), *Josephus and the History of the Greco-Roman Period*, pp. 141-60.

Rappaport, U., 'Jewish–Pagan Relations and the Revolt against Rome in 66–70 CE', in L.I. Levine (ed.), *The Jerusalem Cathedra: Studies in the History, Archaeology, Geography and Ethnography of the Land of Israel* (Jerusalem: Yad Izhak Ben Zvi Institute, 1981), I, pp. 81-95.

—'John of Gischala: From Galilee to Jerusalem', *JJS* 33 (1982), pp. 479-93.

—'John of Gischala in Galilee', in L.I. Levine (ed.), *The Jerusalem Cathedra: Studies in the History, Archaeology, Geography and Ethnography of the Land of Israel* (Jerusalem: Yad Izhak Ben Zvi Institute, 1983), III, pp. 46-57.

—'Where was Josephus Lying—In His *Life* or in the *War*?', in Parente and Sievers (eds.), *Josephus and the History of the Greco-Roman Period*, pp. 279-89.

Rengstorf, K.H., *A Complete Concordance to Flavius Josephus* (4 vols.; Leiden: E.J. Brill, 1973–83).

Rhoads, D.M., *Israel in Revolution: 6–74 CE: A Political History Based on the Writings of Josephus* (Philadelphia: Fortress Press, 1976).

Roth, C., 'The Debate on the Loyal Sacrifices, AD 66', *HTR* 53 (1960), pp. 93-97.

Sanders, E.P., *Judaism: Practice and Belief 63 BCE–66 CE* (London: SCM Press, 1992).

Sauliner, C., 'Flavius Josèphe et la propagande Flavienne', *RB* 96 (1989), pp. 545-62.

Schalit, A., 'Josephus und Justus: Studien zur Vita des Josephus', *Klio* 26 (1933), pp. 67-95.

—'Die Erhebung Vespasians nach Flavius Josephus, Talmud und Midrasch: Zur Geschichte einer messianischen Prophetie', *ANRW* 2.2 (1974), pp. 208-327.

Schürer, E., *The History of the Jewish People in the Age of Jesus Christ* (rev. and trans. G. Vermes, F. Millar and M. Black; Edinburgh: T. & T. Clark, I, 1973; II, 1979).

Schwartz, D.R., 'KATA TOYTON TON KAIPON: Josephus' Source on Agrippa II', *JQR* 72 (1982), pp. 241-68.

—'Josephus and Philo on Pontius Pilate', in L.I. Levine (ed.), *The Jerusalem Cathedra: Studies in the History, Archaeology, Geography and Ethnography of the Land of Israel* (Jerusalem: Yad Izhak Ben Zvi Institute, 1983), III, pp. 26-45.

—'Josephus on the Jewish Constitutions and Community', *SCI* 7 (1983–84), pp. 30-52.

—'On Drama and Authenticity in Philo and Josephus', *SCI* 10 (1989–90), pp. 113-29.

—*Agrippa I: The Last King of Judaea* (TSAJ, 23; Tübingen: J.C.B. Mohr [Paul Siebeck], 1990).

—'Temple and Desert: On Religion and State in Second Temple Period Judaea', in D.R. Schwartz, *Studies in the Jewish Background of Christianity* (WUNT, 60; Tübingen: J.C.B. Mohr [Paul Siebeck], 1992), pp. 29-43.

—'On Sacrifices by Gentiles in the Temple of Jerusalem', in D.R. Schwartz, *Studies in the Jewish Background of Christianity* (WUNT, 60; Tübingen: J.C.B. Mohr [Paul Siebeck], 1992), pp. 102-16.

—'Felix and *Isopoliteia*, Josephus and Tacitus', *Zion* 58 (1993), pp. 265-86.

—'Josephus on Hyrcanus II', in Parente and Sievers (eds.), *Josephus and the History of the Greco-Roman Period*, pp. 210-32.

Schwartz, S., 'The Composition and Publication of Josephus's "Bellum Judaicum" Book 7', *HTR* 79 (1986), pp. 373-86.

—*Josephus and Judaean Politics* (CSCT, 18; Leiden: E.J. Brill, 1990).

—'Josephus in Galilee: Rural Patronage and Social Breakdown', in Parente and Sievers (eds.), *Josephus and the History of the Greco-Roman Period*, pp. 290-306.

Shaw, B.D., 'Tyrants, Bandits and Kings: Personal Power in Josephus', *JJS* 44 (1993), pp. 173-203.

Smallwood, E.M., *The Jews under Roman Rule: From Pompey to Diocletian* (repr.; SJLA, 20; Leiden: E.J. Brill, 1981 [1976]).

—'Philo and Josephus as Historians of the Same Events', in L.H. Feldman and G. Hata (eds.), *Josephus, Judaism and Christianity* (Detroit: Wayne State University Press, 1987), pp. 114-28.

Smith, M., 'Palestinian Judaism in the First Century', in M. Davis (ed.), *Israel: Its Role in Civilization* (New York: Harper & Row, 1956), pp. 67-81.

Sterling, G.E., *Historiography and Self-definition: Josephus, Luke–Acts and Apologetic Historiography* (NovTSup, 64; Leiden: E.J. Brill, 1992).

Stern, M., 'The Province of Judaea', in S. Safrai and M. Stern (eds.), *The Jewish People in the First Century: Historical Geography, Political History, Social, Cultural and Religious Life and Institutions* (CRINT, 1.1; Assen: Van Gorcum, 1974), pp. 308-76.

—'The Reign of Herod and the Herodian Dynasty', in S. Safrai and M. Stern (eds.), *The Jewish People in the First Century: Historical Geography, Political History, Social, Cultural and Religious Life and Institutions* (CRINT, 1.1; Assen: Van Gorcum, 1974), pp. 216-307.

Stohl, M., 'The Nexus of Civil and International Conflict', in T.R. Gurr (ed.), *Handbook of Political Conflict* (New York: Macmillan, 1980), pp. 297-330.

Tcherikover, V.A., *Hellenistic Civilization and the Jews* (trans. S. Applebaum; Philadelphia: Jewish Publication Society of America, 1959).

Thackeray, H.St.J., *Josephus the Man and the Historian* (New York: Jewish Institute of Religion Press, 1929).

Tilly, C., *From Mobilization to Revolution* (Reading, MA: Addison Wesley, 1978).

Ulrich, E., 'Josephus' Biblical Text for the Books of Samuel', in Feldman and Hata (eds.), *Josephus, the Bible and History*, pp. 81-96.

Villalba i Varenda, P., *The Historical Method of Flavius Josephus* (ALGHJ, 19; Leiden: E.J. Brill, 1986).

Wacholder, B.Z., 'Josephus and Nicolaus of Damascus', in Feldman and Hata (eds.), *Josephus, the Bible and History*, pp. 147-72.

Walbank, F.W., *Selected Papers, Studies in Greek and Roman History and Historiography* (Cambridge: Cambridge University Press, 1985).

Williams, D.S., 'On Josephus' use of Nicolaus of Damascus: A Stylometric Analysis of *BJ* 1.225-273 and *AJ* 14.280-369', *SCI* 12 (1993), pp. 176-87.

—'Morton Smith on the Pharisees in Josephus', *JQR* 84 (1993), pp. 29-42.

Wright, N.T., *The New Testament and the People of God* (Minneapolis: Fortress Press, 1992).

INDEXES

INDEX OF REFERENCES

JOSEPHUS

INDEX OF AUTHORS